VALUES AND MUSIC EDUCATION

COUNTERPOINTS: MUSIC AND EDUCATION

Estelle R. Jorgensen, editor

VALUES AND MUSIC EDUCATION

ESTELLE R. JORGENSEN

INDIANA UNIVERSITY PRESS

This book is a publication of

Indiana University Press
Office of Scholarly Publishing
Herman B Wells Library 350
1320 East 10th Street
Bloomington, Indiana 47405 USA

iupress.org

Manufactured in the United States of America

First printing 2021

Library of Congress Cataloging-in-Publication Data

Names: Jorgensen, Estelle R., author.
Title: Values and music education / Estelle R. Jorgensen.
Description: Bloomington : Indiana University Press, 2021. | Series: Counterpoints: music and education | Includes bibliographical references and index.
Identifiers: LCCN 2021014975 (print) | LCCN 2021014976 (ebook) | ISBN 9780253058225 (hardback) | ISBN 9780253058218 (paperback) | ISBN 9780253058201 (ebook)
Subjects: LCSH: Music—Instruction and study—Moral and ethical aspects. | Social values—Study and teaching.
Classification: LCC MT1 .J679 2021 (print) | LCC MT1 (ebook) | DDC 780.71—dc23
LC record available at https://lccn.loc.gov/2021014975
LC ebook record available at https://lccn.loc.gov/2021014976

For Iris

CONTENTS

PREFACE

FOR MUCH OF MY WORKING lifetime, I have been in search of meaning at the intersections of music and education. Working within an analytic philosophical tradition, I have sought to understand the meanings of concepts invoked in music education. Excavating beneath the surface of commonly used words and concepts employed in music and education, I have attempted to clarify their meanings, reveal their ambiguities, critique their potentials and pitfalls, and unpack their implications for musical and educational theory and practice. Thinking literally and figuratively, individually and comparatively, critically and constructively, I have embraced the tensions, paradoxes, predicaments, and questions that my method raises. My approach to philosophy reflects the way I see the world and is born as much from my musical and teaching experience as my study of the philosophies of others. In seeking to clarify the conceptual terrain of music education, I have articulated and distinguished ideas, probed their foundations, and practiced a way of reflecting about music and education that I hope others may find helpful. I am conscious of moving outward to the limits of my knowledge while also seeking a fuller and deeper understanding of my sometimes taken-for-granted ideas. My work is organic: each project is incomplete, grounded in questions arising out of my previous writing and generating new questions that demand my attention.

Boldness of philosophical vision means the courage to pursue a line of thought wherever it leads and irrespective of current fashion or circumstances: it not only stands for staking out and embracing the new; it also requires interrogating and confirming the old. I think of my writing as an extended thought experiment influenced to some degree by others' perspectives but primarily following my own questions and creating my own path. In the process, in the way of dialectic, I am caught between the claims of new and old. Having embraced questions, ambiguities, and paradoxes, I hold this position even if it renders my ideas vulnerable to critique by those who, on the one hand, wish me to take up the mantle of transformation and change or those, on the other, who would prefer that I repudiate the new in favor of conservation and tradition. Taking such a fraught position requires courage, but it is the way I must travel.

I underscore the personal character of this writing. For me, doing philosophy is a solitary undertaking, but I treasure the philosophical friends with whom I can converse. Although I have prioritized the tasks of better understanding and articulating my ideas within the philosophical tradition to which I am heir and thereby speaking in my own voice, I have also fostered a community in which philosophers of music education might forward their ideas and be respectfully heard. In searching for conceptual clarity and distinction, this book begins and ends with my own perspectives and commitments. The text was written before the notes that serve a pedagogical purpose in clarifying either a source of my ideas or an illustrative function in suggesting literature that others may wish to explore. This project afforded me the creativity to discover the conceptual scaffolding on which I might hang my analysis, apply it systematically throughout this book, and determine the specific aspects about which I needed to write. In his review of this book, Randall Allsup pictures me inspecting tarot cards and turning them over one by one. He is right that I am searching for meaning regarding these values and reflecting on their salience for music education. I view all the values about which I write as consequential not only for the past but for the future. Imagination and reason are at work in determining what to do about them. Still, I do not see myself as a prophet, magician, or seer delivering wisdom from on high but rather as an investigator who seeks to reflect on the intersections between values, music, and education and share what I have found. I simply bring my perspective to a philosophical, musical, and educational conversation already underway.

If there is one overarching theme in this book, it is that when we speak of values that impact our commitments and actions, the meanings we ascribe to those words are consequential for thought and action. Juxtaposing, as I have, quartets of values that are intertwined in various ways exposes the ambiguity of these words and clarifies how the nuances of meaning in each value may differ depending on its conjunction with others. When we speak about these values and act according to them, musicians and educators need to proceed carefully and critically. We rely on reasoned feeling and felt reason in determining how to move forward. For me, none of these values turns out to be without flaw. I concur with Aristotle that one may have too much or too little of a good thing. I am also mindful of the magnitude of the theoretical and practical problems this book raises for musicians and teachers. When I consider the many possibilities I might have explored but could not take up, the large, disparate, and relevant literature bearing on my topic, the challenge of doing justice to the intersections between values, music, and education within the space of a single writing, and my necessarily personal and selective cast on each musical and educational value, I am deeply aware of the incompleteness and fallibility of this analysis. At book's end, I embrace important questions that await attention. Still, while I have not attempted or accomplished an exhaustive account, I hope that this book serves an instructional, illustrative, and even inspirational purpose of helping readers think about the ways in which values are, can, or ought to be interconnected with music and education.

My objective is modest. I invite you to think through, mull over, worry with, and converse about the values I have examined and decide for yourself what your commitments should be in the specific situations in which you find yourself. This is our individual and collective responsibility and privilege as participants in a humane approach to music education. If my analysis assists you in challenging your preconceptions about taken-for-granted musical and educational values, prompts you to critically reflect on those values to which you are committed, reminds you of values that you might have forgotten, causes you to articulate and support other values that are not discussed in these pages, helps to clarify and shape your music, teaching, and learning, or gives added meaning to your work, this book will have succeeded in its task.

Estelle R. Jorgensen
Yarmouth Port, Massachusetts

ACKNOWLEDGMENTS

THIS BOOK COULD NOT HAVE been written without the help of family, friends, students, and colleagues to whom I have turned for help along the way. To Linda Bucklin, administrative secretary extraordinaire, your careful editorial review during the multiple drafts through which this book passed and faithful record of files so that nothing was lost helped to make the task of writing a joy. To Iris Yob, Randall Allsup, and Patrick Freer, who read the entire manuscript, I appreciate your critical and constructive questions, comments, and suggestions that have enriched this writing, and I thank Iris for helping to prepare the index. You should be credited only for this book's successes; its failings are mine alone. To Allison Chaplin, my editor at Indiana University Press, my thanks for your support of this project throughout the review and publication process. To colleagues who have assisted me at crucial points in the investigation, I express my thanks and acknowledge your assistance in the notes for this book. And to my students, friends, and conversation partners over the years, the inspiration of your words, examples, and friendship has given me courage and lit my way.

VALUES AND MUSIC EDUCATION

ONE

Culture, Humanity, Transformation, and Value

FOUR QUESTIONS LIE AT THE heart of this book: What values ought to characterize music and education? What are their contributions? What are their detractions? How might they apply to musical and educational practice? My present purpose is to unpack notions of selected values and their relationship to beliefs, attitudes, dispositions, and actions in music education. I suggest that none of these values suffices when taken alone, and all have musical and educational detractions and contributions. The values I discuss undergird and shape as they also express and are affected by the aims and methods of music and education. This symbiotic interrelationship between values and musical and educational beliefs and practices underscores the critical role of values in forging theories and practices in music education and addressing philosophical questions about what music and education should be and become.

In this chapter, I focus on four central and interrelated concepts on which the following chapters are predicated: music as an aspect of culture, humanity and humane education, musical and educational transformation, and values and their intersection with music and education. In sketching the overall project, commenting on my methodological approach, and outlining the plan of this book, I emphasize ambiguities in the intersection between values and music education, distinguish concepts that are crucial in my thinking, and provide a context for the chapters to come. In so doing, I follow a time-honored educational tradition of moving rhythmically and cyclically from general to specific and back to general.[1] In the chapters to follow, I think symbolically and intuitively in quartets as I seek a solid foundation for values, beliefs, and practices in music education.

The title of this book, *Values and Music Education*, invokes music education in its commonly understood sense of a cross-disciplinary field at the intersection of music, education, and culture. Construing music and education problematically and ambiguously suggests that music education is a multifaceted and pluralistic enterprise.[2] With this in mind, I draw from various musical and educational traditions as I relate values to music and education. While musical and educational values may overlap, they are not necessarily coextensive. Music can serve as a metaphor for education just as education can serve as a metaphor for music.[3] Although this idea remains implicit in the present writing, I write not only for those who think of themselves as music educators but for teachers willing to consider music as figurative of general education and musicians open to the potential of music construed as educational enterprise.

I critically examine some clusters of values with a view to determining how they may guide music and education. This enterprise extends a line of investigation in my earlier work predicated on the assumption of certain values—for example, civility, humanity, justice, freedom, inclusiveness, and equality.[4] It is also situated in an interdisciplinary literature spanning fields of music and the arts, philosophy (aesthetics and ethics), anthropology, and education. For example, during the past two decades, Philip Alperson and his colleagues, Keith Moore Chapin and Lawrence Kramer and their colleagues, Julian Johnson, Liz Garnet, Jerrold Levinson, and Jayson Beaster-Jones have been among the philosophers, musicologists, ethnomusicologists, and anthropologists to grapple with issues of musical value.[5] Others, such as Thomas Regelski; Paul Woodford; Robert Walker; Randall Allsup and Heidi Westerlund; Elizabeth Gould; Hildegard Froehlich; and David Elliott, Marissa Silverman, Wayne Bowman, and their colleagues, have focused on musical values and their connections with ethics in music education.[6] And still others, including David Carr, Joe Winston, and Donald Blumenfeld-Jones, have engaged the intersections between ethics, aesthetics, and education.[7]

Ethical issues in music and education are complex and fraught.[8] At a time of economic, political, religious, and social polarization in the United States and abroad, the realities of human greed and scarce resources arising from human action and natural phenomena have fueled cultural polarization and exacerbated a struggle between the forces of conservatism and liberalism, nationalism and globalization. Thomas Byrne Edsall posits that it is easier to sustain democratic institutions and civil discourse in a time of expansion and plenty: when resources are scarce, unemployment is rife, and economic disparity is rampant, competition for scarce resources provides fertile ground for contention, conflict, and inhumanity.[9] While Edsall looks to economics and politics to explain this polarization, others cite the surge of religious fundamentalism and various social reasons.[10] Massive population migrations and technological changes have exacerbated these social and cultural tensions and worsened social unrest and resentment. Whatever the precise causes, it seems clear that economic, political, and religious factors are among the reasons for societal polarization. The ideological divides around the world reflect differing value sets that are as much socially forged as psychologically grounded.

Movements toward the inclusion and equality of minorities and previously marginalized groups in the latter part of the twentieth century and early part of the twenty-first century have been resisted by those with a conservative bent who fear a challenge to the established or traditional order of things. A backlash against liberal approaches to immigration; diverse cultural expressions; equality in terms of gender and gender identity and ethnic, racial, religious, and other minorities; and the claims of redressing the effects of colonization and dispossession and redistributing wealth from rich to poor has fueled a struggle in public spaces over the primacy of different value sets. Declining civil discourse, corruption, and competition for scarce resources have made it more difficult to cooperate with others who are different to solve the intractable issues in society at large at a time of increasing globalization. These realities have polarized and even paralyzed the nation's democratic political institutions and rendered society vulnerable to extremist ideologies from within and without. Beyond the United States, other countries face similar disparities in the distribution of resources along with increasing societal and cultural rifts and fractures and possibilities for strife, revolution, and war.

Notwithstanding these challenges, the third decade of the twenty-first century constitutes a poignant moment for musicians, teachers, and students to examine and reexamine the values that should undergird and characterize music education. Around the world, racism; inequality; poverty, with its attendant problems of food insecurity, hunger, homelessness, and limited access to health care; injustice, with its related issues of policing and incarceration; corruption; violence; domestic and international terrorism; and environmental neglect and destruction are among the systemic evils exposed during the international COVID-19 pandemic. It is not surprising that national and international movements for economic, racial, social, and environmental justice have ignited here and abroad as the bill for conquest, slavery, oppression, corruption, and human and environmental exploitation has come due. In some ways, music and education have been transfigured by the pandemic; in other ways, they remain the same.[11] Tumultuous times have appeared throughout history, and I see no reason why this should not be the case in the future.

At times like this, music educators need the humility to listen to and hear the voices of those who have been marginalized and suffered anguish, pain, and violence. Moments of distress, dislocation, awakening, and upheaval open windows to rediscover, reassess, and recommit to humane values that point toward the good and promote healing and well-being.[12] To this end, I seek musical and educational values that are timeless and widespread throughout the human family irrespective of our differences, that awaken and give musical voice to the dispossessed and marginalized, along with those who have been heard in the past but who now need to accommodate change.

What is a philosopher's obligation in tumultuous times? I return to Friedrich Schiller's philosophical advice to the artist: "Live with your century; but do not be its creature. Work with your contemporaries; but create what they need, not what they praise."[13] This is a remarkable and timeless insight. I think of Herbert Read's *Education through Art*, published in 1943 during the height of the Second World War but focused on the possibilities of art in bringing joy and enlightenment rather than on the chaos around him.[14] Rereading him today, I find his ideas seem fresh and relevant to our time; I wonder whether writing this book focused on art was a respite for him from the tumult and trauma of the time. I return to Jacques Maritain's *Responsibility of the Artist*, published in 1960, in which he reminds artists that their first obligation is to their art—a responsibility Read obviously felt during wartime.[15] Maritain's advice still feels apropos to a tumultuous time when musicians first need to take care of music. Nor can I forget Hannah Arendt's *The Origins of Totalitarianism*, published in 1951 but still an important lesson now.[16] Published six years after the end of a world conflagration and a decade after the rise of the movements she contemplated, Arendt's groundbreaking treatise required time for her to reflect on the causes of the cataclysm that had convulsed the world. I learn from these scholars of the past that the work of philosophy cannot be hurried. As conditions change, in periods of unrest or quiet, it is incumbent on musicians and educators to take the time needed for reflection before rushing too quickly to opine on the present moment. Tumultuous events may open new possibilities, just as they may necessitate reexamination of common practices. Still, irrespective of change or continuity, a long view of music and education can help illumine what is of greatest importance for musical education, especially the values that should characterize them.

Opening spaces for dialogue about music and education requires self-reflexivity in interrogating taken-for-granted ideologies and repudiating simplistic either-or thinking; it also necessitates a disposition of generosity. Ideologies often serve as counterpoints or foils to others and are grounded in values that tend toward both good and evil. This position accords with Aristotle's view of virtue as a "golden mean" between too much or too little of a good thing and Confucius's belief in the importance of balancing opposing views and otherwise extreme positions in coming to wisdom.[17] It also reflects my dialectical view of self, world, and whatever lies beyond. This said, my reading of history suggests that humane ideals are more fragile and the moments in which they shine brightly are fewer than those in which the forces of inhumanity reign supreme. On the one hand, there is the ever-present danger that those ideals associated with the interests of powerful establishments will win out over interests that would unsettle and challenge that power. On the other, advocates for change may overlook the power and stabilizing influence of tradition and evoke a backlash by those who feel themselves displaced from their cultural roots.

Musicians and educators are challenged to find a path in the messy ground of practical realities that offer good and evil on either hand. The fragility of humane ideals also requires special emphasis and sustenance as musicians and educators seek to create a better world. Still, it is important to conserve the best of what traditions can offer while also transforming them for the better. Dialogue concerning these important matters needs to be grounded in generosity of spirit as one seeks to grasp what others wish to say and do in ways that are respectful and empathetic. Open-mindedness and openheartedness make it possible to look beyond human limitations and inadequacies, seek to see and hear what others are trying to say, and build bridges of common understandings with those who hold to disparate ideas and practices. Rather than focusing on what is wrong with or missing from another's point of view or practice, one needs to look beyond imperfections to seek the wisdom that might be gleaned from the other's insights.

It may be helpful for readers to approach this book as something of a thought experiment, as a space in which to rethink values and value clusters in music education. This can be accomplished by decentering or setting aside for the moment prior allegiances and preconceptions and critically, constructively, and empathetically considering the meanings, advantages, and disadvantages of these values.[18] This self-reflexive stance of examining and reexamining one's beliefs and practices resonates with Deanne Bogdan's notion of "situated sensibility," in which she fuses the "disassociation/reintegration" of musical and literary sensibilities.[19] In so doing, she illustrates a process whereby music educators can imaginatively see their own ideas and practices through the eyes of others, reintegrate these disparate ideas and practices into their own now wider and nuanced understandings, and imagine how their situations might be more humane. Taking the time to excavate the words that stand for conceptions and seeing them from different vantage points afford opportunities to reflect on how the particular cast I have given them reinforces or contradicts readers' understandings, which are sometimes explicitly embraced and other times taken for granted. I do not seek to establish who is right and who is wrong but rather to unpack various values and justify and critique my position regarding them. It is necessary to sit awhile with each value and see how it suits. Akin to any experiment, this process cannot be rushed. My point is to prompt readers to contemplate their own musical and educational values and better understand, critique, and justify their commitments and those of others. In so doing, readers may become wide awake to persistent and systemic challenges that characterize music educational thought and practice and seek more expansive, practical, and humane ways by which to improve the situation.[20]

My "this with that" dialectical approach resists either-or dichotomous thinking and postmodern mash-ups—states of dynamic flux that repudiate binaries. Situated thought and action is complicated and messy, yet for me it comes closer to the lived lives of musicians, teachers, and students than categorical and limited either-or views. As a music student and teacher, I have confronted sometimes difficult-to-resolve choices concerning such polarities as intellectuality-sensibility, receptivity-activity, freedom-control, community-individuality, literacy-orality, process-product, ecstasy-restraint, compassion-justice, spirituality-materiality, dialogue-silence, universalism-elitism, form-function, and populism-classicism. If my experience is on the mark, these and other conundrums inevitably place teachers and students in the "eye of paradox," where polarities are both a help and a hazard.[21]

As a matter of public policy, music education requires commitments that enable concerted action in the phenomenal world. What values ought to guide policy makers as they work through the host of sometimes competing and conflicting interests among and between various subjects of study and in the ways of establishing them as aspects of general education and culture? How can policy makers forge practical approaches that take these values into account? In the past, it has been tempting to dictate standardized educational approaches—a way of thought and action that silences difference, as it may encourage resistance and subversion. This approach has had mixed results and has yet to effectively address the complex nature of today's world and the subject matter being studied. It has been challenging, for example, to include in general education the many artistic traditions that coexist in today's diverse societies and to celebrate the idiosyncrasy and divergence of these arts when they are undertaken in societal and educational environments that emphasize values of standardization, normalization, and domestication.[22]

My present objective is to construct sets of values that I hope can be helpful to musicians and educators of many sorts. Here, I am searching for commonalities that lie beneath the differing skins of belief systems and practices. It has been fashionable in recent decades to look for differences in musical and educational practices. While these efforts have been invaluable in demonstrating the diversity of ways in which people come to know music among other things, it is all too easy to lose sight of the common elements that unite these characteristically human (and, hopefully, humane) systems of belief and practice. I hope that teachers, students, and educational policy makers will find this analysis helpful as they reflect on their own ethical commitments and public policies in the arts and education among the various aspects of cultural life.

MUSIC AS AN ASPECT OF CULTURE

Focusing on culture as a principal educational endeavor resurrects and reenergizes an ancient theme in both East and West. Claude Lévi-Strauss writes of culture in metaphoric terms as the difference between the "raw" and the "cooked."[23] Culture is built, as Northrop Frye notes, on imaginative life and is manifested in the arts, religions, myths, and rituals developed by human beings as ways to create a lived life that is richly imaginative and enacted.[24] For this reason, Deanne Bogdan argues, the role of imagination is crucial in culture and requires education and reeducation.[25] Beyond belief systems, culture plays out in ordinary day-to-day lives, in political governance, legal principles, commercial ventures, religious rituals, artistic performances, and domestic arrangements. It embraces all the expressions of human intelligence manifested in a host of differing beliefs and practices.[26] Institutions and societies form around certain shared norms, rules, and expectation sets that provide a measure of stability and order to human interactions. Education, construed broadly, is the process of enculturation whereby the beliefs and practices that constitute a culture are transmitted and transformed from one generation to the next.[27] It is not surprising that the ancient Greek word *paideia* stood for both education and culture.[28] While its modern interpretation is emphatically transformational, the view of education as enculturation remains. John Dewey notices the overlap between education and culture and the importance of culture as a means/end of education.[29] Notwithstanding the important contributions to educational thought of other conceptions of education, such as training, schooling, pedagogy, eduction, and socialization, the educational notion of enculturation focuses on the broad process of cultivating cultural life that expresses human imagination.[30]

Thinking of this cultural life figuratively, as Lévi-Strauss suggests, emphasizes preparation, refinement, erudition, virtuosity, complexity, and distinctiveness as qualities toward which culture naturally tends.[31] As an imaginative venture, culture abounds in exceptional instances, in the transcendence of or divergence from ordinary forms of expression codified in rule sets and expectations within social groups, institutions, or societies. Artistry and aesthetic awareness are critical components for envisaging the ideals to which a people aspire culturally and the means whereby their aspirations are at least partly achieved. Every musical tradition I have studied has practitioners whose communities acknowledge them as chief musicians and exponents and the architects of their most important musical rituals. This has been true from antiquity. For example, the delight in outstanding and sophisticated artistic skill is evident in the complex religious rituals developed by the ancient Mesopotamians; some of these ceremonies took many days to enact and required the assistance of the society's finest singers, instrumentalists, and liturgists to perform.[32] In suggesting that culture is "cooked," Lévi-Strauss highlights culture's imaginative and disciplined qualities; imagined ends are realized through a variety of means that require ingenuity, perseverance, and skill to construct and perceptiveness, feeling, and understanding to grasp. Culture's tendencies toward the erudite and exceptional give rise to esoteric cultural practices as classical traditions arise out of vernacular music. For example, jazz and rock music take on the trappings of classical music in their appeal to a relatively few exponents or experts and in the mode of their transmission and conservation. Yet if they are to thrive, they need to maintain their rootedness in ordinary and everyday musical expressions.

Culture is also enacted and dispositional. It is concerned principally with realizing ideas in the phenomenal world. Donald Arnstine argues that education concerns the cultivation of dispositions—that is, tendencies to act in certain ways.[33] Values constitute the principles that prompt, inhibit, guide, govern, prescribe, and proscribe dispositions to act or not act in certain ways. It is hard to imagine achieving such practical ends without experiencing what is made, often through participating in the process of how it is made. This experiential engagement with culture requires that education be enacted rather than just intellectualized abstractly, that culture be approached through immersion in it rather than only through the study of it. In such an education, the enactive and experiential qualities of the arts point to an education embodied and construed experientially in ways designed to cultivate certain dispositions to action. Regarding music as an instance of culture does not require the assumption that the arts are culturally normative; on the contrary, science, technology, and commerce offer differing cultural perspectives. Still, in today's world, the educational claims of science, technology, and commerce are too often thought of normatively and as more pressing than those of the arts because they are closely allied with the establishment's political and economic aspirations and with utilitarian and material ends. My focus on music among the arts and humanities seeks to redress a lack of emphasis on personal, subjective, sensual, and spiritual benefits too often out of the public eye.

This position is not a new one. Neil Postman laments a societal preoccupation with "technopoly" and advocates for the importance of a "thermostatic" or "isomorphic" principle in which education emphasizes that which is overlooked in society.[34] Arnstine and Vernon Howard, among others, use examples from the arts as figurative ways of understanding general education, and June Boyce-Tillman suggests that education needs to refocus on spiritual ends and on what she calls "subjugated ways of knowing" that have been marginalized, repressed, and silenced in industrial and postindustrial Western society.[35] Among those who see the arts as central to general education are writers such as Harry Broudy, who elaborates on the "enlightened cherishing" cultivated through study of the arts as vital to general education; Philip Phenix, who underscores the centrality of aesthetic knowing as a component of a comprehensive education; Howard, who illustrates the role of imagination as a focal point for learning and the ways in which this can be accomplished through instruction, example, practice, and reflection; James Fowler, who posits a connection between strong arts programs and strong schools; Ralph Smith and his colleagues, who note the importance for culture of education in the arts; and Maxine Greene, who argues for the educational role of the arts as vehicles for imaginative thought in schooling.[36]

Regarding education figuratively as music underscores the importance of the arts as a component of general education. I suggest that the values that should underlie music educational thought and practice ought also to exemplify education generally. This is not to posit, as does Herbert Read, that all schooling should be organized around the arts or be seen only within the context of the arts.[37] Elsewhere, I make the case that metaphorical thinking provides useful ways of understanding music and education.[38] A spiritual and figurative approach offers a counterpoint to the excessive materiality and literality of our time and affords useful insights into how education should go forward in the future. Importantly, music instances subject matter that needs to be approached experientially through participating in it—a quality that is important in coming to know a culture.

Although making music is crucial to understanding it, thinking of music as culture also necessitates regarding music educationally as a humanity, as a way of grasping human ingenuity and the cultures to which it has given rise and that it expresses.[39] This is not to undermine the imperative of music as an artistic enterprise but simply to emphasize its role in culture generally and the importance of regarding it as a way of understanding the human condition. Thinking about music in this way goes well beyond notions of music construed as a practice or as what people do to grasp its broader educational role as a vehicle of human expression, a means of constructing individual and communal identity, and an opportunity to understand self and others. Music helps define, construct, and express who we are as human beings, individually and collectively.[40] It needs to be understood in terms of other cultural expressions—such as the other arts as well as myths and religions—and the perspectives it offers into personal and subjective understanding. Aesthetic, religious, anthropological, sociological, psychological, philosophical, historical, and other approaches to music provide means whereby this wisdom can be attained.

HUMANE EDUCATION

At the outset of this work, I underscore the premise that music and education should be humane undertakings in support of a civil society.[41] Philosophers have long distinguished between what it is to be *human* and what it is to be *humane*. One may consider a human as *Homo sapiens*, a species of mammal with physical characteristics distinct from other species. Friedrich Schiller might use the term "natural man"—governed by such physical, psychological, and social needs as food, shelter, friendship, procreation, and safety—to capture this view of humanity.[42] Schiller's "natural man" is amoral, not governed by moral commitments but solely by animal instinct and training. Bereft of ethical imperatives, this human is like the boys trapped on a deserted island in William Golding's novel *Lord of the Flies*—slave to instinct, passion, and desire, and devoid of civility or ethical constraint.[43]

By contrast, Schiller gives us the "moral man"—a civilized and cultured person who is governed by ethical commitments forged through the exercise of reason but also shaped by aesthetic sensibilities and feeling. Schiller follows Plato in the belief that the object of education is the good—that people who might otherwise live as animals are brought to live, by the exercise of reason and commitment, to values that constitute an expression of the good. Both Plato and Schiller agree that artistic and aesthetic commitments are consistent with the pursuit of the good as a means and end of education. They might see a humane person as one whose life is governed by ethical and aesthetic commitments that point toward the good. Notions of paideia and the cardinal virtues, for example, constitute different expressions of desirable human conduct and how such values should be determined.

Rather than a single universal notion of the good, the "multiplicities and pluralities" of today's world, as Greene would describe things, underscore the complexity and situated character of issues surrounding the ideals of human belief and conduct.[44] Notwithstanding important differences in conceptions of the good, some values resonate historically and continue to guide belief and practice today. Together, they can be taken as symptomatic of widely held *goods*, even if not definitive of a universally held or monolithic conception of the *good*. To be humane is to accede to, live by, love, or identify with these virtues or ethical ideals, albeit contested, ambiguous, and in the process of becoming.[45]

VALUE AND VIRTUE

When referring to desirable traits or qualities such as wisdom, justice, joy, fidelity, reverence, patience, taste, and love, I prefer the word *value* over *virtue*. Both words share common attributes. They connote ideals or attributes that are aspired to—even if imperfectly realized—in the phenomenal world; they are normative and philosophically grounded propositions governing what should be rather than what is. In the West, the notion of virtue has a long-standing association with universalistic and monolithic theological and religious prescriptions and proscriptions framed in terms of rule sets controlling or guiding human conduct dictated principally by Judeo-Christian theological belief.[46]

Although values are rooted in the religions, I want to think of them more inclusively within the context of other societal institutions. Rather than be co-opted by the alternative claims of virtue ethics, consequentialist ethics, and situational ethics, as Regelski envisages the main ethical possibilities for music education, I prefer to steer a middle course between these differing perspectives where each may have a place from time to time.[47] This is often the ground where women and other minorities find themselves. Witness Carol Gilligan's classic claim that women see the world contextually and their ethical mores are framed in different terms than those of men and boys; Nel Noddings's interrogation of the ethics of the Jewish story of Abraham and the sacrifice of his son, Isaac, and her discussion of the ethical imperatives in education from a feminine perspective; and Raimond Gaita's discussion of values within the anticolonialist frames of minority racial and ethnic positions.[48] Notwithstanding the important contributions of virtue ethics to moral education and, I think, for example, of the work of Carr, Jan Steutel, and their colleagues, virtue may be overly intellectualized, especially in its philosophical formulation in the Christian conception of cardinal virtues (in which particular principles are accepted on the basis of their theologically grounded rationality).[49]

For me, a value is a principle that guides conduct and is held dear, even loved, as much as lived by, and in which heart and mind are intertwined inextricably. I prefer this conception over virtue because it foregrounds a quality of personal attachment or emotion with which the principle is regarded. It explicitly highlights the role of cognitive emotions and emotional cognitions, identified by Israel Scheffler and Iris Yob, respectively, in human intellection and value formation.[50] Despite Aristotle's conception of virtue as being interrelated with the life of feeling, it is possible to lose sight of the role of emotion in virtue. Virtue's emanation principally from a theologically privileged position of power can also render it authoritative, definitive, and impersonal while conceptions of value seem less pretentious, more relativistic, and sometimes more subjective. This latter more modest and embodied ethical perspective is consistent with the tenor of my previous writing on music and education.

EDUCATIONAL TRANSFORMATION

Conceived as ideal and actual, values point toward a transformational view of education. Rather than a rational vision that suggests education inexorably improves throughout history, I see it in a state of becoming sometimes better and sometimes worse. Whatever the educational situation at a given place and historical moment, the humane principles that educators hope to achieve are revisited and contested from place to place in each generation. These educational values reflect as much as affect the changing conceptions of the ends themselves and the plans intended to realize them. My previous thinking about the need for transforming music education is grounded in a perennial educational predicament: the present situation is inadequate, imperfect, even harmful, and educators hope to create through pedagogical means a better situation than the one they inherited and in which they presently find themselves. The artist's vision of mastery and struggle toward an imagined end is a compelling metaphor for the educator's predicament writ large.[51] When one thinks about values, one holds in view not only what presently is but also what one hopes to achieve. All along the way, like the artist, one may come closer to the imagined end; as one does so, the end seems to change and recede. As imaginatively construed entities, values are dynamically construed; like the arts, they are subjectively and objectively understood. This imaginative quality lends further credence to the view that the arts can provide important insights into educational values.

My thinking about music is particularly pointed in an educational environment that for the past half century, at least, has been concerned principally with material ends—notably, demonstrable achievements of instruction directed to literacy and numeracy. True, these objectives have been resisted by appeals to aesthetic and performative experiences concerning aspects of knowing beyond the literal and discursive and having to do with the cultivation of imagination and figurative ways of knowing and doing.[52] Still, it is tempting for arts educators to undertake and defend their work in ways designed for the benefit of those with limited and literalist educational mindsets rather than with the purpose of persuading policy makers of the shortsightedness of their materialistic perspectives by exemplifying different approaches more suited to the arts. Too often, with the best of intentions, music educators in the United States have been the vanguard of the other arts in putting the weight of professional thought and practice behind broader educational efforts to assure measurable results in literacy and numeracy; the assumption underlying this move seems to have been that not to do so would render the profession a proverbial ostrich with its head in the sand and out of sync with prevailing educational beliefs and practices.

It is also worth remembering that music education policy makers have quarreled over values from the dawn of the introduction of music to the publicly supported schools in Europe and North America. In the United States, Elam Ives Jr. and John Dwight were among the musicians to challenge Lowell Mason and his colleagues on the view that music education is best offered within publicly supported schools.[53] For Ives and Dwight, musical instruction needs to be conducted by musicians for musical rather than wider educational ends, and it should focus primarily on those students who possess musical aptitude and interest in it; such musical purposes cannot be assured in publicly supported schools. Ives's subsequent career as a singing schoolteacher after his involvement in the Hartford Experiment in 1830 and his early collaboration with Lowell Mason as joint author of *The Juvenile Lyre* demonstrate his regard for the natively developed and privately supported singing schools as appropriate vehicles for enabling musician-teachers and their students to do, teach, and learn music on their own terms. Instrumentalists such as the Benjamin brothers and the many band masters who founded town and amateur bands throughout the United States during the nineteenth and twentieth centuries advocated for and developed freestanding music educational institutions in order to accomplish what they saw as sound instrumental ends.[54] During the twentieth century, persistent tensions among the various professional associations for music education; choral, vocal, and instrumental music; organ and church music; community music; jazz; and popular music in the United States arose out of differences among musicians about the values that ought to exemplify music making and receiving and the means and ends of music education.[55] Some musicians believed that music education within public schools was a mixed blessing and that other organizations and institutions beyond state-sponsored schools were needed to provide music education for music's sake as well as its other educational purposes.

These disagreements over the values that should undergird music education reflect larger conflicts over the values that ought to underlie educational and cultural policy. We remember that music was among the first subjects of study in the emergent common schools in the United States.[56] Following in the wake of Prussian precedent, nineteenth-century social constructions of humanism in the United States suggested that in a well-ordered society in which citizens participate actively in their government, the education of all citizens is necessary for the public good. Some, particularly the poor, are unable to afford to educate their children, and it is necessary for the state to provide a system of general education accessible to all. Initially, common schools might offer only basic education, but gradually, expectations grew of a system of advanced education as well. With that expansion, philosophical and methodological differences arose over the values that should undergird this education and how they should be manifested and controlled.

Every institution in which education is conducted has its own values and its attendant benefits and pitfalls.[57] The challenge for educators in the present century is to find ways to work together across these varying and sometimes conflicting institutional and personal perspectives and practices to collectively realize the best of their benefits and avoid the worst of their pitfalls. Accomplishing such a daunting objective requires grasping the values that drive these myriad beliefs and practices and, in better understanding them, working out practical ways of institutional cooperation. As I have argued in earlier writing, solving the systemic problems of music education in all of the institutions involved in music education and within society more generally requires systemic change, as it also necessitates a transformation in personal commitments; it is hard to envisage such a project in the absence of personal, organizational, and institutional cooperation.[58] My present argument is that identifying values to which musicians and teachers might commit and examining their respective strengths and weaknesses can assist musical and educational policy makers from different institutions to find common ground, decide how they may work together, and determine the limits to that cooperation as they seek to collectively leaven the cultural lump of society at large.

VALUE CLUSTERS

In examining some of the musical and educational values in these pages, I employ clusters of words to stand for a group of intertwined yet distinctive values. Gilles Deleuze and Felix Guattari describe a "pack of wolves" to evoke the complexity of construing the wolf simultaneously as species, member of a pack, and individual animal.[59] For them, this metaphor reveals the dynamic flow of complexities and interrelationships between things. While I would prefer a gentler and less aggressive metaphor, Deleuze's and Guattari's "pack of wolves" evokes the complexity of describing human values and the importance of nuance and ambiguity as a means of connecting and distinguishing things. Nuances are crucial to the arts. For example, the selfsame musical piece may be performed differently while also authentically or in ways acceptable to exponents of a musical practice; the interest in a performance often inheres in the subtle ways in which a musician divergently interprets a score or improvises a piece. As I suggest in *Pictures of Music Education*, nuances are crucial in music education as in education generally; educational policy makers may quarrel as heatedly over a nuance as they may over a significant difference in an idea or practice. It may also be that a collection of nuances adds up to important and more general distinctions. My present depiction of clusters of interrelated values illustrates the musician's and artist's penchant for nuance just as it also problematizes these value clusters by rendering them at once more definitive and ambiguous.

The organization of this book is simple. In chapters 2 through 10, I focus, in turn, on nine value clusters: artistry, taste, skill, and style; reverence, humility, awe, and spirituality; dignity, dispassion, restraint, and discipline; love, friendship, desire, and devotion; joy, happiness, pleasure, and celebration; fidelity, persistence, patience, and loyalty; curiosity, imagination, wonder, and open-mindedness; wisdom, understanding, knowledge, and mastery; and justice, equality, fairness, and inclusiveness. Each chapter is designed to be read independently and in any order, and reiterations and resonances emerge throughout the book. Some readers may prefer to read the chapters in order and others may wish to begin with chapters that draw them in immediately and then move on to others.

A word about my choice of values. Those about which I write have piqued my imagination and interest, bear underscoring at present, and are exemplary rather than an exhaustive or comprehensive listing of values that music educators ought to obtain. In developing this list, various questions guided my thinking—for example: Where are the gaps, fissures, and oversights in my past ethical writing about music education? To which values am I most committed in my own practice? Which values are, for me, of the utmost importance for music education now? Which values collectively exemplify something of the sweep of music and education that I have observed and participated in throughout my working lifetime? Which values have been overlooked, forgotten, or foregrounded in recent musical and educational scholarship? Which values are likely to resonate practically with musicians, teachers, and students? Which values can be dealt with in the scope of a single book? Which values must be laid aside for future attention? As I reflected on these and other questions, a provisional list emerged to form the basis of each chapter. When writing was underway, and as the project came into clearer view, I continued to refine my list in much the way that Vernon Howard describes as the artist's "vision of mastery."[60]

Regarding my analytic method, I examine each value cluster and draw on examples from music and education to ground the analysis. I tease out some of their attributes and unpack their advantages and disadvantages for music and education.[61] I show that the values that comprise each quartet are mixed blessings and that musicians, educators, and other cultural workers need to carefully determine how to apply them to the specific situations in which they find themselves.[62] Regarding each value as if it is conceptually independent from the others is somewhat unrealistic, practically speaking. Still, this approach allows me to examine critically each value's qualities or symptoms, glimpse its consonances and dissonances with other interrelated values, and consider its practical implications for culture and education. Cumulatively, these chapters exemplify responses to matters raised at the outset of this chapter—namely, those values that might characterize music education and education more generally, their defense and critique, and the ways in which they apply to educational and cultural practices in pursuit of a civil society and for humane ends. While not intended as an exhaustive list, they exemplify some of the values that one might expect to be present in humane music and education.

In chapter 11, I rethink my generative questions by way of a meta-analysis that traces emergent commonalities between the various value sets, examines the theoretical resonances with aspects of music and education, illustrates the usefulness of a self-reflexive approach to decision-making in sketching practical predicaments that musicians and teachers face when applying values in their music educational practice, and concludes on a personal note with the meaning of this analysis for music and education. Rethinking these values allows musicians, teachers, and those interested in their work to better grasp, interrogate, and defend their own diverse musical and educational beliefs and practices. In so doing, they may also contemplate "the one and the many," the ways in which people are distinctive, and the commonalities that unite dwellers on planet Earth.

The epilogue reveals some of the questions, gaps, and surprises that arose in this writing. Among the questions, I wonder whether there are intersections between my earlier study of models and metaphors of music education in *Pictures of Music Education* and the values I portray here. While my sketch of values and associated music education metaphors and models may seem to hold true, at least generally, these intersections are not always self-evident. Values, metaphors, and models thought about literally and figuratively only complicate the ambiguity of music and education.

In sum, addressing matters of the values that ought to guide music and education as well as their defense, detractions, and applications to musical and educational practice, I offer a cultural perspective on music and posit a humane view of music education in pursuit of civil and decent society. Given the predicaments facing musicians and educators and my preference for values rather than virtues, I identify quartets of values that intersect with music and education. My approach to each quartet is analytic, systematic, and open-ended. It remains to unpack the various quartets of values that intersect with music and education and see where they lead.

TWO

Artistry, Taste, Skill, and Style

I BEGIN AT THE HEART of things with a quartet of values—artistry, taste, skill, and style—that share much in common with other values I will discuss later, such as curiosity, imagination, wonder, and open-mindedness and wisdom, understanding, knowledge, and mastery. Although they focus specifically on the theory and practice of music, they are also shared with other arts and subjects I have studied, so much so that music and the arts can serve as metaphors for learning more generally.[1] These values are important (in different ways and to differing degrees) to all aspects of lived life, although artists may demonstrate them to an exceptional degree. From antiquity, they have been regarded as ideals for all citizens. In ancient Greece, for example, they are to be found in the conception of *paideia*, and in the European Renaissance, they are regarded as normative for educated people, especially those in the upper classes.[2] One may quarrel over the precise ways in which these values were expressed in the past and with the failure to extend them to everyone, regardless of social status, gender, ethnicity, language, religious affiliation, or any of the other barriers that separate people. They are still contested today. John Dewey is among those to hope that these values might exemplify everyone within a democratic and decent society and that they might be modeled and cultivated within general education.[3] Donald Arnstine, Seyla Benhabib, Harry Broudy, Maxine Greene, Jane Roland Martin, Martha Nussbaum, and Herbert Read are among the writers who, prior to the twenty-first century, argued for the place of the arts and culture in democratic education and society.[4] These thinkers follow the train of philosophers in previous centuries who saw an important place for the arts in education because the arts assist in inculcating values of artistry, taste, skill, and style.[5] More recently, writers on music education have advocated variously for these values as crucial for a democratic education—qualities that have been embraced by philosophers and practitioners alike.[6] While they might be represented somewhat differently from time to time, they remain resilient values in music education conducted across a spectrum of institutions, from elementary to advanced levels of instruction.[7] In this chapter, I unpack each value in turn and examine its contributions to and detractions from music and education. It becomes clear in this discussion that these values are conceptually distinct but overlap and differ in emphasis.

ARTISTRY

The word *artistry* was borrowed from the Latin and French. Originally, it referred to those who cultivated the arts, especially "those presided over by the Muses (history, poetry, comedy, tragedy, music, dancing, and astronomy)." Its meaning subsequently included the humanities and the fine arts. Within higher education, an artist was acknowledged to be "skilled in one of the seven liberal arts; a learned person; a scholar; a philosopher."[8] Its academic connotations are clear in the formalization of university degree requirements during the Renaissance.[9] A different and more practical meaning connotes an artist as "a person who practises any creative art in which accomplished execution is informed by imagination," a "public performer or actor," a "person skilled in a visual art, as painting, drawing, sculpture, etc.," or, even more broadly, a "person who displays talent and creativity in a manual art, craft or in other skilled work."[10] The ordinary dictionary meaning of *artistry* refers to taken-for-granted assumptions of what is meant by the arts, criteria for people and things that are considered to be artistic, and characteristics displayed by artists in terms of their "ability" and "execution."[11]

With these differing meanings in view, I begin with the assumption that artistry is theoretically and practically ambiguous in respect to what counts as an art, who may be regarded as artists, and which displays of skill, technique, or erudition count as artistic. Although artistry is often taken to be a practical and skill-oriented display, I want to forward its older, theoretical, and even figurative references to theory and scholarship and its mythic and spiritual roots in service of the Muses. To see artistry this way is to envisage it as pertaining to the life of spirit and sense, to devotion to other(s) and focus on self, and to thought and action. Artistry's ambiguous and even paradoxical character is evident in my "this-with-that" dialectical approach that opens both opportunities and challenges for music and education.[12]

The role of imagination, or what Vernon Howard describes as the "vision of mastery," plays a crucial role in artistry.[13] Whether in scholarship in academic fields or in displays of fine arts, artistry requires the exercise of the mind's construction of images of the possible. The fine arts provide apt ways to vividly portray or express imagination through paintings, sculptures, plays, musical performances, dances, poems, and the like. Each artistic tradition has its own beliefs and practices exemplified in sometimes long-held traditions of expectations accreted over time. Practitioners and their publics are more or less knowledgeable about these expectations, which become normative, and they can judge artistic exhibitions within these imaginary frames. Aaron Copland, Susanne Langer, and Northrup Frye are among the mid-twentieth-century writers to acknowledge imagination as a crucial aspect of human development and the role of artistry as a means of expressing imagination in the phenomenal world.[14] Following and diverging from Francis Sparshott and Philip Alperson, music education writers such as David Elliott pay particular attention to the social practices that are important constituents of the arts, notably music.[15] More recently, Elliott and his colleagues have posited the applicability of "artistic citizenship" as an end of music education and music's contribution to cultivating artistic citizens of a democracy.[16] Rather than thinking of the arts formally, in terms of mental constructions, these writers emphasize their practical character in transforming thought into distinctive practices, rituals, and actions. Whether the emphasis lies in formal and intellectual actions or phenomenal actions and practical constructions, the notion of artistry as an imaginative activity seems to be a commonly agreed-on characteristic. Artists are engaged in the process of transforming possibilities into actualities and ideas into practices construed propositionally and procedurally. These tasks are undertaken within frames or constraints of commitments and expectations that are acknowledged by artists and their publics. Whether it is an imaginative mathematical formulation or theory, an elegantly crafted philosophical argument, an engaging program of study, a distinguished scholarly article, or a moving song, dance, or poem, imagination is on display in myriad ways that are adjudicated by exponents of the traditions that apply to them.

In every case, artistry is process as well as product, the end conceived as ideal toward which the artist strives as well as the means whereby this end is achieved. As such, it is in a dynamic state of becoming, as the ideal changes along the way with growing experience, maturity, and wisdom. Differing means are employed to achieve this changing end. An imagined ideal seems to recede from me as I approach it, and I have the sense of never quite realizing the perfection of the vision I imagine. I might be pleased with a performance, but my critical eye discloses some things that might be executed better, flaws that might be corrected, opportunities that might be seized.[17] Hearing another's performance, reading another's work, listening to another speak opens the prospect of other ends that I had not imagined and other means that I had not previously employed. The vision of mastery that Howard articulates serves as a source of inspiration motivating me to seek to improve as well as an imperative for focusing my efforts in certain directions. As such, it has an educational purpose toward improving and even transforming my beliefs and practices.

Artistry is framed by distinctive beliefs and practices that are socially as well as individually constructed. Artists' imaginations are shaped to a large degree by the social contexts in which they work. Artistry is predicated on power relationships that define artists' powers and prerogatives and, where possible, sustain their livelihoods. These power relationships and their associated status are defined in terms of the social frames in which the arts are created and experienced. In music, the traditions in which musicians have been steeped from early life, the palettes of sounds they have heard, the systems of musical sounds with which their audiences are familiar, and the rituals that are part of lived life and in which music is made and received affect the possibilities that are explored and the musical events that are enacted.[18] Across multiple traditions, improvisation plays an important role in musical performances and multi-art events that celebrate or mark important moments in a people's collective life.[19] In the musical cultures of which I am aware, especially gifted musicians intimately know the rituals in which the arts play a part. These are the artist dancers, singers, painters, costume creators, and instrumentalists who lead communal rituals as the first among equals and who are relied on to create the rituals in which people participate. Musicians and their musics are associated with social class. In some musical traditions, musicians are regarded as a class apart from the rest of the people by virtue of their spiritual or supernatural power and their knowledge of powerful incantations involving what, when, how, where, and why particular music is created and experienced.[20] Some musical communities may be more exclusive than others, involving an elite cadre of musicians who may either be prepared through a sometimes long and arduous process or come to fame relatively quickly or easily because their music making is accessible and gives voice to the aspirations and experiences of their public. Their audiences fulfill a distinctive role in receiving and appreciating the music performed by artists and engaging imaginatively with it. Historically, musicians have cultivated a social status that separates them from others as a way of preserving their livelihood. Throughout much of musical history, it has been common for them to pass musical secrets from one generation to another through their family lineage.[21] Musician guilds, unions, associations, and the like have helped to solidify their power and prevent others from usurping their responsibilities and thereby their livelihoods. These groups are, in the United States at least, somewhat vulnerable at present.[22]

Artistry is also characterized by the possession and execution of specific skills. Craft forms an important aspect of artistry, and artists often refer to these skills as their craft. Whether it is instrument making, performing, composing, improvising, producing, or even listening or seeing, skill sets are required. Rather than construing artistry as just the productive aspects of art, I also want to think of demonstrations of the artistry involved in seeing and hearing or in the acts of receiving them. For example, a music critic listens skillfully and draws on a host of philosophical and theoretical assumptions as well as a knowledge of how this music is made. I think of the artistry, for example, of a brilliant and evocative concert program, concert review, or published article. For me, Donald Francis Tovey's classic volumes of essays on musical analysis seem fresh and engaging decades after they were written.[23] The masterful way in which he evokes music within the written word and his choice of expressive language to depict it remain, for me, stellar writing that I seek to emulate in my own work. With this broad definition of what counts as artistry, it follows that the skill sets required are both intellectual and practical, transcending the phenomenal world to include skills that are cognitive and spiritual. Within music education, a great deal of attention has been paid to the technical skills, or what some, such as Thomas Regelski, describe in Aristotelian terms as *techné*.[24] Regelski and Elliott advocate attention to these practical and socially informed skills within music education philosophy.[25] My own perspective, and one that they may share at least partly, is that the craft artists employ goes beyond mere technical prowess to include important intellectual skills that together comprise the building blocks of artistry.[26] In this view, artistry is not only and fundamentally about execution, about how the arts are made, constructed, composed, improvised, or otherwise produced, but also about the thought on which these actions are contingent. Be it a symphony conductor leading a performance, the musicians within the ensemble, or the music critic reviewing the performance, all are in their respective and specific ways thinking conceptually and imaginatively and doing their art in ways that are understood by their audience as exemplary, moving, or competent.

Artistry's spiritual connections are crucially important. Plato's notion of play as an ideal and serious matter still resonates today.[27] Throughout the intervening centuries of the Christian era, musicians have ascribed their gifts to God and composed in honor of St. Cecilia, the patron saint of music.[28] June Boyce-Tillman, Iris Yob, and other writers in music and arts education have noticed the spiritual dimensions of musical experience, and composers have also thought of their music as sacred, as going beyond the world of the senses to touch the soul.[29] In the East, for example, in the Northern Indian classical tradition, musicians have practiced the spiritual discipline of *riaz* in which the act of practicing and perfecting one's performance is a spiritual as well as a physical activity.[30] In vernacular traditions, the music of shamans—for example, those of the Hmong people of Laos, whose music I have witnessed—is deeply spiritual and also carries supernatural power in warding off evil spirits.[31] Whether it's a North American spiritual or performance of the Australian aboriginal didgeridoo, these musics carry a pathos and power that is spiritual as well as sensual. The more one understands these musical traditions, the greater one's grasp is on the depth of meaning and soulfulness conveyed in the music.

Among its advantages, artistry's focus on the practical and social aspects of doing music, among other arts and subjects, is active and passive and aligns well with the challenges of music and other classrooms. When learners demonstrate their learning, there is an immediate feedback that is motivating to and readily grasped by participants and observers alike. Before they have reached the capacity for formal operations or abstract thought, very young children can intuitively perceive and express underlying theoretical principles and rules governing their actions. Across the span of human development from very young to very old, artistry is a source of delight to artists and their publics. In music, whether it be very young children engaged in a Suzuki violin program or elderly performers in an assisted living group home, fostering artistry as an objective of music education constitutes a practical and direct way to experience music joyfully and a motivation for further learning.[32] For music teachers working with students, this direct, holistic, and immediate grasp of what music is and how it goes is a powerful motivating force for learning.

Although artistry focuses on procedural knowledge—that is, know-how or knowing how something is made—rather than propositional knowledge—that is, knowing that such and such is the case—I do not wish to suggest that artistry is exclusively procedural rather than propositional.[33] Rather, since it is so pervasively practical, artistry necessarily involves a knowledge of undergoing or how to go on in doing something. Israel Scheffler's distinction between these two forms of knowledge is useful in insisting that propositional knowledge needs to be accompanied by procedural knowledge.[34] While many academic subjects may focus on propositional knowledge, even in those subjects it is important to also know how to do them or undertake them. Although knowing these procedures is crucial in music and the other arts, scientists, mathematicians, historians, and psychologists are among the academics that also require a knowledge of how to do their arts and sciences. For me, this intersection between knowing about something or that such and such is the case and knowing how to do it is so palpable that, practically speaking, the two aspects can be thought of as the Janus faces of a whole and inextricably connected.

In its dependence on the senses and its evocation of the human spirit, artistry expresses modes of knowing that are too often devalued in an otherwise banal and materialistic existence. Demonstrating artistry is an expression of what Langer aptly termed *feeling*, or human understanding that cannot be put into discursive propositions.[35] Feeling does heavy duty for Langer, and some may rightly quarrel with her stress on feeling as the "life of mind."[36] Still, her ideas resonate with the work of musicians and artists and the role of knowledge beyond the purely rational that is a part of human intellection. I am drawn to her grasp of the ways in which sense, affect, and intellection resonate with each other. She is ahead of her time in arguing for a holistic and embodied view of the human mind in which words and other discursive symbols often fail and one is left with the unsayable or unknowable, with that which can be enacted in music among the other arts, rituals, and myths. Artistry is the means of articulating a range of human feeling that would otherwise be left unexpressed. Since music and the other arts are principal vehicles for artistic education, they merit a central place in education—an argument that Philip Phenix has made in his systematic educational plan.[37] Phenix argues persuasively that the arts belong in general education because they constitute an important way of meaning making. His taxonomy of these ways of meaning making accords with Nelson Goodman's ways of world making.[38] Phenix articulates the principle that general education ought to systematically attend to the gamut of types of meaning making. Since artistry provides direct experience of the arts, it follows that it would offer a potent means of education in the arts. Further, as a means of meaning making, artistry constitutes education. The artist's unfolding vision of an end-in-view is the essence of an experiential education. It may be for this implicit if not always explicitly stated reason that music performance, among other forms of artistry, has played a central role in education since antiquity.

Among its detractions, it may be tempting to think that one form of artistry is normative or suffices for all. Still, as Langer notices, the arts share common characteristics, and they also differ one from another. In her view, it is possible for one art to overpower another, as sometimes occurs when arts combine in ballet or opera. In music, one tradition may co-opt another. For example, Western classical music is a meld of musics that have been absorbed into it, and its boundaries are fuzzy. Chinese music incorporates Western music just as Western music incorporates Chinese music. In a time of internationalization and globalization, many musics represent a mix of traditions. Still, these melded musics are also distinctive, and the artistry required in one practice differs from that in others. Each demonstration of artistry is bounded and limited. It is important to resist the notion that one form of artistry stands for them all. Mine is a fallibilistic view that insists that each artistic expression is only one of many possibilities. In an age of rising authoritarianism, these possibilities subvert the hegemony of the one right way of thinking, being, and doing.

Also, the focus on the practical aspects of the arts may create an elitist approach to arts education. For example, a musician may take longer to acquire the requisite craft through which to make music than to gain propositional knowledge about music. In musical traditions with sophisticated compositional and performative techniques and extensive repertoires, this reality may result in an elite cadre of musicians who are separated from their audiences by what may sometimes be a gulf of disparate performing skills and experiences. Just as an athlete trains extensively to compete at a high level, so professional musicians in the Western classical tradition prepare for virtuosic performances that may be well beyond the capabilities of their audiences. Within popular music, a garage band might spend a long time absorbing and mastering instrumental and vocal techniques required to become a professional rock band.[39] Their crafting of the musical and spectacular aspects of their performance also distinguishes them from many in their audiences, who have not devoted the same time, energy, and expense to practice and preparation. Given the pervasive availability of music around the world, expectations of performance standards are easily accessible online, and the prospect of performing at or exceeding these standards is even more daunting. Music or other arts programs that emphasize artistry are likely to have narrower appeal for those students who are not prepared to invest significant time, effort, and expense. This reality, along with the intensiveness of teaching and learning artistry, makes it an expensive educational undertaking.

Focusing on a "vision of mastery" and seeking to reach it is not for the fainthearted. Some people lack the persistence, desire, or imagination to continue until a goal is reached. Perfectionists may never be satisfied with their achievements, and the constancy of high expectations may discourage and even demoralize them so that they are not willing to open themselves to the artistic process. Some may prefer not to make the attempt, rather than try and fail to meet their expectations and those of others. The matter of desire is important, especially for those who are drawn to other activities and whose passions lie elsewhere. My sense is that desire is a particularly important driver toward artistry, and much hangs on the personality, character, and abilities of the person involved. This reality renders artistry a value that is sometimes selectively relevant, especially to those devoted to exceptional levels of performance.[40]

It is also possible that with the focus on performative and procedural knowledge, teachers and their students may overlook the importance of propositional knowledge. Scheffler advises teachers not to conflate these two forms of knowing. Seeing how something is made does not equate with its discursive character.[41] In music performance programs conducted in schools, too many students fail to gain a comprehensive and systematic propositional knowledge of music at the same time as they acquire high levels of ensemble playing skill. Although it is important to focus on the performative and technical aspects of artistry, it is also necessary to build a strong conceptual foundation for music.

TASTE

The word *taste* comes originally from the Old French *tast* and the Italian *tasto* and originally meant "to touch." Its reference to the act of touching or touch later referred more specifically to the act of tasting or "perceiving the flavor of a thing with the organ of taste." In some cases, it referred to "a small quantity" of alcohol "as admits of being tasted." This specific and literal meaning then took on figurative reference to "mental perception of quality; judgement, discriminative faculty" or "the fact or condition of liking or preferring something; inclination, liking *for;* appreciation." The conditions of "enjoyment, pleasure, 'relish'" then came to refer normatively as "the sense of what is appropriate, harmonious, beautiful," especially the "discernment and appreciation of the beautiful in nature or art"—notably, "the faculty of perceiving and enjoying what is excellent in art, literature, and the like." Taste also denotes the "style or manner exhibiting æsthetic discernment; good or bad æsthetic quality; the style or manner favoured in any age or country."[42] Its use as a verb also reflects a change from literal references to encompass figurative meanings and from sensory to perceptive qualities.[43] These usages suggest that taste is educable and can be shaped over time. Musicians and educators are "taste-makers." The acts of composing, improvising, performing, and producing are educational as much as musical in cultivating one's own taste and the tastes of one's audiences and students.

Among its characteristics, taste is tactful. This may seem to be an unusual place to begin. Still, I want to rescue the ancient references of taste and tact to the sense of touch. Taste is rooted in the senses, and the metaphor of touch remains an important characteristic. True, taste has been more explicitly linked to the gustatory sense. Still, the bigger point that I want to capture is that taste refers to the direct engagement of one's senses. Tact, like touch, is sensitive.[44] This is the sort of touch that takes care with subtleties and details and is aware of texture, form, and nuance. It is a careful and thoughtful touch that invokes feeling as well as finely tuned discrimination. Taste, figuratively construed, is a matter of this type of touch. In terms of music and music education, for example, these qualities are evident in the way one sings or plays an instrument. The Peking operatic singer employs a widely different tonal palette than the Italian bel canto singer, yet beneath it all is a vocal and bodily awareness of one's voice and a sensitivity to matters of touch in the carefulness with which the repertoire is performed. Watching a Peking opera master class in Beijing, I was struck by its affinity to master classes with which I am familiar in Western conservatories. Notwithstanding the wide differences in the musics being transmitted, all these teachers are equally concerned with cultivating tact or touch in their students. In very different repertoires, they are all preoccupied with expressing nuances of feeling though their voices and bodies.

Also, taste requires imbibing something and taking it in. This is an active and receptive process of directly experiencing something with one's senses. Yet there is also restraint in the taking. Just as one cannot taste a wine without sipping it in small quantities, one cannot taste a music without participating in it at least to some degree. In so doing, there is a receptivity, open-mindedness, and willingness to be surprised by this music, to allow it to speak directly through its sounds and sights without prejudice. It is impossible to cultivate taste without also teaching for the quality of welcoming surprise. Yet, as Scheffler notes in his defense of surprise as an educational value, too many teachers and students are closed-minded, seeking either to repudiate surprise or defend against its possibility.[45] A music teacher who preplans every moment of a music rehearsal and allows no possibility for the unexpected inevitably, if also unwittingly, teaches for closed-mindedness. Randall Allsup critiques the well-meaning tendency to constrict openings and foreclose possibilities to experience the unexpected, rhapsody, or surprise.[46] Instead, he posits an approach to music instruction that values openings and, in the words of Maxine Greene, "multiplicities and pluralities" in music education to which these openings necessarily tend.[47] This direct and participatory engagement in teaching and learning is experiential in the sense that one is actually caught in a predicament or situation in which one opens oneself to another person or thing; this opening impacts one in sometimes profound and transformative ways.[48]

Further, taste entails intellection, including reason, perception, intuition, and feeling. As an imaginative activity, it requires discrimination, critical and constructive thought, and sensory responsiveness. As with artistry, these intellectual powers can be developed through the educational process. The means whereby these powers are developed are both informal and formal. They are also clearly affected by the specific home environments and social contexts in which people grow, mature, and live out their lives. For example, children in homes, neighborhoods, and religious communities in which vernacular and popular musical traditions are regularly heard naturally absorb these sounds and sights, which become part of their musical taste. For this reason, music educators often speak of music appreciation, in which the response to music is expected to be positive in the sense of valuing what is going on in the music.[49] Where the young are specifically taught songs or instructed in playing instruments, their musical tastes are deliberately directed in ways that sometimes enlarge their musical horizons and other times bifurcate their musical tastes. Too much musical education has resulted in what I think of as a form of musical bifurcation or, worse, schizophrenia, in which students learn those musics that their teachers or administrators believe should constitute the basis for their musical taste while also absorbing those musics around them, about which they sometimes feel conflicted. Too often, their tastes do not mature to a point where they are integrated so that what they do or wish to do accords with what they believe they should do. For those musicians who come from the East and have imbibed a Western musical taste, there are times when the Eastern music speaks past Western norms and they acknowledge deeply held preferences that sometimes lie buried beneath their cultivated Western musical tastes.[50] The same is true of youngsters who grow up on a diet of rock music but subsequently take up the study of Western classical instruments. As classically trained musicians, they find themselves drawn to popular musics that sometimes go in very different directions from those musics to which their education has been directed. Too few embrace these differing tastes and integrate them within their lives. Rather, the pleasure that ought to be associated with a broad musical taste can be replaced by dutiful devotion to a music deemed by others to be suitable for and worthy of one's time and energy.

Furthermore, whatever the musical tradition, taste becomes normative. As Immanuel Kant puts it, taste involves "the faculty of estimating an object or mode of representation." In music, one expects others who are participants in the music to agree with one, to share similar beliefs and expectations, and to act in ways that fall within the expectations of the tradition.[51] In earlier writing, I have referred to this reality as a "sphere of musical validity," a shared mindset characteristic of every musical tradition I have studied.[52] As such, taste is a matter that is affected by power relationships where those wielding the greatest power are in a position to influence the taste of other less powerful people. For example, where a society's establishment embraces a form of music as emblematic of its high status, it is natural for those who aspire to its power and prestige to adopt this music as the basis for music education. From the beginning of publicly supported American music education in the early nineteenth century, classical music emanating from Europe was uncritically regarded as the appropriate basis of school music instruction. Music considered to be of lower status, including that emanating from the United States, such as jazz, the spirituals of Appalachia and African Americans, and vernacular popular music, was regarded as beneath the serious attention of music teachers trained almost exclusively in Western classical music. In this way, the bifurcation between popular and vernacular musical traditions and those of Western classical music too often resulted in musical taste that failed to integrate the music people believed they should enjoy on the one hand and the music they enjoyed on the other. During the past half century, music educators have increasingly realized the role of power in the construction of musical taste and the importance of an integrated musical taste that values musical traditions for their unique contributions and melds aspects of these disparate musical traditions.[53] In order to acquire such a catholic musical taste, it is necessary to understand musics comparatively and grasp the beliefs, practices, and rule systems that apply within the particular musical traditions in which one participates. Acquiring musical taste in its descriptive and normative senses and integrating one's musical taste as the smorgasbord of one's musical experiences are educational tasks that contribute to what Abraham Maslow terms "self-actualization"—or personal or spiritual well-being and flourishing.[54] Such an approach contributes to a sense of personal integrity, wholeness, and transparency.

Among its advantages, taste is an important marker of distinction for those musics that have strong intellectual appeal. It seems particularly relevant as a value in classical traditions from East and West that have extensive repertoires and require considerable preparation in the requisite skills for performance and in which there are clear delineations between musics that cultivate different and specialized classes of people—the composers, improvisers, and performers on the one hand and the audiences for whom music makers compose, improvise, and perform on the other. These specialized roles in classical musics did not always exist. Consorts of musicians playing for their own pleasure music sometimes composed by one of their own presaged concerts in which musicians performed for audiences. Still, over the past two centuries, one sees growing specialization in these various roles.

The notion of taste as requiring direct experience of or with music, as one might sip a drink in order to taste it, has the advantages of encompassing theory and practice and of thinking of them holistically. In this view, those who have performed, improvised, and composed are able to understand a music intellectually and grasp how it is made. This value underscores the importance of performance, improvisation, and composition and creative writing about music in general education. Even in the absence of a full-blown theory of musical activities, music educators have long understood the power of doing music. One thinks, for example, of a typical instrumental lesson of Plato's time in which a lyre or singing teacher might face the student directly.[55] Plato probably envisaged this model of music education within his educational plan. For him, this active involvement in music making needs to come early in the schooling process and becomes a vehicle whereby a citizen acquires musical taste.[56] Importantly, Plato understood that students inevitably go on to subsequent important learning. Nevertheless, the early establishment of musical taste serves as the bedrock of *paideia,* the acquisition of culture. Of course, Plato's world was simpler than ours in its exclusion of most people and in its lack of concern about multiple traditions and perspectives. It sought only to establish the taste of this place and the narrow interests of the establishment. Taste is therefore regarded as unproblematic, and Plato assigns the acquisition of virtuosic skills to slaves. He approaches musical understanding through participating competently in communal rituals of which music is a part.

Taste also permits us to accomplish much with little. Depth is valued over breadth. In wine tasting, rather than gulp down a large quantity, one savors the sight, smell, and taste of a small quantity. This is a powerful educational principle. Plato did not expect all students to undergo lengthy and time-consuming performance instruction or to acquire virtuosity. Indeed, as in other musical traditions, students are discouraged from too much musical instruction at the expense of other often more important objectives they are expected to pursue. The principle of accomplishing a lot with a little requires teachers to select subject matter that can accomplish the most with the least time and effort. Zoltán Kodály is convinced it is possible to cultivate musical taste with fifty-four well-chosen songs.[57] I am sure he did not mean to restrict music educators to this precise number of songs. Still, he articulates the principle that a carefully selected and limited repertoire is crucial in music instruction, and its effects are potentially transformative. It may be this principle's resonance with their music education programs that leads many music teachers to be concerned about the songs and pieces they selectively teach to the young.

Among its disadvantages, musical taste can be used to subjugate personal desire and impulse as a means of social control. The power exercised by influential people in establishing and ensuring a musical taste as normative effectively disempowers those musical traditions that are considered outside the established norms. Since marginalized and excluded traditions are also part of identity construction, the exclusion or marginalization of some musical traditions effectively excludes and marginalizes those who practice them. One sees this in the exclusion of indigenous traditions from the music curricula in early publicly supported schools in the United States—a means of disempowering Native Americans, African Americans, and rural Americans whose oral and shaped note traditions cultivated in singing schools of the late eighteenth and early nineteenth centuries were bypassed in favor of European music and instructional methods.[58] Lowell Mason's sol-fa system, consonant with John Curwen's English sol-fa system, was intended to cultivate the literacy required for classical music. In the process, those who practiced indigenous or vernacular musics were regarded as outside the musical mainstream for the purposes of musical education.

The cultivation of musical taste is also associated with musical institutions that tend to become powerful and difficult to dislodge. Once established, institutional norms in taste are often conservative and resistant to change. I have mentioned the bifurcation of musical taste and the differences between what music teachers may be prepared to teach and what students may desire to know. Although music educators realized this difficulty in the 1960s, during the intervening decades, many music conservatories have continued to prepare music teachers within a comparatively narrow range of musical traditions in which the Western classical tradition is normative. Notwithstanding the growing interest in the study and teaching of popular music among music teachers, conservatories have resisted change. Cultivating a broad catholic musical taste has yet to be realized fully in music education at the tertiary level. It is still unusual to encounter, for example, Appalachian fiddle music in American conservatories, though such traditions continue to flourish in some of the rural places in which musicians may teach.[59] Even within the classical tradition, conductors of recent orchestral pieces often encounter resistance among their audiences to music that is most daring in its departure from earlier styles and sounds. For these various institutional reasons, emphasizing musical taste can constrict rather than expand musical horizons.

Besides cultivating a certain snobbery about one's taste, in which one regards one's own preferences and judgments as superior to those of people with whom one disagrees, musical taste may overemphasize qualities of perceptive sensitivity and judgmental restraint and underemphasize the importance of surrender, ecstasy, and abandonment to the medium, be it music, visual art, drama, ritual, or something else.[60] Thinking of taste in intellectual terms overlooks sensory responsiveness in which conscious appraisal of music or another art form is less relevant than the leisurely and bodily response to its sounds or sights. Native Americans may judge music by its power to evoke dance.[61] In the dance, or in the process of evoking trance, the point of the music is not so much appraisal as arousal. And it must be admitted that the intellectual characteristics of taste may be more relevant to some musics than to others.

SKILL

Skill is often associated with notions of artistry, particularly regarding artists' craftiness or expertise in utilizing the means and media at their disposal to create an artful painting, composition, performance, or piece of scholarship. It connotes artists' creative powers. The English word *skill* has Nordic roots and once referred to such things as "reason," "intellectual power" and "discrimination," "a sense of what is right or fitting," and "a wise or sensible act." It also came to be ascribed as the "capability of accomplishing something with precision and certainty; practical knowledge in combination with ability; cleverness, expertness."[62] Construed as a verb, skill once meant to "separate," "divide," distinguish, "part from," "care," "allege in argument," "understand," "comprehend," "have knowledge of," and "know how to do something."[63] Some of these meanings have fallen into disuse; indeed, using *skill* as a verb has likewise faded. I want to rescue this evocative and ambiguous word as both noun and verb, think of skill conceptually and practically, and tease out some of its richness and detraction from music and education.

Among its characteristics, skill is a form of knowledge, especially know-how—that is, knowing how to proceed in music, visual art, literature, or some other art form. For Scheffler, this is procedural knowledge or "seeing how it was made."[64] Such knowledge need not necessitate that one grasp what is done propositionally because one can learn a skill by trial and error and without a deep knowledge of the ontological qualities of a thing. I may teach pianists to play a piece without communicating what I am trying to achieve and by simply demanding that they imitate exactly what I am doing. Many musical traditions employ this approach in inducting the young through imitation and repetition. Here, I prefer to think of skill as enriching propositional knowledge and combining with it such that, as one learns the "what" of a subject, one also learns how to do it or vice versa. My view of skill sees theoretical understanding and practical knowledge as intertwined and including comprehension, understanding, and practice. Practically speaking, *knowing that* and *know-how* constitute different aspects of skill as I conceive of it.

Also, in our time, skill is often employed in educational discourse to refer to technique or the specific aspects that comprise a subject. In music, for example, skill is often a matter of nuance and distinction. Details matter, and the precise techniques a musician employs emphasize the specific features of a composition, improvisation, or performance. Percy Scholes saw this clearly in his story of taking guests to his home in the Swiss countryside out on a balcony to see the view.[65] As he tells the story, some took in the details of the landscape and commented on specific features, and others seemed not to see the details. He wants musicians to notice the details because they represent the richness of musical pieces. Along with the capacity for nuance and distinction, *skill* also refers to the cleverness and expertise with which music is experienced. When one performs skillfully, the performance appears magical or effortless. Paying attention to the details allows sometimes complex skills to appear almost superhuman, especially to those who possess limited skill themselves.

Skill takes time, patience, determination, and practice to acquire. Musicians may understand an interpretative principle in performing a composition, but, as I noted earlier, accomplishing a vision of mastery in practice is another matter that may require concerted practical effort to realize. Howard also makes this point regarding the teaching of singing where singers do not always know what they are up against or what to look for, and, at least early in the educational process, they must trust their teachers to help them discover what to do.[66] These practical aspects sometimes seem prosaic and crafty. Much turns on developing routinized actions that often fade from the foreground and seem instinctual to musicians. Virtuosity and grace emerge after the specific practices have been so internalized and mastered that musicians can toss off difficult passages with ease while focusing on the musical whole being created. Accomplishing these feats often requires the discipline to continue to refine the specific practical aspects until they seem almost second nature. This process is not merely a matter of repetition. It also involves critical analysis in evaluating what one is doing and how one needs to improve toward an imagined ideal.

Further, skill is a matter of applied imagination. Mary Reichling elaborates on the role of reason, intuition, feeling, and perception required in the creation of images of what should or might be created.[67] For me, hers needs not be an exhaustive list of dimensions, but they illustrate some of the complexity of imagination in skill development and demonstration. Reason entails the powers of deduction, induction, and analogical thought that enables one to figure out how to broach the gap between what one wishes to accomplish and what one can do at the present. Intuition offers a holistic intellectual grasp of what one is doing, what one needs to do, and how to achieve the desired results. Feeling demonstrates and evokes cognitive, emotional, and bodily experience that cannot be expressed propositionally but is enacted through such means as the arts, rituals, myths, dreams, and religions.[68] Perception allows one to make sense of a host of sensory stimuli in the arts, be they visual, auditory, tactile, or something else. Each of these dimensions of imagination is interrelated with the others and involves skill sets that are applied, in turn, to the specific things being created, be they artistic, scientific, or of some other realm. Rather than being monolithic, skills are multifarious, often specific to the given task being undertaken, yet sharing commonalities as evidence of the work of imagination.

Among its advantages, skill embodies knowledge. Abstract knowledge about something is not only acquired intellectually but also enacted physically and emotionally. Such knowledge combines the senses, has emotional valence, and brings reason and imagination to bear on what is learned. As such, it enables learners to express what has been learned through actions as well as concepts expressed verbally. Playing an instrument skillfully is a holistic form of knowing in which mind, soul, and body are one—a state of being akin to the generalization that Alfred North Whitehead terms "wisdom."[69] The resulting holistic approach to teaching and learning transcends atomistic means and ends by allowing learners to grasp not only the whole but the many elements that comprise it.

That skill is observable in the phenomenal world renders it amenable to assessment in an educational world preoccupied with monitoring instructional effects. Skill makes public that which may otherwise remain private. It assists teachers in determining what has been learned and how to most effectively proceed toward further development. Since this learning is demonstrable and public, teachers can evaluate the level or extent of students' mastery and tailor future challenges to best fit with students' present skills. This possibility contributes to improving the efficiency and effectiveness of learning and teaching. Resources can also be allocated to areas where they are most needed and efficacious.

Skill employs different modalities, be they tactile, visual, or auditory. All of the arts make differing demands, and those who seek to master them bring different predispositions and experiences to the required tasks. It is not surprising that the arts appeal differently to people whose physical, emotional, and intellectual capacities also differ. Developing skill requires sensitivity to the challenges each skill presents to a learner with a specific repertoire of physical, emotional, and intellectual capacities. The necessity of beginning with the individual learner in skill development is a humane and student-centered approach to education. A teacher needs to begin precisely where the students are and devise strategies that will permit them to progress successfully without becoming overwhelmed or discouraged on the one hand or bored or insufficiently challenged on the other. It may be this necessity and the need for teachers to focus on their individual students that has made private musical instruction one of the most successful and enduring forms of education, with a history stretching back to the earliest historical records.[70] Since the learning is also concrete as well as abstract, the very young who have not yet developed capacities for abstract thought are enabled to intuitively grasp the heart of musical principles before they may comprehend the theoretical principles that underlie their actions.

The apparent magical quality of cleverness and expertise in skill is inspirational in learning. Seeing and hearing or touching something that has been brilliantly executed prompts aspiration on the parts of learners. Music teachers who have conducted their students in choral or instrumental ensembles know the encouragement and motivation prompted by a brilliant performance that has been received enthusiastically by an audience. An audience immediately recognizes virtuosity and may respond in shouts or whistles, or in a host of other ways that acknowledge the wizardry that has been displayed. Sometimes, a profound silence may take hold before the audience cheers. I have referred to the motivational impact of virtuosic musical displays as a "demonstration effect" in which others want to emulate what these musicians have shown.[71] As a musician, Lowell Mason understood the power of example at the dawn of the American school music movement and sought to establish the value of music in the general elementary school curriculum.[72]

Importantly, skill requires practice to develop. Its acquisition is a form of delayed gratification that requires time and effort. In an age in which digital media evoke expectations of instant gratification, mastering an instrument or musical practice stands in stark contrast, with its development of patience, forbearance, determination, and resilience required to master a skill. The drudgery of repetitive motions and the often stepwise procedures that need to be employed as one develops a technique are out of fashion in a world filled with the enticements of vivid media and instantaneous results. Yet these are the very qualities required for living a happy and fulfilled life and transcending the obstacles and sorrows that one inevitably encounters. Cultivating a disciplined approach applies not only to a skill set or an art form but by extension to the rest of life. By requiring reason, feeling, perception, and intuition in imaginative thought and action, skill fosters a high level of thought and action.

Among its detractions, focusing on skill may emphasize practical aspects and procedural knowledge and may overlook theoretical matters concerning what is being done. It may be tempting for teachers to assume that seeing how something is made suffices for a thorough understanding of it when, in fact, such an education may be unnecessarily narrow. In music, for example, an exclusive focus on performative skills may be understandable, especially given the public nature of musicking. Still, such an emphasis may miss the wider and more abstract conceptual knowledge that also requires systematic development. When this occurs, students may be shortchanged in their broader musical understanding. It is also easy to become preoccupied with the development of skill for skill's sake rather than grasping its important role in achieving a comprehensive knowledge of music making and receiving.[73]

Focusing on skill may also foster an elitist approach to music and education and value those who demonstrate high ability or expertise over those of more ordinary talent. Especially given the individual nature of instruction required to develop skill and the often individualized and costly instructional programs, whether in apprenticeship, small group, or individual studio settings, it may seem imperative to focus on those who evidence high aptitude for the instruction. In music conservatories, for example, this selectivity of instruction and the high demands on students to produce work at professional standards is doubtless elitist because of the time and effort required to cultivate skill in performance, history, theory, composition, ballet, opera, and the like. Music education programs in such environments naturally tend toward preparing teachers and musicians to teach in ways that they have been taught and that accord with values characteristic of music conservatories. In the West and East, these values are typically those of the classical music traditions. Too often, this reality results in a gap between the interests and capacities of music teachers and the skills desired by ordinary students in publicly supported schools. Also, the skills possessed by graduates of such institutions may not be those possessed by popular musicians and the present-day music industry where employment opportunities may present. Although this reality of disjunct skill sets and the tensions between those skills associated with high-status music and those associated with low-status music are ameliorating somewhat, the values of high-status music remain normative. Focusing on skill highlights these tensions and discontinuities because undertaking a musical practice requires commitment to that tradition, and this commitment necessarily impacts one's identity and social status. Many students may desire a general grasp of music but are not necessarily willing to commit to a musical tradition, especially one outside the popular mainstream of their experience. So the development of musical skill may appeal more narrowly, especially when the technical demands are high. As a result, many people may be excluded from a musical program built around the acquisition and demonstration of skill. This is particularly the case in a world in which there are often many distractions and interesting alternatives to explore beyond this music.

The effort required in practice and discipline may be out of sync with prevalent societal values. Providing an education that emphasizes delayed gratification requires discipline, persistence, and diligence in the face of obstacles in one's way to producing exemplary performances, improvisations, compositions, and the like. Work and play are required. In a society that does not prize those values, it is likely that the difficulties of excelling in skills may surprise the young who find it necessary to develop them in an environment in which the expectations of them are higher than those they have encountered up to this point. This reality is likely to make it even more difficult for learners to achieve the expected results than if they had grown up from an early age with the selfsame expectations of discipline, persistence, and diligence. They will have more work to do than if they had applied themselves from early childhood. It is also possible that in seeking to help their students reach the desired level of competence, teachers will turn what should be joy-filled instruction into the drudgery of work. When this occurs, students are trapped in constant drudgery without a continuing sense of success and high morale needed to inspire them to continued effort, and emphasizing skill can become destructive and demoralizing.

Emphasizing skill focuses on the craft by which art is made. Craft's practical nature and its requirement of sometimes sophisticated understandings of procedural knowledge may cause it to be depreciated in favor of artistry that appears inspirational, effortless, and transcendent. Howard notes that rather than bifurcating art and craft, it would be better to think of "craft art" or "arty craft" in which both aspects meld.[74] Without the craft or the skill set whereby an art is made, art falters; without an overall artistic statement, craft is prosaic. These intersections may be lost where the crafty aspects of art are depreciated or deemphasized. When this occurs, artists do not possess the techniques that allow them to mine the artistic possibilities that might otherwise be possible. Their craft limits their capacity to imagine and realize what may practically be created.

STYLE

As with *artistry, taste,* and *skill,* the word *style* is ambiguous, serving as both noun and verb, and having a wide array of meanings. Some might see it as skill "turned up a notch" with the addition of artistry. Its origin in the Latin *stilus* evokes a "stake or pale" that also serves as a weapon. It also refers specifically to a "sharp pointed instrument for writing on a tablet." *Style* developed to refer to the manner of written communication and declamation and to describe "the manner of expression characteristic of a particular writer . . . literary group or period . . . or of a writer's mode of expression considered in regard to clearness, effectiveness, beauty, and the like." In referencing the "manner of discourse," *style* means such things as the "form of words, phrase, or formula, by which a particular idea or thought is expressed." It also connotes aspects of approach and fashion, to the "method or custom of performing actions or functions, esp. one sanctioned by usage and law." Its artistic use is spelled out more specifically as a "particular mode or form of skilled construction, execution, or production; the manner in which a work of art is executed, regarded as characteristic of the individual artist or of his [their] time and place; one of the modes recognized in a particular art as suitable for the production of beautiful or skilled work." Along the way, style also means a "definitive type of architecture," a "kind, sort, or type, as determined by manner of composition or construction, or by outward appearance." It is viewed not only as a way of doing things but also a "way of describing historical events, e.g., baroque, classical, and romantic" periods. It covers such things as the "manner of executing a task or performing an action," "fashionable air, appearance, deportment, etc.," and a way to describe one's own preference or taste in visual art, music, or other artistic form.[75] As a verb, style variously means to "give a name or style to" something, to "name or address with honorific title," to "order, direct to a purpose," to "design, arrange, make, etc., in a particular (esp. fashionable) style," and, more recently, to "show off, especially when fashionably or ostentatiously dressed."[76]

Among its characteristic musical and educational features, *style* denotes certain socially ascribed ways of thinking and doing music, among other things that are agreed on by the members of communities of practice.[77] These beliefs and practices are educational and take on normative valence as attributes that ought to be followed by the exponents and adherents of a musical tradition. Earlier, I described a "sphere of musical validity" as the mindset and practice of a musical group in which members share understandings and follow practices that are adhered to and promulgated as exemplary.[78] As a social phenomenon, musical style is organic and dynamic, as particular fashions come and go. Musical rules are contested between those who seek to challenge or change the tradition and those who seek to conserve it in space and time. Across the places in which music is made and taken by musicians and their publics, preferences, nuances, and stylistic differences emerge, consolidate, and decline. Across times, the music typical of an historical era likewise changes, enabling historians to describe each era as a style. All the musics of which I am aware can be described at least generally in terms of certain typical characteristics that together comprise a style.

Style both distinguishes and disciplines. The metaphor of a sharp instrument that inscribes an ancient tablet evokes these twin roles. Because it describes, delineates, and differentiates beliefs and practices, it provides an analytical or conceptual tool for examining and appraising music, art, drama, literature, dance, and the other arts. It offers an educational means of preserving beliefs and practices that may otherwise be transient and ephemeral and constitutes a source of social stability. It arises out of a widespread human desire for immortality and the hope that what is made here and now might last into the future. Style also disciplines because it insists on certain characteristics as normative and presumes that others ought to agree that this is the case.[79] It serves as a basis to criticize, demean, ridicule, ostracize, shame, or otherwise punish those who depart from its precepts and to insist on compliance with its beliefs and practices. Musical competitions, for example, are predicated on common stylistic assumptions and practices, and musicians are ranked according to their conformity to these rules. Performers whose performances are stylistically normative are often ranked higher than others whose performances are individualistic, idiosyncratic, and challenge taken-for-granted stylistic rules.

Although style is socially informed, it is also deeply personal and embodied. Each musician, for example, imbibes a tradition's rules, personifies them, and brings to that tradition an imaginative perspective that makes this music uniquely their own. We recognize artists and musicians by their distinctive "voices," or what they seek to communicate and the ways in which they express themselves artistically and musically. In every musical tradition with which I am familiar, informed listeners expect ambiguity, difference, and idiosyncrasy among performers, composers, and improvisers. In the sciences and the arts alike, people approach and solve problems that reflect agreed-on approaches that characterize the groups and institutions of which they are members in quite personal and idiosyncratic ways that sometimes challenge and counter the group consensus. So style needs to be thought of psychologically, individually, and personally as well as socially, collectively, and communally. In music, as in the other arts, these stylistic individualities evidence the richly ambiguous possibilities of sound, color, texture, and shape that appeal to such senses as hearing, sight, and touch.

Style is a synthesis of characteristics that are dependent on the skills of musicians and audiences alike. Within music, these specific attributes concern the formal or theoretical properties and practical improvisatory, compositional, or performance skills musicians display—elements that audiences variously grasp. Although there is a natural interest in developing skills of music making as a means to inculcate a sense of musical style, music teachers also recognize the importance of an audience's grasp of what is going on musically, hence an emphasis on educating audiences as a primary purpose of music instruction in general education.[80] In addition to understanding the particularities and mastering the specific skills required within a musical tradition, style also requires what Langer refers to as an "articulated" whole or what Whitehead might see as "generalization" or even "wisdom."[81] For Whitehead, style is "the last acquirement of the educated mind."[82] Here, the particular characteristics or skills are interrelated and integrated in ways that produce a unity, prompting a cyclical process whereby the romance of intuition and the reasoned and systematic understanding of instrumentalism are, in turn, synthesized into generalization. One need not accept Whitehead's tripartite and cyclical educational vision to acknowledge the crucial point that the individual constituent skills are not separate ends: style emerges where they are integrated and together comprise a unified, coherent, and imaginative whole.

Among its contributions, style serves as an important point of departure for and end of creative expression. It requires a formal or informal education to acquire and master. There is a grace in the execution of a musical performance, a painting, a sculpture, a theater piece, or whatever the artistic medium that comprises a compelling artistic statement. Whether it be a painting or drawing by Salvador Dali or Frida Kahlo, this grace is witnessed in the details and nature of their execution, the development of a personal style, and the deeply symbolic convictions that an informed viewer may recognize across these artists' oeuvres. Creativity occurs within the context and even discipline of style as it also contributes to new forms of artistic expression. Viewed in this way, style prompts education in and through art as it also flows from it. Learning and experimentation are fundamental aspects of artistic thought and practice, and style provides a holistic educational means and end. Style values an education in the arts for both artists and their publics. It requires artists and audiences to be literate in an artistic tradition in the sense of understanding it intimately while also contributing to the pluralistic and multifaceted ways in which literacy may be viewed. As Phenix would argue, style contributes to aesthetic modes of knowing that are essential to general education.[83]

Style also acknowledges the power of fashion in shaping what is taught and learned, the importance of social influences on the individual, and the seeming effortlessness and "flow" of a creative performance. It appears graceful and effortlessness only when artists have mastered their media and produced unified and compelling works. Witnessing this grace, artfulness, and integrity evokes admiration on the part of the audience that is knowledgeable of this art form as it also allows critical examination of it. The more one knows of this style, the more one may be inspired by a brilliant music performance or artistic exhibition and wonder at artists' work when they excel. Socially informed practice is not merely fashionable or decorative; it also serves a spiritual purpose in education in unifying those who share similar understandings and thereby solidifying not only the art but the group whose practice it is. Notwithstanding the power of fashion and social pressures to conform, style is individualistic and creative in its departure from fashion and the status quo. These creative and idiosyncratic elements of style stand out in bold relief because of the powerful backdrop of social and artistic conventions and expectations.

As an embodied mode of knowing, style is humane in its focus on artists and their audiences. In studying a composer's style, for example, one comes to know about the person who made the composition and to see the music as subject rather than mere object. In so doing, style not only elevates one's mode of thought and practice but values those who do the music and undergo the education. Thinking stylistically emphasizes the value of individual experience and public understanding. During this writing, my visits to the Chihuly Collection and the Dali Museum in St. Petersburg, Florida, prompted me to think about music of the period in fresh and compelling ways and to see the work of artists as sharing a common humane bond. These visits prompted my reflection on a performance I had heard before of works by Rossini, Mendelssohn, and Beethoven by the Sarasota Orchestra conducted by Han-Na Chang. I pondered the many ways in which a sense of style, be it musical or artistic, reflects the contexts of time and place in which musicians and artists work and their own personalities and preferences. These works were not only compelling in their sensory appeal but evocative of reflection on my experience and human experience more generally. They revealed what I already knew or did not know, and the time spent with them was meaningful and inspirational. As such, style opened windows on life as education and education as life.

Among its detractions, style may serve to impede and smother creativity that repudiates it. Such is the power of fashion and social approval that artists and musicians who travel a different path may meet criticism, ridicule, and ostracism. Where approval of one's artistic work is monetized and provides a source of livelihood, there is a strong incentive to do that which is socially approved and fashionable. For music teachers working with young people who are strongly influenced by peer approval, it may be tempting to pander to the popular and fashionable in which young people are naturally interested rather than introducing them to styles that are unpopular and sometimes difficult to master because they are further from their experience. Focusing just on styles that are popular restricts the array of other styles that might be explored and stunts the musical and artistic development of the young.

Since style requires a systematic education in the arts, there is a danger that this idea will be understood too narrowly. The fine arts are predicated on oral and written traditions that have accreted over time. Whether it be vernacular traditions commonly practiced or more esoteric traditions practiced by a few, these bedrock ideas and practices need to be mastered in depth before one can depart intelligently from them. The classical fine art traditions stretch back to antiquity and have been preserved in artifacts and written and oral traditions passed on from one generation to the next over millennia. Style requires a literacy in these arts and an understanding of how present beliefs and practices came to be. Music, as do the other arts, needs to be studied in the richness of its multifarious traditions so that the young come to see how the development of classical traditions relate to each other and to the vernacular and popular traditions around the world. When using the phrase *systematic education*, I do not refer to the study of just classical music. Rather, I think of a broad, deep, and inclusive approach to musics that focuses on their roots and how the present sights and sounds emerged. To accomplish this objective requires valuing improvisation, musical literacy and notation, orality and its cultivation, and a historical and geographical grasp of the spread of musics and their intersections with each other and with the other arts. It is likely that the idea of a systematic musical education will be interpreted too narrowly, privilege a few traditions, devalue others, and further exacerbate divisions between different traditions and styles and those who value them. This said, I still see great value in focusing on and extending the systematic understandings within the fine arts traditions that often draw from the popular and everyday world. Watching people crowding Dali and Kahlo exhibits, listening through mobile devices to commentary on each work about aspects they may not have otherwise noticed, I was struck by why one would not also want to do the same thing in music. Education in these traditions keeps them alive. Thinking too narrowly about what constitutes a systematic musical education or failing to focus sufficiently on the classical in music deprives people of knowledge that is important in living life artistically and aesthetically.

Since there is so much to know about music to acquire a grasp of its style, there may be a danger in focusing on the theoretical to the exclusion of the practical skills of music making and centering on the past rather than the present. In either case, the cultivation of a musical taste that deprecates various musical traditions or fails to emphasize sufficiently the making of contemporary music provides a myopic view of music and musicking. It may also lose out on learning musical skills that will carry over into the rest of lived experience and fail to grasp opportunities of transforming rather than simply transmitting past traditions. As such, it may fail to sufficiently engage the musics of minorities or those who are in less privileged and influential social positions. For example, the musics of the Americas have strong classical threads and vibrant vernacular and popular roots. Where Eurocentric musical traditions prevail in educational institutions in the United States, the musical heritage of American natives and immigrants from other cultures may be bypassed, and their musical voices can be silenced. Where people cannot make and do these musics and they do not count as worthy of serious and playful engagement, the notion of who we are as Americans and human beings is distorted and diminished. More broadly, a truly inclusive view of music and education requires an international and global perspective—a daunting imperative where too many music teachers are trained too narrowly and ethnocentrically.

Developing a sense of style requires focusing on specific aspects of making and receiving music, among other subjects; there is a danger that one may never arrive at a point of generalization, where one internalizes and makes this knowledge one's own and develops one's own confidence in matters of taste and style. When there are so many details to master and limited time in the educational process, one may simply run out of time to integrate these specifics in a unified whole. As I have already observed, Zoltán Kodály offers an approach to this predicament: through a limited repertoire of well-chosen songs, he advises, it is possible to learn the character of music.[84] His approach was to learn folk songs in a classical way such that while young children sang the songs of their native land, they also imbibed musical skills that could translate into many different musical traditions. Through expanding their repertoire to international musics, Kodály teachers forged approaches that took an even broader view than what Kodály envisaged in his time. One need not adopt all the elements of Kodály's methodology to envisage approaches that include various musical traditions and yet also approach them systematically in the sense of providing oral and literate skills that will enable learners to branch out into all sorts of musics after their formal education is complete. It will be necessary, however, to master the details, internalize knowledge, and develop confidence in one's own style throughout the educational process and not just at its end. A repertoire-based approach such as that Kodály advocated holds promise as one way to achieve this end, and there are doubtless many others.

Artistry, taste, skill, and style are theoretically distinct and practically interrelated values at the heart of what musicians and educators do. Besides being appropriate for musicians and artists, they also constitute democratic ideals for all citizens. What musicians think and do concerning artistry, taste, skill, and style can be seen educationally, and what educators think and do can be viewed musically although these values play out variously. *Artistry* refers to what it means to be an artist; *taste* draws on notions of tact and touch; *skill* entails intellectual power, discrimination, precision, specificity, and nuance; and *style* draws on the metaphor of a sharp-pointed stake, pale, or stylus that delineates as it also discriminates musical and educational discourses, practices, and approaches. This quartet of values is richly ambiguous and requires imaginative approaches to cultivate. Each has promise and is flawed; each is potentially transformative and stultifying. Since these values tend toward diversity and away from authoritarianism or the insistence on one right way of thinking and doing, musicians and educators are caught in a paradox as they seek to apply artistry, taste, skill, and style to their musical and instructional situations.

THREE

Reverence, Humility, Awe, and Spirituality

I TURN NOW TO A contrasting quartet of interrelated values long associated with the religions. These values, like those of artistry, taste, skill, and style, are grounded in feeling and cognition. While artistry, taste, skill, and style may tilt more to the material and sensual, reverence, humility, awe, and spirituality seem closer to the immaterial and transcendent. Here, the soul takes flight, and while these values can be understood and conceptualized intellectually, their import is felt and intuited rather than reasoned deductively and inductively. Rooted in ancient times, and sometimes forgotten during the intervening millennia, they are enjoying renewed interest and being embraced in secular education for not only what they offer the study of the humanities, arts, and sciences but, equally importantly, how they evoke personal consciousness and self-understanding and inform human existence and experience.[1] For example, spirituality is the focus of some research and practice, especially by philosophers, religionists, and social scientists working at the intersection of music and education.[2] Notwithstanding the pronounced secularity of music education in our own time, these values are of interest to musicians and educators in religious and secular settings. As we unpack them, it becomes clear that they overlap one another and despite their differences, they share certain commonalities. My approach in this chapter is to begin with their ordinary dictionary meanings, evoke some of their characteristic features, and trace some of their advantages and disadvantages for music and education. I turn, first, to reverence.

REVERENCE

The word *reverence* emerges in the Anglo-Norman and Old French.[3] Its ordinary dictionary meaning as both noun and verb connotes ideas of deep respect, veneration, esteem, and admiration for, and deference to, persons or things because of their status, position, rarity, or sacred character. For me, these important intellectual characteristics fail to capture the depth of feeling that generates them. To revere a person or thing suggests a worshipful attitude, the sense that one is on holy ground, even unworthy of the person or thing one addresses or to whom one pays reverence. In the face of infinitude and the mystery and awe of that which lies beyond ordinary human comprehension, words fail, and one prostrates oneself, bows in obeisance, and, in deep love, gives thanks for a precious gift bestowed to one who is undeserving of it. Reverence is depicted figuratively in the metaphor of religious worship. Within the liturgy of the Christian tradition, for example, the faithful gather in sacred space and time, set apart from the ordinary and secular world; acknowledge themselves as dependent on God, the angels, and a panoply of saints; esteem, admire, and venerate these beings; and walk softly in this place. The things and people with whom they are associated are, by extension, worthy of the same deep veneration and love. Actions are more powerful than words as believers genuflect, kneel, or stand silently, or pray or sing alone or with others. The mass, service, or other sacred rituals by the community of Christian believers evoke the mystery of the relationship between Christ and his church. Likewise, in other faith traditions—for example, in Buddhist temples, Hindu shrines, Jewish synagogues, Muslim mosques, and sacred groves—believers give gifts to God or the gods; remove their shoes; kneel; pray; chant prayers and pleas for assistance; make sacrificial gifts; recite, chant, or read from sacred scrolls and books; remember and retell sacred stories; or reenact sacred rituals.

Music has been a part of sacred ritual since the ancient world, and it has also imbibed this rich tradition of reverence. Musicians' powers are believed to come from the gods. As acolytes of the priests in religious ceremonies, they play an important role in the social system in which they, too, represent the power of the gods. In various societies around the world, musicians are regarded as vehicles through whom the gods communicate to ordinary people. This association of music with the supernatural may cause the musicians to be feared. Where music is believed to constitute an agency of supernatural power, strict rules circumscribe the times and places in which it can be performed and the specific people who may perform it.[4] It is not surprising that the classical traditions, like certain vernacular traditions from which they emerge, also take on attitudes of veneration for the music performance and the composers, improvisers, and performers who make it possible.[5] For example, among the Indian classical traditions, the practice of *riaz* is a spiritual act of worship, a discipline that also acknowledges the power of the guru or *ūstad* who, by virtue of his exceptional artistry and virtuosity, is revered by his students and emulated by them.[6] As signs of their devotion, they purchase food and gifts for him, do menial tasks for him, and, as his disciples, regard themselves as lowly followers of a person who is far higher in status and power than they are. They are in awe of him as a musician and teacher who holds great power over their musical progress, and they are utterly dependent on him. Today's popular musical spectacles likewise reveal "stars" whose personae command the deep admiration and esteem of fans who regard them as almost superhuman beings.[7] Every turn of their lives is lauded and recorded in ways evocative of the worship of gods in earlier times, and they live in mansions set apart from ordinary people, paid for by those who attend their concerts, acquire their recordings, and crave their appearances.

Reverence is passionate in its commitments and intensity of belief. It is based on a conviction or judgment that the thing or person being revered is worthy of respect and honor. While reason plays a crucial role, the emotions are central to intellectual experience, and respect emerges from this emotionally charged intellectual engagement. One may revere the virtuosity and artistry of musicians and hold them in deep respect. This intellectual judgment also has an emotional valence of admiration that colors the thought, and the word *appreciation* connotes this emotionally tinged valuation. Words, concepts, and ideas ultimately fail to satisfy, and it becomes necessary to express and enact deep-seated beliefs in various ways. People often want to share with others their admiration for the things and people they have discovered; they want to tell others about their experience and enact their beliefs and commitments, sometimes in solitary action and other times communally. Susanne Langer might say it is necessary to psychically distance oneself from or objectify the thing or person that one is appraising to be able to grasp its qualities dispassionately.[8] For her, this act of appreciation is exemplified in the judgment of a work of art as one considers its various aspects and regards its integrated aspects along with the whole. With reverence, however, the experience may be both transcendent and immanent. One may be in awe of a subjectively and imaginatively grasped mystery of infinitude and reach out to touch it if possible and, at the same time, also feel an intimate connection with it in desiring it for oneself. In this way, intellectual assent is accompanied by emotion, whether it be a cognitive emotion such as surprise or the joy of verification that accompanies reason, or the emotional cognitions such as the arts and religions in which reason centers on feeling.[9]

Reverence is both a state of becoming and achieved actuality that sets apart those persons or things who are revered or those who revere them from the ordinary and prosaic. One's estimation of the thing or person being revered and the ways in which this judgment is manifested develops, grows, and changes over time and in space. For example, as their knowledge broadens and deepens, performers gain richer insights into the repertoire they perform, and their reverence for this musical tradition may grow. There is an important dimension of sacrificial giving of one's self, one's time, and one's all to the persons or causes one reveres. I think of those performers who study, perform, and record a composer's complete works or who mine the oeuvre of a specific performer, and who revere this music or that musician. They go to extraordinary lengths in service of this music to give their time and attention to its study. Their depth and breadth of understanding of this music prompts their students and audiences, in turn, to hold them in deep respect and reverence. Others recognize the prowess of these musicians and deeply respect and honor the sacrifice that has made it possible; they revere the few not only for their own sake but because of the rich traditions that stand behind them.

Reverence goes beyond thought to enactment, beyond respect to commitment, and beyond mere assent to desire and love to act in certain ways. When I visited Cambodia's Killing Fields, our guide, a Buddhist, wore a shawl about his shoulders as a symbol of his reverence for this sacred place and as a mark of honor to those who had been undeservedly shot or bludgeoned to death at the hands of others who cared nothing for their suffering and only for their extermination. This simple act expressed or demonstrated his reverence in ways that words could not adequately convey, and it profoundly impacted those of us who journeyed to this place with him. Such acts of reverence, whether on occasions of celebration or mourning, are often collective and communal. This widespread desire to share one's commitments with others plays out in religious rituals and public ceremonies. It is also the basis for efforts in publicly supported education to bring the young to shared commitments in the company of their fellows. Lucy Green notices that music may both affirm and celebrate on the one hand and repudiate and alienate on the other.[10] When music affirms and celebrates the people who make and receive it, it can constitute an important way by which students experience reverence.[11]

A sense of the holy, of sacred time and space in which education is enacted, apart from ordinary and profane time, is crucial to reverence. Iris Yob describes the educational experience within the frames of sacred space and time.[12] She thinks of the school as a special place apart from the rest of life—an idea that seems surprising at a time during which efforts have been made to align schools more with and as a part of the rest of life. Yob asks us to consider that treating the educational process as separate from the rest of life, grounding it in notions of deep respect for the knowledge being gained and the people involved in the process, and engaging perennial and important existential questions such as "where did I come from?", "where am I going?", and "what is my purpose here?" dignify education and humanize it. These aspects move the focus of education from the ordinary toward the extraordinary, from the sensual toward the intellectual and moral, from the profane toward the sacred. This approach situates education on higher ground, as worthy of deep respect and honor. In a democracy, although education separates those with the ability, desire, and willingness to expend effort to gain knowledge from others who are unable, uninterested, or unwilling, one hopes that wisdom can be possessed by the many rather than the few.

Among its educational advantages, reverence values the community gathered in the presence of a subject of great worth. Such an education cannot be about trivialities but about knowledge that is consequential and of enormous importance. Although knowledge is objectified in its separation from those gathered about it, it is also subjectified in the experience of those who gather in its midst. Where learning is oral, and the community of learners gather about a teacher, the teacher is object in the sense of possessing knowledge and subject as the personification of this knowledge. Parker Palmer and Maxine Greene are among those to advocate this dialogical and communitarian approach to education.[13] Subject matter that concerns important existential questions confronting human beings invests the instructional situation with consequence for the rest of lived life. In the presence of such perceived value, all bow before it. I think, for example, of a music class I witnessed in Japan, where teacher and student bowed to each other before and after the lesson on an ancient myth sung and played.[14] In Dewey's view, this intensified and heightened form of experience can be esthetic.[15] It evokes the kind of spiritual experience that Abraham Maslow described as "peak experience."[16] Although music is related to the rest of life, in a sense, the process of music and education is separate from the world of ordinary experience. Time in music making and receiving intensifies the ordinary and separates one from everyday considerations while one is engaged with it. This apartness from the humdrum and prosaic seems extraordinary and captivating in its intensity and joy.

Reverence values the embodied mind in the educational process. Within this frame, music education is an intellectual process in which one can appraise the qualities of the revered persons or things. Still, these things being prized are also embodied in rituals, performances, or artifacts of one sort or another. Reverence suggests the notion of a mind embodied in a holistic and personal approach to knowledge rather than a mind divorced from body.[17] Musical rituals are inseparable from the meanings that give rise to them or to which they contribute. Langer grasps this fundamentally presentational or, I would prefer, performative character of musical meaning.[18] She realizes that music takes place in the phenomenal world as a fundamental part of lived life. Especially at a time in which the intellectual values of music education are sometimes downplayed in favor of sensual values,[19] such an approach to music cultivates an attitude of deep respect and humility. It suggests a corrective to pervasive cynicism, disrespect, and inhumanity in society and what Neil Postman would call a "thermostatic" educational approach that constitutes a counterweight to values prevalent in society.[20] In emphasizing things that are fragile and rare rather than resilient and ever-present, musicians and educators make a place for music that may not be in the public eye and systematically sustain it in times and places where it might otherwise disappear. They help to preserve the variety of the world's musical traditions and create opportunities for cross-fertilization between various musics.

Among its disadvantages, reverence is fragile, and its power may be abused. This process of setting apart is elitist rather than universal, no matter that one may hope for it to be generally shared. The reason for this reality lies not so much in a conscious effort to exclude the many as in the fact that few may be willing to put forward the effort required to understand things that are not readily accessible. This pedagogical moment is fleeting. Its present-centered quality and focus may mask asymmetrical power relations that subjugate certain knowledge and learners and cause them to be apathetic, uncritical, and disempowered.[21] Those in the pedagogical situation may focus so much on transmitting traditional beliefs and practices that they neglect the claims of change and transformation where needed. Focusing uncritically on a subject of great worth may devalue ordinary experience and mask the power of those who can dictate which knowledge is considered of most worth. That which is rare, esoteric, and guarded by gatekeepers who ensure its value may come to be revered more than that which is ordinary and plentiful. There may even be a violence in the insistence on certain ways of making, receiving, and coming to know music and the silencing of those who disagree.[22] An unproblematic and unproblematized approach to knowledge in reverence may also suggest certainty where there is none and cultivate dogmatism and narrowmindedness in a pluralistic world.

The dominance of tradition and the relative inaccessibility of knowledge in reverence may suggest the importance of the teacher as intermediary in the process. The teacher may pontificate, in the words of Ivan Illich, as "pastor, prophet, and priest."[23] This teacher-centric approach to music education in which the teacher directs the learner's learning can degenerate into what Paulo Freire would term "banking education."[24] Rather than inviting learners to construct their own meanings and contribute actively to their own learning, reverence may cultivate student passivity and foster a lack of engagement with the subject matter.

HUMILITY

The word *humility* has distinctively Western and even Christian roots. Coming from the Latin and the French, it refers to qualities such as meekness, self-abasement, unpretentiousness, and having a lowly view of oneself—the opposite of pride.[25] Humility is a deeply rooted educational value throughout the Christian era, especially in monastic, cathedral, and parish schools. It is also exemplified in the life and work of Johann Heinrich Pestalozzi, who sought to emulate Jesus in his teachings and whose interest was in serving poor and working-class children.[26] The architects of publicly supported music education in the United States stressed what they saw as Pestalozzi's views of their responsibilities toward the poor and the working classes in developing a raison d'être for public education.[27] Systems of public education in Europe and North America were originally developed with a view to cultivating humility as a means of preparing working-class children as workers for the industrializing economies of the nineteenth century. Moreover, the Renaissance ideal of humility as a feminine value fostered the docility men expected of their wives. In music, the claims of humility contributed to the cult of the "piano girl" and the amateur who performed only in domestic settings and limited women's musical aspirations and musical training.[28]

Humility begins with one's own sense of insufficiency and inadequacy and one's dissatisfaction with oneself.[29] In Judeo-Christian thought, for example, this self-consciousness arises from a pervasive sense of sinfulness and guilt embedded in theologies and religious systems that emphasize sin and its consequences in humanity. This mindset is rooted in the Jewish account of creation, in which women are portrayed as particularly culpable in bringing evil into a perfect world, and other stories such as that of Noah's flood, in which a vengeful God destroys much of the creation. It continues in the Christian account of the crucifixion of Jesus, deemed necessary for the redemption of a sinful humanity. As Mircea Eliade notes, stories of creation, the struggle between good and evil, and notions of redemption and renewal are widely found among the world's religions. In differing ways, these religions portray humanity as inadequate, fallible, and ultimately powerless against natural and supernatural forces.[30]

The idea of humility is also linked to what Vernon Howard calls the artist's "vision of mastery."[31] For Howard, artists imagine an ideal composition, improvisation, or performance that they attempt to render in the phenomenal world. For some musicians, this vision appears more or less fully clothed, and the artist constitutes the medium whereby the musical event appears completely. For others, this vision develops piece by piece as the artist gradually crafts the composition, hones the improvisation, or creates the performance. This approach has less of a sense of effortlessness and is more a matter of developing the skills needed to construct a desired end. Whichever the approach, for musicians, there is a sense in which one discovers more and more of the possibilities of this vision, such that the vision itself changes over time and may sometimes appear to move even further away the more one progresses toward the imagined goal. For example, when musicians return to repertoire they have performed in the past, their earlier interpretations may seem inadequate for the present. The musical score or practice is ambiguous in its meaning, and there are differing possibilities in how it may be rendered. The musicians' experience may also have widened and deepened their understanding of this music, and they may now desire to create something that seems to be even more compelling. They may possess technical and interpretive skills that differ from those they had in the past. These realities prompt a sense of humility in the face of the possibilities yet to be realized in performing this music. The desired end seems elusive and defies a sense that one has attained a comprehensive knowledge of it or found the best interpretation possible. One may be pleased with this performance but not necessarily satisfied with it.

Some musicians are what Aaron Copland calls "classical" in their tendency to lose themselves in the music they are performing, such that the claims of fidelity to the music are more important than their own individuality and prowess; they regard themselves as servants of the music they are making. Others are more "romantic" in their more individualistic and idiosyncratic ways of performing; these performers draw attention to themselves rather than to the music.[32] Somewhere in this murky ground, musicians strive for both fidelity and individuality in interpretation; too much of the "classical" emphasis makes for a less personal interpretation, and too much "romantic" emphasis detracts from the music and becomes self-exposure rather than self-expression. Confronted by the possibility of too much or too little humility in musicking, Aristotle would probably plump for the "golden mean" that permits a certain degree of self-effacement in making music while also welcoming the counterpoint of pride that directs personal attention to musicians doing what is needed to create and bring this music to life.[33]

The notion of meekness as an attribute of humility connotes ideas of gentleness, kindness, courtesy, graciousness, docility, and obedience.[34] These qualities are related to notions of tact described by Max van Manen as desirable attributes of teaching.[35] They are also often attributed stereotypically to women. Within a feminine ethic of care, Nel Noddings sees such qualities as desirable and essential to humane education.[36] The deference to others, concern for their well-being, consideration for their feelings, grace in dealing with others, and willingness to follow the rules that govern the instructional situation seem essential for achieving the kind of dialogical education for which Freire, Greene, and Palmer hope.[37] In the absence of these qualities, I cannot see how one undertakes a truly humane education. Since people of differing genders are engaged in education, these values cannot remain those of just women teachers; everyone should demonstrate them. This premise requires educating all musicians and teachers in ways that foster these values even though they are too often regarded stereotypically as feminine traits.

Graciousness, or the quality of possessing grace, is a mark of humility as well as humanity. Musicians of all stripes admire speed and virtuosity, the overarching sense of fluidity and effortlessness that is pleasing to eye and ear.[38] Grace suggests that expectations concerning music are met in a pervasive sense of style. When all is as it needs to be to compose a piece of music, create a riff in a group improvisation, or perform a piece of music, musical experience appears light, full of joy, or bathed in pathos as needs be, and the music that is made constitutes a whole that is pleasing to the senses. The fluidity of being in the moment as one engages in this musicking is akin to what Mihaly Csikszentmihalyi refers to as "flow."[39] Theologically, of course, grace connotes benevolence in the face of lack of merit, and thankfulness.[40] I suppose there is grace when one knows that the composer, improviser, or performer has done their best, though the result may not be perfect in every way; overall, one recognizes that what has been created is graceful. There is also grace in the humanity of the interaction between those who make and receive music in instructional situations. Graciousness is evidenced in a benevolence and kindness to others in ways that may not be merited by the others' words and actions. Teachers may hope that by their lived example, they may cultivate a generosity of spirit among their students that allows them to treat others not as their words and actions merit but rather in appealing to their better selves. Such graciousness in our dealings with others and theirs with us has its own sense of style that is sometimes termed, somewhat prosaically, professionalism. This grace is cognizant of the fact that mistakes form the fabric of all musicking and human interaction. Faced with what Isaiah Berlin, invoking Immanuel Kant, thought of as the "crooked timber of humanity," music teachers and their students can practice grace as an aspect of humility in their music making and receiving and in their interactions with each other.[41]

Among its advantages, humility is the beginning of education and a counterpoint to arrogance and self-satisfaction, or the sense that one has no need to improve oneself and that one is self-sufficient and possesses all the knowledge one needs. As Israel Scheffler notes, some may take refuge in dogmatism, gullibility, or skepticism as a means of refusing to rethink their positions or consider alternatives to what they know or can do.[42] Learning begins with the learners' acknowledgment that they may have something to learn. In that moment, one may grasp that others possess skills and understandings that one desires to possess; one admits insufficiency, that one does not know all there is to know. Up to the point at which a learner acknowledges this vital reality, no matter how much a teacher might wish to teach, learning does not take place. One's arrogance, self-sufficiency, and self-satisfaction stand in the way of challenging one's worldview, one's knowledge, or one's skills. Still, I am uncomfortable with the connotation of humility as self-abasement, the idea that students must diminish themselves to learn from their teachers. Such a view would constitute an inhumane view of educational humility that necessitates the diminishment of students to establish and reinforce the power of the teacher. Rather, a generous interpretation of humility suggests that learners grasp that they need knowledge and skills that will help them become better musicians or persons. Such pedagogical humility is the beginning of the process of acquiring knowledge, know-how, and wisdom.

Humility also facilitates humane and artistic approaches to education. It supports a caring educational ethic that respects all the participants in the instructional situation, values their differing perspectives, and supports a dialogical approach to education in which all involved can participate openly and without fear. It also fits nicely with the nature of music and musicking and the artistic humility that is generated by the ambiguity of musical meaning, and the musician's pursuit of an artistic vision that changes and is clarified over time. The musician's devotion to excellence in composing, improvising, and performing in a musical tradition reveals a humility that prizes virtuosity and grace as it also recognizes the challenges of bringing to life this music in this situation. Since one's prowess as a musician is often tested at the limits of one's knowledge and skill, there is a sense that one is fortunate when the composition, improvisation, or performance comes off well. One is heartened by the success but hopeful for something better in the future.

Still, humility has a dark side in which women and minorities already suffer from too much of it. Male protagonists of religions address the notion of pride, the antithesis of humility, as something one must strive against. Women sometimes resist this idea by suggesting that men who suffer from too much pride need religious observance and lessons in humility the most. For example, rendered as marginal worshippers by not being permitted to sing, and separated physically in the synagogue, Lubavitcher Hasidic women regard Sabbath services as particularly necessary for men, and from time to time the women absent themselves from these services in the belief that they are less in need of lessons in humility and religious faith and practice.[43] For women and minorities, who are often reminded of their deficiency and lower status, a lack of sufficient pride and confidence and an excess of humility may constitute an evil to be overcome. Women may require a greater sense of personal power, entitlement, and confidence to not only fulfill domestic duties but take a greater role in public life. Although it is important not to oversimplify these matters, too often, humility is a gendered value in which those who most often proclaim the need of humility are most in need of it themselves. Since humility is stereotypically a female value, persuading men who act from a sense of entitlement to demonstrate humility can be a challenging undertaking.

Humility can also serve as an agent of repression by powerful societal institutions and those who represent them. Beginning with a sense of guilt, underscoring people's sinfulness, and undermining their confidence and self-worth are discouraging and constitute a negative way to undertake the work of education. Identifying pride as an unmitigated evil can contribute to a sense of worthlessness that impedes personal growth and development. Teaching people to humbly accept their positions in society and not to contest the imbalances and inequities in the social order contributes to a stratified society with little upward mobility; it empowers the ruling class, often a minority, enables it to impose its will on the great majority of people, and breeds passivity on the part of the vast majority of the population. The only way out of this situation, for Freire, is to empower the oppressed, strengthen their pride, and provide them with the skills to individually and collectively change the circumstances of their lived lives.[44]

AWE

Originally, the word *awe* derived from Old Norse connoting an attitude of "immediate and active fear," dread, and terror. Absorbed into general English use by the thirteenth century CE, its meaning changed to incorporate Christian notions of a divine being. It came to mean "dread mingled with veneration, reverential or respectful fear," a "feeling of solemn and reverential wonder, tinged with latent fear, inspired by what is terribly sublime and majestic in nature," and a sense of "profound reverence."[45]

Awe is prompted by such things as the difficulty encountered in satisfactorily, easily, or fully addressing existential questions—"Who am I?" "Where did I come from?" "Where am I going?"—that go to the core of the mystery of human existence and a profound sense of one's frailty in the face of the power of the natural world. For Yob, awe may be engendered not only by events in the natural world but by displays of intellectual and artistic prowess and virtuosity that seem superhuman.[46] The realities of evil and mortality are among the predicaments that prompt fear of the unknown and the unexplainable. In his play *Freud's Last Session*, set in England at the outbreak of World War I, Mark St. Germain portrays Sigmund Freud and C. S. Lewis's dissatisfaction with the answers found in science and religion and the fear both experience in the face of suffering and death.[47] Rudolf Otto invokes this awe in the notion of *mysterium tremendum et fascinans*—a sense of overwhelming and compelling fear and mystery.[48] Where music is assumed to possess the power of appeasing the gods or arousing certain emotional and physical states, not only is there the dread of the wrong people performing the wrong music in the wrong way and in the wrong time and place, but the awe of music's power transfers itself to the musicians. They are to be feared by those who are not musicians, and they themselves fear for their own performances. Musicians often suffer from performance anxiety, or the dread that they will fail in their music making or break one of the many taboos surrounding musical performance.[49] In short, the entire process of musicking may be invested with awe that feeds into itself in a vicious cycle.

Dewey sees the artistic experience as intensified and extraordinary. He uses the word "consummated" to describe this heightened state of consciousness that is culminated, fulfilled, and satisfied. For him, artistic experience is "consummated" whereas ordinary and prosaic experience is "unconsummated."[50] It is done and undergone, active and passive, constructed and received. Such is the power of the intensification of this experience in moments of consummation that one is awestruck in the face of its extraordinary power. The fact that such experience lies beyond one's control and is unpredictable, unexplainable, and serendipitous leaves one feeling that one has stumbled on it or it has been given to one rather than earned by one's own efforts. Moreover, such moments bring a sense of joy that this experience has come unexpectedly and dread that it may never come again. I know of no more potent attraction to young musicians than the experience of this intensity: it serves as a powerful vehicle of intrinsic motivation. It requires the focused energy of mental concentration just as it also energizes the musician.[51] At its end, one is both exhausted from the energy expended in its making and receiving and refreshed by the wonder and awe at what has occurred. For example, to watch the impact of the experience of Western classical music by instrumentalists and singers in the Congo, the members of the Kinshasa Symphony Orchestra and Chorus, as they perform Orff's *Carmina Burana*, is to see commitment, joy, and awe in the face of an extraordinary experience of music from another place and time out of the realm of their ordinary lives.[52]

One of the important aspects of awe is the sense of transcendence, of excellence, of surpassing the taken-for-granted and creating something exceptional. For Bennett Reimer, this idea has its counterpoint in what he calls "profundity," or a sense of depth and vastness.[53] Whether it be up or down, height or depth, transcendence surpasses common experience, and, like reverence, awe derives from a sense of limitlessness, of possibility, and of infinity. Maybe it was this transcendent quality that prompted the ancients to think of music as an exhibition of supernatural power.[54] Hildegard von Bingen thought of music as "the breath of God," a concept that resonates with the Indian notion of "tala."[55] Music's ambiguity, its seemingly inexhaustible possibilities, and the impossibility of its containment require imagination and reason to mine and leave one in awe of the fact that one has excavated some of its potential or viewed and heard a part of its treasury. In exploring these possibilities, musicians also have the sense of discovering themselves. For music lovers, this lifelong process may leave them more in awe at the end than at the beginning. Moreover, the greater the transcendence and profundity of a music, the more fascinating it can be. Music teachers may experience their students coming to love best the music that seems the most transcendent and profound and at which they worked the hardest. I watch the joy and concentration on the faces of members of the Kinshasa Symphony Orchestra and Chorus as they perform Beethoven's Ninth Symphony.[56] The transcendence and profundity of this piece impacts their lives in compelling ways. Honing the required skills requires devoting themselves to practicing this piece in the villages and towns from which they come, as they raise their little ones, care for their homes, and trudge the long miles of pathways far from modern conveniences to meet the public transportation that carries them to their rehearsals. Their experience of this music is a window into another culture and a different way of being in the world; they can know it even though they may never travel to the place and time from which it arose.

Awe is a powerful emotional experience. As with the values of reverence and humility, it is enacted as well as known intellectually, a bodily experience that engages the whole person. It demands a physical response and action. One bows down, falls silent, takes off one's shoes, covers one's head, lowers one's gaze, and, in a host of other ways, acknowledges that one is in the presence of divinity, the unexplainable and unaccountable, or the extraordinary. One is drawn to this more powerful and incomprehensible other and cannot but acknowledge one's relative powerlessness, finitude, and fallibility. As Scheffler would have it, the cognitive emotions of "joy of verification" and "surprise" surround one's intellectual grasp of the situation; as Yob suggests, the emotional cognitions apparent in the arts, religions, and myths are evident expressions of human feeling.[57] Still, like reverence and humility, awe goes further than cognition and affect to impact the entire physical self. One is caught up in and captivated by this moment. Langer might say that psychic time (or what she calls "virtual time") seems to stand still, so engrossed is one in this present moment.[58]

Among its contributions, awe fosters exceptionality, artistry, and virtuosity. For Kirk Schneider, knowing majesty and splendor as well as fear and dread allows one to experience the full panoply of existence, the heights and depths of feeling, and the paradox of transcendence and immanence.[59] This experience is so important as to constitute the basis for general education. Much of life is prosaic and ordinary, but the moments in which experience is heightened to an intensity that evokes wonder and dread allow one to better grasp one's possibilities and limitations in the face of infinity. In music education, the experience of awe encourages teachers and students to surpass ordinary expectations and to develop their musical proclivities to the utmost. Such a musical education hopes to realize "visions of mastery"—imagined constructions that are realized musically and represent the highest aspirations of each musical practice. Awe values speed, grace, and virtuosity. The attainment of musical skills that evoke a personal sense of style also represent the hopes of this musical tradition. When a brilliant composition, improvisation, or performance evokes superlatives that also leave musicians and audiences in awe at the achievement, these exceptional, artistic, and virtuosic musical events inspire to greater effort and improved musicking. At the same time, when failure surely comes, or when others can do what one cannot, awe fosters humility in the face of transcendence.

Importantly, awe addresses life's most important questions. In the presence of the ultimate finitude and finality of life, music education construed in terms of this value offers opportunities to reflect musically on these questions. For Zoltán Kodály, only the most exceptional music serves the interests of music education. To this end, folk music conjoined with the best of the classical tradition offers musical simplicity and complexity united in an artistic approach to music education. For him, this repertoire should resist commercially driven mediated music, constitute the best of music, possess "intrinsic value," and cultivate good taste. In his view, "bad taste in art is a veritable sickness of the soul." He continues, "Nothing is too great to write for the little ones," and it is important to do one's "best to be great enough for them."[60] Kodály wants young people to experience music as artful, as a transcendent and profoundly important human undertaking. In our time, it might be said that all the traditions that constitute today's musical mosaic deserve the very best efforts to bring them alive, and they offer many ways to engage life's most important questions. Ultimately, as one strives to experience awe, these musical undertakings are humane in their tendency to improve the lives of human beings by offering opportunities to transcend the prosaic and often humdrum realities of ordinary life.

On the other hand, among its detractions, just as fear and dread may motivate one to do one's musical best, too much emphasis on awe may inhibit music making and receiving. Awe, as humility and reverence, represents a double-edged sword. Too little or too much of a good thing can constitute an evil. A conductor who strikes fear into musicians may help focus their efforts during rehearsal, but too much fear may frighten them and render them unable to enjoy the music making experience. Performance is risky. Most musicians report that some anxiety helps focus their minds and prepare them for performance. Still, all may not go as planned. The presence of too much fear and dread inhibits musicians from focusing on the task at hand in a performance, and its physical effects may be deleterious to an ability to perform this music as one should.[61] For this reason, I wish to find the point of Aristotle's "golden mean," somewhere in the middle ground between the extremes of too much fear and not enough of it.

Focusing excessively on transcendence rather than immanence and profundity rather than the ordinary may overlook the fact that much of human experience is not extraordinary or awe-inspiring. When one values only musical exceptionality and artistry, one fails to notice that much joy arises out of people's everyday musical experience. Think of a jazz band playing an informal Sunday afternoon concert to an audience gathered under a banyan tree in the Selby Gardens of Sarasota. There are no pretentions of awe on this occasion. Rather, audience members enjoy picnic food and drinks and hear music as a background to their chatter, or listen to, sing along with, and dance to the band's music. The applause after each piece is hearty, and people enjoy this experience of visiting with friends and family in a beautiful garden. Thinking about this occasion of ordinary musicking, with its importantly social appeal, reminds me that much musical experience has personal appeal to ordinary people who do not aspire to extraordinary feats of musicality. I imagine that if the band on this occasion were not comprised of professional musicians, or if the music were poorly played and sung, those who attend this informal concert might not enjoy it so much. Yet for most of the people present, this activity constitutes a lovely way to enjoy a Sunday afternoon, simply sitting and listening, socializing, dancing, singing along, and otherwise applauding the musicians' efforts. Awe is memorable because it is set against this quite ordinary musical activity. Awe may be valuable when its pursuit constitutes a counterpoint to the widespread engagement in ordinary musical experience rather than a substitute for it.

SPIRITUALITY

The word *spirituality* is rooted in the notion of "spirit" and thought of as "the quality or condition of being spiritual" or "attachment to or regard for things of the spirit as opposed to material or worldly interests."[62] With spirit, I think of qualities or things that are distinct from the material or phenomenal world, incorporeal or immaterial as opposed to corporeal or material. Rooted in the Latin *spiritus* and *spiritualis*, *spirituality* in the West draws particularly on Christian theological distinctions between the mind, body, and soul or spirit, in which the incorporeal soul or spirit animates or gives the body its living quality. Hildegard of Bingen calls this spirit *anima* in her morality play, *Ordo virtutum*.[63] Philosophers and musicians have long recognized this quality of livingness and breath in music that seem to animate the performance and render it spiritual. More recently, Peter Kivy describes a resilient theory of musical meaning based on people's recognition of their lived lives in music's dynamic qualities. Deanne Bogdan regards the shiver and shimmer in musical pieces as a spiritual quality and sees the evidence of music's spiritual quality in musical performance.[64] For Langer, imagination endows music with a sense of vitality and a living quality that resonates with the living beings who create and partake in it. Music seems to possess "vital import" for musicians and their public.[65] Although experienced in the phenomenal world, music is also ethereal and imagined. Still, the immateriality of these sonic images, while conceptually distinct from the material and phenomenal images and physical making and receiving of music, are, practically speaking, interconnected with music's sensual properties in a holistic musical experience.[66]

The ambiguity of spirituality is of special interest to musician-educators. Yob points to the historically resilient association of notions of spirituality with religion and references Otto's notion of *mysterium tremendum et fascinans,* which is associated with the sense of mystery and awe when one is in the presence of the divine or confronted by monumental natural phenomena and human creations.[67] In her account, spirituality and awe may share common elements. Still, transcendence is not the only possibility; as with reverence, one may also experience immanence, a deeply subjective and passionate felt life evocative of emotions other than awe, such as joy or pathos. Rather than being restricted to religious experience, spirituality may be manifested in a range of different encounters associated with the religions, arts, and sciences. What joins these experiences of spirituality are their abstract qualities, their focus on the immaterial rather than the material (that is, things not seen rather than things seen), the figurative and imaginary rather than the literal and prosaic, and, probably most importantly, the ways in which they evoke wonder, awe, and humility. For Yob, one type of spirituality does not necessarily suffice for all, and while spiritualities may overlap, it is important for teachers and students to experience an array of them within the educational process. This ambiguity of spirituality and the connections between the religions and the arts and sciences as sources and manifestations of spirituality suggest that music educators need to think of spirituality among the means and ends of their work. Also, just as musical study may provide a window to religious study, so, too, may the study of the religions open one to musical experience—all of which can foster spirituality in a variety of ways.

What does it mean to experience music spiritually? Importantly, one is focused imaginatively on the sonic properties of music rather than visual or other social attributes of its practices. This requires intelligent and abstract attention to, and thought about, music as an objective thing as well as a subjective reality—a view that has been criticized in some quarters of music education in recent decades.[68] This intellectual view of music relies on imagination (which is reasoned, intuitive, perceived, and felt) in making sense of the music, quite apart from all the other practices and social meanings that are attributed by its musicians and audiences.[69] Rather than experiencing mere passionate arousal, one reflects on and thinks about music, both in the moment of musical experience and after the music has ceased. As such, it is a species of thought that Donald Schön calls "reflection-in-action"—a lively in-the-moment engagement of body, mind, and spirit that animates music and makes it meaningful in an ethereal and noncorporeal way.[70] Engaging in music through feelings and thought necessitates understanding the vocabularies of the means by which music can be thought about—that is, its "articulate character," in which the various musical elements fit together to animate the whole and musicians employ myriad means to design and create the sounds that captivate attention and imagination.[71] For Langer, "articulation is its [music's] life, but not assertion; expressiveness, not expression."[72] Music construed as object and subject, a dynamic thing in the process of becoming, is profoundly mindful. The intellect is captivated through all the means of music making and receiving, doing and undergoing, whether it be musical composition, improvisation, performance, or listening.

For David Carr, regarding music as a spiritual undertaking also implies a strong moral and even religious component, in which music is in service of ethical ends.[73] He and his colleagues emphasize the moral quality of spirituality in education and conceive of spiritualities ranging from religious and attitudinal to psychological accounts.[74] This association of music and morality is rooted in ancient thought and expressed by philosophers such as Plato, who assumed that the musical modes have particular ethical valence and proposed that music in education should be strictly censored in order to ensure that the young are educated toward "the Good."[75] This idea also remains resilient in our own time. Regarding spirituality as a virtue in music education implies, for Carr, that repertoire should be carefully selected to promote the moral purposes of education. In making this case from an ethical and educational perspective, Carr's proposition resonates with ideas forwarded by musician-educators. Among them, as I have already noted, in view of the dangers he sees inherent in mediated music, Kodály prods music teachers to select the best of classical and folk repertoire to cultivate the aesthetic and moral sensibilities of the young.[76] Suzuki also highlights the spiritual dimensions of music and its role in fostering empathy, humanity, and nobility of character.[77] Drawing on the ideas of ancient Chinese and modern pragmatic philosophers, Leonard Tan speaks to the importance of instrumental music education as a means of fostering moral thought and action.[78] In making connections between spirituality and morality, all of these writers see the purpose of music education as going beyond coming to know music and as impacting the development of the young as humane, noble, and moral people. These authors' interest is enriching the lives of those who participate in music education in its many different forms.

Among its advantages for music and education, spirituality moves the focus away from the material and visual toward the immaterial and the aural. This is particularly important as a foil to the pervasive materialism and visual preoccupation of our time. Meanings ascribed to sonic stimuli are often diffuse, ambiguous, subjective, fleeting, and fragile. Where visual presentation is hegemonic in contemporary society, young and old may not listen and hear as they need to, and they are less equipped to deal with the ambiguity, subjectivity, and immateriality of human communication. At a time in which sight is often valued over sound, music educators who take a thermostatic view of their role in society and culture may wish to emphasize those things that are not valued in the wider society and culture in order to bring sights and sounds into better balance.[79] This imperative of balance between too little and too much sight and sound is Aristotelian in its search for the "golden mean" between the senses and Eastern in its value of balancing sometimes contesting or conflicting goods. The same may be said for the importance of offering a counterpoint to a societal focus on materiality by emphasizing the immateriality of a spiritual experience of music.

Moreover, this immateriality, ambiguity, subjectivity, and fragility of musical sound prompts the development of imagination. Such thought values holistic and intuitive thinking, critical thinking, sensory perception, and expressive thought and action. An intellectual emphasis in music education helps develop ways of thinking that can be helpful in ordinary daily life and is beneficial to teachers and students by enabling them to gain a richer, broader, and deeper understanding of music and the wider culture of which music is a part. To think of music and education intellectually is to see the value of music as a humanity as well as an art, to grasp not only what this music is and offers but what it shows one of oneself and others. Ambiguity, fallibility, and mortality are inescapable aspects of the human condition, and emphasizing spirituality as a value in music education helps foster the dispositions to deal imaginatively and constructively with these existential realities.

Nevertheless, among the detractions of spirituality, its ambiguity makes it difficult to apply as a matter of public policy. In the political realm especially, where economic values are prized, it is often necessary to be able to specify the qualities that characterize spirituality, and its diffuse, nebulous, and immaterial qualities make it difficult to do this, especially in an environment in which material and literal educational ends are prized. Where people face a daunting labor market and where economic conditions are harsh, it is easy to understand an impatience with education that concerns ends that may seem irrelevant to the present. Focusing on spiritual things may also suggest an unduly atomistic approach that bifurcates body and spirit and prizes spirit over body.[80] Such a view goes counter to holistic notions of the body that resist such a bifurcation. It is also easy to slip into a view of music that opposes the senses to the spiritual and pits the physical against the intellectual qualities of music, giving primacy to spirit and mind over body and denigrating the physical appeal of music. A Dionysian view of music challenges this perspective of music education by advocating for the physical appeal of music as an objective of music education. In this view, teaching people that the body is evil and that passions need to be suppressed may undermine one's image of self and repress the full development of personhood.[81] Although Friedrich Schiller advocates that education in the arts is a means of lifting people from a natural state in which they are ruled by passion to a state of moral development, he admits that historical evidence does not bear out his claim.[82] People do not necessarily act better because they are artists or appreciate the arts, even though he hopes that they do.

Moreover, as with reverence, humility, and awe, spirituality's long association with religion presupposes an asymmetrical worldview in which the powerful speak on behalf of the powerless, in which some expressions of spirituality are valued over others, and in which some traditions are reified and embraced uncritically. The primacy of mind over body, of the restraint and restriction of the body, of certain views of morality over others in which passion may play an important role, may combine to create a myopic and one-sided music education. Such an approach may emphasize those musics with intellectual appeal and focus on work and discipline over play and celebration. Viewing music as an agency of moral development in terms of its efficacy in prompting people to act more humanely and civilly is also fraught in its promise of ends that may be impractical and unachievable even if steadfastly hoped for and acted toward.

Several conclusions emerge from my discussion of the values of reverence, humility, awe, and spirituality for music and education. Reverence evokes veneration and respect, and a sense of wonder, awe, and mystery; humility references qualities of meekness, a sense of inadequacy, especially in relation to imagined ideals of mastery, tact, and grace; awe connotes fear and dread, especially regarding the mystery of human existence; spirituality is thought of in terms of such qualities as immateriality and noncorporeality and in its associations with the religions, arts, and myths. Despite the promises and pitfalls of these interrelated yet conceptually distinctive values, and the impossibility of any of them sufficing without detraction, I want to hold on to them, conscious of the good that is possible and the dangers they present. As values embedded in a life of feeling but also intellectual, they also constitute a pointed reminder of the importance of the immaterial world of the spirit, of things unseen rather than seen, and of the multiple ways in which human subjectivity can be expressed. If musicians and educators are watchful, then reverence, humility, awe, and spirituality can constitute beacons that light the paths of music and education.

FOUR

Dignity, Dispassion, Restraint, and Discipline

THE VALUES OF DIGNITY, DISPASSION, restraint, and discipline have been prized in music and education from antiquity and reflect the primacy of reason and scholarship, the formality long a part of music, especially its classical traditions, and education, and the role of emotion as servant of intellect. These values may be regarded as a corrective to reverence, humility, awe, and spirituality in the sense that they are grounded in the primacy of reason over feeling, and they emphasize the phenomenal rather than the spiritual. They are expressed in such ways as the gravitas and decorum of formal and higher education and the academic privileges and responsibilities conferred by the award of credentials, certificates, diplomas, and degrees. Music and education that espouse these values are regarded as serious undertakings, and their processes and results are thought to be consequential and life changing. Accordingly, all those engaged in this work are supposed to act with dignity, dispassion, restraint, and discipline.

Although these values have been evident in traditional approaches to music education—for example, in the conduct of large choral and instrumental ensembles—they are under pressure in certain quarters. Some writers challenge the reification of intellectualism in education, refuse the mantle of the master in the apprenticeship model of musical education, and urge popular culture and informal approaches to instruction that embrace different values.[1] In the face of these critiques and against this backdrop, it is important to revisit these values and ask: What do they mean? What good do they add to music and education, and how do they detract from them? Although dignity, dispassion, restraint, and discipline are interrelated, I examine each in turn to see what they hold for music and education.

DIGNITY

The word *dignity* originates in the Latin *dignus*, meaning worth.[2] I begin with a notion of dignity that refers to aspects of nobility, stateliness, and gravity associated with persons and positions of high social rank in a stratified and classist society. This conception emphasizes the social and public character of dignity where judgments are based on expectations of conduct in a hierarchical society and the public behavior of the establishment and upper class is considered normative. For example, references to dignitaries suggest that some people may possess dignity because they were born into a high class where they are expected to act in certain ways or because of their positions of trust and high office. The nobility and gravitas in their behavior may be considered normative by others of lesser social status who seek to emulate their behavior and, by so doing, attain higher status. Yet irrespective of one's social status or position, matters of appearance and conduct and style and manner mark dignity. To say one possesses dignity is to say that one's behavior is esteemed by others. In this conception, appearances rather than moral character may be seen to mark dignity. One's actions bespeak the qualities of nobility, stateliness, grace, and style associated with persons of high class or who hold high office. In this conception, a rake who acts immorally in private may possess dignity so long as his public actions and observable behavior are consistent with expectations of him based on his birth or position, and his private conduct remains hidden from view. To say he possesses dignity relies on social judgments of his behavior as appropriate to his social class or high position.

Still, public appearances do not necessarily reflect the entire gamut of private thought and behavior. In counterpoint to this social view of dignity, educators have long emphasized an intrinsic and internally generated dignity that emanates from a deep spiritual and moral commitment within the person irrespective of social class and position. For example, Friedrich Schiller distinguishes the conduct of the "moral man" in contrast to the "physical man," and Johann Heinrich Pestalozzi reveals the dignity of the poor in his *Leonard and Gertrude* and *Evening Hour of the Hermit*.[3] This view of dignity focuses on dispositions to act in particular ways that emerge from an individual's beliefs, attitudes, and commitments.[4] Here, the hope is that one does not merely acquire a veneer of dignity, but one's actions are consistent with one's beliefs, attitudes, and commitments. This is a transformative view of education that hopes for dignity to emerge from one's private thoughts and personal commitments. It suggests that one's behaviors change as one's ideas change and one's developing personal commitments drive one's actions.

For teachers and their students, acting with dignity and decorum in ways that suggest nobility, style, poise, elegance, restraint, and gravitas recognizes that personal image has an important impact on the nature of social interaction. Irving Goffman is among writers in the last century to suggest the profound impact of the various ways in which people present themselves to others.[5] This reflexive consciousness of one's appearance to others suggests a social consciousness of the impact of one's image on the nature and quality of one's interactions with others. Given this consciousness's social and psychological importance, Howard Gardner posits it as an intelligence that can be developed educationally.[6] As social activities, teaching and learning are impacted by image. An awareness of how to influence others, hopefully for the good, is an important aspect of general education. The public hopes that those responsible for general education will produce citizens who are prepared to participate fully in shaping society in the future. Being disposed to act with dignity constitutes a means by which people can discourse civilly and persuasively, act humanely and respectfully toward others, and navigate practically the various power relations within society. If dignity is to be developed through the socializing processes of education, then musicians, teachers, and their students need to cultivate it in their classrooms and all the other places in which they engage in music, teach, and learn.

Acting with dignity requires the exercise of self-control and self-discipline, in which reason and intellect have primacy. This view relies on the agency of human beings, on their ability to respond to, shape, and reshape their personal experiences and the communities of which they are a part. For John Dewey, self-control is the Janus face of freedom, and its development is necessarily communal and social.[7] This being the case, democratic ideas need to be expressed throughout the educational process if democratic societies are to survive and thrive. Rather than taking hedonistic, egocentric, and impulsive action without thought for the consequences for others, one restrains passion and impulse. One thinks and acts intelligently and empathetically in sensitive, careful, measured, and thoughtful ways that consider the needs, interests, and rights of others. One acts as if oneself and others are persons of worth.

Among its contributions of dignity, education distinguishes and separates people as it also creates communities of those with shared interests and attachments. Ironically, those who aspire to dignity and who act with restraint, style, and elegance stand apart from others who act boorishly, please themselves, and lack knowledge, self-control, and discipline. Philosophers in West and East alike regard dignity as an educational good that needs to be manifest in society and in all those involved in education, be they teachers or students.[8] Without emphasizing the formality on which decent societies rely, education is bereft of the very elements that make it possible for people to improve their social lot and build and maintain civil and humane societies.[9]

Dignity commands respect and inspires others. One's personal grooming, deportment, dress, actions, and speech imply a sense of gravitas. Notions of what it is to act with dignity vary from time to time and place to place, and the ways in which musicians and teachers present themselves to their audiences and students differ. Professional dress and decorum require restraint on the musician's and teacher's part. Doing this may mean resisting the impulse to present oneself to one's audiences and students informally as a means of minimizing the social distance between oneself and one's listeners and students. Dignity suggests that some separation between musician and audience, teacher and student may constitute a good in commanding the respect of audiences and students and revealing the differences between where these audiences and students now are and where they might be. Modeling professionalism in appearance and action allows musicians and teachers to demonstrate how professional people should act. It can also inspire audiences and students to act in ways that accord with the importance of what is being sung and played, said and done, taught and learned.

Rituals rely on dignity, especially the sense of occasion and a knowledge of how one needs to behave in the public events that mark all civilized societies. Iris Yob notes that educational rituals characterize schools as sacred places and times.[10] Emphasizing the formality that marks these times and spaces evokes for musicians and their audiences as well as teachers and their students a sense of wonder, awe, and a respect for "the many mansions" of beauty, knowledge, and wisdom that may be theirs.[11] Education and music are thereby elevated above banal, ordinary, and prosaic things; dignity constitutes a search for wisdom that goes beyond the skills needed to earn a livelihood and prosper economically to concern important spiritual and existential questions of life. An inside-out approach to dignity can be personally and collectively transformative. Disparities of social class, economic circumstances, gender, ethnicity, language, and religion are among the barriers that are a source of despair, distress, and rage for those who are or believe themselves to be oppressed and shut out from participating fully in society. Those who have never learned to act in dignified ways from an early age may find it difficult to acquire these skills later in life. Paulo Freire recognizes that the poor are especially excluded from the higher reaches of society due, often, to their lack of an education that develops their dignity in ways as fundamental as an ability to read and think critically about their circumstances.[12] As people come to see themselves as worthy, their self-respect grows. Valuing dignity can facilitate learners' personal and social development, develop their self-confidence, and immeasurably enrich their lives in a host of ways. Emphasizing dignity as a musical and educational value constitutes a means of overcoming these barriers, reducing these disparities, and empowering all to participate fully in society.

Notwithstanding these contributions, the ambiguity of inside-out and external manifestations of dignity means that some dignified expressions may mask evil intention and thought whereby some seek to maintain power over and intimidate others. Throughout history, powerful people have regularly resorted to the trappings of dignity to enhance and maintain their image and power, and music has often been a means whereby this dignity is projected.[13] This crucial role of music has meant that musicians have often been the pawns and playthings of unscrupulous rulers for their own ends. Witness the role of musicians in creating spectacles as a means of creating and projecting dignified images and propaganda, the musical ensembles that accompany military parades and warfare, or the use of chamber music to enhance the atmosphere, elegance, and pretention of private social events attended by people of high social status. The possibility of dignity being used for miseducative purposes is also very real, especially when it is superficial, does not emanate from one's thought and feeling, or fails to evidence integrity or consistency between thought and practice in private and public life.

There is also the problem that dignity tends to make conduct expected of persons of high social status normative. As such, it may maintain classist and elitist attitudes and behaviors and, in so doing, a conservative mindset opposed to social change of any sort. This preference for a stratified social order in which a privileged class exercises power over most of the people leads those without power to emulate their betters and remain complicit in their subversion and even oppression. Historically, the upper classes have had the benefit of an education denied to the great majority, and they have learned to act with dignity in ways that are considered normative. Democratic ideals in decent societies have led to social movements throughout history to remove inequities and undertake social change in directions intended to promote greater equality among people. To this end, proponents of the great movements of democratic education—notably, the promotion of inside-out approaches to dignity within formal education—have sought to remove this special privilege by providing opportunities for all people to be included in its benefits. They have sought to subvert the forces of exclusion of those who do not know how to behave in a dignified manner by developing in all citizens a sense of self-respect, showing them how to behave in formal social events, and helping them develop the skills to do so. Notwithstanding these proponents' efforts, appeals to this hope have sometimes been made by unscrupulous people to manipulate the public. When this occurs, the public might be expected to be leery of notions of positive social change and aspirations to create a better social order.[14] Still, in decent societies, for those who seek a humane education, it is imperative to provide opportunities for everyone to know what dignity means and how to be dignified.[15]

DISPASSION

In its ordinary usage, *dispassion* is construed as the "freedom from passion" and the "absence of emotion," as both noun and verb.[16] It is in counterpoint with its root, passion, from the Latin words *passiōn-* and *passiō*, referring originally to a sense of pain and suffering and, subsequently, to "sense relating to emotional states," particularly "strong, controlling, or overpowering emotion[s]" such as anger, rage, desire, fear, and so forth.[17] Passion is not only a noun but a verb meaning "to show, express, or be affected by passion or deep feeling" or "to excite or imbue with passion."[18] For Epicurus, the idea of a "moderation of feelings" was a source of happiness.[19] If one pays "attention to internal feelings and to external sensations in general," one may "rightly trace the causes" of one's "mental disturbances and fear."[20] In his view, "Unhappiness comes either through fear or through vain and unbridled desire."[21] Noting the roots of the notion of dispassion in the ideas of Epicurus and the other Stoics, the eighteenth-century essayist William Temple described dispassion as "great tranquillity of mind" and "indolence of body" where passions are subdued, tempered, and diverted; the mind is quiet; and calmness and reason prevail.[22] The ambiguity of the word as both noun and verb suggests that this calmness of mind is not only a state of being but an active process of tempering and subduing the emotions, both as means and end. Rather than giving way to a fit of anger or a temper tantrum, a dispassionate person seeks to hold emotion in check and subdue the rage or frustration she or he may feel. This ambiguity suggests that dispassion may remain a value one seeks, even if one is imperfectly or incompletely successful in subduing strong feeling and maintaining calmness.

Among the contributions of dispassion, Temple evokes the garden and gardening as metaphors for the ideal of the calm state of mind that characterizes the work of philosophy just as it represents, for Epicurus and the Stoics, a way to achieve happiness. Temple thinks of Epicurus as the philosopher of the garden. Among the first to have a garden in Athens, Temple wrote, Epicurus "passed his life wholly in his gardens; there he studied, there he exercised, there he taught his philosophy."[23] For Temple, "no other sort of abode seems to contribute so much, to both the tranquillity of mind, and indolence of body, which he [Epicurus] made his chief ends." As Temple put it, "The sweetness of air, the pleasantness of smells, the verdure of plants, the cleanness and lightness of food, the exercises of working or walking; but above all, the exemption from cares and solicitude, seem equally to favour and improve both contemplation and health, the enjoyment of sense and imagination, and thereby the quiet and ease both of the body and mind."[24] For Albert Sieveking, this quietness and calmness suggests a nexus between "the Garden Spirit and the Soul of Universities and Academies."[25]

Sieveking agrees with Epicurus that the work of teaching and education can best take place in the midst of a garden, where restfulness, calmness, and freedom from the tumult of ordinary life are to be enjoyed.

Dispassion also values the beauty of the settings in which instruction needs to take place. Where educational form follows function, the importance of the beauty of natural and architectural surroundings for teaching and learning are overlooked, and the curriculum is devoid of music among the other arts, the effect is stultifying and depressing. I am intrigued by the power that Temple attributes, not only in the example of Epicurus's life but in his philosophy, to the importance of natural surroundings in fostering dispassion. Romantic philosophers such as Jean-Jacques Rousseau based Émile's education in his home and garden and emphasized a natural education.[26] Likewise, other educational philosophers such as Johann Heinrich Pestalozzi valued the natural world, and Pestalozzi's music master, Joseph Neef, regularly led students out into the countryside to sing.[27] As they selected songs for young children to sing, nineteenth-century pioneers of music's introduction into publicly supported general education recognized early the importance of a consciousness of nature in an urbanized and industrialized age.[28] There are myriad songs in the early songbooks used in schools about the beauty of the natural world and the inspiration it brings. Notwithstanding that many youngsters were growing up in towns and cities that were often crowded, polluted, and devoid of natural beauty, music teachers were quick to recognize the importance of fostering children's imaginations and giving them respite, if just for a while, from the cares of schooling and their daily lives. I want to extend Epicurus's evocation of the garden as an appropriate context for education to the importance of the arts in the school curriculum. The persistent idea that music is a time of recreation in the school day symbolizes this simplicity, restfulness, and quietness of mind that Epicurus sought for himself and his students. Paradoxically, even as music constitutes a means of recreation and a rest from the study of other academic subjects through its playfulness and entertaining quality, it also effectively prompts learning in unexpected, imaginative, intuitive, and felt ways. It can provide the unstructured space and time for students to gain spiritual insights into the existential questions that puzzle or worry them. If students' minds are not cluttered with constant objectives and expectations that fill every moment, music can allow students an opportunity to reflect and come to understandings of their own.[29]

Temple further grasps the importance of "indolence" in achieving a dispassionate or calm state of mind. Indolence, or idleness and laziness, is often decried as an educational sin in our time, preoccupied as contemporary society is with productivity and busyness.[30] Still, ceasing constant activity, procrastinating, and relishing a lack of obligation to work or to do something productive in every waking moment are needed if one is to come to wisdom. Far from an evil, indolence can constitute a good in freeing one to simply be and to allow music, education, and the experiences of life to happen to one. This notion is not far from Dewey's conception of the "passive" aspect of artistic and educational experience as one "undergoes" it and opens oneself to it.[31] I am probably not alone in having experienced a flood of insights when away from work, walking by the seashore, in the woods, in the garden, or at a concert. During this rest and relaxation, even though I may not be conscious of thinking about a difficult problem, new and different questions, ideas, and solutions may flash into my mind unbidden. This luxury of letting the experience of the moment happen when it is ready in leisure is, for Dewey, an overlooked and compelling aspect of the arts and education. I wish for more of it in music and education.

Dispassion also constitutes a means of fostering a civil society. For the Stoics and Epicureans, dispassion is the way to happiness, and reason holds the emotions in check and guides moral conduct. Violence ensues where people have not learned or are unable to exercise self-control. Some incite others to violence, arguing that certain causes are just, the ends can only be achieved through violent behavior, and the ends justify the means. Yet civility requires the capacity to hold one's feeling in check, exercise reason, and participate in solving disputes peacefully. In our time, violence is too often manifest through the media and in the public spaces, and it is especially challenging to foster civility. Nevertheless, if civility is to thrive in decent societies and people are to know happiness of the sort the Stoics and Epicureans valued, dispassion is a crucial value.

Nevertheless, dispassion also has a dark side. Elevating reason above emotion or feeling may devalue those aspects of life that are felt rather than logically reasoned. For Susanne Langer, such a view prompted her *Philosophy in a New Key*. She forwarded the notion that although Western philosophy emphasizes reason and propositional discourse through discursive symbols, much of life experience is felt rather than reasoned, enacted rather than propositionally thought about, and represented through nondiscursive rather than discursive symbols.[32] In education, the preeminence of reason and propositional thought and the study of discursive symbols in fields such as mathematics has led to the "subjugation" of music, among the other arts, religions, myths, dreams, and rituals.[33] The focus on rational and patriarchal ways of knowing associated with education has denigrated the cultivation of passion, emotions, senses, and feelings and ascribed to them a negative valence. These "lower" qualities are too often associated with the experience of girls and women, and, in the process, they and the females associated with them are devalued. Such a view fails to grasp that passion, emotions, senses, and feelings provide the spark of life and add immeasurably to the enjoyment of life's pleasures for all people. Reducing people to a state of monochromatic calmness of dispassion removes the intensities of passionate commitments that constitute the full measure of the richness, height, and depth of human experience. Holding passion too much in check or considering passion as an unmitigated evil restricts the multidimensionality of pleasure and pain and thereby the full expression of one's humanity. Letting go and surrendering oneself to one's passions can be a source of creative expression, delight, and sorrow that one may not imagine if one dwells only in a garden holding oneself in constant check.

There is also the danger that one may put up with too much evil, and one's dispassion may breed apathy and passivity. Some evils need to be righted, and the sacred scriptures of the Abrahamic faiths of Judaism, Christianity, and Islam, at least, point to the importance of rage and indignation in pursuit of righteous causes. Proponents of these faiths notice that one cannot and should not remain calm in the face of evil. Dewey's important distinction between "self-expression" (for example, using one's anger in productive ways) and "self-exposure" (for example, having a temper tantrum) reveal how passion can constitute a good when it serves as a means of self-expression through such means as music and the arts.[34] Apathy and passivity in the face of circumstances that demand change may, by neglecting to act, constitute evils of omission, of not acting when one should. Focusing on the importance of dispassion as a musical and educational virtue may lead one to neglect the importance of the limits of dispassion and of the imperatives for passion, especially in cultivating the arts. Navigating this territory is challenging for teachers and their students. When people and institutions trample on freedoms or evil is done, passionate action on behalf of change may be required. Directing rage and indignation in productive ways is a form of self-expression that Dewey would applaud as an artistic and educational good. Musicians, teachers, and students need the courage of their convictions to think and act passionately on behalf of ends and means to which they are committed.

Dispassion also suggests that reason operates independently from felt life and can exercise control over feeling, desire, and emotion. In practice, especially in music, one's thoughts are a meld of intelligent thought, emotion, and physical and psychical states. Reasoning includes cognitive emotions and emotional cognitions that are also impacted by one's senses, physical state, and well-being.[35] It is well understood that reason does not exist alone, devoid of the other aspects of one's body; it is a part of the mind and body and, as such, does not dwell in a metaphysical realm entirely apart from other aspects of mind and body; it is also shaped socially and environmentally.[36] Given the complexities of these interactions, a conception of "reason alone" without emotion or feeling seems simplistic and naïve. In the vicissitudes of poverty, homelessness, violence, disease, death, natural disasters, and wars, it is difficult to imagine that one could attain a state of dispassion and that one's passions would not sometimes betray one. Conceived as a state of being, and notwithstanding one's efforts to attain it, dispassion seems a value that is ultimately out of reach.

RESTRAINT

The word *restraint* has a long history in musical and educational thought and practice. This originally Norman and French word is used principally as a noun and originally referred to "an act of binding, restricting." Throughout its history, it has been thought of variously as an "ordinance or injunction which imposes a restriction," "an embargo," "an act of restraining, checking, or stopping something," "self-control" or "moderation," a "restraining force or influence" or "a means of restraining a person from a course of action, or of keeping a person under control," "deprivation or restriction of a person's liberty" and "restriction" or "limitation."[37] This ambiguity, suggestive of external discipline or coercion on the one hand and self-imposed constraints on one's impulses and desires on the other, is evident throughout the world's musical traditions and educational systems.

Restraint can be active and passive. It is active in the sense that one exercises and imposes rules that limit, check, or prevent one's actions or those of others (for example, passing laws, enacting regulations, or limiting freedom of movement by means such as imprisonment). It is passive when one is the subject of actions by others that limit, check, or prevent one's actions. In these senses, restraint may serve a good purpose by preserving the safety and well-being of the society or the community. Taking children on a field trip or ferrying touring musicians from place to place may require imposing certain rules that ensure that all can arrive at the destination safely and ready to play or sing. Still, the perspectives of those on this journey depend on whether participants have the power to enact the restraints or are merely the recipients of others' determinations. In its active sense, restraint may constitute a means of empowerment whereby one makes decisions that limit one's own actions; in its passive sense, restraint can be disempowering when one must accommodate oneself to the decisions of others even when they do not seem justified. For this reason, Dewey argues, wherever possible, democratic education should be based on social control whereby students share in devising the limits imposed on their actions. In this way, they learn that democracies necessarily limit their actions while also fostering and preserving liberty for all.[38] Likewise, Freire contrasts banking education in which students' actions are limited by the dictums of others with liberatory education where students participate in setting these possibilities and limits.[39] For Dewey and Freire, it makes a world of difference whether restraint is conceived and practiced actively or passively. My own view is that active and passive notions of restraint are important for the practice of music and education and fall in the messy ground between these theoretical polarities. Here, musicians, teachers, and students need to determine which approaches fit the circumstances in which they find themselves.

Among its advantages, restraint is consonant with the idea of education as a means of socialization and enculturation in which the older generations need to pass on to the young the traditions bequeathed to them. If society is to continue, or a musical tradition is to survive, some stability in social expectations is required. The young need to learn obedience to rules and regulations conveyed by their elders, and they need to accommodate restraint that is both active and passive. For a society or a musical practice to maintain itself, people need to be able to act in the expectation that others will behave in certain ways. The alternative, at its logical extreme, would be anarchy, musical or otherwise, and the breakdown of civility and expectations of the restraint exercised by self and others. It is not always possible for the young to be consulted on the ways in which instruction should be carried out. Sometimes, teachers need to make decisions that restrain their students' options and that they deem to be in their students' best interest. For this reason, Dewey's democratic education constitutes a meld or a synthesis of both active and passive forms of restraint. Although teachers or conductors, as leaders of their classroom communities or musical forces, sometimes require obedience and restraint from their students or musicians, Dewey would hope that they seek to create conditions where the students and musicians can also participate in forming the rules that restrain their conduct insofar as possible. In the practical worlds of music and education, this is a messy process. If my own experience is on the mark, musicians and teachers who seek to work in this juxtaposition of active and passive notions of restraint are in a paradoxical situation in which they face conflicting pressures. They do not always arrive at the right balance of active and passive restraint, notwithstanding their desire to do so.

Restraint can also help prepare people for the world of work. From the beginning of music education in the industrial age, schooling was envisaged as a means of preparing people to work obediently in factories, shops, offices, and other places in which their actions would be restrained by others. Nineteenth-century architects of school music, such as William Woodbridge, argued for the importance of vocal education and each child's accommodation of the needs of the chorus as a means of forwarding these industrial ideals. As cogs in the vast enterprise of capitalism, where most workers were restrained by their bosses' decisions, restraint was crucial in developing the skills that most workers would need to earn a livelihood. Large musical ensembles such as bands and choirs served as the means of preparing the young to participate in this world of work. With the dawning of the information age, restraint of a different kind was needed for a different world of work. Creative and entrepreneurial skills and independence required restraint of a more active sort. Workers needed the ability to restrain themselves in ways that would allow them to survive in a very different reality. Here, the paternalism once practiced by large corporations was replaced by disinterest in the plight of workers who were treated increasingly like self-employed widgets or replaceable units responsible for their own well-being and survival. These sorts of skills may be fostered in small ensembles where musicians exercise shared participation in their own governance rather than the large ensembles of the past. Yet the resilience of large ensembles in school music programs reveals the power of tradition in music education and the influence of large corporations and pervasive technologies in which workers are prepared to function as interchangeable parts of a smooth-running machine and where restraint is persistently passive.

Like dispassion, restraint, especially when active, fosters self-control and moderation. Educators have long believed that their work is internal—namely, to cultivate the disposition to restrain one's impulses and control one's passions. Education has a fundamentally restrictive and constraining influence on the young. This is far from being an inhumane undertaking, as the exercise of self-control suggests that one does not require external pressure to act in certain ways. For Schiller, the point of aesthetic education is the development from a "natural" person governed by passions and impulses to a "moral" person able to act moderately and reasonably, even when one is disinclined to do so or when one's passions and impulses come to the fore. Moderation assumes, like dispassion, that reason can control conduct and restrain feeling in ways that point to the good.

Notwithstanding its potential contributions, restraint can also negatively impact the work of music and education. It seeks to prevent rather than to enable, to limit actions by prescription and proscription rather than assist musicians, teachers, and their students to act positively toward desired ends. Restraint specifies and enforces limits on what should or should not be done, but it does not necessarily provide the means whereby people are enabled to act in desired ways. When viewed passively, it may serve to legislate certain norms and state specific rules rather than inspire to improved action. In its appeal to extrinsic rather than intrinsic motivation, restraint may fail to constitute the humane approach to conduct for which it may hope. As such, it may constrain rather than foster musical and educational growth.

There is also the possibility of limiting liberty. I have noted that Dewey is careful to describe freedom and social control as means of fostering a democratic society in which both aspects need to be present in educative experience. The personal and collective emancipation for which Freire hopes as the basis for his liberatory approach to education may be overlooked in restraint's emphasis on limiting thought and action in certain prescribed ways. Such an approach may also emphasize tradition at the expense of music's and education's crucial transformative role in challenging the nature and limits of traditional beliefs and practices. Notwithstanding the importance of limits in creative expression, it is possible to squelch those who are inclined to burst the bounds and restraints of tradition and forge new ways of seeing and acting in the world.

An illusion of restraint in the active sense may cover the fact of imposed constraints from above or outside. What may appear to be humane and liberatory may turn out to be manipulative, and musicians, teachers, and students may possess little real control. For example, behind the scenes, musical and educational policy makers may be arranging or manipulating circumstances in such a way that musicians, teachers, and students appear to be able to exercise self-restraint, but they are really being constrained by others. The impact of realizing that one is being hoodwinked or conned is especially galling because one's intelligence is insulted. For me, the veneer of democracy is particularly irksome and even oppressive. Having lived with these working conditions, I wish there were fewer instances of musical and educational administration that pretends to be what it is not.

It is also possible that musician teachers may value passive and quiet students over those who are rambunctious and noisy. Restraint may be interpreted to focus on constricting physical activity in the learning process. Keeping students quiet and docile may be miseducative in that some students may learn best through modes that emphasize physical movement and practical activity rather than book learning while seated quietly. When learners are required to attend class and sit quietly for hours at a time, it is easy to understand their feeling of being restrained in the classroom with few periods for exercise or their sense of imprisonment and resentment toward teachers or administrators. Valuing restraint may emphasize book learning of a sort that is alien to the needs and interests of many young people, especially musicians. Maria Montessori's focus on school activities and the importance of movement and sensory response to things in the child's world seeks to remedy this overly intellectual, bookish, and passive approach to restraint. She emphasizes the importance of physical and emotional engagement with things in the phenomenal world.[40] As such, Montessori seeks to model an approach to restraint that is self-motivated and hopes for its growth in the hum of activities involving physical and practical action on the part of enthusiastic and sometimes boisterous students. Her educational approach resonates particularly with the experience of many music teachers involved in working with students in performance settings.

It is also important to investigate the restraints that are imposed on and by musicians, teachers, and their students. The claims of tradition and the expectations based on certain norms may need to be challenged, even at the risk of unsettling the status quo. In *Transforming Music Education,* I suggest that systemic changes are needed in music education assumptions, values, and practices.[41] These changes necessitate reworking a host of musical and educational restraints that impact music, teaching, learning, instruction, curriculum, and administration. They fly in the face of the traditional restraints that affect music education in different ways and are fostered by normative thinking and standardized and homogenous approaches to school music. Opening music education to an array of formal and informal approaches to transmitting knowledge about a wide array of musical traditions unsettles the hegemony of large and sometimes militarized musical ensembles in the school curriculum. It also prompts the development of an array of different restraints that, in turn, require critique in a never-ending process in search of an elusive ideal.

DISCIPLINE

The word *discipline* is rooted in the Latin words *disciplīna* and *discipulīna.*[42] Construed as noun and verb, *discipline* has conveyed various meanings over time, including "teaching, instruction, training, branch of study, philosophical school or sect, system, practice, method, orderly conduct based on moral training, [and] order maintained in a body of people." Its Christian usage connotes such notions as "moral law," "obedience to divine law," "divine warning or punishment," "religious doctrine," "monastic rule," "chastisement," and "scourging." Discipline is also interconnected with discipleship (notice that *discipulīna* is predicated on *discipulus*—that is, a disciple, or one who follows a discipline as a way of life). Given this wide conceptual swath of references, I focus on its musical and educational meanings. Throughout musical and educational history, both sacred and secular, discipline has been regarded as fundamental to musical tradition and formal education. It has been invoked especially regarding Western classical music, among other classical traditions.[43]

Thinking of discipline as an educational method and objective evokes Dewey's means-end continuum, in which method serves as both an end and the means to yet another end.[44] For example, the means whereby one learns a musical practice serve as ends along the way and bases on which yet other more advanced ends become possible. Pedagogical approaches are not simply additive to the musical practices they serve. Rather, they are infused with the values that underlie those beliefs and practices. The ways in which subject matter is taught and learned express the values underlying the traditions themselves. Since the exponents of a practice agree on certain methods and ends, discipline in this sense connotes a specific rationality expressed in ways of thought and practice that neophytes internalize as they are educated in a musical tradition. This is how it has been interpreted, for example, in the notion of discipline-based music education.[45]

Regarding discipline as orderly conduct is akin to ideas of restraint, dispassion, and dignity in its insistence on acting in prescribed ways within specific constraints. Discipline is predicated on the claims of reason in governing conduct and ensuring that emotional response is within certain limits. It also emphasizes the need to conform to expectations in public spaces. Rooted in systems of rules that give rise to these expectations, discipline implies that rule sets have been internalized by exponents who not only live by them but love to live by them. These rules and expectations express moral purposes and ends. For example, musical practices such as jazz embody ethical values of mutual respect, communal musicking, and self-expression within the group's performance. This tradition as it is practiced in New Orleans, for example, gives voice to those who make and receive it, provides a sense of self-respect and empowerment, and constitutes a means of livelihood particularly for black musicians in a color-conscious society.[46] The rules under which the tradition operates embrace democratic values that attract musicians and listeners irrespective of color from other parts of the United States and around the world. Its moral valence has been recognized by critics and protagonists alike.[47]

When regarded as a musical system, tradition, or school, *discipline* spans both theory and practice. It entails the philosophical and theoretical propositions, assumptions, expectations, beliefs, attitudes, and values that underlie the practical aspects of music. Irrespective of whether a musical tradition is notated, its theoretical underpinning and superstructure may be articulated formally or informally and understood implicitly or explicitly. For exponents of and participants in this music, these understandings are interpreted and shared in varying degree. They are critiqued by exponents and public alike and employed in the evaluation of musical compositions, improvisations, and performances in which music plays a role. Likewise, the performance practice of the music is agreed on to varying degrees by its exponents, and it is adjudicated and contested according to publicly held expectations. This practical and procedural knowledge is precise and rule governed. Proscriptions and prescriptions of actions constrain musicians to a specified range of actions within which they are expected to operate. Divergences from expected actions may or may not be permissible and will surely be noted by both musicians and the public.

Thinking of discipline as training entails both positive and negative elements, utilizing encouragement and reward of desired attitudes and actions on the one hand and constraint and punishment of undesired attitudes and actions on the other. Whether this training relates to either the theoretical or practical aspects of a musical tradition, positive and negative reinforcements combine to move neophytes and exponents toward the desired thoughts and actions. Although the emphases and methods of training differ from one tradition to another, from place to place and time to time, the musical traditions I have studied ensure ways and means whereby musicians and their public come to understand what is expected of them and possess the skills required to do and participate in this music. Although there are many informal means of acquiring knowledge, instruction is often a formal process that relies on demonstration (and sometimes instruction) by skilled exponents. Where music is orally transmitted as a part of communal rites, learning the songs, dances, instruments, and lore interconnected with the music is a part of training for the rituals that mark the onset of adulthood. The preparation to undertake these rituals is necessarily rigorous, and expectations to conform to certain beliefs and practices are high. The stakes are particularly high when spiritual power is believed to attend musical performance. Exponents of musical traditions and their publics regard their own practices as consequential, possessing gravitas, and worthy of dignity, and training plays an important role in ensuring the continuation and subsequent flourishing of these beliefs and practices.

Among its musical and educational contributions, the idea of discipline as both means and ends constitutes a way of empowering those involved in coming to know a musical tradition. Israel Scheffler points to the educational importance of the "rule" approach to teaching.[48] In contrast to models of teaching that dictate the educator's task as impressing students much as one might stamp and impress a mold or that rely entirely on the students' insight into knowledge, the rule approach suggests that the teacher's central task is imparting the rules that govern systems of thought and practice. Scheffler's concept of rule has much in common with Jerome Bruner's view of the importance of conveying the systematic order of the subject matter.[49] Once students grasp the system of the subjects they are studying, they have the means to extrapolate beyond the specific matter to other new circumstances to which these rules more or less might apply. For Scheffler and Bruner, these rules and expectations constitute keys that unlock a universe of other understandings. Having access to these keys enables students to learn for themselves, independently of the teacher, and constitutes a source of self-growth. This democratic idea is a source of personal and collective freedom. Paradoxically, by focusing on discipline, one comes on a means of freedom.

Discipline also creates the framework and the order necessary for creativity to thrive. Ironically, the willingness to constrain behavior within a musical discipline, for example, provides the basis for creative action within those limits. Creativity is most evident against the backdrop of the order created within a musical practice.[50] Rules need to exist before it can be apparent where and how they need to be broken in creative ways and where the limits set by the tradition might be challenged or subverted. These creative divergences from the norm are best understood where the rules underlying a tradition are clear. In this view, creativity is grounded in discipline and does not exist without it.[51]

Thinking of discipline as a procedural as well as propositional matter broadens the musical and educational enterprise beyond knowing about such and such to "seeing how it was made" from the "inside-out" perspective of a practitioner.[52] Grasping the systematic and rule-bound nature of a particular tradition is crucial to acquiring procedural knowledge—that is, how to do something as opposed to knowing about it.[53] Vernon Howard unpacks the sometimes complicated ways in which musicians, among other artists, come to know the rules that govern an artistic practice.[54] Examining this process from the perspective of singers who are learning their craft and art, he views the changing perceptions of aspiring artists from rule-governed to rule-covered behavior throughout their artistic education. While procedural understanding may be particularly important in artistic, professional, and practical subjects, it is also central to academic and theoretical subjects such as history, literature, mathematics, and the sciences. As such, the education of artists may constitute a metaphor for education generally.[55]

Notwithstanding the contributions discipline may make, there is also a dark side. Discipline relies on the power of tradition as a basis for expectations regarding appropriate conduct. This tradition is difficult to unseat because it comes with the force of sensus communis, or common sense and taken-for-granted assumptions about beliefs and practices that are accepted as normative. Although it is important to interrogate this tradition and to inquire as to the ways in which it may err, the power of the order and system that comprise a discipline may make it difficult to contest or interrogate it. The challengers to a system are dependent, to some degree, on the means at their disposal to change the system, and these means are often controlled by the powerful establishment within a tradition. A musical practice, for example, is predicated on continuity of expectations, and where these are subverted, the practice is undermined. Those with a vested interest in the status quo may lose power if this challenge is not thwarted. Consequently, change, when required, may be difficult to achieve because the system is oriented toward stasis.

Thinking of discipline in terms of punishment of the sort evident in religious views of chastisement, scourging, and violence may emphasize negative rather than positive reinforcement in music, teaching, and learning. For much of educational history, discipline was thought of principally in terms of punishment, both psychological and physical, and corporal punishment was believed to be essential to inculcating desired behaviors in publicly supported schooling in the West into the present century.[56] Within traditional approaches to music education, for example, anthropological and ethnomusicological evidence of the elders beating musical rhythms into youngsters illustrates the persistence of beliefs about the interconnections between physical and mental experience in the musical training of children.[57] Regarding discipline as punishment for evil or undesirable conduct relies on the power of negative reinforcement as a potent means of training. Rather than encouraging desired conduct in humane ways, this stern approach sees punishment for wrongdoing as a powerful incentive for people to avoid the behaviors proscribed in the tradition. Pestalozzi was among those to seek a more positive and humane view of the education of children that resists this view and urges educators to rely on encouragement rather than punishment.[58] This idea is recast by modern educators such as Dewey (influenced by his wife, Alice), Montessori, and Martin,[59] and Shinichi Suzuki and his wife, Waltraud, who advocate love for one's students as a basis of music education.[60] I have also forwarded a positive view of discipline in music education that hopes for humane instructional approaches and rejects punishment as a principal means of discipline. This view is evident widely in the music education profession, even if music educators do not always do as they say they believe.[61]

In its emphasis on the intellectual aspects of the subject matter, discipline, as with dignity, dispassion, and restraint, downplays the role of the senses and emotions in learning. In overintellectualizing education, emphasizing discipline may afford insufficient attention to the humane and affective aspects of education or, as Langer might suggest, the "education of feeling."[62] Even though the arts can provide an important metaphor for education generally, focusing on discipline may paradoxically emphasize the academic subjects closely associated with cognition and undervalue the arts and other practical subjects. The focus in the arts may likewise be on conceptual aspects rather than on the distinctively "feelingful" ways of thought and action that characterize them. Accordingly, their most distinctive aspects may be downplayed in favor of the sort of intellectual objectives that characterize other academic subjects.

In sketching the values of dignity, dispassion, restraint, and discipline, I emphasize the social qualities of dignity that are both internally generated and superficial, the moderation and calmness of feeling construed metaphorically through the garden of dispassion, the hope for a check on excess and self-control and moderation of restraint, and the systematic and orderly conduct of discipline related to the notion of disciple, the follower of a discipline. These values are ambiguous, share commonalities while varying in emphasis, contribute to music and education, and are problematic in one way or another. Contrasting with reverence, humility, awe, and spirituality, they rely heavily on intellection and reason in keeping emotions in check, although they may also hope for something of their wonder, mystery, feeling, and otherworldliness. The process of contesting the norms that govern music education needs to be ongoing from one generation to the next and one place to another. Without such interrogation, traditions may become ossified, and change may be more difficult to achieve when needed. Although each may constitute an unattainable goal, it is worth preserving for its possibilities. For those who would hold on to these values, the challenge becomes one of avoiding the worst of their detractions. Navigating this fraught territory amid theory and practice and developing practical solutions appropriate for pedagogical situations constitute important challenges for musicians, teachers, and students.

FIVE

Love, Friendship, Desire, and Devotion

THE INTERCONNECTED QUARTET OF VALUES addressed in this chapter—love, friendship, desire, and devotion—is deeply rooted in a musical and educational lineage stretching back to antiquity and evident in cultures around the world. These values constitute the heart and soul of human existence. In contrast to the values of dignity, dispassion, restraint, and feeling, they embrace rather than check the life of emotion, feeling, and sensation. This counterpoint is crucial in balancing the differing claims of intellect and emotion, mind and body, and thought and action in the entirety of human experience. Grounded in the metaphor of the heart, they emphasize different qualities and point in different directions, some of which are in tension with others. Like reverence, awe, humility, and spirituality, their experience tends to be more subjective than objective; still, the character of this subjectivity differs in its corporeal and sensual rather than intellectual and spiritual qualities and concern with things seen rather than unseen. Here, I think of these values from a perspective framed by the musical and educational traditions with which I am familiar. As I unpack each in turn, I also critically examine some of their contributions and disadvantages with a view to rescuing these values for musical and educational practice.

LOVE

Love is among the most enduring musical and educational values.[1] It is espoused by musicians who speak of themselves as "amateurs" who do music for the love of it and by teachers who posit love as a grounding educational principle.[2] Despite its wide usage, its meaning is ambiguous. It is construed as noun and verb, experienced objectively and subjectively as a dynamic process in the sense of becoming, done and undergone, thought and felt. Cultivated particularly in those spaces where intimate interpersonal bonds are forged in private life, it is also evident to differing degrees and in various forms in public life. It is present in schools, religious communities, businesses, and musical organizations, among the myriad ways and different institutions in which human beings relate socially. My focus here is on pedagogical notions of love. I tease out the senses in which one may speak of love educationally and examine some of its associated notions of friendship, desire, and devotion.[3] Doing this helps to clarify this cluster of values and grasp their contributions and detractions in the broad musical and educational enterprise.

Thought about in terms of its ordinary usage, as "affection and attachment," love can be defined as a "feeling or disposition of deep affection or fondness for someone." It typically arises "from a recognition of attractive qualities, from natural affinity, or from sympathy and manifesting itself in concern for the other's welfare and pleasure in his or her presence." This attraction and attachment can also be directed toward "a group or category of people" or "one's country or another impersonal object of affection."[4] In each case, the notion of love differs somewhat.

Conceiving of love as directed beyond people and toward a wide array of objects opens possibilities that are both sacred and secular. Love can be construed in religious terms. In the Abrahamic faiths, believers see it as "the benevolence and affection of God towards an individual or towards creation," "the affectionate devotion due to God from an individual," and "the regard and consideration of one human being towards another prompted by a sense of a common relationship to God."[5] In polytheistic and animistic traditions, adherents may be attracted to some gods whom they regard as beneficent even as they seek to appease others whom they fear. Those who deny the existence of god(s) may sense mystery, awe, and wonder in the face of life and the natural world or may acknowledge an impersonal providence or natural principle to which they may be attracted and attached.[6] Within secular life, love may also be construed as a "strong predilection, liking, or fondness" for objects such as money and social status, a feeling derived from both the possession of these objects for their own sake and from the benefits that accrue from their possession. Musicians, along with other artists and their publics, speak of their love of music or the other art(s) they practice or appreciate.[7] This deep affection and attachment often leads them to go to sometimes extraordinary lengths to cultivate the requisite skills, live a life in pursuit of their art, and make sacrifices to attain and maintain it.

Love is also conceived sexually and physically as enactment and holistic fulfilment. To make love can connote physical and sexual acts driven by lust, physical desire, or instinct to the exclusion of other emotional and intellectual attachments or commitments. It can also refer to "an intense feeling of romantic attachment based on an attraction felt by one person for another; intense liking and concern for another person, typically combined with sexual passion." When one speaks of being "in love," one means a state of being that, while enacted sexually, may also fuse physical, emotional, and intellectual attraction as a consuming passion. This holistic expression of love has a moral dimension that moves beyond the merely physical to embrace one's attraction to and regard for one's beloved and one's responsibility for, commitment to, and duty toward this person. It is natural, then, to speak of the other as one's "love" and, as in times past, to imagine gods such as Cupid, Amor, Eros, and Venus as the personifications of love.[8]

Love is also conceived of as "an abstract principle." For example, Samuel Coleridge wrote that "love is a desire of the whole being to be united to something, or some being, felt necessary to its completeness."[9] As Virginia Woolf posited, "Love. Hate. Peace. Three emotions made the ply of human life."[10] Coleridge rooted love in desire and feeling, in a longing for completeness to be found only when one unites with something that, or someone who, one feels is necessary to complement one and fulfill what one lacks. For Coleridge, love is grounded in one's feeling of incompleteness and desire for completeness that can be found only outside oneself. In a different vein, Woolf construed love figuratively as one of three constituent emotions of human life. Her metaphor of ply suggests that love is part of the very fabric of human life, its material or its warp and weave, and necessary to the human condition. Love is not only pervasive, but it also evidences distinctive features of resilience and manifestation demonstrated differently from time to time and place to place.

Thought of as a verb, love is something enacted. It means to hold someone or something precious or "dear" and to "entertain a great affection, fondness, or regard for" "a person, a thing personified," or "a quality or attribute."[11] Such is this attraction that one is "unwilling to part with" this person or thing or allow it to "perish," and one may be willing to give one's life or sacrifice all to possess it. Love is expressed spiritually and physically, performed practically rather than only thought about or spoken. This enactment may be far more powerful than ideas about or words of love. Words fail as a means of expressing this powerful emotion, and loving acts of kindness, tenderness, devotion, and commitment count far more than the words that are said. Importantly, one takes "pleasure in the existence of (a virtue, a practice, a state of things) in oneself, in others, or more generally."[12] Love is not only a gift to others but reciprocal in the pleasure it brings to the giver by having been given and received. This reality makes unrequited love, or love that is spurned or unreturned, that much more bitter for the lover.

Where is pedagogical love to be situated within this richly ambiguous construction? Among its qualities, thinking of love in terms of depth of affection and attraction toward persons and things differs from construing it in terms of purely physical desire or romantic or sexual love in that its objective is spiritual rather than sensual, and its expression is physically reserved rather than seeking sexual consummation. On the teacher's part, interested love, or the natural affection of people who are attracted to each other, is tempered and accompanied by what some would see as disinterested love—that is, the love that looks beyond those who are naturally attractive or deserving of one's love to those who are dependent on one and for whom one is in a position of trust. In her notion of caring, Nel Noddings is at pains to take account of this affection, moral obligation, and commitment even toward those who are unlovely or undeserving.[13] Seen in these ways, the sexual expression of love between teacher and student constitutes a betrayal of the teacher's position of trust in relation to the student. Pedagogical love is principled as well as practical in ways that seek to see the student in terms of future possibility rather than merely present reality. It is felt and expressed in affection and touch while also conscious of decorum to preserve the teacher's position of trust and recognize the student's vulnerability. Such love is deeply spiritual in a holistic sense of personhood while also enacted in the phenomenal world. Coleridge's principle of need as a basis of love is intriguing for its possible pedagogical implications. It rings true in anecdotal evidence of those teachers who have spoken to me of their need to teach and of a grief experienced when they no longer can and of students who have expressed to me their need for assistance and direction as they seek the learning they deem necessary and that they feel they lack. Moreover, the passional attachments that pedagogical love suggests are manifested, for example, in the love that music students often express for their instrumental and vocal teachers and the love that they have for the music(s) they practice. In this ancient and widespread approach to musical education, the love that binds teachers and their students sometimes persists for a lifetime, and for students, this deep affection and attachment often merge into a form of reverence for their teachers. It can be witnessed in individual and small group instruction and large instrumental and vocal ensembles. Akin to religious expressions of love, teachers and students believe they are in a sacred space, standing on holy ground, and they see each other as infinitely precious. Construed as noun and verb, pedagogical love is a dynamic process and a state of being. It is experienced in the moment and over time. As both unidirectional and reciprocal, requited and sometimes unrequited, pedagogical love profoundly affects all aspects of teaching, learning, instruction, curriculum, and administration, both facilitating and hindering these pedagogical processes.[14]

Concerning love of music, the power of the social and contextual aspects of music making and receiving is such that musics do not have the same attraction for everyone.[15] For example, a teacher skilled in a classical tradition may work with students who are primarily interested in other vernacular traditions, or vice versa. Since the mid-twentieth century, music teachers have become increasingly ambivalent about which musical traditions they should teach. Some still make it their raison d'être to foster the Western classical tradition. They embrace its repertoire in their choirs, bands, orchestras, operas, chamber ensembles, and studio teaching. Others reject this purpose, preferring to focus instead on popular and vernacular musics that are more accessible and attractive to the young. Classical traditions are critiqued for their elitism, classism, sexism, and irrelevance, among a host of failings that these musics are seen to possess.[16]

Without a concerted focus on classical musics in general education in the West, classical music may remain a peripheral and elite aspect of culture with a relatively small group of devotees and institutions, as it has for much of its history.[17] This was certainly the concern when advocates of music education promoted its introduction into elementary school curricula in the early nineteenth century. Their hope was to enlarge access to classical music that had theretofore been primarily restricted to a privileged elite. Especially since the mid-twentieth century, school music teachers have found it more difficult to cultivate a sense of attachment to classical music and much easier to build on an already persistent attraction to popular and vernacular musics forwarded in the pervasive mass media. Capitulating to popular taste rather than fostering less accessible musics that rely on musical education for their sustenance shortchanges students by failing to develop their imaginations and stretch their minds and hearts. There will always be popular culture because it is accessible and attractive to ordinary people. In the absence of education in more esoteric and classical traditions, these traditions become more isolated from the public. They become what they were before the efforts to democratize these traditions; they are experienced by a small and privileged upper class or those supported by these patrons with the wealth and education to appreciate and sponsor them. One teaches the young to love classical music in the hope that they will grow attached to and support it—a value consistent with a long tradition of musician teachers who have hoped to democratize classical musics and extend opportunities to the public to come to love them.

In today's world, musical traditions that in the past might have been separate are often fused and changed by contact with other traditions. The reality of today's globalized music is that Western classical music has become an international tradition that has absorbed musics from Africa, Asia, North and South America, Eurasia, and Australasia. The same is true of other ancient classical traditions and newer popular traditions. Likewise, popular musics, jazz, and other classical musics have also taken on elements from Western classical music. Film scores regularly employ a pastiche of musics side by side or woven together within a specific musical tradition. Classical musicians such as Itzhak Perlman collaborate with popular musicians such as Billy Joel and perform klezmer music. Yo-Yo Ma's

Silk Road Ensemble brings together Western classical musicians and traditional and classical musicians of the East.[18] While some musics have become pervasive internationally, it has also been important to sustain and advocate for the local and vernacular traditions that represent the specific places in which people live. Alexandra Kertz-Welzel sees the tensions between nativist and local identities and an international consciousness of the world of musics.[19] These tensions need to be resolved within each society. Musicians and teachers hope to sustain and conserve local musical heritages while also broadening musical horizons outward to the wider world. In fact, cultures are intent on sustaining the local musical customs and traditions that are a mark of distinction and difference from others. For example, if young Indians are to come to a rich understanding of the fine arts today, knowing the classical traditions of north and south India is important, just as it is for young Americans to know the classical traditions of the Americas. If music education is to go beyond national and regional bounds to encompass the world of musics, young Indians could also be expected to acquire some knowledge of Western classical traditions, just as young Americans would benefit from becoming acquainted with Indian classical traditions. As the young gain this broad international knowledge of some of the world's great music traditions, albeit from different perspectives and to different degrees, their musical horizons widen, and they may experience a growing attachment to less accessible musics beyond the vernacular and mass mediated musics already well known to them.

Still, where mediated music is pervasive, Zoltán Kodály recognized that a knowledge of one's own musical culture cannot be taken for granted.[20] The young need to learn the folk songs of the places in which they live. The links between folk traditions and the classical traditions that grow out of them should provide mutual sustenance one to the other. Notwithstanding the need for critiquing all these musics, young people need to come to love and cherish classical music as they do other more familiar musics. Those steeped in classical traditions also benefit enormously by expanding their horizons toward a love of popular and vernacular traditions. This is because all these musical traditions are expressions of our differing and common humanity around the world. All are of value in one respect or another. All are limited in one way or another. There may be those who profess no love of music. In this admission, they often refer to a specific genre or style of music, or they admit a lack of interest in or inability to make sense of the sights and sounds that may count as music. One may hope to develop their sensitivity to sound, ability to notice a music's details, and, if possible, through one means or another, open their eyes as well as their ears to music. Still, just as love is directed specifically toward a person or thing, experienced musicians and teachers know that while people may come to love a specific music, this love may not necessarily translate equally to every music.

Among its advantages as a musical and educational value, love takes a humane and holistic view of the people involved in the instructional process and the subject matter, and it constitutes a source of pleasure for them. Although the subject matter is crucially important, finding opportunities to build on affection and attachment between teacher and student offers the prospect of personal transformation and growth. One might also expect to encounter joy, happiness, and pleasure in love—aspects that can enhance motivation to teach and learn and the entire musical and educational process. Love resonates with musical and educational making and receiving, an absorbing dynamic that brings delight in the moment and sustains teaching and learning over the long term. For those, such as Shinichi Suzuki, who believe wholeheartedly in its pedagogical efficacy, love is a means of inspiring teachers and students alike.[21] For Suzuki, there is the joy of Mozart coupled with the child's mastery of a violin piece. This is a pervasively positive view of music education that hopes not only to enrich music but to enrich the hearts, minds, and lives of those who participate in it. As principled action, pedagogical love also constitutes a powerful means of moral development in the young and in society at large. Fostering a love of classical and other esoteric musical traditions stretches minds and hearts beyond the ordinary to the extraordinary, toward musical grace, style, and virtuosity as manifested in these traditions, thereby fostering and stretching imagination and enriching human experience. By extension, classical musicians need to stretch their musical imaginations beyond the confines of the classical tradition they practice and that are rooted in the vernacular to other musical traditions with which the musicians may be less familiar—traditions that display their own grace, style, and virtuosity. This openheartedness may enable such musicians to find ways to bridge these traditions, create new forms of music, and open connections to those whose identities are bound up with these musics. It also enables them to critique the musics they practice and forge more humane approaches to them.[22]

Love's appeal as an educational value needs to be tempered with a recognition of its dark side. It may be false, mask deceit and opportunism, and appear to be something it is not. Given the power of attachment between teachers and their students, it may be easy to slip into confusing pedagogical and sexual or romantic love. At a time in which sensuality is admired and cultivated in expressions of contemporary culture, it may be especially difficult to maintain the distinction between pedagogical and sexual or romantic love. Some teachers may abuse the trust of their students and prey on them in the name of pedagogical love just as some students may seduce their teachers. There is also the possibility that disinterested love may go against personal inclination. It is more difficult for teachers to work with students who are unlovable, hostile, ungrateful, arrogant, and offensive than with those who are lovable, affectionate, grateful, teachable, and courteous. The same goes for students who may find that it goes against the grain to work with teachers whom they find unattractive and whose approach is unappealing. Disinterested love may be more difficult to accomplish than interested love, and it may not suffice as an educational principle. Teachers may also pit some musical traditions against others and fail to grasp the currents that flow through them all. By their one-eyed approach to their own preferred musical practice, or by taking an either/or mentality that divides rather than unites musical traditions, they may exclude others from participating in it and thereby coming to love it.

Although on the surface, love may be an attractive music educational value, it may be an insufficiently powerful force in general education, especially where disinterested love is also required. Its compelling advantages for enhancing motivation and helping to create a pleasurable educational environment may be offset by the dangers of false love that abuses trust and confuses pedagogical and romantic and sexual interest. Given the strength of sexual desire, the hope in pedagogical love for spiritual, holistic, and principled thought and action may be overwhelmed. So anticipated joy and pleasure may not eventuate, and instead, manipulation and discontinuity between professed values and actions may emerge. It may be difficult to bring students to a love of those musics with which they are unfamiliar, and teachers may capitulate to student impulse. Rather than finding the ways and means to entice students with the values of other less accessible musical traditions, they may pander to their students' impulses by focusing on a limited range of musics that their students already enjoy. This approach may stunt the students' musical development.

FRIENDSHIP

The English word *friendship* is rooted in Northern European languages and is defined literally as "the state or relation of being a friend."[23] In today's ordinary usage, the word *friend* has become more amorphous than it once was, designating on the one hand "a contact on a social networking web site" who may or may not be well known to the other and on the other hand "a close acquaintance," a person "with whom one has developed a close and informal relationship of mutual trust and intimacy." One may speak of a friend as a person or a thing, be it cause, association, or country. Once thought of as an antonym of *enemy*, *friendship* has connoted a range of helpful and supportive people and things, be they "a person who wishes another" or "a cause . . . well," "a sympathizer, helper, patron, or supporter," "something that is helpful, reliable, or beneficial," or "something that improves or enhances a person's lifestyle, appearance, [and] security." Friendship is exhibited by "friendliness" and "amicableness," the "friendly feeling or disposition felt or shown by a person or group of people (for or to another)." It is also enacted in "friendly or helpful" ways that might be "typical or characteristic of a friend." For example, nation-states speak of friendship as an "accord, alliance, peace" and "a state of mutual trust between allied nations or peoples." As such, friendship reflects a "capacity to unite harmoniously" and the notion of "affinity" or "correspondence" one with another.[24] As with love, friendship is thought of figuratively and literally, spiritually and sexually, as noun and verb. For example, George Herbert describes an old friend metaphorically as a "mirror."[25] Thought of as a verb, to friend someone is now understood in terms of social media as adding a person to one's list of digitally connected people. Unlike love, the closeness of association varies widely, and its sexual connotations are often euphemistic rather than literal. Its emphasis lies more in a supportive and amicable disposition and the ability to associate together in ways that are agreeable, mutually beneficial, and peaceful. The emotional warmth, mutuality, shared interest and commitment, reliance, and trust in and with others foster tranquility and harmonious relationships between people. As with love, friendship is enacted as well as embraced as an abstract principle.

Friendship is a persistent value in philosophical discourse among men, and although it is also found among women, it remains a pervasively male idea in philosophizing throughout the ages. Forest Hansen reminds us that Plato's symposia evidence the value of friendship as a basis for doing philosophy and talking about ideas within the educational process.[26] Still, this was a conversation mainly among men, and it remained such in educational philosophy during the following centuries. For example, Jean-Jacques Rousseau wished his protagonist Émile's teacher and mentor to be his friend, in the sense of an older brother who is affectionate and supportive of his younger sibling and who can guide his young charge into a wider knowledge of the natural world and prepare him to develop a sense of morality and purpose as he reaches puberty.[27] The word *fraternité* can be construed as a metaphor for friendship in its reference to the affection, support, trust, and mutual purpose between brothers. This gendered notion of friendship can overlook the equally important power of sisterhood and relationship forwarded by women authors, such as bell hooks, who have posited the importance of mutuality and united purpose that need to characterize the support of women for each other.[28] hooks seeks to redress the long history of marginalization and a socialization that has too often spawned competitiveness and distrust among women and made it more difficult to realize the affection, mutuality, and trust that friendship implies. Jane Roland Martin faults the prescriptions of educational philosophers for the education of girls and their isolation from each other in the academy.[29] In her reading, Rousseau seeks to enlarge Émile's world and offers him friendship, but his recommendations for Émile's sister, Sophie, are disastrous for home and society. Sophie is denied friendship and remains imprisoned in the narrow confines of her mother's kitchen and home until she is married. Drawing on the writings of nineteenth-century American women, Martin enlarges the notion of friendship between the genders and promotes an education for women and men that subverts gendered notions of friendship and opens the possibility of friendship not only between women but between women and men. At a time in which women still earn less than men for the same work, in which equality, mutuality, and trust within and between the genders is still far from realized, friendship broadly construed remains a crucial value in realizing human potential. Notwithstanding regressive, repressive, and reactionary forces allied against friendship in its broadest meaning, this inclusive view of friendship remains a means of enhancing personal happiness and creating a more humane society.

Friendship is characterized by egalitarian relationships, mutual respect, trust, face-to-face engagement, and fidelity. Thought of educationally, teachers and students are fellow learners in pursuit of wisdom, and the social distance between teachers and students, and students and their fellows, is minimized. All the participants are regarded as persons of worth and of more or less equal standing. In this view, teachers teach from their greater knowledge rather than out of their superiority over students granted by the position they hold. In such an education, students may also teach their teachers as well as their fellows. As Randall Allsup notes, this dialogical approach to education resists vesting education solely in the teacher conceived as master.[30] Mutual respect entails a civil and humane attitude that values others. Indeed, friendship relies on valuing others as well as oneself. It seeks out differences, prizes and respects them, and sees them as complementary to one's own limited understandings and practices. Notwithstanding that friendship is sometimes thought about in terms of the online, virtual communication of social media, it has historically relied on face-to-face communication that is unfiltered by technology. This is because friendship reveals vulnerability that is evident in the phenomenal world but can be disguised in virtual time and space. Sometimes, friendships can be forged through letters, in videos, and on today's internet platforms, but my sense is that this virtual world approaches the ideal of face-to-face direct communication possible in lived life only in the phenomenal world. Fidelity, or faithfulness, is the capacity to remain committed, supportive, and constant over a long time. One counts those friendships that persist over a lifetime as among the most precious. This is true in education, as in life generally.

Thinking musically about friendship highlights the attitudes of hospitality toward musical traditions that Martin Marty advocates in terms of the religions and that Patrick Schmidt, drawing on Jacques Derrida's notion of hospitality, suggests should characterize the ways in which music teachers and their students should approach musical traditions.[31] This openness and generosity of spirit also resonates with Charlene Morton's notion of cosmopolitanism, in which one acknowledges the flaws in one's own cultural expressions as one also welcomes the perspectives of others.[32] It also accords with Kertz-Welzel's idea of international and global understandings of music that are filtered culturally.[33] For me, these various conceptions of a welcoming of those musical traditions that are not one's "home" fosters the sorts of openings for which Maxine Greene and Allsup hope.[34] Borrowing Coleridge's notion of need for the other as a driver of musical friendship suggests that musical hospitality is not only desirable but essential to music education. Approaching music, teaching, learning, instruction, curriculum, and administration in this way offers a welcoming, humane, and civil approach to music and education that puts people at the heart of these enterprises and resists limited either/or thinking and practice. It opens to the diverse ways in which people come to know and experience music and the wider worlds of their various cultures. It also offers a positive approach to seeing, as Raimond Gaita puts it, the "common humanity" beneath the myriad differences in musical traditions and cultures.[35]

Among the contributions of friendship as a value in music and education, the emphasis on the humanity of the musical experience and on the entire educational process elevates both music and education to the highest importance in human society. Culture is the product of human imagination, and coming to know it in ways that express the ideal of friendship enables one to better understand oneself. Notwithstanding the importance of the social claims of music making and the role of music education as an aspect of public policy, music's individual and psychological benefits have been forwarded by music education writers in the past.[36] The value of friendship insists that these emphases persist. Friendship also highlights the role of positive motivation in musical education. It works through encouragement rather than punishment, and it hopes for the best in people rather than their worst. It seeks to build common and shared understandings, imaginative and critical thought, and the intellectual capacity to embrace complexity and ambiguity. It resists fundamentalist thinking, literalism and uncritical thought, dogma and prejudice. Cultivating friendship develops intellectual and emotional capacities, promotes personal growth, and fosters the peace and tranquility that comes from a deeper understanding of those who come from differing backgrounds. Thinking of oneself as a fellow learner with one's students and minimizing the social distance between one's students and oneself, as would be typical of friendship, cultivate and exemplify humility on the teacher's part and help to foster the resilience and courage that students need to acquire.

Nevertheless, friendship may have a dark side. One hopes that one's friends want the best for one, but this is not always the case. Thinking of Immanuel Kant's metaphor of the "crooked timber" of human nature suggests that one's friends have their own idiosyncrasies and shortsightedness, biases and blind spots, self-interests and desires.[37] No matter how well-intentioned, they do not always see what is best for themselves or others. One's friends may lead one toward evil. One's self-interest may cloud one's judgment of the other's needs and wishes and cause one to mislead the other. This is also true in education. Inexperienced teachers may fail to grasp the importance of social distance between themselves and their students—a distance that may be an important aid to relating to their students as authority figures. Education is inherently asymmetrical in its power relationships between those who possess knowledge and those who do not. This is as it has always been. It is naïve to disparage the important role this asymmetry can play in providing a basis for students to trust in their teachers and a means whereby teachers can pass on their wisdom to students. With greater knowledge and experience than their students, teachers may know what students need to know for their long-term development as opposed to what students desire to know in the moment. Some boundedness in the relationships between teachers and students can prove important in clarifying the roles and responsibilities of both. This distance can assist teachers as they seek to direct and control the actions of their students and develop their critical thinking and independent thought and action. Still, it may also result in student passivity and require students to sacrifice their own interests and desires to become what their teachers wish them to be. In music, as in other subjects where performative skills need to be acquired, the master-disciple pictures can play an important role. Over the years, many music students have told me that their relationships with their master teachers were among the most valuable and precious aspects of their musical preparation. One who is clearly an expert practitioner in what one teaches is in a very different situation than a neophyte who hopes to become an expert. Especially in great traditions, the challenges of developing one's musical craft and gaining artistic competence in a distinguished musical tradition separates experts from neophytes and makes it difficult to establish a more egalitarian relationship on which friendship depends. This may also be true in some vernacular traditions where there is also the expectation that the music will be performed correctly. For this reason, friendship may follow later, after the neophyte has developed into an exponent. Moreover, the claims of education go beyond friendship, which cannot be relied on to sustain instruction. Where music teachers have little choice over who and what they teach, their obligations reach to all the students in their care, irrespective of whether they are friends. Teachers and students may have friendly relations, but other values may be more prominent while the instruction is ongoing.

DESIRE

Although desire has long been an educational value, it became theoretically prominent during the latter part of the twentieth century, especially in the work of feminist scholars who advanced the notion of desire in musical and educational thought and practice.[38] From antiquity, educational participants employed or expressed the language of desire and relied on teacher and student "gaze" and "embodiment" in their musical instruction.[39] In the ancient academies, medieval centers of higher education, classical traditions of East and West, and indigenous traditions around the world where teaching and learning is a matter of choice, it was incumbent on students to express their desire for learning and persuade their teachers of this longing so that teachers would also desire to teach them.[40] The explicit language of educational desire emerged out of the feminist challenge to the progressive intellectualization, rationalization, technologization, and commercialization of publicly supported education during the nineteenth and twentieth centuries. Ironically, a renewed emphasis on competency-based education within online higher education in the twenty-first century relies on a widespread desire for credentials on the part of midcareer professionals.[41] In this milieu, student desire for these credentials is catered to within the framework of professional requirements for certification. On the one hand, the rise of educational positivism together with the increasing technologization and commercialism of education created a climate in which desire was sidelined, and it fell to feminists to resuscitate desire and reinstate it as an explicit educational value. On the other, the emergence of technological means of distance learning and the increasing cost of education put a premium on student desire for credentials and cost-effective and rational approaches to an educational process in which desire is sidelined and minimized. Given these tensions between desire and the educational means to address it, it is not surprising that the language of desire has attained prominence not only in educational discourse but especially in the work of feminist scholars in music education including Deanne Bogdan, Eleanor Stubley, Julia Eklund Koza, Roberta Lamb, Marie McCarthy, Elizabeth Gould, and, in a different vein, Allsup.[42]

The word *desire* comes from the French and Italian, and as a noun it is a "fact or condition of desiring; that feeling or emotion which is directed to the attainment or possession of some object from which pleasure or satisfaction is expected; longing, craving; a particular instance of this feeling, a wish."[43] Construed as a verb, it means "to have a strong wish for; to long for, covet, crave."[44] As with the other values in this quartet, desire is ambiguous, being both noun and verb, object and subject, emotion and thought, idea and enactment.

Among its qualities, desire is felt. It falls in a realm Susanne Langer describes as "non-discursive" symbolism of the arts, religions, myths, rituals, and dreams that everyday linguistic symbols and propositional language fail to capture.[45] As such, it is primarily expressed through enactment, done rather than simply thought about. In counterpoint to Israel Scheffler, Iris Yob might characterize desire as an emotional cognition rather than a cognitive emotion, as thought about emotion rather than emotion that accompanies thought.[46] In a dialectic vein, desire could be thought of as both emotional cognition and cognitive emotion. Although desire is among the deepest human qualities, it is also something that humans share with other living creatures. It may also be driven by sexual impulses seeking fulfilment. John Dewey speaks of desire in terms of "impulses" that, for him, constitute the basic motivation for learning and that are central to educative experience.[47] Notwithstanding their differing perspectives on feeling and its place in the arts and education, these writers see desire as emotion/thought, as a fundamental, if also instinctual, human quality that is bodily at its core.[48]

Desire is also an intense wishing, longing, even craving for someone or something. In its most robust sense, it becomes a want/need—that is, one's wants are also felt as needs, and there is an urgency to their fulfilment. Like interested love, this is a powerful force that impels to action and is not easily assuaged. Such longing may arise internally, or it may be created by external means. For example, some students may, from a very early age, long for musical instruction and wish to perform. Others may meet a teacher who inspires a desire for musical instruction during the school-age years or later in life. In such cases, musical desire may have lain dormant, to be ignited when circumstances transformed what had been unconscious and latent into a powerful motivating force. Whatever the circumstances of its arousal, desire becomes a conscious experience. It may be thwarted by circumstances such as those acknowledged by Susan Laird as a "musical hunger" for piano lessons that she was not able to take because of her parents' inability to pay for them.[49] Or it may be cultivated in productive ways conducive to subsequent growth, as described by Dewey.[50]

Further, desire has an object-in-view and the hope for satisfaction or pleasure on its attainment. Dewey uses the word "consummation" to refer to an artistic experience that fulfills its object—namely, the creation of an artistic experience and the undergoing of it.[51] For him, the impulse and its satisfaction are part of an interconnected process or continuum of means and ends. This means/ends tension suggests that desire is never ultimately fulfilled. Its object or its "vision of mastery," as Vernon Howard would describe things, seems to keep receding.[52] I like this dynamic view of desire as something that moves toward the thing hoped for and, in its fulfillment, prompts yet another and more distant end. This view seems to resonate with the musical experience I have known. From this perspective, desire is an ideal never fully realized and points to yet other possibilities. Its consummation along the way is never final, although each moment offers immediate joy and the prospect of future delights. This possibility continues to motivate musicians throughout their lives.

Moreover, desire is embodied—that is, it is expressed through one's bodily actions. One does what one is as a human being. Music and education that embrace the ideal of desire treat all those involved in the musical and educational process holistically rather than atomistically. One's body shapes one's thinking in important ways, just as one's thinking impacts one's body. Liora Bresler and her colleagues think in terms of "moving minds" and "knowing bodies."[53] Mind is dependent on body and inextricable or inseparable from it, and vice versa. In this construction, music education cannot be just about a collection of concepts to be learned, emotions to be expressed, or psychological and motor skills to be trained. Rather, it necessarily concerns the persons, the individuals who collectively make up the musical and educational process. It comprises the beliefs and attitudes to be passed on to the next generation and the dispositions to act in ways consonant with those beliefs and attitudes. Music and education are physical—they fundamentally concern one's body, deportment, and "presentation of self" to others.[54] To neglect the body in music and education is to neglect the self and the desire that drives one's actions. If music and education are to contribute to happiness, as Noddings would doubtless hope, they need to take the body and its desire into account and foster growth that honors it.[55] Only in this way can they hope to cultivate the understanding and acceptance of self and one's personhood that is essential to psychological well-being.

As a bodily phenomenon, desire is revealed in the physical processes of what theorists have termed the "gaze."[56] I think of the word *gaze* as a metaphor, in which one's seeing stands for the full range of senses whereby we take notice of things and of others. To gaze is not only a visual experience, although this is important. For me, this metaphor stands for all the senses—sight, sound, taste, smell, and touch—whereby we are consciously aware and mindful of the things and people around us. Musical and pedagogical gaze are special ways of "seeing." They do not judge the other, deprecate the other, ignore the other, or repudiate the other. Rather, they reach out to the other, accept the other, delight in the other's difference, bow to the other, and seek to see and hear things the way the other might see and hear them. To gaze is to take account of, to notice, to value, to reach out to, to accept, even to surrender to the other. One longs for communion with the other and to learn from the other. One hopes to ignite desire in the other. Gaze constitutes ambiguous musical and pedagogical means whereby musicians, teachers, and students are profoundly authentic and present to each other in ways that evidence activity and passivity, strength and vulnerability, attachment and reserve, and desire to help and willingness to let go. One longs not only for openings but for closings, for the culmination and satisfaction that come with assuaging desire and for the possibilities that closings have for more openings in the future.

Among desire's contributions is a holistic approach to music and education. It sees the one and the many, and the whole surpasses the sum of its parts. Langer's apt term "articulation" refers to the absorption of the various parts into a greater whole.[57] For music and education, knowledge and self are interconnected, and knowledge is constructed by the individual just as the individual is impacted by the surrounding environment. As Alfred North Whitehead suggests, the end of education is wisdom, in which the various aspects of knowledge come together in a gestalt, a sense of the totality of one's world view, a unity—a paradox that Plato recognized when he spoke of those who can grasp the one and the many.[58] Desire values the body and repudiates the notion that the body is inherently evil—a view that bumps up against beliefs propagated by the Abrahamic faiths. It also affirms the power of human sexuality in its varied manifestations as a part of human interaction, be it musical, education, religious, or whatever. Happiness is construed as an end of music and education, and this involves education and artistic expression in the domestic and private as well as social and public spheres. The subject matter of such education values aspects of normal daily life as it also explores and cherishes those aspects of culture that are more esoteric and less accessible. Desire suggests, for example, that the music that has physical appeal to prompt people to dance, a musical value consistent with a Dionysian experience of celebration and revelry, is valued in musical instruction.[59] Even within more intellectually oriented musical traditions, the physical appeal of the music is recognized as a part of its spiritual experience. An education grounded in desire values enactment and physical engagement in learning. Musical education is inherently performative and experiential, immediate and virtual, physical and theoretical. Since enactment and the joy it brings spurs one to further desire, the doing of the subject matter motivates intrinsically in encouraging one on to further experiences. Such an approach works affirmatively in ways that emphasize celebration.[60] Since a sense of self is focal to such music and education, and because people differ in the specific things that affirm them, the musical and educational ends of valuing desire are open-ended and diverse and inevitably result in pluralities and multiplicities.[61]

On the other hand, desire may have flaws and limitations. Sexual desire may be confused with desire for knowledge. This is beautifully illustrated in the Swedish film *Så som I himmelen* (*As It Is in Heaven*), in which a professional conductor retires to the village where he grew up and becomes a charismatic cantor and leader of the village church choir.[62] In confessing her love for him, one of his choir members tells him that he must surely know that most of the women in the choir have fallen in love with him. True, the village choir is thriving; there are more people in it than in the congregation. Still, some of the men of the village, including the pastor, fear this power. I have witnessed the suspicion and jealousy of those who resent the power that charismatic ensemble leaders seem to hold over their musicians. The value of desire may prove unacceptable within religious circles where it is taken to be evil. Dionysian approaches to music education surely run up against the power of a pervasively negative view of desire. In conservative Christian discourse, for example, jazz and rock music have been associated with evil just as Western popular music has been considered evil in conservative Islam.[63] Since these religions have often suppressed desire, overcoming these deeply held religious values to see desire constructively and positively may prove impossible, practically speaking. Pedagogical gaze may be mistaken for sexual desire. This may be due to others' interpretations of ambiguous gestures and actions. In the film *As It Is in Heaven*, the conductor is focused on conveying the joy of musicking and inspiring his singers to sing well. The physicality of music making in which his singers seek to find their own tones and become united as they improvise around the sound that they are individually and collectively generating may play a role in blurring the lines between the sexual and the artistic aspects of musical experience. This ambiguity gives rise to the possibility of misinterpreting the actions of others. Moreover, the person-centeredness and diversity that emerge in an open-ended desire-generated music education may subvert taken-for-granted assumptions and make it difficult to formulate public policy. In any social system, agreement is needed on those beliefs and practices that are regarded as beyond the norm. Inevitably, some values and practices become prominent, and others are marginalized. The diversity that emanates from focusing on desire as a musical and educational value may resist domestication and limitation and may be difficult to accomplish practically speaking, especially where beliefs and practices lie outside the norm.

DEVOTION

In counterpoint to desire that connotes sensual dimensions of attraction, the word *devotion* evokes, for me, spiritual dedication manifested in action. *Devotion* comes from the Latin *dēvōtiōn-em*, a "noun of action from *dēvovēre*, to devote." Originally, it referred to earnestness in religious duties and obligations and "a feeling of devout reverence and awe" toward a deity, a "devout impulse or desire," an "act of worship," a "form of prayer," a "solemn dedication" or "consecration." Later, it took on a secular connotation of "being devoted to a person, cause, pursuit, etc., with an attachment akin to religious devotion; earnest addiction or application; enthusiastic attachment or loyalty."[64] Within classical traditions, for example, *devotion* is often used to describe the relationship of musicians to the tradition they practice and to the relationship between music teachers and their students. This is the case, for example, in the North Indian tradition where students express their devotion to their teachers by performing services and giving gifts to them. Students also seek to demonstrate their devotion to their teachers and the music through the practice of *riaz,* a spiritual experience akin to religious obligations in which musicians manifest their devotion to their artistic tradition.[65] These close-knit groups of teachers and students are also evident in the Western classical tradition in North American conservatories described by Henry Kingsbury and Bruno Nettl.[66] I embrace the ancient meaning of *devotion*—namely, a dedication to a calling or a spiritual or sacred purpose manifested as a lifelong commitment. As with the other values in this quartet, devotion is ambiguous. This spiritual attachment to persons and things is thought and felt, grounded in belief and manifested in action, done and undergone, formal and informal, sacred and secular, and means and end.

Among the qualities of musical and pedagogical devotion, there is a strong attachment and loyalty to the people involved in the instructional process and the subject matter that is actively undertaken and passively undergone in formal and informal ways. Devotion concerns the musical tradition(s) being fostered and practiced and the other persons (including teachers, students, and significant others such as friends and family members) involved in this process. This spiritual attachment is felt intellectually and emotionally as emotional cognitions and cognitive emotions.[67] The choice to live a life of devotion to some person or cause is freely taken, enthusiastically embraced, and undertaken with great affection for the enterprise. As a habit of mind and action, both thought about and done, devotion is manifested formally in disciplined ways with sets of codified rules and expectations and informally through idiosyncratic, serendipitous, and opportunistic ways via rules and expectations that may be dynamic and not codified. For example, in contrast to the Western classical music tradition, in which expectations of students regarding practice are widely shared, musicians pick up aspects of popular musical practice in various ways, and expectations of devotion are more contingent, open-ended, and diverse.[68]

Expressions of devotion on the part of teachers, students, and the musical traditions to which they adhere serve, on the one hand, to invite people to enter the musical practice and, on the other, to exclude those who do not manifest the required devotion. Devotion's power comes because of the spiritual commitments that lie behind or beyond actions. Practices are not ends in themselves but manifestations of intellectual commitments that are regarded as of vital significance. The exclusive quality of devotion seems more evident where the rules undergirding a tradition are highly codified and standardized across the tradition, extremely demanding, or virtuosic. The more virtuosic a musical tradition or instrument, and the higher its artistic and temporal expectations of musicians (including its technical demands, complexity, and size of repertoire), the more its practice can exclude the practice of other musics or other activities because there is less time to devote to other things. This is also true for educational practices that are both inclusive of those who demonstrate an attachment to this subject and exclusive of those who do not. The choice to take part in certain activities may exclude the possibility of taking part in others. The more demanding the practices, the fewer the people who may be willing or able to make the sacrifices to attain them.

Pedagogical devotion is an imaginative activity that absorbs one's attention. Rather than conceive only of the single-mindedness of religious devotion as a metaphor for musical and educational devotion, I prefer to think of devotion as directly implicated in and evocative of the spiritual nature of music and education. Devotion elevates music and education above the ordinary, banal, and material to focus on important spiritual and existential questions of life. Its single-mindedness requires focusing one's attention on a thing or person with a specific end in view. As each end is reached, its attainment motivates and provides the means to focus on yet other more challenging ends in a dynamic means-ends process. Performing a musical tradition or studying with a person in a focused way imbues the musical and educational process with a spiritual quality that helps to make possible a high level of excellence in the thought and practice of this tradition.[69] Consequently, exponents become separated from others who are not able or choose not to go to the trouble. This focus has the quality of consecration in which exponents set themselves apart or are set apart from others in ordinary life by their dedication to the practice. This consecration is akin to that of the religious who are set apart from the laity and pursue a different way of life from those who are not so dedicated. As such, devotion imbues music education with a sense of the sacred that carries enormous import and significance in the lives of its practitioners and public.

Devotion offers important contributions to music and education. Among them, it prompts loyalty to the musical tradition, its exponents, teachers, students, and the public, along with faithfulness and persistence—qualities regarded as characteristic of a civil society since ancient times.[70] Beside devotion's reliance on the exercise of free will and the importance of choice in determining which people and causes one will devote oneself to, it is felt, thought about, and enacted. In earlier writing, I have theorized that choice and free will on the part of both teachers and students are more likely to result in happiness for those involved in the instructional process than situations in which there is an absence of choice.[71] The longstanding tradition of musical instruction under conditions of choice is evident in the success and persistence of individual and small-group instruction as one of the most effective means of music teaching and learning. Devotion also takes a holistic view of mind and body, rational thought and feeling, and blurs the lines between the abstract and the phenomenal, theory and practice. Within music education, it offers the prospect of an integrated and balanced approach to musical instruction that focuses on the people as well as the musical tradition(s). Its sacred quality honors the challenges of mastering musical traditions and the virtuosity and grace of its outstanding exponents. Realizing the challenges in becoming an exponent of a tradition subverts the expectation of immediate reward and gratification. Devotion suggests that some things worth having are hard won, often at considerable sacrifice of time, effort, and money. It acknowledges the requirement of mental concentration, focus, and mindfulness if exceptional results are to be achieved. Rather than focusing on the acquisition of small bits of knowledge, devotion seeks to express a way of life as a musician or citizen of a civil society. It emphasizes the importance of ritual and the need for continued practice if one is to continue to be an exemplary musician, especially in a distinguished tradition. Devotion emphasizes high standards, embraces excellence in a musical tradition, and recognizes the importance of virtuosity, grace, style, and esotericism as markers of human imagination and creative thought and practice. In this view, standards constitute ideals to which exponents ought to aspire, so it becomes important to articulate them clearly in the musical and educational process. These markers are crucial in an environment in which extreme relativism repudiates standardization and accepts all musical traditions as of equivalent merit.

Notwithstanding these potential contributions, there is also a dark side to devotion. It is possible that devotion may come to focus on the burdens and obligations of a tradition and lose its heart and driving force. Langer speaks of "generative ideas" that are transformative at first but later become buttoned up and restricted by rules and dictums that codify and stultify them, and in so doing, the spirit that spawned the initial ideas is lost.[72] As such, the ideas are all but destroyed by well-meaning disciples who literalize, codify, and clutter them with prescriptions. If joy is not at its heart, devotion may burden practitioners of a musical tradition with the claims of its outward manifestations, and in so doing, these musicians may lose their musical souls as spirituality evaporates. It may become exclusive and obsessive to the exclusion of other goods. Focusing so much on the sacred character of music and education may also fail to emphasize sufficiently the importance of the secular and those musical traditions and practices that are the stuff of ordinary, everyday life. Devotion can too easily be rendered as what one does, as the doing of rituals and the undertaking of specific obligations, rather than as letting go and allowing experiences to happen serendipitously. Sean Steel posits the value of a Dionysian emphasis on ecstasy in music education that embraces surrender and those moments in which one is out of control; for him, since ecstasy is the point of rock music, its study and practice need to be parts of the music curriculum.[73] Still, ecstasy is to be experienced in other musical traditions—for example, in Native American traditional musics that serve principally to arouse ecstasy and the desire to dance.[74] Indeed, it seems that ecstasy of one sort or another, whether mystical or sensuous, can be encountered in all of the musical traditions with which I am familiar. Focusing on devotion may also result in exclusive and elitist approaches to music education that overlook the claims of affording ordinary people the opportunities to experience musical traditions that would otherwise be inaccessible to them. Devoting oneself to a musical tradition may leave one insufficiently critical of its musical and educational practices and of the need to transform it toward more humane ends.[75] Further, it is possible that an obsession with standards can marginalize, if not destroy, imaginative and diverse musical expressions. This is especially the case when one set of musical standards is hegemonic and other different standards are considered of lesser worth.

In teasing out the various meanings for music and education of love, friendship, desire, and devotion, we find that love is both interested and disinterested, spiritual and sensual, expressed in touch and decorum, sacred and secular, centered on the people and the subject matter of music and education, and evocative of joy and moral development. Friendship is defined to include women and girls as well as men and boys among which attachments vary in closeness. Desire is construed broadly and holistically as intense longing, both want and need, that is felt and enacted with the hope of fulfilment, satisfaction, or consummation. Devotion has a strong spiritual and religious connotation of worship, prayer, and consecration that elevates music and education above the banal, ordinary, and material aspects of life. The analysis reveals commonalities such as affection, attachment, felt thought, and enactment regarding persons and things as well as distinctive features and shades of meaning. For each of the intertwined yet differing values in this set, the possibilities of good and evil on either hand pose significant challenges for musicians, teachers, and their students, who apply them to their individual situations. The conditions in which musicians and teachers must often work may diminish their freedom of choice and make attempting to secure the good while avoiding the evil of each of these values difficult to achieve. Still, I see no way forward except to acknowledge that while I am drawn to them, they present complications and predicaments that musical and educational policy makers need to carefully address in determining what to do.

SIX

Joy, Happiness, Pleasure, and Celebration

THE QUARTET OF VALUES—JOY, happiness, pleasure, and celebration—I examine in this chapter offer yet another cluster that, like love, friendship, desire, and devotion, is grounded in subjective emotional life and feeling but of a differing character and expression. These contrasting values together illustrate something of the richness and multidimensionality of emotion, feeling, and corporeality. They constitute the spice of life, and it is no wonder that they have long been considered a part of humane music and education. Although interrelated, these values have differing and sometimes conflicting nuances that merit exploring with a view to seeing what their possibilities are for music and education in our time. I begin with their ordinary meanings, describe their characteristics, and sketch their contributions and detractions for music education. First, to the matter of joy.

JOY

The word *joy* comes from Middle English and Old French words meaning joy and jewel. The connotation of a jewel as something precious and delightful remains in the contemporary idea of joy as "a vivid emotion of pleasure arising from a sense of well-being or satisfaction; the feeling or state of being highly pleased or delighted; exultation of spirit; gladness, delight."[1] Its vividness, brightness, and intensity in a positive rather than negative sense make it a desirable feeling that people want to experience. In the past, educators have appealed to joy to make the learning process more attractive and less onerous. If students experience joy throughout their educational experience, it is assumed they will want to learn. For educators such as Johann Heinrich Pestalozzi and Maria Montessori, the home is the metaphor for a joy-filled education, schools need to address the claims of family life in what Jane Roland Martin calls the "schoolhome," and joy constitutes what John Dewey might describe as an educational means-end.[2]

Joy is also a spiritual experience that epitomizes a sense of triumph over obstacles and the exultation when one achieves a desired end. It emerges within what Susanne Langer would term "felt life," and it is often expressed in the arts, myths, rituals, and religions.[3] The ways it is expressed are imaginative and ambiguous, known and enacted through gestures and rites. These entail languages and modes of expression that are grasped widely and different from one society and culture to another. Musical expressions of joy occur throughout history and in the myriad musical traditions in today's world. The metaphor of the jewel in its exquisite cutting and setting of a rare, highly prized, and valuable stone captures the joy in a finely wrought piece of music where every aspect has been honed to achieve the musician's vision.

There is a playful quality to joy. By *play*, I mean the inventive character of joy, to delight for hedonistic purposes and for its own sake rather than for other utilitarian purposes. Play encompasses serious purpose and intellectual meaning, and it satisfies intellectually, emotionally, and physically. As Northrop Frye explains, its imaginative quality is a particularly developed feature of human culture.[4] Play exists for its own sake as much as for the sake of other things, and it provides intrinsic justification for whatever is done. Joy resonates with musicking as a mode of playful expression. When musicians speak of playing their instruments, they refer not only to their technical facility but to the associated joy of musical play.

Joy is personally experienced. Although its spiritual and subjective character is felt individually as well as collectively in groups, the differences among people mean that what brings joy to one person may not bring it to another. These differences may be matters of degree and kind. A musical piece may evoke or express an individual's joy differently in terms of the intensity of joy experienced, whether it evokes or expresses joy or other emotions, or its ephemeral or persistent character. Thinking about joy requires attending to its individual and interpersonal character. As an affective state, it is thought of in psychological or in psychosocial terms.

Given that joy may sometimes be ephemeral and at other times more persistent, can one rely on something so impermanent? While joy is sometimes fleeting, it is a desired state of mind that motivates people to seek experiences that generate it, rendering it, practically speaking, an ideal. To exclude joy as a value because it may be ephemeral would also exclude others that are experientially based. Emotions may be fleeting, but the ideas, beliefs, attitudes, and values with which they are associated may persist beyond an immediate experience of joy itself. Such experiences also remain in memory as normative states to which people aspire. Since joy is experiential, one may not know joy until one has first lived it in one form or another. So it is necessary to provide opportunities for the young to know joy in general and artistic education.

Thinking of joy idealistically requires that people live their lives in accordance with their dispositions, talents, beliefs, attitudes, and values. Dewey refers to these deep-seated and personal drives as impulses. Joseph Campbell characterizes such a lived life as "following one's bliss."[5] For me, a life lived in the pursuit of joy manifests integrity when one's actions accord with what one most prizes and one is elated by one's triumph over the obstacles in one's way. The pursuit of joy need not be a solely hedonistic purpose. Joy may also emerge when one focuses on the needs and interests of others and pursues aspects other than joy. It may arise almost as a byproduct of seeking these other purposes. Whether one seeks it directly or it emerges in seeking other ends, joy remains something to be aspired to, and it serves as a powerful motivating force that reinforces other ends.

Leonard Tan writes of joy as an artistic ideal.[6] Drawing on ancient Chinese philosophy, he proposes that artists hone a craft or skill to such a degree that their virtuosity spawns joy, and they are delighted at the sheer prowess and effortlessness that they have demonstrated. This sense of grace, virtuosity, and what Mihaly Csikszentmihalyi might characterize as "flow" sparks a joyous response on the part of the artist.[7] Joy is both a means and end of artistry in its myriad forms, and artists' efforts are also a source of joy for themselves and their publics.

Thinking of joy figuratively, as something precious, much as a jewel might be, also invokes the intellect and the exercise of judgment. Joy is associated with intellectual triumph or, as Israel Scheffler expresses it, "the joy of verification."[8] Reasoning through a problem and finding after all that one's solution turns out to be productive or rings true can be exhilarating. There is joy in triumphing over a problem that once stood in one's way. Rather than pure emotion or emotion alone, joy is inevitably intertwined with thought. One can appreciate a finely wrought art piece when one grasps the extent and nature of the skill and virtuosity required to construct it. In a sense, the more one knows about an art form, the better position one is in to appreciate and value it, and the more intense one's joy when one experiences an exemplary performance or witnesses a superb creation. Whether made with a view to contemplation or to be danced, sung, or acted, those in the know or the art's experts and exponents are apt to be especially joyful when they participate in or witness a brilliantly wrought performance or artifact. Experiencing joy, then, requires a grasp of the social and cultural milieu of which the art is a part as well as the rules and expectations that guide its practice. To some extent, one may be able to transcend one's cultural limitations, but how much more telling this experience can be for those steeped in the tradition.[9]

These judgments might be thought of as cognitive emotions or emotional cognitions in which emotion and cognition, while different in emphasis, are inextricable.[10] The ambiguity of judgments that Immanuel Kant would describe as thought grounded in or about feeling underscores the ambiguity of joy.[11] Such notions help to justify music in general education. They also suggest the importance of the social and cultural contexts in music instruction and the imperative of developing the skills needed to understand and do this or that music with integrity.

Among the contributions of joy to the thought and practice of music and education, music provides an apt means through which people may come to experience and express joy, through which joy may be evoked, and through which lived life may be enriched and brightened. Having experienced joy in musical experience, young and old alike are more likely to recognize and possibly seek it in the rest of human existence. This spiritual sense of exultation lightens the rest of life and helps give it meaning and purpose. Joy experienced in this circumstance can spill over into others, and its intensity may prompt people to want more of it. Its experience positively reinforces the thoughts and actions that led to the experience of joy in the first place. Thinking of joy as a means and end of education requires constructing situations that are evocative of joy for all who are engaged in the educational process. One imagines teachers and students doing the educational activities they desire to be doing and studying subjects in ways that bring them joy. If music education is about and for joy, then a teacher's first study needs to be to ascertain the means and ends of music and education that bring joy. Although this is a liberating process, and it is hard to imagine joy when one is enslaved or dehumanized, paradoxically, joy sometimes emerges out of discipline and constraint. A joy-driven music education is not a free-for-all that involves teachers pandering to their students' whims and fancies. Instead, there are often limits on student choice, the process may sometimes be effortful and routine, and discipline provides a means of forging ahead and breaking new ground.

Also, a joy-filled music education emphasizes the development of virtuosity and musicality. Such an education is manifestly skill-driven and performative, thought of broadly in terms of performance, improvisation, composition, and listening, among other aspects of musical experience.[12] As one does music, hones one's proficiencies, and comes to be virtuosic in one's practice and thought about music, a joy in the sheer elegance and grace of one's musical mastery emerges out of one's efforts. However, obstacles stand in the way of achieving the "vision of mastery" that musicians seek to realize.[13] Sometimes, the greater these obstacles, the more musicians experience exhilaration in surmounting them. A conductor who has struggled with an ensemble for mastery in the preparation of a challenging yet exquisite piece of music well knows the joy that can erupt after the ensemble has performed the piece brilliantly. Ensemble members, conductor, and audience alike may be moved to tears or shouts of joy after the performance has ended. This experience is almost magical in its effect of replacing the cares of life with joy, at least for a time. This joy is not mere sentiment. Rather, it is a transcendent and empowering sense of confidence that one can accomplish this and more; it is also an immanent sense of knowing that suffuses one's being with light. This joy becomes not only an end but a means toward other ends. The ensemble and its conductor are encouraged to go beyond this experience to master yet more challenging or different repertoire and thereby to grow as musicians and people. Having experienced this joy in the presence of musicians making music, audiences also desire more of the experience of joy and seek out opportunities to witness it and possibly make music themselves.

Embracing joy as an ideal involves taking a humane approach to music and education. In this view, music education is about the people in relation to the music, about approaching music in ways that bring and express joy for the people. It is about enriching the human experience and suffusing it with joy. The curriculum is not just about the subject matter of music but also, importantly, about the ways in which people come to engage music along with their other subjects of study. Rather than conceptual learning that focuses entirely on the subject matter and stops short of the idiosyncratic ways in which people learn, a joy-filled approach is built with respect to these specific people with a view to the kinds of experiences that are most likely to enable them to experience joy. Such experiences differ from time to time and from place to place. Instead of carving up the subject matter in ways that do not necessarily address the interests and needs of specific teachers and students, joy is more likely to be found in a ground-up approach, in which teachers and students are engaged in the kinds of musical experiences where they have the greatest aptitude, interest, and skill.

One of its detractions is that joy is an ambiguous construct. Its subjectivity may mean that finding joy in large heterogeneous instructional groups may be more challenging. In such situations, students and teachers have far less choice of each other or of what is taught and learned than in individual or small group instruction, where teachers and students may choose each other and the instructional approaches that resonate with and fit them. In school music, instruction is often conducted in circumstances that leave little choice. Even when there is choice, conductors need to know how to evoke joy. Too many large instrumental ensembles are not joyous but filled with anxiety, tension, and even distress. Musicians adore conductors who are joyous and know how to foster joy in their musicians; I see this joy in their demeanor, body language, and faces. It is often more difficult and expensive to arrange conditions where teachers and students can exercise the choices possible—for example, in private studio instruction. The more teachers and students can select each other and exercise some choice in the material they will teach and learn, the more likely they are to stumble on joy. In the financial stresses that constrain publicly supported education, it is sometimes challenging to create situations that could lead to joy for all rather than just for some.

Since joy often comes in the pursuit of other ends, it may sometimes be a byproduct of seeking other ends. For example, the pursuit of artistry, of mastery in one's chosen field, may yield joy along the way. C. S. Lewis also speaks in religious terms of being surprised by joy and of coming on it unexpectedly.[14] I have already noted Scheffler's comments on the educational power of surprise and the joy of verification, of realizing that what one expects to happen occurs.[15] For him, joy derives from the application of intellect that is a principal driver of education. When teachers set students musical problems to solve and provide them with the tools to solve them in creative ways, and students find interesting solutions, the joy of verification emerges almost after the fact of the pursuit of the musical problems themselves. Notwithstanding that joy is necessarily interrelated with the pursuit of other objectives, and it may be in the background, it still lurks there. Yet musicians and educators may not be prepared to set musical problems for their students and enable these learners to solve them. It may be necessary to subvert state-mandated objectives to explore the kinds of musical problems that students are interested in. Although it is simpler to set up a directive system of music education than to organize it around creative problem solving, some music educators have proposed these sorts of solutions. I think of R. Murray Schafer's music educational emphasis on composition and improvisation published over three decades ago.[16] Still, too many music teachers do not feel comfortable creating and improvising music in ways that lead to open-ended results and ambiguous solutions.[17]

It may be tempting for music educators to imagine that the pursuit of joy requires abandoning labor and discipline and focusing on students' immediate interests. Alternatively, teachers may become so absorbed in the labor and discipline of developing musical skills that they leave joy to happenstance. Both alternatives are mistaken. The first fails to take advantage of the educational imperative to hone one's musical skills; it sells teacher and students short by expecting too little of them. The second does not plan for joy to be experienced all along the way; if musician educators do not hope to evoke joy, it may never appear. For me, it is better to risk the possibility of needing to avoid pitfalls along the way than to not pursue joy at all.

HAPPINESS

In their Declaration of Independence from Britain, the founders of the United States enshrined "the pursuit of happiness" along with life and liberty as self-evident truths and a priori goods.[18] By happiness, these writers imagined that equality, economic well-being, and democratic governance would lead to happiness.[19] Following in their train, American philosophers of education, such as Nel Noddings, write in praise of happiness as a value in publicly supported education.[20] Still, Noddings challenges the current educational practice of focusing almost exclusively on academic subjects such as language, mathematics, science, fine arts, the social sciences, and humanities. She also criticizes the neglect of important domestic knowledge that is crucial to happiness—for example, making a home, parenting, care for animals, and environmental stewardship. June Boyce-Tillman describes this devalued knowledge that is typically overlooked in education as "subjugated ways of knowing."[21] Boyce-Tillman includes music as one such area of knowledge that is often not regarded as of equal worth to other school subjects. For Noddings, if one is to construct education around happiness and its cultivation, it is necessary to unpack the meaning of happiness and the ways in which it can be achieved in education through the study of subject matter that goes beyond traditional academic fields. She suggests that if educators are to take happiness seriously into account, the purposes and means of education need to be thoroughly rethought and reconstructed.

My own approach in thinking about happiness as a musical and educational value is to begin with ordinary dictionary notions of happiness as "the quality or condition of being happy," "good fortune or good luck in life generally or in a particular affair; success, prosperity," "the state of pleasurable contentment of mind; deep pleasure in or contentment with one's circumstances," "an instance or source of pleasure or contentment," and "successful or felicitous aptitude, fitness, suitability, or appropriateness; felicity."[22] Although some of these meanings have fallen into disuse, happiness is a state of mind that is often taken to result from luck or good fortune. It also includes success in reaching one's objectives or in obtaining things that are or are considered desirable, including prosperity. Further, there is a certain fitness, aptitude, or match between oneself and the circumstances surrounding one. The emphasis in these dictionary definitions is not on the intensity of emotion that one experiences so much as one's state of mind. References to luck and fortune suggest that happiness emerges out of factors that go beyond one's control. Unpredictable events and natural and human-caused disasters seem capricious, and fortune seems to smile on some people more than it does on others. Some people experience more personal and family tragedy than others. The social, economic, and physical health and well-being of families to whom one is most closely tied differ markedly, and the opportunities to realize one's aspirations may be more limited than for others. Religious and political proscriptions and prescriptions may make it difficult for some people to realize their aspirations. Historically, this has been the case especially for women, ethnic minorities, and those who are differently gendered. Some people suffer from a predisposition to depression and melancholy, with less aptitude for happiness than others who are naturally predisposed to being cheerful. Some may make wiser choices than others, and unwise choices may set up a train of circumstances that are less felicitous in their effects than wiser choices might have been. These individual and social factors help to create a sense of luck or fortune that assists or impedes achieving happiness.

The view of happiness as a state of mind, of thinking about oneself and the world beyond, is, as Noddings point out, an ethical one.[23] There is an emotional quality of this thought that focuses on one's dispassionate obligations and responsibilities as well as one's passionate attachments and responsibilities to those for whom one cares. The existential ubiquity of suffering and evil requires a view of happiness that allows people who experience sorrow from time to time to nevertheless treasure the bright moments and times in life. For Noddings, this entails valuing home and home life, connecting with those nearest and dearest, and offering hospitality to others. One cares for one's family members, children, parents, and extended family members and the animals that one welcomes into the family circle. One cares for those who suffer and who are in need. One exercises responsibility in seeking to create humane social policies within society. One cares for the human spirit in its myriad manifestations. One cares for the natural environment and the creatures and plants that inhabit it. Without such carefulness, Noddings claims, happiness is elusive because these are human needs, and without their satisfaction, notwithstanding external trappings of success, one cannot be happy.[24] I like this view because it is clear-eyed about the sorrow and death that is a part of the human condition and because, like joy, one can be surprised by happiness's unexpected appearance. Still, happiness is not fleeting, as joy may be, but a more settled state of mind. It looks beyond the difficulties one confronts to grasp a deeper and abiding sense of meaning in one's life. One's aptitudes resonate and fit with the ways in which one lives. Like joy, this resonance contributes to integrity or a sense of transparency and wholeness in being and doing what one is best suited to do and wishes to do insofar as circumstances permit.

Among the contributions of this view for music and education, musicians and teachers seek to create congenial circumstances that are appealing for themselves, their colleagues, and their students. They seek the happiness of their fellows and students in instruction as well as at its end. The curriculum, instructional methods, and administration of the music program are geared toward a musical and educational process that motivates musicians and students intrinsically and rests more in prompting people to learn than in disciplining and constraining them to undertake projects that lack inherent interest and attractiveness. Music classes provide exactly the times and places in which schoolchildren can experience happiness. Creating these opportunities requires teachers to study the kinds of activities and classroom environments that can foster happiness. This is a humane view of music and education that posits that people learn best when they are happy and enjoy the projects on which they are working. Such a musical education, for example, puts a premium on the appeal of the musical repertoire studied, the activities undertaken, the relationships fostered, and the happiness of all participants engendered.

Also, Noddings' emphasis on happiness suggests that the values of domesticity and informality are particularly important for music education.[25] Lucy Green is among those to explore notions of informality in music education with reference to how popular musicians learn.[26] Employing techniques of teaching and learning characteristic of popular music widens the range of instructional possibilities in music beyond formal and didactic approaches to include aspects of imitation, repetition, successive approximation, playfulness, peer-to-peer instruction, and approaching instruction from a need-to-know basis in which learning is contextualized and immediately applied in musical experience. Also, knowledge may be picked up idiosyncratically in doing things that are not necessarily thought of as pedagogical and in musical games.[27]

Notwithstanding the important contributions of music and education geared toward happiness, detractions also lurk. This approach can overlook the fact that education is sometimes a painful process in which one must unlearn habits, attitudes, and beliefs that one has previously acquired. Musical skills sometimes require hard work to develop, and the rewards are not always immediate. Building instrumental technique and musicianship can require extended practice that may be dull and irksome and require patience, fortitude, determination, and perseverance over years. Many things that are worthwhile in life must be diligently sought after, and focusing on happiness as a sole raison d'être for music and education overlooks the importance of other values that may or may not always generate happiness in the present moment. Negative reinforcement may sometimes be a powerful motivation toward musical learning. It is important to learn what one should both do and not do. These important limits in the musical and educational process may run counter to an immediate experience of happiness, even though they may or may not generate happiness in the long run. Taking these caveats into account tempers enthusiasm for happiness as a musical and educational value.

Difficulties also arise for music educational programs that rely on informality and serendipity as a basis for instruction. Green is careful to situate informality within a larger and formal curriculum. Other sorts of informal learning, such as those available on the internet, rely more heavily on the student's interest in certain phenomena. Allowing students to follow their interests and impulses may be associated with happiness, but, as Dewey argues, focusing on student impulses may stunt a student's growth over the long term.[28] Rather, it is more likely that students will grow when teachers plan instructional programs that focus on their long-term development. Although one might hope to combine a strategic plan and happiness all along the way, things are not always this simple. Sometimes a teacher may need to foreground the claims of determining what students need to know over what might bring them happiness at present. Planning instruction for groups of students also means that students learn the important democratic principle that their own individual happiness may need to be accommodated insofar as possible within the group's best interests. One of the challenges for mass music education is to find instructional approaches that best meet the needs and interests of an entire group while also promoting the possibility of happiness for as many as possible. In these circumstances, individual happiness may be compromised somewhat, depending on the nature of the group, and notwithstanding a teacher's hope to create the possibility of happiness for everyone. There is also an important distinction between public and private life, and students need to be attuned to formality as much as to informality. Although one might hope that happiness may feature in public life as well as private life, this is possible only to some extent.

PLEASURE

The word *pleasure* comes from the Anglo-Norman and refers to "the condition or sensation induced by the experience or anticipation of what is felt to be good or desirable," "a feeling of happy satisfaction or enjoyment," "gratification," and "delight." An opposite of pain, its connotations range from valued physical sensations to "the condition of judging something to be satisfactory" and relate to matters of "will, desire, and choice."[29] Rather than regarding pleasure purely in sensual or sexual terms as desire, its meanings range broadly to cover physical sensation, affect, and thought. Pleasure is not only experienced in the moment but anticipated and remembered. Kant's invocation of aesthetic pleasure as judgment that arises out of feeling and elicits enjoyment has special relevance to education in the arts where sensation, emotion, and thought combine in gratifying ways.[30] Contra notions that pleasure is connected solely to the satisfaction of bodily appetites, pleasure, in the Kantian view, has an important intellectual basis as a cognitive emotion that emerges from the exercise of judgment, one of a trilogy of types of reason that also includes pure and applied reason.

The ambiguity of pleasure, incorporating desire and judgment, has important implications for music and education. Like joy and happiness, pleasure resonates with Langer's conception of "feeling," a broad conception of sensation-emotion-thought that is particularly manifest in the arts.[31] Importantly, it is grounded in human sensuality and sexuality, which constitute aspects of human nature. In musical cultures around the world, song, dance, and instrumental music play important roles in rituals connected with life events such as birth, puberty, courtship, marriage, and death. Since music expresses desire, sometimes covertly and sometimes overtly, societies have an interest in directing, validating, and delimiting its expression. From antiquity, philosophers have directly addressed desire by proscribing and prescribing musical expressions as part of general education.[32] Empirical researchers have also sought to understand the ways in which sexuality is and should be manifested in music education, whether in such things as the commonplaces of music, teaching, learning, instruction, curriculum, and administration or as a means of personal expression, identity formation, socialization, or enculturation.[33]

Thinking of pleasure as affect emphasizes the ways in which it can be anticipated, imagined, and reflected on as well as experienced in the moment. Whether the object is to satisfy physical desire or to experience the emotions that surround musics and musical events and are inseparable from them, pleasure is anticipatory, experiential, and reflective. Mind and body are thought of experientially and holistically, and bodily desire is thought of ethically as either a good to be celebrated or an evil to be controlled or even repudiated. Throughout the Christian era, theologians have quarreled over the natural state of the body as either something evil that needs to be denigrated and constrained or something good that needs to be cultivated and enhanced; they have disagreed over whether pleasure is something to be constrained or celebrated. Augustine frets over the possibility that music's sweetness will lead him away from contemplation of the divine.[34] Pleasure, in his view, has a negative and potentially sinister connotation. By contrast, Martin Luther asserts the power of music for physical and spiritual good and the pleasure that music brings as a gift of providence.[35] Likewise, for Jean-Jacques Rousseau, pleasure is something to be celebrated as a natural part of human experience.[36] Sean Steel embraces pleasure as an aspect of a Dionysian approach to rock music education that celebrates physical abandon and erotic delight.[37] These conflicting theological and philosophical notions of the body and pleasure mean that educators are often ambivalent about pleasure as an unmitigated good and ideal to which teachers and their students should strive. Its unbridled and hedonistic quality is often regarded askance by those who seek instead to tame or domesticate physical desire—a view that Friedrich Schiller embraces in his distinction between the natural and moral "Man" and the tendency of education to point more toward morality than pleasure.[38]

From its inception in publicly supported general education, music education has been justified principally for its social, moral, and spiritual purposes rather than for the pleasure and delight that it brings. This reality puts school music at odds with much musical experience outside school, where music is more often valued for the pleasure it brings those who make and receive it.[39] Still, writing about her response to the Mozart *Clarinet Quintet in A Major*, K. 381, Maxine Greene remarks that "there is pleasure to be found in letting the sound flow through and around one, moving into reverie, sitting passively and allowing the sweetness of it (or the sprightliness or percussiveness) make one feel good."[40] Like Peter Kivy who thinks of listeners who experience pleasure when listening to music,[41] Greene would find a place for pleasure in education in music among the other arts. Overlooking this important quality fails to capture the richness and physical nature of the musical experience.

Among its contributions, pleasure as an end of art and of music education is affected by a complex web of personal and social understandings, preferences, and practices rooted in cultural beliefs and mores. In certain rituals, music is sometimes composed, improvised, performed, sung, and danced to as a means of evoking fear, distress, and pain. Some music appeals more to intellect than to physical desire. The makers of certain musics may hope to unsettle, irritate, and alienate their public. While some people may value a certain music, others may disdain it; one musical piece is not necessarily and unequivocally related to pleasure and another to pain. Rather, music may evoke a range of responses all the way from pleasure to pain. This being the case, it is difficult to see how pleasure could be the end of all music education in a way that would satisfy all musicians and their publics equally. It is more likely that pleasure as a musical and educational value is contingent on the musics, people, and contexts in which music is made and received. This ambiguity may make it difficult to rely solely on pleasure as a means and end of a monolithic approach to music and education. Still, it opens to a rainbow of possibilities where different musical traditions can thrive.

Irrespective of whether pleasure is construed mainly in terms of hedonistic desire or as a cognitive emotion associated with dispassionate contemplation, music and education grounded in pleasure hope to appeal to those who have a stake in it. The specific quality of this appeal may vary significantly, whether to body or mind and whether singing and dancing or examining musical scores with a view to expressing and enacting them in performance. Play evokes pleasure as well as happiness, and musicians and educators naturally regard it as an important aspect of informal as well as formal music education.[42] The positive emotional valence of pleasure animates learning—that is, it brings learning to life. Rather than what Alfred North Whitehead describes as "inert knowledge," such musical education tends toward vital knowledge that is felt as much as rationally grasped.[43] As it does this, it motivates teachers and their students to desire more such experiences and to seek to achieve them. Pleasure serves as an intrinsic source of motivation for learning.

Still, the danger lurks that overemphasizing pleasure may cause teachers to capitulate to their students' present desires and impulses, rather than taking a longer view that seeks to assist them toward individual and collective growth. Emotion and desire may be fleeting, and focusing mainly on pleasure may lead teachers to chase the mirage of present sensation and appearance rather than aspects of more lasting value. One may hope to encounter pleasure all along the way to knowing music and its connections with the rest of life, but it does not suffice to rely on it entirely. The pleasure one takes in this music at this moment in time may be a function of familiarity and life's experience to this point. Pushing beyond the present horizon of knowledge to musical traditions that are unfamiliar may be discomforting at first. Years later, after one has become acquainted with other traditions, they may be a source of pleasure. Even should one never come to the point of deriving pleasure from them, one now has a broader view of self, others, and the varied ways in which people express themselves musically across times and places.

Pain proves resilient in education and can even be an important teacher. I hope for a humane education, and it is difficult to acknowledge this reality, but I must do so. School musicians have devised instructional methods and curricula that have generally eschewed pain in favor of pleasure; they hope to render musical instruction pleasant and avoid pain at all costs. Although children's rights are enshrined in the United Nations charter, the United States is not a signatory to this charter, and children here and abroad are still regularly abused physically and psychologically. Physical punishment and psychological abuse have been outlawed in modern schooling in the West; nevertheless, they are resilient and persist in some places.[44] Worse, pleasure is sometimes interwoven with pain, as the stories I have heard of differently gendered students and teachers in music programs attest. Too often, music teachers and students work in acoustically harmful sonic environments despite the hope of music educational policy makers for safe and painless environments that are conducive to health.[45] The persistence of abuse and violence in music education programs and unsafe acoustic environments in which teachers and students must work are deplorable. Still, it should also be said that sometimes educative experience is painful. It can be distressing for a boy to learn that at the rate of his present progress, he may never achieve the level of performance that he hopes to attain. It can be disappointing for a girl who longs to play an instrument to understand that another may better match her physical characteristics and personality and thereby ultimately bring her joy. It can be a source of grief for an adult whose hearing loss requires redirecting energy from performance to scholarship as the focus of creative work. Learning what one cannot do is sometimes very painful. Yet education is all about discovering that our aptitudes and capacities constrain our development in certain ways as they also enable our development in other ways. Despite one's hope for unmitigated pleasure in music and education, pain sometimes plays an important educative role.

CELEBRATION

The word *celebration* comes from the Latin, as a "noun of action" rooted in *celebrare*, to celebrate. Simply put, it refers to the "action or an act of performing or observing a religious or formal rite or ceremony," "an act of celebrating a significant or happy day or event," and "an act of public honour or recognition."[46] Celebration connotes a ritual that is performed within a set of rules that define it and is understood by the community of participants. Its formality and public character give it an aura of solemnity, even if it may also be a joyous occasion.

As a ritual enacted within socially prescribed and proscribed rules, celebration is also felt, and there is an emotional valence to the events that are remembered and the persons who are honored. For this reason, Langer includes rituals among those activities that express or are about aspects of life that escape discursive language and must instead be enacted.[47] These ritual acts are symbolic in ways the participants grasp. Christopher Small analyzes the symphonic concert as one such musical ritual whose meanings are understood by performers and listeners alike.[48] For him, all who participate in central and peripheral ways in this ritual are musickers who together comprise the community of those whose identities and ways of life are defined, at least in part, by partaking in the ritual. A musical ritual expresses the commitments, beliefs, and values of a music's exponents and public. The whole is suffused with the joyous participation of musicians and listeners alike. Iris Yob describes these emotions and thoughts that are communicated and felt by participants as "emotional cognitions."[49] For her, rituals articulate and express emotional life in formal and richly symbolic ways of thinking about them.

To its credit, unlike the emphasis on informality in Nodding's conception of happiness, the intensity of moments of joy, and the sensuous nature of pleasure, celebration is characterized by ritual formality. Thinking of music and education as celebration implies affirmation that is governed by specific rules and expectations of belief and conduct on the part of a music's public. Not only is one affirmed personally and subjectively by this musical ritual, but one acquires knowledge of and identifies with the musical traditions that govern a musical practice and the wider community of which one is a part. Constraints on hedonistic behavior in celebration are devised according to specific normative values, beliefs, attitudes, and practices on behalf of the group. This sense of the public as opposed to private expressions of feeling psychically distances one from the raw emotion and allows one to enact it ritually in more elegant and moving ways than one might do while in the grip of an immediate felt state. This idea is akin to Dewey's metaphor of the "expression" of wine from grapes.[50] For Dewey, artists encounter and surmount obstacles in transforming subjective feeling into publicly accessible celebration. Rather than self-exposure, musicians engage in self-expression as they create compositions, improvisations, or performances of already composed pieces that are publicly accessible.

Celebration assumes that those who experience music identify with and are affirmed by it. Green notices that some music is alienating to musicians and their publics, and she contrasts celebration with alienation.[51] In today's often multicultural societies where multiple music traditions are evident, all the members of a society do not necessarily share the same beliefs, attitudes, and values about music.[52] The multiplicities and pluralities evident in contemporary societies mean that in school music, some teachers and students may feel affirmed by a musical piece and others may be alienated by it. A musical performance designed as celebration may not turn out to be such for all the participants and to the same degree. This reality opens possibilities for developing an open approach to music education that rejoices in multiplicities and invites students to come to know music through a host of musical traditions and alternative formats.[53] Such a music education celebrates the musical variety accessible in a place and time and offers various pathways to students that affirm them musically and in other ways.

To its detriment, the necessity of finding those musics that are affirming to students may lead music teachers to focus on their students' present musical tastes. In today's world, these tastes are shaped mainly by commercial interests, mass media, and family traditions. In school music, student musical tastes may sometimes collide with those of teachers whose musical affiliations are shaped by professional musicians. The lack of alignment of institutional influences on music education and the lack of time devoted to musical instruction in schools may make it difficult for teachers to persuade their students of the value of other musics that are less immediately accessible to them. Relying on formal education alone to cultivate the rules and expectations of practices overlooks the many informal ways in which music is picked up as one participates in it in lived life. Youngsters who have grown up in a jazz music or a classical music tradition may be affirmed by its inclusion within the school curriculum. Others who have never heard live music concerts and whose entire lives have been shaped by playing recorded popular music on a digital device may continue to feel alienated by these musics even if they attend school music classes for several years. Finding and agreeing on a repertoire that should be known by all students to fulfill the claims of celebration is a particularly daunting undertaking in today's school music programs. Industrial Age music education constitutes an inertia against Information

Age music education approaches that are multifarious, digital and acoustic, and change-oriented and require different teaching, learning, and instructional skills than those in monolithic and standardized mass music educational systems.

Making music in the sort of "robust praxialism" that Philip Alperson desires for music education requires doing and undergoing music and an extensive and intensive musical program in general education.[54] Music of whatever practice should be well done, and doing a music competently is much more time-consuming than learning about it or hearing it. For this reason, construing music as celebration requires teachers to be expert musicians and necessitates the investment of significant time in musical instruction—characteristics that are too often lacking in school music. Luther's view that a classroom teacher must be a musician or "I will hear nothing of him" commits educational policy makers to a very different strategic approach than supplying classroom teachers with minimal musical preparation in the ways that are typically undertaken in the West.[55] The most qualified musicians are often located in high school music departments rather than elementary schools, where there are fewer music specialists. It is quite impractical to grasp the rules of musical practices and identify with them in the ways required in music education cast as celebration unless teachers at every level are also musicians and there is sufficient time allocated for music instruction in the school curriculum. Attempting to develop musicianship in children when teachers lack it themselves is a case of the blind leading the blind and makes limited sense in terms of public policy. If celebration is to work practically as a value for music education, significant resources are necessitated to ensure that music teachers are musicians with enough instructional time at their disposal. Nevertheless, since the nineteenth century when music entered publicly supported schools, too often, expert teachers and instructional time in music have been in short supply.

When thought of metaphorically as a jewel and as a vivid emotion, joy also has a spiritual dimension. Happiness, as a particularly American ideal, involves a pleasurable state of mind that is partially out of one's control and affected by individual and social factors. Pleasure evokes an array of delightful sensations all the way from sensual and sexual desire to emotion, thought, and judgment. Celebration is a rich idea that, when thought about ritualistically as enactment, is heavy with symbolic meaning. Although these values play out sometimes similarly, being rooted in emotional and physical life, they have differing implications for music educational practice whether in terms of informal or formal approaches to instruction. Their potential power rests in the possibilities that the emotional power of joy or delight, the commitment and contentment of happiness, the sensuosity and intellectual satisfaction of pleasure, and the affirmation and validation of celebration provide sources of intrinsic motivation for musicians, teachers, and their students. None of these values, taken alone, suffices, and all have different contributions to offer. It remains to music and education policy makers to figure out how to retain the best of what they offer and avoid the worst in the specific situations in which music and instruction are ongoing.

SEVEN

Fidelity, Persistence, Patience, and Loyalty

THINKING ABOUT FIDELITY, PERSISTENCE, PATIENCE, and loyalty evokes the role of a dynamic tradition as a crucial element in music and education and the master and apprentice metaphors for capturing the roles of musician, teacher, and learner. In contrast to values of love, friendship, desire, and devotion and those of joy, happiness, pleasure, and celebration that seem closer to subjective and emotional life, these values arise in the life of mind and are expressed in specific actions. Since antiquity, they have been manifested in accumulated musical and educational beliefs and practices that have played an important part in decisions about which musics to foster and which educational perspectives to embrace. At a time heavily impacted by changing technologies, political realities, and social mores, it may be tempting to focus on change, opt for a musical and cultural education in search of novelty and difference, and downplay, subvert, or upend tradition.[1] I hold a more complicated if also problematic position that regards tradition as a living thing in tension or dialectic with innovation.[2] Notwithstanding the critique of tradition that must necessarily be mounted, it also constitutes a good that contributes to stability, ritual, collective memory, identity, and shared possibility in social groups and institutions. In music instruction, these values are often evidenced particularly in studio settings in the classical traditions of East and West and glimpsed in vocal and instrumental instructional manuals and treatises. They are also apparent in teacher preparation programs and in the development of researchers. Drawing on the master and apprentice metaphors that are pervasive throughout classical and vernacular musics of the world, they are especially important where practical skills need to be learned through an extended period of practice.[3] While fidelity, persistence, patience, and loyalty may be especially important in private and small group settings and at advanced levels of instruction, they also relate to general education in schools conducted under the auspices of various institutions, be they government, religion, musical profession, family, or commerce. Though these qualities are intertwined, I unpack them in turn to examine their attributes, contributions, and detractions for music and education.

FIDELITY

The word *fidelity* comes immediately from the French word *fidélité*, rooted in the Latin words *fidēs*, *fidēlitāt-em*, and *fidēlis*, meaning faith and faithfulness.[4] Although it has religious connotations in its reference to a vision or set of principles, I want to think of fidelity particularly in terms of its musical and educational usage. Its references to beliefs and associated practices are crucial, and, practically speaking, I see them inextricably intertwined. Fidelity is manifest in mental assent to beliefs that are also carried into practice in the phenomenal world. Donald Arnstine might consider fidelity to be a "disposition"—that is, a tendency to act on a specific belief or belief system.[5] Assent to and action on behalf of this belief suggests that one finds the belief sufficiently compelling, justifiable, and motivating as to prompt action. A disposition begins in private interior life and may become public and visible to others in one's actions. I think of fidelity as a thought-action that is manifest, to some degree, in the phenomenal world of musical or educational practice. For example, violin teachers' belief in the importance of achieving certain technical and interpretative skills lead necessarily to the practice of an approach to violin instruction and the cultivation of specific dispositions in their students. Rather than regard musical concepts and musical actions as if they were distinct and separate, they seek to cultivate an imperative for students to act on their beliefs. Students may also come to belief through their actions. That is, these violin students may also play themselves into beliefs about violin performance. There is a symbiotic relationship between belief and practice so that beliefs may also be reinforced and transformed by actions.

Faithfulness connotes "unswerving allegiance," loyalty, truthfulness, and commitment to people, ideas, or things and provides a compass for belief and action, not only musically or educationally but spilling over into the rest of one's lived life.[6] Rather than flitting from one perspective to another, fidelity points adherents in certain directions and enables them to navigate multiplicities of possibilities with a clear sense of purpose. It serves as a north star by which to find one's way through sometimes complicated decisions. The decision to commit to someone or something narrows and focuses one's field of view as it also opens various possibilities arising from that commitment. One cannot learn everything, but one can learn something. Learning opens options to pursue its outcomes in ways that would not be possible in the absence of commitment. Time constraints to learn and play repertoire necessitate pianists making choices about which musical tradition(s) and pieces within those traditions to perform. Time spent learning to play one thing necessitates giving up something else.[7] Whatever they choose to pursue, their repertoire choices both limit and enable them as pianists. These choices provide a means of navigating a multiplicity of repertoire possibilities and achieving satisfaction as they pursue their pianistic objectives within a finite field of view.

Fidelity conveys an implicit honesty, sincerity, truthfulness, and transparency of thought and action that may be thought of as integrity—that is, one is true to one's word and one's stated belief. This clarity of perspective and action suggests a point in which one arrives at what Alfred North Whitehead would think of as wisdom, a place of unity, integrity, and wholeness where knowledge is useful in a host of ways.[8] Here, one seeks truth and acknowledges it irrespective of its inconvenience or the duties and obligations it brings. Eschewing cynicism on the one hand and skepticism on the other allows the possibility of surprise in which one's dearly held beliefs and practices may be challenged and one may need to rethink what one has learned and come to value in the past.[9] If young singers realize that their past vocal practices have been deleterious to their singing, they must now consider the ways in which what they have learned will cause them to change their ideas about their vocal practices in the future. These may be transformational moments in which they may decide to pursue what they now understand to be greater truth than they have known in the past, no matter the cost. At this point, they come to realize that if they are to follow a new path, their actions and beliefs will need to be united; they will need to conform to their new beliefs and be scrupulously honest about who and what they are and may become as singers. They must count the costs and possibly risks of following what they believe to be truth wherever it leads.

Fidelity also entails a sense of duty in which one can be trusted to keep to one's allegiance and promises. One fulfills one's "word of honour, oath, or pledge" as a duty or an obligation, and one's integrity is manifest in one's "honesty, truthfulness, trustworthiness" in keeping one's word.[10] In Western conservatories, music teachers inculcate a sense of duty in their students.[11] They often prepare their students as their disciples and instill in them an imperative to faithfully practice, prepare for their lessons, and fulfill obligations to them personally as well as to the musical practices they personify. This is also true in classical traditions in the East. In India, for example, students were traditionally obliged to provide for their teachers' comfort in material ways.[12] Practice was a spiritual exercise (e.g., *riaz*) that students had to undertake and undergo as part of the process of becoming and being musicians. Students were required to demonstrate their fidelity as a precondition for their teachers being willing to impart knowledge to them, hence the requirement of a period of initiation and trial before students would be accepted as disciples. Wisdom was valued for its own sake as for its source of livelihood, and teachers sought to ensure that knowledge would be transmitted only to those who could be trusted to guard it and be faithful to it.

Among its contributions, fidelity provides for a sense of stability in a social practice. Absent the commitments of fidelity, it is hard to imagine how a social group or musical practice can be sustained over time. One's fidelity extends to the people with whom one associates and the practices in which one participates. As such, fidelity contributes to the mutuality within the community and the cohesiveness of the social group. Since fidelity is enacted, adherents share in rituals that are enacted repeatedly. A teacher's musical and pedagogical beliefs translate into lessons, practice sessions, and performances that, to some extent, become codified and taken for granted as rules that govern behavior. Enacting these rituals in the company of others forges a sense of collective memory. School terms begin and end, lessons have typical elements that follow in order, performances are remembered for their specific character, and teachers have their inimitable ways of interacting with their students. All of this helps forge a sense of identity as an individual member of the musical community. There is a collective sense of the shared possibilities and responsibilities of becoming a musician, an educated person, and a member of society. Also, the idea of fidelity may conjure up the idea of the teacher as a gatekeeper to the profession. Acceptance of slipshod work does not benefit a profession, as it allows malpractice and miseducation to thrive. Fidelity to standards of excellence is therefore an important criterion for admission to a profession.[13]

Although it may seem ironic, fidelity also promotes organic change and difference. Tradition is dynamic and evolutionary. Imagination leads to ambiguity that is manifest in divergences, differences, and distinctions. Even as musicians remain faithful to certain musical ideas and practices of which they are a part, they seek to rework and even reinvent them. They challenge taken-for-granted assumptions. They seek fresh musical ideas as they rework others. They critically examine the forms in which they work and the very sonic possibilities on which they draw. Underlying all, there are deep commitments to this music in which they are steeped and the people with whom they work and play. Fidelity may be tested in historical moments of profound change, such as ours, when musical traditions mix and collide and fundamental assumptions are challenged. It seeks a way to reconcile what can be reconciled and to negotiate differences in and challenges to beliefs and practices that can and should be worked through. It also acknowledges the dissonances and discontinuities that cannot be bridged. In this time of global and cultural upheaval, efforts such as those by Silkroad constitute a means of dialoguing across musical traditions to find common musical ground.[14] Silkroad's performances cultivate broader understandings of the various musical traditions represented by the performers and their audiences. In this way, musical fidelity is recast more broadly.

Among its detractions, fidelity may fail to take a sufficiently critical view of knowledge. A belief system and a musical or educational practice may be in error. Deconstructing the classical concert tradition, for example, Christopher Small points to problems that may lurk beneath a social system of rituals that he sees as elitist, classist, and exclusive, that benefit privilege and entitlement, canonicity, and those who stand to gain by it. In his view, this tradition represents the exercise and even abuse of power by impresarios, managers, and conductors of the musicians with whom they work.[15] For Small, the concert hall spaces, musicians, patrons, and protocols are indicative of power relationships that too frequently benefit the wealthy, powerful, and upper class and exclude most people. Were he to see the Wiener Philharmoniker perform its Sommernachts Konzert on the grounds of the Schönbrunn Palace as broadcast on PBS, the symbolic import of the concert's location would not be lost on him. Even though the orchestra plays in an informal setting, it does so on the grounds of one of the Austro-Hungarian Empire's chief palaces, in a setting of pomp and privilege, with the most favored patrons seated on rows of chairs nearest the orchestra while the great majority of the audience are seated informally on the grass farther away. Notwithstanding the orchestra's hope to increase its audience and the enjoyment of those who have come to this concert, as it plays a repertoire associated historically with nobility, the performance can also be read as patronizing to those who lack wealth and status. It may also be seen as a representation of the music that the conductor and concert organizers believe the audience should enjoy. In this 2016 performance, I notice a paucity of women musicians, with entire instrumental sections comprised only of men—a holdover from a time when women were excluded from its membership. While I am glad for the presence of a sprinkling of women in its ranks and for this sign of the beginnings of inclusiveness, I am reminded of the continuing sexism not only in this orchestra but in the Western classical tradition.[16] If fidelity is to be intellectually honest, it needs to be self-reflexive; adherents need to interrogate a tradition's problems at the same time as they foster the best in this music. Although one might wish this were always the case, fidelity may cover blindness to the claims of change or refusal to admit that change is needed.

Blind faith contributes to the loss of the animating spirit of a musical practice. Criticisms, tensions, resistances, and obstructions serve to energize ideas and practices as they are debated and contested in the public spaces. Trust in traditional belief and practice may prompt too small a view. It overlooks the fact that critique, resistance, and change may indicate fidelity to a larger vision or greater principle that has yet to be fully realized. Seen in this way, it is possible that fidelity may help to guide change. For Susanne Langer, disciples pose a danger for transformative ideas, and Randall Allsup is right to be concerned about the making of disciples as an end of music education.[17] Disciples tend to reduce the possibilities of generative ideas to systems of prescriptions and proscriptions that can stultify a tradition and even destroy it. As the original ideas and practices are ossified, they lose the power, inspirational quality, and immediacy they may once have possessed. Throughout the history of musical education, systems of thought and practice were erected around once fresh ideas. As time passed, faith in these systems cluttered them with what Émile Jaques-Dalcroze aptly described as "ridiculous pretensions," especially in the hands of those unequipped to believe, practice, or forward them.[18] Israel Scheffler cautions against the dogmatism and skepticism that emerge in the absence of open-mindedness and critical thought.[19] Paul Woodford regards such blindness as one of the crucial challenges facing music education in our time. For Woodford, the democratic process requires an intellectual education in music as in other things.[20] I see the anti-intellectualism manifested in blind faith, sectarianism, and reductionism, too evident in education and society, as destructive of animating ideals by literalizing ideas that were once figurative and codifying and hedging them about with rule-bound systems.[21] In the process, generative ideas lose their extraordinary dynamic power and are rendered limited and prosaic.

PERSISTENCE

The verb *persist* is of Latin origin and means "to continue firmly or obstinately in a state, opinion, purpose, or course of action, [especially] despite opposition, setback, or failure."[22] The noun *persistence*, immediately from the French, refers to the state of persisting, where one continues to hold to particular beliefs and practices in spite of obstacles or even lack of success or collapse. Persistence is not transitory or momentary but "lasts" and "endures" in a "continued or prolonged existence or occurrence."[23] It may also have the negative connotation of obstinacy in that one may hold on to one's beliefs and practices tenaciously, possibly too long, when change may be warranted. The possibilities of persistence as a musical and educational value are promising and problematic. Still, it is worth rescuing the best of what persistence may offer, especially in the face of its possible derogatory references.

Persistence relates especially to notions of the arts and education that envisage the necessity of a "vision of mastery"—that is, an imagined end to the process of striving to overcome obstacles that stand in one's way in achieving an objective.[24] This view finds support, for example, in John Dewey's view of art as being made through the process of being pressed or "expressed," just as grapes are expressed into wine or literally wrung out into wine.[25] For Dewey, artistic creation requires persistence in withstanding or undergoing this "wringing out" process. Absorption, concentration, and commitment are required to create musical pieces, paintings, sculptures, poems, or plays. Dewey believes that the arts are never merely done but are also undergone often in the face of impediments that require skill and intelligence to overcome. Extending Dewey's view of art into educational experience, Herbert Read, Maxine Greene, and Vernon Howard are among those to see the need for imaginative and critical thinking as a means of persistently cultivating artistry throughout the entire educational process.[26] For Leonard Meyer, grasping the meaning of classical music and its attendant emotional valence requires a process of coming to know its constituent elements and developing the repertorial expectations on which this music is grounded. This takes time and persistence to accomplish.[27]

Cultivating the capacities and dispositions to foresee possibilities and persist in the face of challenges and obstacles is required to realize a vision of mastery or the extraordinary and intensified experiences that are possible in the arts. This principle is especially important in those endeavors that rely on practice over an extended time to hone the skills that are required to bring an artistic vision to life in the phenomenal world. Persistence empowers and motivates teachers and learners throughout the creative process to achieve their artistic and educational objectives. Within musical performance, practice is both a technical and an artistic matter of honing the skills needed to create the sounds and polishing the musical ideas and feelings they express. Practice and performance require qualities of resilience and fortitude that enable musicians to stick sufficiently with specific approaches and objectives in the face of setbacks and failures along the way to realizing imagined visions that evolve during the music making process.

Notwithstanding the crucial role of persistence in artistic thought and practice, some musicians and educators have developed pedagogical approaches that rely on what I think of as a theory of pedagogical immediacy. This is the notion that the rewards for children's musical efforts should come quickly, music can be performed without necessitating much skill, and children need not struggle for musical perfection in every respect. For example, Carl Orff and Gunild Keetman's *Schulwerk* is predicated on the idea that children need not grasp sophisticated musical concepts or possess advanced technical skills to be able to improvise and perform classroom music successfully.[28]

While immediacy may play a valuable role in general music education in certain situations, it is at odds with the mores of every musical tradition I know. Rather, mastering these musical traditions requires persistence in developing skills through extended practice and over a long period of time. For example, writing about music education in pre-Independence South Africa, John Blacking tells the story of how his failure to correctly perform certain details of Venda music so distracted one of the performers that she was unable to go into a trance state. In a musical performance that was expected to induce or be associated with trance, the performance failed because of his lack of skill that, he concluded, was due to his not having been born Venda.[29] His story illustrates that in the traditional music of the Venda people, it is essential to get all the musical details right. The requirement of exemplary skill is accompanied by low tolerance for error. This reality also means that only a few people are encouraged to become the Venda's chief musicians. For Blacking, the unsophisticated character of the singing of Christian hymns in the schools attended by Venda children in pre-Independence South Africa constituted an affront to the Venda vernacular musical aesthetic. As Lucy Green illustrates, while the skills may differ, popular, traditional, and classical music traditions all require skill.[30] Once one admits that there are acknowledged ways to compose, improvise, perform, produce, and listen to a specific music that are considered by exponents and adherents to be "right" or "correct," musical education necessarily requires inculcating these skills in the young. The more sophisticated the musical demands and the higher one's aspirations, the more important persistence becomes as a means of meeting these expectations.

Among its advantages, persistence as an educational value is particularly appropriate to social and cultural undertakings that often occur over long periods of time. Educational change transpires over decades and centuries; it takes time for educational results to be manifest in the lives of students, for educational changes to work their way through the educational system, and for their impact to be fully apparent. Persistence and commitment over the long term are required if one is to fully realize an educational vision. The history of the elementary and secondary school curriculum in the United States is rife with faddishness and a failure to persist over the long term.[31] Curricular change in this country gives the impression of "tinkering" toward various Utopian visions.[32] By contrast, studio music teaching has remained remarkably persistent in its approach and effective over centuries in preparing young performers at high levels of virtuosity and musical maturity.

Persistence also brings its own rewards. As a music teacher working with musicians of various ages, I was struck by the fact that these musicians often came to value the repertoire that was the most challenging and required their persistence in surmounting stylistic, technical, and interpretative obstacles along the way. They prized the music that cost them the most effort to gain. Meeting its challenges provided them with a sense of exhilaration and triumph when they were eventually able to perform it effortlessly and artfully. Their acquired skill was a source of joy especially when they were no longer preoccupied with the technical challenges of performance but could focus, instead, on interpreting this piece with all the tools they had learned. As they studied this challenging repertoire, they also learned to persist, and this disposition in turn aided them in acquiring still more advanced skills. Empirical evidence suggests the possibility of a transfer effect of music listening and training to other areas.[33] It seems reasonable to expect that persistence acquired in music instruction may transfer to some extent into daily life and allow people to cope more effectively and constructively with difficulties and failures throughout life.

Among its detractions, an excess of persistence may lead to obstinacy, unwillingness to adjust and change one's beliefs and practices in the face of evidence of the need to do so, and closed-mindedness to the possibilities of alternative ideas and practices. Obstinacy is evident at all ages, and some students are more prone to belligerently resisting change than others. Closed-mindedness can be seen in what Scheffler calls "dogmatism," or an unwillingness to criticize beliefs and practices or doubt their veracity.[34] For Allsup, fundamentalist imaginations are characterized by an emphasis on facts, literal thought and interpretation, a lack of toleration of ambiguity, and the repudiation of divergent cultural perspectives.[35]

Relying excessively on persistence may be insufficiently age-appropriate or sensitive to the needs, interests, aptitudes, and abilities of students and discouraging to those in the music educational process. The claims of immediacy also have an important place in musical education. For example, immediacy may be particularly important for the very young or for those who, as Whitehead might say, are approaching subject matter from an intuitive or "romantic" perspective.[36] In working with young and amateur musicians, I found it helpful to balance repertoire in which persistence was required with more accessible repertoire where the rewards were more immediate. Some people are less persistent by nature, and accessible repertoire can help motivate musicians as they work on more challenging repertoire that requires greater persistence. Focusing excessively on the problems to be overcome may also fix attention on the problems themselves. It may fail to acknowledge the teacher's pedagogical responsibility to build bridges to understanding that will make the student's path toward growth as seamless as possible. Valuing persistence to such an extent that one demoralizes and discourages a student can stunt and even prevent further growth and development.[37] Every student does not aspire to a high level of virtuosity as a musician, and even gifted and ambitious students are not equally at home with repertoire or able to sing or play it equally well. A teacher's challenge is to match repertoire with students in ways that allow them to shine at each stage of the learning process. For example, Daniil Trifonov's teacher, Sergei Babayan, looked at Daniil's hands and began his instructional program with a study of Chopin's piano oeuvres. After

Daniil gained additional musical maturity, they moved on to a study of Brahms concerti. Although Babayan says that good teachers set out to deliberately break the rules of a tradition and teach their students to do so, he does so not to repudiate the tradition but to transform it for the better.[38] Above all, he wishes for Daniil to grow and excel as a pianist now and in the future.

PATIENCE

Patience (from the French *pacience* and Latin *patientia*) has long been regarded as a virtue that connotes endurance through problems and provocations, calmness, a willingness to wait and defer gratification until later, and constancy and diligence in achieving one's desired ends.[39] Within music education, patience has long been prized as a musical and pedagogical value. It concerns persons and things and is evident in artistic and educational processes and products. I think of patience not only as a noun but in the active sense of exercising patience or acting patiently. As with the other values in this quartet, it is an enacted belief, attitude, and disposition, and it bears fruit in the phenomenal world.

In our technologized, commodified, and commercialized present in which there is a premium on time and a monetary value ascribed to it, efficiency and immediacy are often valued over time-consuming activities that require patience to complete. Where there is a premium on the use-value of time, there may be little tolerance for slowness and for taking the time needed to relish each moment as one also overcomes obstacles along the way in what is sometimes an inefficient process. Instead, impatience in search of speed and immediate results may be preferred over patience that endures and even embraces slowness.[40] Patience can seem almost archaic and ill-suited to a fast-paced world where young and old are tethered to electronic devices that deliver immediate results. The educational preoccupation with product and efficiency influenced by corporate thinking of the twentieth and twenty-first centuries has been challenged by philosophers, such as Jane Roland Martin and Nel Noddings, who have advocated a humane approach to education in which the imperative of efficiency is decentered by a focus on the needs and interests of the people involved and their enjoyment of the process.[41] When slowness is considered as a good, patience is revalued as a means of achieving worthwhile and long-term educational and musical ends. Patience is not only empowering, but it resists forces that would dehumanize music and education.

Tolerating the "faults or limitations of self and others" is among the qualities of patience.[42] To be patient is to admit that all human beings have limitations, and perfection is out of reach for most of us. Although musicians and educators might strive for it, there is still a sense that a piece or performance might have been improved and that more could be known about this subject or about the others with whom one works and plays. Patience tolerates the imperfections and limitations of others, oneself, and the things that have been created. It persists in seeking to improve what can be improved while recognizing what is unattainable at present by these people in this situation. This is a hopeful mindset in which one exhibits a positive attitude and an uncomplaining demeanor. There is also a calmness and acceptance of the reality of the situation even as one seeks to improve it.

Patience also entails the important quality of "waiting," or the ability to take the long view and defer gratification.[43] To wait is to allow time to pass for the hoped-for ends to be realized. For example, after posing a question, a teacher pauses to allow time for students to reflect on the question and frame their responses rather than rushing headlong on to the next question. It requires a long-term view in which one realizes that sophisticated practical skills sometimes require a long time to acquire. Since propositional knowledge may be acquired more quickly than procedural knowledge, it is often in the acquisition of procedural knowledge of music that patience is particularly required. This reality suggests that patience is especially important in teaching and learning the practice of music. Taking a longer-term view of a musical or pedagogical situation requires teachers and their students to put off the desire for immediate gratification to achieve a longer-term goal. As with persistence, patience involves developing and demonstrating the capacity to wait for greater and more long-lasting rewards that follow diligent practice for a prolonged time.

Endurance in overcoming "obstacles and difficulties that are sometimes painful" and in being "longsuffering when provoked" are other crucial aspects of patience.[44] The pathway to worthwhile objectives is sometimes difficult. Obstacles are encountered in the artistic and educational process and these are sometimes frustrating to overcome. Like persistence, patience endures these difficulties. Teachers and students may be provoked and distressed by the difficulties they encounter or by people who may deliberately stand in their way and prevent them from reaching their desired goals. While it may be tempting to portray the educational process as filled with light and happiness (and we might hope that this is the case for much of the time), it is important to acknowledge that difficulties may need to be endured along the way. Patience enables these difficulties to be met more successfully.

Patience also suggests qualities of "constancy and diligence."[45] Thinking of the waiting process as active rather than passive allows one to do all that is possible to accomplish the hoped-for-objectives. Rather than a mindless activity, patience is the kind of waiting that remains fixed on the objective and faithful to it. One is diligent in striving even when one encounters problems, distractions, and difficulties in the attainment of the desired ends. Patience focuses on a specific end-in-view and stays with it despite these challenges and the tantalizing possibilities of other means and ends that may seem easier to attain. This fortitude serves to restrict as well as enable those involved in this musicking or this educational process and facilitates teachers and their students reaching the desired end. Having decided to master this repertoire, these musicians stick with it until they eventually reach their goal of performing it well. As they remain with this enterprise, they gradually hone the skills needed to interpret the piece and perform it intelligently with grace and style. The values of virtuosic speed, versatility, and grace that Howard espouses can only be won as musicians and educators exhibit patience in meeting performative and interpretative challenges on the path to performing in exemplary ways.[46]

Among its contributions, exercising patience is a hopeful and empowering undertaking consistent with democratic and humane practices of music and education. On one hand, it entails imagining a hoped-for end, be it a composition, improvisation, or performance that may be not quite within one's capacity at present. On the other, it enables learners and musicians to carefully work through the process of achieving or realizing this end and hone the skills needed to make the vision a reality. It facilitates the process of overcoming the difficulties in one's way and thereby enables musical and educational growth. Although patience may be important in musical traditions that prize virtuosity or at advanced levels of musical instruction in the professional preparation of classical musicians, it is also at work in popular and vernacular traditions. Green describes popular musicians who patiently listen to recordings, gradually hone their skills through imitation, trial and error, and successive approximation to their imagined ideal such that their performances come to approximate or surpass exemplary recordings by other musicians. Trial-and-error learning by successive approximation is evident as the musicians try, fail, try again, succeed, and, through practice, persist until their performances pass the tests of their own expectations and public affirmation. Patience empowers these musicians to improve their performances through informal learning just as the classical musicians in my earlier example may be empowered to improve through patience in their formal learning. Since formal and informal learning are present in classical and popular traditions, patience is needed in them all.

Patience is necessitated by and cultivated through high musical and educational expectations by teachers and students. Teacher expectations have been shown to significantly impact student expectations of themselves and their subsequent achievement.[47] For example, a teacher's high expectations in terms of repertoire choice may suggest a significant gap between what a student is presently able to accomplish and needs to be able to accomplish to succeed. The wider this gap, the more patience may be required in moving from actuality to possibility, from what is now known and can presently be done to what needs to be known and could be done. Hopefully, teachers seek to navigate this gap carefully by ensuring that the steps forward are attainable by their students at every stage. Still, the steps are sometimes more ambitious, and it is necessary for teachers and students to remain focused on the longer-term objective. Realizing these practical expectations requires and helps students develop patience and learn how to succeed at each point. Students sometimes surprise themselves and even their teachers when they achieve more than they might otherwise have imagined because of their teachers' high expectations of them.

The value of patience is also particularly important as a corrective at a time in which impatience is fostered in contemporary society and by technology. Accepting one's limitations and those of the others with whom one lives and works is crucial to creating and maintaining a civil and humane society. Patience reminds us of the value of slowness, attention to detail, the value of active waiting, and the importance of taking the time needed to produce results that are exemplary. It contributes to what Neil Postman terms a "thermostatic" view of education that constitutes a corrective for values that are marginalized or subjugated in present society.[48] As Martin writes, paradoxically, creating a memorable education is a matter of focusing on the present while also realizing that the educational process is long and patience is needed if it is to succeed.[49] Emphasizing short-term gratification misses the possibilities of longer-term goals that point to wisdom, a life lived fully and well, and the creation and sustenance of cultural life and a humane civilization. An education for and in patience is memorable because it brings alive the learning and integrates it with the rest of lived life. For Martin, the progressive education she received in her early school years lasted a lifetime; many decades later, the songs and poems patiently taught by teachers and memorized by students could be recalled with light in old age as a source of inspiration, joy, and consolation.

Still, patience may mask important detractions. Excessive reliance on patience can emphasize educational work rather than play and result in drudgery and frustration. Joy constantly deferred in search of future reward may lead to an educational process in which few points of light punctuate an otherwise dreary process of always looking forward to a hoped-for reality rather than relishing the present moment. For Dewey, education needs to be life lived now, not just the promise of life to be lived in the future.[50] Particularly in early childhood and throughout youth, it is crucial to consider the development of individual students, their varied personalities and musical proclivities, and their instructional levels. Teachers also need to pace instruction in ways that cultivate patience while also keeping the capacities and interests of students foremost in mind and joy ever present.

One can be too patient, so willing to forgive musical limitations as to fail to create a composition, improvisation, or performance that could be within the reach of musicians. An excess of patience can mask laziness and an unwillingness to expend the effort needed to insist on the attainment of pedagogical or musical objectives within their reach. When time is expensive and in short supply and other more efficient methods and approaches would take greater advantage of time and resources, excessive patience may squander precious resources and fail to take advantage of the opportunities at hand. Some people are naturally more patient than others, and some instructional situations require more patience to navigate than others. The satisfaction that teachers and students derive in specific situations may be partly due to the match between their expectations and their patience in expending the time and effort required to meet these expectations. Still, especially in group instruction in general education where resources are scarce, teachers are obligated to use them wisely. Offering music education in the hope of captivating student interest in music or uncovering yet unrealized musicality is an expensive undertaking. There are practical limits to patience and matching teacher and student expectations. It may be for this reason that Jaques-Dalcroze advised music teachers at early stages of education to offer a short and rich course of musical instruction, identify those with musical aptitude, and then focus resources on them.[51] Although the two or three years of intensive musical instruction that Jaques-Dalcroze recommends may not suffice to determine whether students can benefit from musical education, his advice serves as a caution of the dangers of too much patience in publicly supported education.

Impatience may constitute a good when it motivates people to exert the effort needed to achieve their goals and search for the most efficient pathways to reaching their objectives. Focusing on immediate gratification of impulses may also constitute a hook for those with little interest in or aptitude for music and a means whereby students' interest can be caught. In Dewey's view, impulses may be transformed into growth that has long-term benefit. Martin writes about the songs she was taught in elementary school that captivated her interest and that of her classmates. As a student, she accompanied class singing on the piano, thereby reinforcing the importance of the private piano instruction she received outside of school. For her, the concept-driven and "tuneless" songs she was later asked to teach in her own elementary classroom lacked the zest and interest of those she had learned in school as a child. Rather than teach music for other extrinsic and conceptual reasons, she was impatient to teach a repertoire of songs to her students that were intrinsically interesting to them and that they would remember throughout their lives. Lacking the immediate interest of the songs she experienced as a child, the music education that she was obliged to offer her students fell far short of the joy she and her classmates had known in music class as children. She realized that if her students were to come to love music as she had done, she must subvert the directives she was given and build on their impulses.[52]

LOYALTY

The word *loyalty*, from the "Old French *loialté* (modern *loyauté*)," is closely related to fidelity while also manifesting qualities of persistence and patience. Its ordinary dictionary usage suggests such meanings as "faithful adherence to one's promise, oath, word of honour," "faithful adherence to the sovereign or lawful government," and "enthusiastic reverence for the person and family of the sovereign."[53] Although it is a noun, I conceive of loyalty in the active sense of doing and undergoing. As belief manifested in action, it is, like the other words in this quartet, a thought-action. Its European roots lie in the feudal oath of allegiance sworn from vassals to their lords. From ancient times, loyalty has been seen in the obligation and fealty of subjects to their royal and noble rulers and powerful others above them in social, political, and religious hierarchies. It is also evident in the *paideia* of ancient Greece as a virtue that should characterize citizens of the republic.[54] I want to rescue this word from its socially stratified beginnings and apply it to democratic societies that are decent in the sense of respecting all human beings and treating them civilly and equally before the law. Loyalty is a traditional value, and I see it manifest in the respect accorded to people and other things, whether they be beliefs, practices, rule systems, or whatever. For musicians and teachers, loyalty is evident in their relationships with their students, and they are loyal to the musical traditions they espouse and the educational systems in which their instruction is located. As with the foregoing values, I see loyalty as a double-edged sword, as having benefits and detractions and thereby requiring care in the ways in which it is manifest in music education.

Among the attributes of loyalty, respect is a critical element in a democratic society. I think of loyalty as directed toward beliefs, practices, and people within a free society where loyalty is not so much commanded as earned, and the people and things toward which one is loyal need to be worthy of being emulated and highly regarded. Parker Palmer depicts the educational community gathered about a subject of great worth and the mutual respect between the participants and their respect for the subject matter.[55] For classical musics of East and West in which long and erudite traditions are considered by their exponents to be worthy of respect, teachers also come to exemplify and personify a tradition and are revered for their distinction as musicians and scholars. In such musics, many are called but few are chosen, and only the best and most loyal of the aspiring musicians are selected from among those who may aspire to a music's practice.[56] Other musical traditions aspire to the trappings of classical music. I think, for example, of references to classic rock; the academic teaching of rock, hip-hop, jazz, and traditional musics; and the cadres of distinguished musicians, teachers, and scholars of these traditions. Loyalty to a music is inspired by the respect exponents have for each other and for the tradition. In the musical traditions with which I am familiar, respect is accorded those who exemplify virtuosity and faithfulness to the rules governing a tradition as well as the courage to break those rules in innovative ways and thereby transform the tradition. Aside from the spiritual power that may be manifested by musicians or adherents to their performances, loyalty is demonstrated in a deep respect on the part of musicians and public alike to this music. Loyalty may be commanded by those in power, and the musicians themselves may convey power in their performances, but loyalty is, at root, a matter of respect for the music itself and for those whose music it is.

Loyalty also involves adherence to and mutual regard for others within the musical and educational community. It is hard to imagine how one can remain faithful, persistent, and patient in the absence of a community of like-minded others with whom one shares beliefs and practices. Maxine Greene highlights the importance of community in shaping one's imagination of how things might otherwise be.[57] In their performances, chamber musicians demonstrate loyalty not only to the music they are playing but to their fellow musicians who make it together. Each seeks to excel while wishing the same for the others, and all are acknowledged for their contributions. All have important parts to play in cooperatively creating and re-creating this music. Respect for one's fellows is as critical as respect for music qua music. As such, a specific performance becomes a link in a chain of performances that stretches back through time to remembered musicians, performances, and stories that gave rise to this music and these musicians. This performance also becomes a means of embracing their individuality while at the same time unifying them as a performing group.

Beyond respect, loyalty is manifested in affection, devotion, and even reverence. Duty alone may not satisfy as a motivation for fealty to a person or tradition. Rather, when respect transforms into appreciation and delight in the subject matter and people with whom one associates, close and long-term bonds are forged in loyalty, and the whole takes on a sacred or spiritual dimension. As with reverence, there is the sense of standing on holy ground in the face of awe and mystery. As with fidelity, not only does one live a dutiful life and fulfill one's obligations to a musical tradition or to those with whom one has chosen to associate, but duty is colored with affection and warmth of regard. When difficulties emerge along the way, as they must surely do, loyalty to these people and musics emerges as much out of love as respect. One is better able to persist and to be patient over the longer term when one loves what one believes and does.

Commitment is another crucial aspect of loyalty. In former times, oath taking was a solemn and formal occasion at which one swore one's allegiance to causes and people, and one's word was one's bond. One's honor was at stake, and one bound oneself in an obligation to service that was unbreakable unless one should be released from it by the other person or by death. One's integrity was at stake, and an oath required a transparency and consistency of one's words and actions with the oath taken. At a time in which teaching's historic character as a calling or vocation is too often devalued as a mere source of livelihood, loyalty reminds us of the commitment and sacred calling that teaching and learning once manifested and that they might still possess. Iris Yob is among those to argue for the value of schooling that possesses this sacred character not only in religiously sponsored education but more broadly in general education.[58] Construing education as enculturation necessitates music teachers cultivating a way of life and exemplifying it for their students. Inducting students into a way of life is also evident in various grounding metaphors and models of music education that have been evident since antiquity and exemplify a spiritual character. In a host of differing ways, personal commitments and allegiances to musical traditions are at the heart of musical instruction, and loyalty fosters and expresses these commitments to belief and a way of life.[59]

Among its contributions, loyalty potentially transforms music and education in profoundly spiritual and humane ways. As they commit to following a vocation or way of life and to each other, musicians, teachers, and learners find meaning and discover dignity in what they do. Although music and education may not be valued highly in contemporary Western societies, both activities stand for grand purposes and lofty ends.[60] They point to the betterment of society and the enrichment of individual experience, to the cultivation of humanity, civility, mutual regard, inclusivity, and empowerment. They offer transcendent and immanent experiences that make life worth living well. They point beyond the material to the spiritual, to what Langer terms the "presentational" or performative—the life of feeling beyond those things that can be expressed discursively or propositionally through words, mathematical symbols, and the like.[61] Writing especially to teachers of religion and the arts, Yob points to the power of myth, ritual, and music among the arts in cultivating spiritual experience beyond merely material educational ends.[62]

Loyalty is also the glue that bonds and strengthens social practices of music. In solidifying the personal ties between music musicians and audiences, loyalty helps to link expectations to actions. Through participating in musical rituals, it strengthens the shared beliefs and practices of the musical community. These shared practices become part of a social tradition that is transmitted from one generation to the next. The continuity of these expectations and practices provides stability in the tradition. As it solidifies over time, the tradition is also systematized, codified, and more easily transmitted by didactic means. This clarity of expectations on the part of musicians and their publics further serves as a means of binding the musical community together around shared musical beliefs and practices. Institutionalizing music also codifies the means of its transmission; it provides a basis for musicians to gain a livelihood and devote themselves fully to its practice, and it potentially enriches this musical tradition.

Loyalty also contributes to the quality of instruction by focusing on the interpersonal attraction that enhances the instructional process. The "reciprocal empathy" between teacher and student, in which loyalty is a key component, is typical particularly of studio instruction in the Western classical tradition.[63] I have hypothesized that this small-group and individual instruction in which teachers and students choose each other, what and how they study, and where there is mutual regard is among the most effective and productive forms of musical instruction.[64] Its success lies partly in the role of individual choice and commitment of teacher to student, student to teacher, and student to student. This affection colors the ways in which teachers and students communicate with each other, whether musically or pedagogically. Daniel Trifonov and his teacher Sergei Babayan illustrate this loyalty at work. The love between them is deeply spiritual and expressed musically in their joint performances. On embarking on a professional career, rather than distance himself from Babayan, Trifonov retained strong ties to his teacher, revering him while also bringing his own artistic acumen to his performances. Their joint performances are magical and unified, and their separate roles of artist teacher and artist student seem to be lost. Each brings something complementary to the performance: from Babayan, a maturity, assurance, and rhythmic intensity; from Trifonov, a melodic liquidity and virtuosic intensity. The musical fruits of loyalty are there to see and hear.[65]

Among its detractions, loyalty may be coerced, and feeling between teacher and student may be manipulated. The possibilities of coercion and manipulation, especially in the teacher-student relationship, may reinforce rather than challenge the unequal power relationship in music instruction. Abuse of power, manipulation, intimidation, and other forms of coercion may create a façade of loyalty that is forced rather than freely given, undemocratic rather than democratic. As Dewey might say, this coercion can be miseducative because it may stunt and hinder student growth rather than assist it. Where music is strongly institutionalized, expectations are codified, social relationships between musicians, teachers, and the music's public are hierarchically ordered, and music serves as an agent of power (as it often does), loyalty reinforces traditional power relationships when subverting and overthrowing them may be required. Codifying and systematizing beliefs and practices may also cause exponents and the music's public to lose the spirit of the ideas that prompted them. Loyalty may fail to critique these relationships and ideas when they need to be unmasked and interrogated. The ever-present possibility of abuse of power requires rethinking loyalty in the sense of understanding an act of critique as an instance of loyalty rather than disloyalty. Seeing loyalty this way entails being critical for the sake of making the musical tradition and the means of its transmission more humane and civil and cultivating the circumstances for creative expression on the part of the music's exponents. Still, those in the possession of power within a musical tradition may thwart efforts to contest those power relationships that preclude rich artistic expression and inclusive and humane approaches to music education; they may cast critique as an act of disloyalty subject to punishment or discipline.

Requiring loyalty as a precursor to instruction, as is the case in some Eastern classical music traditions, can be elitist and authoritarian. For music teachers desirous of attracting a large population to the musics being studied in the context of publicly supported schools, it is difficult, even if possible, to provide the types of musical instruction that rely on choice in the ways that studio instruction can. Throughout its history in the West, school music has been a means of general education in which the purpose is not so much to prepare exponents of a musical tradition as to introduce them to various musics with the intent of providing a basis for more informed musical choices. Still, some school music teachers audition students for membership in their classes and ensembles and exclude those who fail to demonstrate loyalty. The demand for loyalty as a precursor to instruction can be read as undemocratic when students are excluded from acquiring knowledge that they need to possess to make informed decisions about the musics to which they will be loyal. Demanding loyalty as a precursor to instruction opens the possibility of excessive elitism and an authoritarian approach to instruction inconsistent with the claims of general music education in decent societies.

In unpacking the interrelated values of fidelity, persistence, patience, and loyalty, I emphasize their association with vital traditions and metaphors of the master and apprentice evident in music and education. Fidelity connotes integrity, truthfulness, and allegiance to ideas and practices and its commitment to duty; persistence emphasizes the need for holding on to convictions and practices and enduring over the long haul in the face of obstacles; patience highlights calmness, endurance, and willingness to defer gratification; and loyalty highlights respect, faithfulness, mutual regard, affection, reverence, and commitment and is the glue that binds together musical and educational communities. Although the values of fidelity, persistence, patience, and loyalty offer important contributions to music and education, they are ambiguous and potentially flawed. The crucial challenges raised for musicians and educators include practical matters of determining approaches that express the best each value offers while avoiding the worst and applying this value in ways suitable to their own musical and educational situations. Such decisions also need to be made individually and collectively in ways that embrace the humanity at the center of music and education. Still, without these values, the professions of music and education, the quality of musicianship, and the interest and understanding of musical audiences will falter for lack of excellence, intelligence, and commitment fostered by fidelity, persistence, patience, and loyalty.

EIGHT

Curiosity, Imagination, Wonder, and Open-Mindedness

CURIOSITY, IMAGINATION, WONDER, AND OPEN-MINDEDNESS are among the values long associated with musical and educational thought and practice. Embracing them means thinking of music and education as profoundly intellectual and passionate undertakings. As with the values of love, friendship, desire, devotion, joy, happiness, pleasure, and celebration, they light up life; as with reverence, humility, awe, and spirituality, they open to things of sense, spirit, and that which lies beyond the mundane and ordinary world of human experience. Rather than the qualities of steadfastness, perseverance, conviction, and consistency that are necessary for fostering traditions as living things associated with the values of fidelity, persistence, patience, and loyalty just discussed, these values have a very different cast. They relate particularly to encountering and fostering change, navigating novelty, experiencing surprise and awe in the presence of virtuosity, and demonstrating humility in the face of human fallibility and mortality. In his essay "Music and the Last Intellectuals," John Shepherd urges the importance of regarding music as a humanity. He argues that music constitutes a part of a well-rounded cultural education, and its study is critical to understanding what it is to be a civilized human being.[1] Although some teachers and musicians think of music and education as humanities, too many emphasize practical musical and pedagogical skills. In taking stock of the interlocking and overlapping values of curiosity, imagination, wonder, and open-mindedness for music and education, and in emphasizing transformation rather than tradition, I examine each in turn and sketch some of their possible contributions and detractions.

CURIOSITY

I dig beneath the ordinary dictionary usage of the word *curiosity* and its pejorative connotations. It is variously defined as the "desire or inclination to know or learn about anything, [especially] what is novel or strange," "inquisitiveness" regarding "trifles or matters which do not concern one," and persons or things that are regarded as strange, surprising, or odd. Here, I distinguish between curiosity and imagination. Curiosity's interest is in the offbeat and unknown; imagination refers to the process of creating mental images. One may be involved in the other. Curiosity may prompt imagination just as imagination may awaken curiosity. Curiosity relates to qualities of things as well as people, to thought as well as action, and is often applied to the work of artists, musicians, and scientists. For example, it once referred to a "curious or ingenious art" or "experiment," a "vanity, nicety, refinement," and a "scientific or artistic interest; the quality of a curioso or virtuoso; connoisseurship."[2] Although others have described curiosity as an educational disposition, my present purpose is to show it as a musical and educational value.[3] In revealing some of its contributions and detractions, I suggest that curiosity constitutes a somewhat mixed blessing.

Among its qualities, curiosity connotes an interest in that which is strange, odd, or novel and out of the realm of ordinary experience. In music, this strangeness, oddness, or novelty is immediately apparent in musical sounds, sights, beliefs, and practices that seem peculiar to those who are unfamiliar with them. The music may seem to be a curiosity, and it may attract or repel those who encounter it for the first time. Learners are often very interested in others and things beyond their experience that seem extraordinary, unfamiliar, and strange. At first, students might be intrigued by music in a fanciful or intuitive way that sparks their interest and focuses their attention. Initially, the otherness of this music may prompt their curiosity. As the initial impulse is transformed into sustained interest,[4] they come to better understand the different other, and curiosity may be assuaged for the moment. Hopefully, teachers redirect their students' attention back to themselves and their musical commonplaces so that the beliefs and practices with which they are identified are critically examined and their curiosity is further prompted. In the process of finding other musics to be strange and being curious about this apparent strangeness of the other, I think of curiosity as Janus faced; one's gaze, first outward, shifts inward to better understand oneself and the musics that constitute one's heritage. One grasps how others might see one's heritage as other and strange. I think of the other as subject rather than object. That is, whatever is initially strange is approached respectfully and empathetically as subject rather than object in a manner consistent with Martin Buber's *I-Thou* relationship.[5] This attitude in assuaging musical curiosity enables teachers and students to better understand the initial strangeness of others' and their own musics. In this way, they come to a broader view of common humanity in its diversity. I also acknowledge that cultivating curiosity is sometimes about creating impulses through the presentation of that which may be initially novel, jarring, and even distasteful to learners. It entails coming to understand these dissonances, grasping their relationships to that which is familiar, arriving at a more constructively critical understanding of oneself and one's place in the world, and being changed by the process.

Curiosity also involves an attention to detail. Percy Scholes recognizes this important aspect of aesthetic experience and employs it in his design of musical appreciation programs for school-age children and adults.[6] For him, attention to artistic and musical details can be readily cultivated by a sustained focus on developing skills of knowing what and how to notice musically. Attending to musical details is a sensual undertaking that relies especially on ear, eye, and touch. The thought involved in curiosity melds sense and intellection, and the details are sensed immediately and intuitively as they are also reflected upon. Such thought may have an affective component evident in feeling.[7] Since attending to musical details necessitates noticing intellectual, sensory, and affective qualities, cultivating curiosity in music education requires that teachers provide opportunities for their students to notice and express this array of qualities. This attention to detail is manifested not only in an ability to discriminate between these qualities but carefulness in valuing discriminations. In education, teachers and students care about the details they notice because they care about and respect the people involved and the subject matter. In this view, curiosity is a manifestation of learners' sense of fallibility about what they do not know and respect for people with whom, and things with which, they come in contact; it is evident in noticing and taking an interest in the details.

Curiosity also connotes an inquisitive interest that pursues knowledge in ways that may appear to be intrusive to others. This desire to know pushes against the boundaries erected by powerful interests and the guardians of musical traditions; it reaches beyond acceptable limits toward the unknown. Where musical practices also express power, are associated with the supernatural, or constitute the means of livelihood protected by exponents, secrets are protected, and musical knowledge is safeguarded against excessive prying by those judged as unworthy.[8] Musical knowledge must be safeguarded because it conveys spiritual, political, economic, and familial power. For much of musical history and in many of the world's musical traditions, the onus is on students to acquire musical knowledge and skill. Knowledge is bequeathed only to those deemed by the guardians and exponents of a tradition as worthy of receiving it. In the West, although universalistic educational values are pervasive in general education, studio instruction is premised on students' curiosity. Teachers selectively bequeath their instruction to those students they deem sufficiently curious, talented, and trustworthy. The common practice of auditioning students for entry to studios and musical ensembles is one means of winnowing those students whom teachers are prepared to teach from those they are not.[9]

Among its benefits, a disposition to curiosity grounds student-centered approaches to learning driven by students' need and desire to know.[10] Student curiosity about the subject matter intrinsically motivates them to further learning. Teachers respond to their students' interest, offer knowledge that students find intriguing and genuinely interesting, and selectively prompt further student interest. In contrast to what Paulo Freire might call "banking" education, this approach is liberating to students and is intended to build on student interest and desire.[11] Instruction is designed to empower students to learn for themselves rather than rely passively on teachers to provide information to them. This inquiry-based approach takes advantage of serendipity and the individuality of each student and tends toward diverse outcomes. Instruction often manifests an improvisatory and rhapsodic character that is not easily standardized but is consonant with an artful education.

The expansive and open-ended educational process prompted by curiosity seeks to deepen and broaden musical understandings and widen musical horizons. Rather than focusing only on exemplary works within a musical tradition, this approach disrupts the canon by revealing counterexamples or exploring odd and different examples that are not normative. This pluralistic approach to music reveals the ambiguity of expectations even within a specific tradition. Curiosity challenges the normativity of expectations and opens the prospect of differences as well as commonalities within or between traditions. When it moves beyond a single tradition, curiosity expands musical perspectives and enables musicians to better grasp the character of the traditions of which they are practitioners from their own and from others' perspectives. Such a process can be unsettling and discomforting to learners, but it fosters humility as they come to understand the diverse ways in which people come to know and experience music. Beginning with knowns and pressing outward toward unknowns, learners grasp how to negotiate being at the edge of their knowledge and skill. As their understanding widens, they gather confidence in confronting apparent musical and cultural difference and otherness. These skills and confidence are particularly important in a world of musical and cultural "multiplicities and pluralities."[12]

Curiosity prompts a comparative educational approach as learners explore similarities and differences within and beyond a musical piece or practice, between aspects that are normative and those that are not, and between various musical traditions, styles, and forms. Comparison allows learners to pursue their musical interests and understand their relation to similar and different musics. Rather than thinking of different musical traditions as incommensurate, this approach fosters an interest in underlying similarities between different musics and the common humanity that is expressed in them.[13] Grasping these commonalities ironically enables learners to make sense of and value the significant differences within and between musical practices. They may seek to meld aspects of musical traditions and learn from different others. This melding process may bring about transformations in the musical traditions themselves.

Music education is also queered in the process. While the word *queer* has been applied in a specialized sense to the different gendering of music and music education, I focus on its ordinary meanings applied to human experience and interpret this word more broadly to value different musical practices that interrogate, subvert, threaten, undermine, and otherwise transform taken-for-granted rules and expectations that have become commonsensical. In his genealogy of queer theory and writing at the turn of the twenty-first century, William Turner admits the slipperiness of the term and thinks of it as a conglomeration of different conceptions.[14] My sense is that the term remains ambiguous as writers resist hard boundaries and embrace the amorphous and dynamic quality of its conceptions. Amid this growing literature, musicologists such as Philip Brett, Elizabeth Wood, Gary Thomas, and their colleagues, Doris Leibetseder, Judith Peraino, and Jodie Taylor, excavate the musical queer in classical, rock, and popular traditions; educational theorists such as Nelson Rodriguez, Wayne Martino, Jennifer Ingrey, Edward Brokenbrough, and their colleagues explore "critical concepts" at the intersection of education and queer studies; and writers such as Elizabeth Gould, Karin Hendricks, June Boyce-Tillman, and their colleagues examine the notion of queerness and its relationship to spirituality, music, and education.[15] The word *queer* that Gould thinks of figuratively as "alchemy" and as exemplifying "ecstatic abundance" shares much in common with my broader use of the term.[16]

Jane Roland Martin makes the point that students are intrigued by the musically queer, or those songs with lyrics that are out of the ordinary and that stick like "molasses" throughout a lifetime so that they are still remembered and can be sung from memory in old age.[17] Focusing on the musically odd and queer, especially when undertaken comparatively, can help the young come to value eccentricity and individualism and gain the courage to follow their own bliss and accept their individual interests and gifts even when they run counter to those of the majority of others. Students may come to see that art is often an expression of and about queerness, oddness, and striking representations out of the ordinary; musical pieces are memorable for their unabashed individuality and in their difference from the norm. So curiosity becomes the basis for a musical education in pursuit and embrace of queerness in the rich panoply of its possibilities.

Among its detractions, curiosity's prejudicial sense of nosiness and lack of respect for boundaries, secrets, and personal privacy may be intrusive and may jeopardize interpersonal relationships. It may undermine the trust and openness to others that is necessary in building educational communities in music and put different others at risk of disclosure. Reading David Gillham's novel *City of Women*, a depiction of the lives of women in wartime Berlin, I realize anew how, although it is tempting to consider secrets as sources of power over others and seek to uncover them, at times throughout history they have held the key to survival.[18] In Indian classical traditions, aside from transmitting knowledge from one generation to another, musical secrets were crucial to economic survival just as they were in Western classical music and jazz.[19] Knowledge is power, and controlling access to it, as in musical guilds and unions, protected musicians' livelihoods.[20] Preparing large numbers of people for musical performance careers without a thought to their ability to earn a livelihood exacerbates the difficulties of finding work as a musician and makes it harder for musicians to survive amid mounting competition from others. Viewed from the perspective of protecting musical livelihoods, knowing musical secrets is a mixed blessing. Musicians opposed to what I have described as the Boston School Music Movement in the mid-nineteenth century, in which music was introduced as a subject into the common schools of Boston, Massachusetts, and others in the early twentieth century such as Émile Jaques-Dalcroze worried about the negative impact of "pretenders." These are the unmusical or unskilled people who can "clutter" the educational system and the musical world and detract from those who are gifted musically.[21]

Flitting from one novelty to the next fails to provide enough educational direction or establish a sense of typical practices required to thoroughly understand a musical tradition. Notwithstanding the tendency of musical canons to be exclusive, sexist, and ethnocentric, establishing a clear sense of a musical practice requires knowing its musical canon.[22] A music's beliefs, practices, rules, and values are evident in its central tendencies and typical examples. Although the odd, queer, and marginal instances are also important, it is crucial for those who desire to become exponents of a musical practice to know its tradition and the basis for its rules and expectations. Since musical practices involve the mastery of practical skills and these need to be developed in orderly progression, careful instructional planning is needed.[23] Organizing around typical instances provides for clear focus and an economical approach to acquiring and mastering the skills required in a musical practice, especially when least-cost approaches to musical instruction are often required.

Learner-centric approaches to education that rely on curiosity also potentially fail to value traditional teacher-led instruction. They may take insufficient notice of the wisdom and advantages of the "banking" education that Freire decries but that may have important educational benefits. Not every student is inquisitive about subject matter that teachers consider of great importance. Where teachers are skilled exponents of a musical practice and students do not know what to be curious about, their curiosity can be awakened and emerge during or after teacher-directed instruction. Relying exclusively on curiosity as the impetus for learning may fail to take advantage of teacher knowledge and expertise in a musical tradition and miss out on what the teacher potentially brings to the instructional situation. Musician-teachers who know a tradition intimately can select repertoire and instructional approaches that provide their students with a comprehensive and intimate knowledge. Viewed this way, "banking" education provides a valuable depository on which students can draw in the future.

IMAGINATION

The word *imagination* was originally borrowed from the French and Latin. Its ordinary dictionary meaning refers to the capacity of "forming images or concepts" and the active process of creating "internal images or ideas of objects and situations not actually present to the senses." Within philosophy, imagination has also taken on technical meanings relating to aspects of mind "considered as engaged in imagining" or "a person's mind, or a part of it, represented as the place where images, ideas, and thoughts are produced and stored, or in which they are contained."[24] It is understood literally and figuratively, dynamically and statically. This ambiguity is represented, for example, in Mary Reichling's model of musical imagination constituted of four interrelated facets: reason, intuition, feeling, and perception.[25] Rather than examine its ontological character, my present focus is on its function as a musical and educational value. To this end, I unpack some of its salient features, briefly sketch its contributions to and detractions from music and education, and demonstrate that its value is a two-edged sword.

Among its characteristics, pedagogical and musical imagination constitutes an ability to recall memories of past experiences and foresee what is theoretically possible and has yet to come into being in the phenomenal world. The capacity for foresight involves being able to consider "future or potential actions or events" without them necessarily being present in the phenomenal world.[26] One way to think of these future potentials is to consider imagination as a sort of conceptual or abstract plan that may range between two extremes—the fanciful or unrealistic and the feasible and applicable. At first, musicians may not foresee this plan fully or perfectly in all its particularities. Gradually, as they seek to realize it musically, the closer it appears to be; it becomes clearer as it may sometimes seem to recede from them. Some musicians may have a fully formed conception or compelling vision at the outset while for others, the conception or vision seems to be modified or transformed along the way. Vernon Howard calls these two contrasting theories of artistic imagination the Athena and Penelope perspectives.[27] For Athena, imagination comes with the force of clear foresight; for Penelope, imagination emerges throughout the creative process. Howard would probably agree that artists may fall anywhere on this continuum. Whether the foresight seems clear at outset or emerges along the way, memory and conception work hand in hand. The capacity exists to conceive of an abstraction, be it idea or action, ahead of its application to, or realization in, theory or practice. Nor does foresight apply just to artistic or other fields in which theory is applied in practice. The derivation of a new mathematical formula or physical theory entails foresight and the ability to draw on known entities in deriving new ones.

Imagination also has the force of expectation. It is the "person's impression as to what is likely"—namely, an "expectation, anticipation." This expectation is active in the sense that thought is linked to action as in the "action of picturing mentally."[28] Such is the power of these images that people fully expect to see them. They already exist in the mind's eye; they are imminent to their creators. Whatever the words, mathematical symbols, sounds, colors, shapes, or materials about or in which people are thinking, images present with such immediacy and animating conviction and force that people are willing and even eager to act on them. These images possess a dynamic quality and "livingness" or "liveliness" that is compelling to their creators and, depending on the skill in their creation, to those who witness or partake in them in the phenomenal world. This assumption lies at the heart of Susanne Langer's analysis of artistic performance.[29] Despite philosophical criticisms of her theory, musicians and artists find her aesthetic theory to be compelling because she seems to have caught the feeling of what they are up to when they create art.

Imagination is a holistic thought-felt-sensed experience that relates the phenomenal and the abstract, the mind and sensory perception, reason and intuition, thought and emotion. There is a strong perceptual component to imagination—namely, "the capacity by which the mind integrates sensory data in the process of perception."[30] Accomplishing this integration necessitates remembering ideas and practices in the past and reconstructing and transforming experience into new possibilities. Various modes of reasoning, be they deductive, inductive, or analogical, are complemented by a gestalt or inductive sense of the whole that seems immediately present. This thought is associated with emotion in what Langer describes as "feeling" or Israel Scheffler and Iris Yob describe variously as "cognitive emotions" and "emotional cognitions."[31] These thoughts and emotions are grounded in a bodily experience that also entails the senses and even the passions. Combining these elements in multiple ways and to differing degrees further suggests that imagination comprises elements that are situational in that they differ from one person to another, one project to another, one time to another, and one place to another.

This ambiguity of imagination resonates well with human situations in which ambiguities, differences, and multiplicities also abound. As Scheffler notices, ambiguity is more common than not in human discourse.[32] In the diverse realms of languages, sciences, and arts, imagination offers ways of making meaning in the face of ambiguities. Unmasking erroneous propositions, ambiguities, and anomalies necessitates innovative and divergent ways of thinking about ideas and evidence and proposing novel and hopefully more authentic and robust ways to think about them. Human propositional discourse about the known and unknown is nuanced and ambiguous. The arts are constructed around ambiguity, and they demand imaginative ways of thinking about and doing them. Maxine Greene thinks especially of the power of community in shaping individual and collective imagination, and the multiplicities and pluralities to which it gives rise.[33] It may seem that instrumental music devoid of textual reference and association is particularly ambiguous and dependent on imagination. Still, music's figurative character is such that imagination is needed even when text or title is present, musical elements are arbitrary, or the music is well-known.

As a creative act, imagination is often inferred from the construction of artistic or innovative products. There is good reason why imagination is defined artistically as the "mind's creativity and resourcefulness in using and inventing images, analogies, etc." or applied to those who possess "poetic or artistic genius or talent."[34] In the invention and construction of commonplace things that have utilitarian value, imagination is ascribed to those things that represent leaps beyond the ordinary or prosaic. Musical imagination is evident in dramatic sonic transformations over the past decades, exemplified in the development of new scale systems, new acoustic instruments, and new forms of electronically produced and manipulated sounds.

Among its benefits, imagination offers ways to think divergently and innovatively that are necessary for sentient beings to flourish. Imagination has enabled pervasive innovation, technological change, and global interconnectedness, and its cultivation through education in and through the arts is crucial to general education. For this reason, Herbert Read believes that art needs to organize education.[35] Howard regards the arts as a metaphor for general education and argues that the learning of all subjects needs to be infused with a spirit of imagination and creative expression.[36] Northrop Frye suggests that culture is a manifestation of human imagination at work. Imagination is an appropriate value not only for our time—a time of pervasive change—but for human civilization throughout time.[37] One of Frye's principal educational commentators, Deanne Bogdan, argues for the need for "re-educating imagination," for critiquing culture and transforming it.[38] Imagination is also possessed by other animals and is an objective of artificial intelligence.[39] Sentient beings are able to shape their actions proactively in the phenomenal world because they can remember and foresee; integrate sense, thought, reason, and intuition in holistic ways; and create images of what is not yet evident in theory and practice. These abilities are essential, for example, in fostering peace, civility, and culture and preserving the world's ecosystem. Greene suggests that imagination is transformative. It "lessens social paralysis," "awakens a sense of decency and humanity," and "offers life, hope, and light."[40] If life as we know it is to flourish on this planet, the realities of the Anthropocene require imagination in finding ways to live in harmony with the natural world.[41]

Aside from its practical value as a means of creating and sustaining civilization and culture and fostering a sustainable interrelationship between humans and the physical environment, imagination has a humane and spiritual purpose. It enables expression of inner thought and feeling and fosters ways of being, thinking, and doing that bring inherent satisfaction and a sense of well-being. For example, Abraham Maslow thinks of "self-actualization" as the highest level of his hierarchy of human needs.[42] Self-actualization is a highly imaginative process in which people derive satisfaction from their situations, are absorbed in them, and can express their thought and feeling in deeply spiritual and satisfying ways. In a different vein, Mihaly Csikszentmihalyi coins the psychological concept of "flow" to evoke the absorption, self-forgetfulness, and effortlessness of creative action in which people are carried along in the moment by a dynamic process.[43] These modern conceptions of imagination at work have their counterpart in the ancient world, where imagination was crucial in the purposes and means of education. Plato viewed imagination as one of the highest levels of abstract thought and play as an educational aim. This play has a serious purpose and is disciplined in its methods.[44] Plato conceives philosophical discourse as the highest level of education and conducts it playfully and conversationally through story, analogy, and metaphor. Imagination's spiritual value in enabling human cultural and artistic expression is particularly compelling at a time of rampant incivility, inhumanity, violence, terror, and war.

The growth of artificial intelligence, the replacement of people by machines in many aspects of life and work, and the pervasiveness of and dependence on technology in everyday life require imagination as a potential solace and respite from technology.[45] Technologies can become oppressive and crowd out other opportunities to think imaginatively and freely and to interact socially in the phenomenal world. Disengaging from the constancy of this technology is a pressing psychological and social need in a technologically driven world.[46] Rather than being enslaved by technology, we need a humane existence that also allows us to express ourselves artistically and think through sometimes complex and important existential questions independent of it. The arts offer opportunities, spaces, and times free of the claims of technological devices that demand our constant attention. They also open ways to imaginatively use technology in productive ways while also providing respite from pervasive technology that can dehumanize existence.

Imagination has its detractions, however. Focusing on imagination alone or thinking of it just in terms of divergent thinking can take insufficient account of the value of convergent thought. Convergent thinking establishes and maintains normative rules that govern thought and practice and enable musical traditions to thrive. Musicians of all traditions with which I am familiar have strict expectations of what constitutes "right" or "correct" practice. Failing to attend to these beliefs and practices ultimately undermines and destroys musical practices. Social conduct is premised on the constancy of specific norms; without them, civilization and culture would dissolve. Because of this, among other reasons, music teachers naturally tend to be conservative in the sense of seeking to transmit these expectations. Imagination is certainly a part of this transmission, and the emphasis, at least at first, is principally on establishing certain convergent expectations and images. For example, Howard describes the singing teacher who has a student (let us think of a young tenor) who both knows and does not know what he is to do.[47] At first, this student is dependent on the teacher to show him the way and assist him in creating the kinds of imagery that are true to the vocal practice he seeks to acquire. Gradually, when he becomes a more skilled singer, the rules by which he was first directed or of which he was once a slavish follower may be selectively broken as he comes to respect, be governed by, and sometimes actively subvert or repudiate those rules.

Imagination also potentially overlooks the importance of closure and even of wisdom. Teaching only for openings may fail to notice the importance of teaching for closings, for bringing a sense of completion, understanding, mastery, and unity to the openings that have been forged. Such closure and completion underscore the importance of logic and reason by which openings are interrogated and commonalities and differences are grasped. True, reason is an aspect of imagination, broadly construed. Nevertheless, the purpose of such closure and wisdom is to encircle the known and to provide a clear sense of purpose for learners. Even though this articulated sense of completion potentially constitutes a springboard to further openings, closure is comforting, reassuring, and an important aspect of allowing learners to integrate what they are learning and make it their own. This closure also allows for reflection on the openings forged and introspection on their importance and relevance to one's already formed perspectives. Although crucial to learning, closure is sometimes forgotten in the emphasis on teaching for imagination and openings. Performing a musical piece constitutes a metaphor for this process. Openings without closings do not satisfy, and both are needed as the possibilities in a score or musical idea are explored, mined, and ultimately constricted. In this way, infinite possibilities become finite actualities that effect closure. Wisdom likewise comes as learners mine the possibilities and ultimately limit them in important ways. The musical discipline or practice of which one is an exponent affects these closures; musical ideas and practices are not only imaginative in forging openings but convergent in insisting on closings. So while imagination comprises an important value in learning, it cannot be the sole value.

Conceptions of a monolithic or unitary imagination are inadequate, yet construing imagination as a plurality of imaginations creates practical challenges for educational policy makers. The possibility of multiple intelligences, as Howard Gardner suggested in 1983, open the prospect of differing psychological "frames of mind" or ways of seeing the world.[48] Gardner's theory resonates with earlier philosophical views such as Philip Phenix's analysis of "realms of meaning" and Nelson Goodman's formulation of "ways of worldmaking."[49] Accounting for the additional complexities of such attributes as gender and gender identity, group membership, social class, ethnicity, ideology, and power in shaping the ways in which people see the world only complicates the situation further.[50] It becomes even more challenging for educational policy makers to specify the sorts of imaginations that need to be cultivated and the ways this should be accomplished. Consider, for example, the importance of taking into account life stages following the work of Erik and Joan Erikson in formulations of imagination.[51] In his portrayal of educational growth as perpetual and the educational process as lifelong, John Dewey forwards the view that education primarily concerns the young, and growth continues and imagination expands toward openings as ends become means to other ends.[52] The Eriksons have a different view in which people pass through life stages from youth to old age, and the differences are such that each stage seems to require a nuanced educational approach. Whereas in youth, imagination may be oriented toward openings and expansions and the educational focus may be toward growth, as one reaches middle age and through later life, imagination changes as people begin to seek a sense of closure that circles progressively inward. Music educators concerned to reach people at all of life's stages need to keep these differences in mind, and theories of imagination need to articulate the role that life changes have on forging closings as much as openings. Thinking of gender, ethnicity, language, religion, and life stage, among the host of other factors that affect imagination, raises the prospect that educational policy makers may oversimplify the complexities that abound in cultivating imagination. They may face significant challenges in envisaging the particularities of opening and closure, developing practical educational plans that confront this ambiguity, and taking account of the possibilities of multiple imaginings.

There is also a dark side to imagination. Greene worries about this potential for darkness especially regarding the problematic nature of freedom and the failure of imagination to escape slavery, subservience, and oppression. The practice of freedom never realizes its promise, and notwithstanding the possibilities it offers, it remains a never-ending struggle.[53] All openings and possibilities do not constitute goods. For example, the German Third Reich imagined a nation without minorities and the disabled. Educating for civility and humane ends repudiates such an imagination and the means to create it and welcomes people of diverse backgrounds and abilities. The prospect of imagination in service of both good and evil requires considering the specific purposes to which it is put and the means of achieving it. Without a consideration of these other educational goods, imagination falters as a value.

WONDER

The word *wonder* comes from the Old Saxon and Dutch and has deep roots in the English language. It is thought of ambiguously as noun, adjective, and verb; process and product; thought and action. As a noun, its ordinary dictionary meaning refers to an "object of astonishment (usually implying profound admiration)," although in the past it sometimes connoted an "evil or shameful action." It is often associated with a "deed performed, or an event brought about by miraculous or supernatural power," be it "a miracle" or an "omen or portent." Wonder also refers to an "emotion excited by the perception of something novel and unexpected, or inexplicable; astonishment mingled with perplexity or bewildered curiosity."[54] As a verb, it means such things as "to ask oneself in wonderment; to feel some doubt or curiosity (*how, whether, why,* etc.); to be desirous to know or learn" or "to be greatly surprised; to marvel."[55] Beyond this array of ordinary meanings, I sketch aspects related to wonder construed as a musical and educational value and tease out some of its contributions and detractions.

I begin with the spiritual dimension of wonder, an idea proposed by Yob, among others in music education.[56] Wonder is at home in the sacred, in times and spaces set apart from ordinary lived life. It connects the natural world with the supernatural or with forces and events that strike awe and fear because of their inexplicability, sheer majesty, and power that lies beyond humanity's power to control. It concerns the deepest existential questions: Where did I come from? What is the purpose of my life? Is there life and existence and a future beyond death? The religions evoke wonder as people seek meaning to the cosmos and the place of humans within it. Supernatural events in religious narratives not only prompt wonder but enjoin the faithful to obey religious dictates. William James is among the early psychologists of religion to posit a human need for the religions as a means of providing comfort in facing daily life, illness, mortality, violence, terror, and war.[57] Not only are the religions sources of ethical values or virtues, but if music and education are to give meaning to the rest of life and concern the questions evocative of wonder, they need to be thought of and enacted as sacred enterprises.[58]

Wonder also acknowledges human fallibility. Lacking omniscience, human partial understanding of self and the world renders knowledge imperfect and inevitably, in some respects, wrong. This mystery and failure to grasp the complete picture means that when learners wonder, they cannot be assured of arriving at the whole truth. Howard posits the importance of reflection as a means of learning music, among other things. Still, that reflection is more or less guaranteed to arrive at an incomplete understanding. As with the other means of coming to know music he discusses—namely, instruction, example, and practice—reflection is bound to be open-ended and ambiguous.[59] One's wondering more or less assures this because one's perspectives are partial and fallible.

Wonder may be prompted not only by natural circumstances and events but by artistic creations, myths, and sacred rituals.[60] This is particularly evident in what Bogdan coins as the "shiver," "shimmer," and brilliant displays of musical virtuosity.[61] Some musical performances are so astonishing that they seem supernatural; words such as *magical*, *electric*, and *stunning* are often used to describe them. It is easy to slide into the romantic image of the musician as a priest standing between the supernatural and phenomenal worlds. In all the musical traditions of which I am aware, some musicians and performers so transcend expectations as to electrify their audiences. These performances are inspiring for those who observe them, and they play an important role in clarifying the limits and possibilities of musical practices.

Wonder is thought with emotional valence, be it cognitive emotions, emotional cognitions, or both.[62] This thought is also holistic and bodily in its combination of sense, emotion, intellection, and visceral response; it is so immediate and powerful as to prompt acknowledgment and action. A brilliant performance may evoke a moment of silence followed by thunderous applause, foot stamping, shouting, and other physical manifestations of appreciation. Alternatively, it may evoke hissing, booing, or exiting a performance that is disliked or feared. Whether joy or fear, approbation or dislike, there is an emotional and visceral response to wonder that impels one to action. Among the arts, music constitutes a powerful way in which wonder is experienced, and wonder-filled musical education is necessarily holistic in engaging mind and body.

Among its contributions, surrounding learners with music evocative of wonder tunes their ears and opens their eyes to possibilities of what they might achieve. It allows them to conceive of "visions of mastery" to which they can aspire.[63] Amazement and wonder at an artist's breathtaking brilliance, virtuosity, and effortlessness reveal the power of demonstration and example as a means of learning. Examples prompt imagination because they clarify possibilities and expectations and prompt wonder at how this demonstration was achieved. The more brilliant a performance, the higher future expectations may become. For this reason, Shinichi Suzuki is concerned with developing a beautiful violin tone by surrounding very young players with the sounds of exemplary violinists, so they internalize these sounds as normative and aspire to make or exceed them themselves.[64]

Wonder also renders music and education more spiritual and humane. Construed as a verb, wonder generates a student-centered form of learning. It relies on learners' desire to know and allows the possibility of doubt and curiosity along the way. As learners realize the limits of their present understanding, interrogate the answers to their questions, and ponder the mysteries they encounter, they grasp their fallibility, acknowledge their humanity, and embrace their individual interests, talents, and perspectives. Wonder widens the possibilities for learning experiences beyond traditional times and places and construes the whole of life as a learning opportunity. Still, musicians, teachers, and students need to be active learners and open to surprise and amazement. As Scheffler explains, cynicism and sectarianism are enemies of a wonder-filled education about "the many mansions" that are a teacher's heritage.[65]

As wonder evokes surprise, like curiosity, imagination, and open-mindedness, it prompts confidence and joy in learning. When learners are captivated by mystery and awe and startled by the unexpected, there is a heightened sense of adventure as new and different learning pathways open for exploration. Surprises add zest to the learning process and contribute to a sense that subject matter being learned is concerned with real and important questions and answers that may not be fully anticipated. Music teachers may evoke wonder through such means as exceptional and virtuosic performances, graphic imagery, high fidelity sound, and attendance at live performances. They can set musical problems that prompt students to wonder how they might be solved. The experience of wondering can be joyful as students ask better questions, gain confidence in engaging with the musically unexpected and even awesome, and better understand the phenomena that induce their wonder, and they are able to elicit wonder in others through musical performances and productions. In these and other ways, wonder fosters musical growth and mastery that, in turn, bring joy to students and their teachers. The confidence acquired in evoking, negotiating, and unmasking musical wonder can ripple out into other aspects of life.

Nevertheless, there is a dark side to wonder. Among its detractions, a focus on wonder may overemphasize results over the process of achieving them. It may prompt fear when the expected results are not forthcoming and learners are unable or unwilling to expend the effort needed to achieve brilliant results.[66] As noted earlier, many musical traditions employ inhumane methods of musical instruction—for example, beating students when they fail to produce correct performances.[67] In the West, some directors have advocated fear as an appropriate motivation for their instrumental ensembles. Unrealistically high expectations of students, especially those of average ability or musicality, may breed resentment, loss of self-esteem, and fear of discipline on the part of students when these expectations are not reached.[68] Fear and a loss of self-esteem may demoralize learners and musicians and have a miseducative result in stunting or precluding further development.

Excessive attention to creating performances that evoke wonder may fail to notice that virtuosity and technical brilliance and wizardry may mask a lack of depth and substance in musical interpretation. Attending just to the superficial aspects of musical performance that may dazzle audiences overlooks the virtues of simplicity and depth of interpretation that may not be outwardly brilliant but are recognized and valued by those who know this music well. Overanalyzing music and overemphasizing technical perfection may also destroy wonder. There is truth in the difference some writers have recognized between the surface of music and its depth and between the manner and substance of music.[69] I prefer to see musical surface and depth figuratively, as integrally interrelated, where the distinctions between them are matters of degree and nuance rather than discontinuous and discrete binaries. In pursuing wonderful performances, it is possible for musician-teachers to fail to notice the processes whereby music is made and received and forget the less dramatic but equally important claims of musical simplicity and its depth of possibilities. Aside from the moments of public performance, there are the invaluable times and places in rehearsals, practice sessions, and informal musicking where music is learned and enjoyed quite apart from the end of a flawless and brilliant performance before an audience. These may also be sources of wonder.

OPEN-MINDEDNESS

In ordinary usage, *open-mindedness* refers to the quality of being "receptive to new ideas" and "unprejudiced."[70] As with curiosity, imagination, and wonder, it concerns thoughts, attitudes, and emotional responses to novelty, difference, and dissonance that are expressed in actions. Here, I describe open-mindedness construed as a value that undergirds music and education and sketch some of its advantages and disadvantages.

Open-mindedness begins with moderation, an ancient idea that sees extreme positions as exclusive, problematic, and even dangerous. For Aristotle, the mean was a fraught situation betwixt too little and too much of a good thing.[71] Moderation is also subject to being too moderate at one extreme and insufficiently moderate at the other. Finding a point between extremes allows one to relish the broad array of possibilities between them; however, as Aristotle observed, the mean is easy to miss. Moderation allows one to dispassionately grasp the multiplicity of ideas and practices and categorize and evaluate them comparatively. In music and education, it requires negotiating the middle ground between ideological and methodological extremes and weighing the advantages and disadvantages of ideas and practices in coming to decisions about what to do and how to do it. Since every good, when taken to extremes, may open the possibility of evil, finding practical pathways between the pitfalls on every hand is a challenge. For teachers, this possibility requires thinking carefully about the ends of their instruction and the methods by which they do their work. For students, it requires imbibing habits of mind that critically reflect on what is learned formally and informally.[72] Without moderation in assessing the universe of possibilities, one is inevitably trapped in sectarianism, bigotry, and cynicism.

The receptivity characteristic of open-mindedness is demonstrated by a willingness to entertain novelty and difference. Embracing the differences among people and musics has exemplified the international practice of music education, as education generally. Philosophical writers on difference and cosmopolitanism in music education also argue that music educators should cultivate receptivity and welcome of the myriad ways in which people come to know music, the diverse musical practices around the world, and their place in music education.[73] This welcome is enshrined in teachers' love for and receptivity to students irrespective of their backgrounds, abilities, and attitudes.[74] It is also evident in the inclusion of the world's musical traditions in the music curriculum.[75] Whatever the ways in which this welcome is expressed, rather than immediately foreclosing possibilities, music teachers and their students need to suspend judgment for a time and consider constructively and critically those things that may initially jar, offend, or be too readily dismissed. Hospitality opens spaces and times where differences and dissonances are celebrated, ideas and practices are thoughtfully and carefully considered, and new possibilities may emerge.

Open-mindedness also stands against prejudice, cynicism, and dogmatism. Prejudice arises when past tradition is followed uncritically and new approaches are dismissed prematurely. When learners arrive at judgments too quickly based on their prior experience and knowledge without considering a wide array of other possibilities, deliberation and critical thinking are shortchanged and possibilities foreclosed. The learners' faith in the validity of their experience is such that approaches, methods, and materials that differ from their own are disparaged, and they are unwilling to consider alternative possibilities. They are impatient with deliberation and critical reflection and assert rather than test positions and practices. Cynicism reveals an unwillingness to hold to a position, even if warranted. As Scheffler notices, it constitutes a defense against the very real possibilities that one will surely be wrong at one time or another. Better to hold to no position or judge none worthy of assent than to see one's position(s) exposed as problematic in one way or another. Dogmatism defends against doubt by being unwilling to challenge one's ideas and practices. This closed mindset inevitably gives rise, in Scheffler's view, to sectarianism and a rigid adherence to beliefs and practices that brooks no dissent or critique.[76] Cynicism and dogmatism constitute different means of protecting one's beliefs and practices against the intrusion of novelty and difference. The rigidity these stances spawn inevitably causes musical traditions to ossify, living ideas to die and barriers to be erected between ideas, practices, and people. Open-mindedness, by contrast, welcomes doubt, difference, and dissent and offers possibilities to connect, meld, and otherwise mix differing people and the musical cultures they represent.

Doubt is an important aspect of open-mindedness. Recognizing one's fallibility and the impossibility of omniscience suggests that decisions must be made on imperfect and incomplete evidence. Skepticism and uncertainty about the merits of beliefs and practices tempers gullibility and enthusiasm in embracing ideas and practices and leaves one disposed to think that there must be something wrong with even the most enticing and cherished beliefs and actions. Being inclined to disbelief rather than belief, to see the dark side of prescriptions and proscriptions, and to challenge and criticize the arguments and evidence that underlie them leads to a search to refute them where possible. Science is predicated on doubt. It insists on maintaining an open mind and ensuring that all aspects of thought and practice are examined without prejudice or bias. Although doubt has been emphasized in scientific approaches to educational inquiry, it has been less evident in practical spheres such as music curriculum and instruction where methodological belief and orthodoxy have been cultivated. Embracing doubt, by contrast, repudiates what Thomas Regelski aptly terms music educational "methodolatry."[77] Instead, teachers develop provisional approaches and procedures that meet the needs of their students in their instructional situations.

Among its advantages, open-mindedness is particularly important in musical meaning making and practice where ambiguities, multiplicities, and pluralities abound. Here, musicians and teachers welcome divergent interpretations of musical scores and invite their fellows and students to embrace the variety of sights, sounds, beliefs, and practices of the world's musics even when their cherished beliefs and practices are challenged. Open-mindedness broadens the musical canon and encourages what Henry Giroux aptly terms "border-crossings" across the "soft boundaries" (as Claire Detels would say) of musical traditions.[78]

Even within a musical practice or piece, musicians, teachers, and their students consider alternative score readings or interpretations than those that are normative. Their reflections open pathways to differing compositional, improvisatory, or performative strategies. Because of this, music students and their teachers are encouraged to mine a host of musical possibilities. Their divergent interpretations give voice to myriad possibilities in musical scales, sounds, systems, performative techniques, and the like.

Open-mindedness also allows young and old to cope with pervasive societal and cultural changes, to better understand different others, and to exercise humility as they face the tensions and challenges in multicultural societies. Learners constructively criticize their societies and cultures and find points of common ground with different others that promote peace. Open-mindedness resists sectarianism, fundamentalism, and authoritarianism and fosters the confidence and ability to confront inhumanity and violence. A crucial aim of music education, as education generally, is the cultivation of dispositions that welcome and critique disparate world views. In emphasizing education for openings, Maxine Greene and Randall Allsup highlight the capacity of the arts and education to broaden educational horizons; they emphasize creative possibilities for people whose particular gifts, inclinations, and experiences predispose them to see the world differently from others.[79] Understanding the plethora of musical possibilities prompts humility when one realizes the limitations of one's own perspectives and practices and others' strengths and contributions. As musicians and educators embrace the dissonances, tensions, and opportunities that arise when musics and educational traditions intersect, meld, and sometimes conflict, it is possible to navigate them in ways that enrich these traditions and those who practice them.

Open-mindedness fosters the dynamic development and flexibility needed to adapt to grow and change. As Dewey observes, growth is central to education; when it is stunted or prevented, education becomes "mis-educative."[80] Open-mindedness seeks and finds solutions that foster growth. This humane approach to education emphasizes the mind and its development as a crucial objective of education. Better understanding of different others and their musical, artistic, and cultural practices helps to connect people to one another and provides the space for empathy to develop. When mind and heart are integrally linked, action cannot be far behind. These are the kinds of dispositions, habits of thought, feelings, and actions that are required in an education for democracy. As Donald Arnstine posits, the arts are particularly important in educating democratic dispositions.[81] My sense is that they accomplish this because open-mindedness is both required and cultivated in their study, and it is not surprising that they constitute a compelling educational metaphor. In opening possibilities for empathy, open-mindedness may also foster peace and tranquility in a world too often consumed by inhumanity, war, and violence.

Still, open-mindedness has its limits and detractions. Among other things, it may mask insufficient commitment to positions and principles and a lack of courage to advocate for them. Cynicism, or the refusal to believe, and radical relativism, or the unwillingness or inability to discriminate between the merits of differing positions, may fail to do the intellectual work of sifting through the various possibilities that claim one's attention. It may leave one rudderless in an ocean of differences and possibilities. Musical education is a profoundly ethical undertaking, and so teachers and students cannot be ethically neutral.[82] Every educational action reflects beliefs grounded in ethical commitments. Excavating a performer's repertoire or a music curriculum allows one to grasp a musician's, teacher's, or educational policy maker's ethical beliefs.[83] Irrespective of the degree to which musicians, music teachers, and their students are explicitly aware of these commitments, they are nevertheless implicit in decisions such as their repertory choices, instructional practices, and learning approaches. The further a performer delves into a musical tradition, the greater the imperative to commit to action. These commitments become consuming passions that foster the courage to defend or challenge the status quo. Whether it be Shostakovich navigating Soviet Realism, classical musicians resisting Mao's dictums in the Chinese Cultural Revolution, or popular musicians opposing the hegemony of the Western classical music establishment, courageous and principled action is required on the part of those who would challenge closed-mindedness.

I am often surprised by the power of closed-mindedness and the vulnerability of open-mindedness. Tyrants and authoritarian regimes thrive on people's willingness to abdicate their power to resist oppression. Open-mindedness sometimes seems to be the weaker cultural, social, and political force. This may be because, as Freire puts it, those who have been oppressed "carry the image of the oppressor within them."[84] Democracy thrives on open-mindedness and withers without it. In democratic societies, although ordinary people have a stake in their decision-making and can seek individual and collective happiness, authoritarians and powerful individuals can take advantage of and thwart the open-mindedness on which these societies depend. Democratic fragility and the associated vulnerability of open-mindedness require constant vigilance, resistance, and concerted effort on the part of musicians and educators to protect open-mindedness and the democracies predicated on it. The short-lived character of democracies throughout history suggests that too many people do not have the stomach for this task.

Hospitality at the center of open-mindedness has conceptual and ethical limits. Nel Noddings argues that one cannot care for everyone or everything equally; some persons and things are more deserving of one's care than others, and without limitations in what or whom one cares for or about, one exhausts oneself in diffuse caring that may have limited value.[85] Applied to education, her approach underscores the necessity of closing some instructional possibilities in order to open others. Her point echoes Scheffler's earlier observation that human choices have implications that inevitably close some possibilities as they open others.[86] The more one does of one thing, the less one can do another thing because of the available time, space, or energy. Such choices also limit the hospitality that can be extended to musics, cultures, beliefs, and practices. Assuming our first duty is to those who are closest whether by familial, religious, geographic, linguistic, or other ties, place is a crucial curricular consideration in music, as in all education.[87] For this reason, musical and educational decisions need to be taken close to the ground of the specific circumstances of music, teaching, learning, and instruction. While musicians and educators might agree on general principles that should guide this work, the ambiguities and diversity of perspectives and practices in music require that individual musicians, teachers, and their students make their own commitments. This relational and situational ethic requires that while philosophers might articulate theoretical possibilities, musicians, teachers, and students need to determine what they should do in their specific practical circumstances. While this may be a messy process, preserving open-mindedness requires it. The result is a tapestry of music educational ideas and practices that escapes a reality of musicians and teachers and their students marching in lockstep, eyes forward, looking to neither the right nor the left, as did Plato's cave dwellers chained in place and gazing on the shadows on the wall.[88]

Regarding the ambiguous and interrelated values of curiosity, imagination, wonder, and open-mindedness from the perspective of music and education, curiosity seeks knowledge and understanding and probes the limits of the known, is predicated on attention to detail, and can be construed pejoratively as inquisitiveness. Imagination creates powerful images and concepts that bring alive possibilities, requires memory and foresight, prompts expectations, is a holistic experience of mind and body that combines thought, feeling, and action, thrives on ambiguity, and is often inferred from artistic or innovative creations. Wonder ponders and bows before the unknown, mysterious, and ineffable. Open-mindedness welcomes the many ways of knowing and being in the world and, with clear-eyed reason, takes time to examine and weigh possibilities before discarding them, and thinks divergently and dispassionately. All these values play out in the phenomenal world and impact music educational practice in profound ways. Taken alone, none suffices. Although they reveal important advantages, when taken to extremes, they are potentially harmful. As musicians and educators wonder and are curious, imaginative, and open-minded, they can devise approaches that address the cultural and societal challenges of our time and meet the specific needs of students, teachers, and the public. These intellectual and practical challenges require the best minds to articulate and negotiate in all the varied circumstances in which music and education are carried on. I wonder what difference these values could make if we saw them in action more generally in music and education.

NINE

Wisdom, Understanding, Knowledge, and Mastery

THE QUARTET OF VALUES—WISDOM, understanding, knowledge, and mastery—that is the focus of this chapter relates to engagement with beliefs and practices that constitute the subject matter of musical instruction. As with curiosity, imagination, wonder, and open-mindedness, they have primarily to do with the mind and intellect, although, in their expansive and embodied character, they encompass theoretical and practical matters of existential significance. Musical traditions central to education are passed down formally and informally from one generation to the next and across a generation. As they are transmitted to and internalized by learners, they are also transformed as ideas are contested by exponents and challenged as one tradition rubs up against another. This living wisdom, understanding, knowledge, and mastery of the tradition is personified by its practitioners. As a "subject of great worth," the material of instruction is encountered individually and collectively by teachers and their students.[1] Ambiguities between theory and practice, subject matter and person, color notions of wisdom, understanding, knowledge, and mastery that I explore in this chapter. These values are nuanced and offer strengths and weaknesses for musicians and educators. Beginning with their ordinary meanings, I unpack each in turn, noting intersections between them. I examine what each value offers for music and education and why it is to be treated with caution.

WISDOM

The word *wisdom* has been rooted in the English language since Norse and Saxon times. The hero Beowulf possesses "wisdom" or the "capacity of judging rightly in matters relating to life and conduct."[2] This relationship to "soundness of judgment" and righteousness links wisdom to other values such as justice, equality, fairness, and inclusion. Although qualities of intellectual acumen in decision-making are resilient in the dictionary usage of this word, I regard them as necessary but not sufficient conditions for the notion of wisdom that I forward. Connecting wisdom with judgment and righteousness or "right doing" is a useful place to begin this analysis. Wisdom refers to an intellectual capacity demonstrated in the activities of decision-making and enactment. Invoking judgment suggests that wisdom necessitates acts of evaluation and appraisal. For Benjamin Bloom and his successors, such engagements reflect some of the highest levels of cognition that subsume knowledge and understanding and evidence capabilities of evaluating and assessing possibilities and making informed decisions about them.[3] While I prefer to see these decisions holistically, informed by sense and affect, they are also profoundly ethical in their invocation of "righteousness." As noted earlier, musical and educational decisions cannot be ethically neutral but invoke deeply held notions of what is "right"; wisdom is contingent on conceptions of what constitutes right belief and conduct. These conceptions are immanent and transcendent, individually formed and socially contested, rooted in religious and other moral prescriptions or proscriptions. As dynamic constructions, these ethical commitments need to be acknowledged as a bedrock of wisdom.[4]

Wisdom also relates to a special sort or degree of knowledge that is "high" and "abstruse." This advanced learning, "enlightenment," and "erudition" originally referred, especially in its early use, to such fields as philosophy and science. It was also used to denote "practical knowledge or understanding," such as "expertness in an art."[5] While this practical connotation seems to have fallen into disuse, I want to revive this meaning of wisdom. It relates not only to expertise in theoretical knowledge but also to practice—for example, expert musical performance, composition, improvisation, and production. The art and craft of musical practice exemplify musical wisdom that is interwoven with expertise in conceptual and theoretical perspectives on this practice. That it is abstruse refers to the quality of wisdom evident in erudite thought and practice. Wisdom values learning and expertise in knowledge and understanding of a subject, field, or practice that may not be widely shared. Reserving its use in this way prizes exceptionalism and excellence in thought and practice. The notion of enlightenment in this ancient use of the word *wisdom* suggests the metaphor of a sort or degree of knowledge that fills the mind, heart, and soul with light that is the antithesis of the darkness of stupidity and folly. This conception of erudition is not absolute. All along the way from elementary to advanced levels of theory and practice, it is possible to conceive of differing degrees of mastery, as June Boyce-Tillman and Keith Swanwick suggest in their cyclical theory of musical learning.[6] Notwithstanding its dynamic character, this evolutionary and relative view of wisdom values pursuit of excellence and mastery at every point along the educational process.

Alfred North Whitehead regards wisdom as a unity or integrity of knowledge that is cyclical in nature.[7] For him, wisdom occurs at the point of "generalization" at which one understands not only the constituent parts of a whole but the whole itself. In Whitehead's view, throughout the educational process, the romance of an intuitive grasp of this whole is transcended by instrumentalism in which one systematically grasps how all the parts are integrated into the whole. Instrumentalism is followed, in turn, by generalization, where romance and instrumentalism merge to become a richly informed intuitive, imaginative, and rational grasp of a contextualized whole. One cycle follows upon another with the end of generalization or wisdom in an education that is, for Whitehead, "religious" in that it "inculcates duty and reverence."[8] All the parts are articulated and interdependent with the others in a unity as learners come to see the significance of a whole as more than the sum of its parts.

Although Whitehead's view might be beguiling, I see wisdom in more dialectical terms. For me, the parts do not always neatly fit together; some aspects are in tension or even conflict with others, the pieces that comprise the whole have their own lives and identities, and differing wholes constitute alternative ends. In regarding wisdom as dialectical, although I find myself in agreement with Plato, who valued those who grasp the "one and the many" in coming to know wisdom, I would go further.[9] Rather than a monolithic view of wisdom, I embrace a plurality of wisdoms. Since individuals encounter knowledge in multiple ways, wisdom is ambiguous.[10] Even within a community of musicians, for example, there are differing conceptions of the many aspects that connect variously to form integrated and disjunct, coherent and disconnected wholes. Conceptions of what constitutes wisdom in a musical practice may be shared, but exponents and the public also disagree about the merits of specific compositions, performances, recordings, and other practices and about those who possess musical wisdom. These individual and communal perspectives on wisdom result in beliefs and practices being affirmed and contested within the institutions, groups, and communities for which they are relevant. What passes for wisdom is ultimately adjudicated by the community or group of experts whose wisdom it is. Judges in international music competitions evaluate the worth of performances by individual contestants and collectively decide which are the best. Likewise, music education researchers adjudicate the value of pieces of scholarship, award prizes and research grants, and publish articles based on their collective estimates of researchers' work. Still, judges in various musical and scholarly traditions regularly disagree with the criteria used and the ends of these performances and this scholarship. In short,

I prefer to think of a multiplicity of wisdoms, adjudicated and contested in the public spaces within and between various traditions.

Wisdom is also profoundly artistic, feelingful, and spiritual. This is a holistic view that sees the intellect conjoined with emotion and sensibility, in which mind is embodied and thought, feeling, and sensitivity are intimately connected. This proposition resonates with Susanne Langer's view of mind as the life of feeling where sense and spirituality come together.[11] The arts, religions, myths, and rituals especially capture this imaginative experience and expression of inner life in what John Dewey describes as a state of heightened intensity and enacted experience.[12] Abraham Maslow conceives of this state as the highest level of human need for spiritual "self-actualization," and Mihaly Csikszentmihalyi thinks of it psychologically as a state of effortless "flow."[13] For me, in wisdom, imagination sets judgment alight, gives life purpose and meaning, and unites all aspects of mind and body, thought and action. Wisdom is known and felt, committed to intellectually and acted on in the phenomenal world. There is an ease and unselfconsciousness while at the same time it may be or seem to be hard won and apart from ordinary, humdrum, and prosaic existence. This profound commitment to ideas and practices is evident in transparency and integrity that are demonstrated to others in a life lived with purpose and conviction. Commitment is not only serious but playful in its joyous embrace of this moment and a sense of its preciousness that radiates to others.

Among its contributions, wisdom values exceptionality demonstrated on the part of scholars and practitioners alike in any musical or cultural tradition. Its emphasis on reaching beyond ordinary expectations toward virtuosity, style, grace, and a seemingly effortless command of ideas and practices to which Vernon Howard points is idealistic and inspirational for exponents and their publics alike.[14] Wisdom also values the single-minded effort and devotion toward reaching for an imaginative "vision of mastery" that may necessitate personal sacrifice on the part of one who seeks to excel.[15] It recognizes the reality that "many are called, but few are chosen"—that relatively few will follow this path.[16] Whether learners seek to be artists, scholars, professionals, or athletes, music and education provide them with transformative means whereby wisdom can be attained. Wisdom serves a crucial role in enabling students to transcend the ordinary and vernacular in search of the extraordinary and virtuosic. Although it may be seen in many walks of life, wisdom is particularly valued in the education of gifted music students who evidence high potential to achieve prowess as professional musicians, scholars, and teachers.

These holistic, dialectical, and ambiguous qualities of wisdom value the human beings at the center of education and their lived lives at the nexus of thought and practice. As part of a humane approach to music, education, and society, wisdom recognizes the cultural embeddedness of beliefs and practices and the diversity of wisdoms around the world. Thinking of these wisdoms as contested and dynamic recognizes the differences and commonalities that animate human beings in different cultural milieus. Rather than regarding people atomistically, as if mind, body, and soul are discrete and independent entities, wisdom is predicated on the belief that people are living beings and all the aspects of human experience are interconnected. The end of education in search of wisdom is integrity, transparency, and light. Importantly, embracing wisdom as a value recognizes that much of human experience is spiritual and feelingful, and an education in search of wisdom is about what can be seen and what remains unseen. As such, wisdom concerns the human need for what Maslow calls "self-actualization" or the deep sense of satisfaction and joy in being true to oneself and expert in those things one values.

On the other hand, wisdom as an educational value may overemphasize exclusivity over inclusivity. Its rigors may be beyond the capacities and desires of some students to attain. It may emphasize an elitist approach that restricts instruction to a few students who are judged to possess the capacity to excel. For example, during much of the Christian era, musical education and participation in liturgical music was limited to a few musically talented boys; girls and those of ordinary gifts and talents were often excluded from an intensive and rich musical education.[17] In the United States, secondary school and college music programs still focus on auditioned ensembles beyond the reach of those students who do not possess the requisite musical expertise.[18] Even in jazz, a tradition that began as a vernacular and oral practice, focusing on wisdom may result in teaching it academically as a classical tradition and, in the process, losing something of its vibrancy and interconnectedness with ordinary life and music making.[19] At a time in which general education is concerned with inclusion and ordinary experience, focusing on wisdom may exclude those who do not rise to its expectations of mastery and exceptionality and may seem out of touch with the ends and demands of practical and vocational education.

Wisdom can be a dangerous thing to possess, especially in anti-intellectual environments in which it is held in low regard or in authoritarian regimes to which it presents a threat. Advocates for democratic education might wish for wisdom to be possessed widely not only because it helps to create individual happiness and sustain democratic institutions but because it acts as a bulwark against anti-intellectualism, resentment, and tyranny that can arise when it is restricted to a few. Still, when wisdom's demands are at odds with and apart from ordinary experience, focusing on the practitioners and exponents who are willing to seek it potentially excludes many from the benefits of musical education. The many who do not attain wisdom may resent the few who do. In some societies, those who possess wisdom may be repudiated, ostracized, or even punished with death.

Just as resentment of Socrates led to his death, throughout history, intelligentsia and artists have been the target of oppressive political regimes and have been persecuted and even killed because of the threat they posed to those who rejected the wisdom for which they stood.

UNDERSTANDING

This originally Northern European word combines two words—*under* and *standing*—to literally refer to "the ground beneath our feet." Understanding is thought of as a noun and as a verb, "to understand." The ambiguity of noun and verb, object and action, invites both literal and figurative interpretations. I want to think of the "ground beneath our feet" as a metaphor for thought that undergirds and constitutes the basis of action.[20] As the act of standing requires something solid and substantial underfoot that enables a person to maintain upright posture, so understanding suggests a solidity of intellectual beliefs on which actions are predicated. The qualities of thought invoked here comprise the foundations on which practices rest. They are predicates to action and the north star for decisions that must be made and applied in practice. Early use of this word also connoted quite the opposite idea—notably, to stand under, "to support or assist; to prop up."[21] In this way, practices might also support, assist, or prop up the beliefs to which they relate or vice versa. The conjunction of these two metaphors relating to the ground on which one stands and one standing under something else and supporting it suggests an interesting ambiguity in this word as both foundational to and flowing from musical and educational beliefs and practices.

Understanding references intellectual power and ability as a central musical and educational means and end. Its ordinary dictionary meaning includes the intellectual capabilities of meaning making, comprehension, reasoning, and judgment and requires the employment of intelligence and sense. I see it holistically as encompassing reason, cognition, emotion, and the physical senses. The exercise of mind as the life of feeling concerned with all aspects of lived existence is a potent means of directing action, enacting change, and responding to those things that lie within and beyond personal control.[22] Notwithstanding the natural development of these intellectual, emotional, and sensory powers and the varied degree to which they may be possessed, they are crucial aspects of individual lived experience and vital to shared social and cultural life. Aspects of judgment, comprehension, meaning making, reasoning, and emotional and physical expression can be cultivated through formal and informal education in and through musical participation among a host of other ways. As a source of individual and collective empowerment, the cultivation and expression of understanding needs to be central to educational and musical belief and practice.

Although understanding can be directed to thought about itself, it often refers to other things. In music and education, intellectual, emotional, and physical powers are applied to ideas and practices that are often interconnected. Understanding primarily concerns persons, beliefs, and practices that are employed in intellectual processes such as comprehension, meaning making, reason, and judgment. Abstract thought in practical fields such as music and education often relate to the ways in which abstractions play out in the phenomenal world. These understandings may be settled and affirmed or critiqued and contested. Cultivating musical understanding requires attention to the ideas and values that underlie and are generated by musical practices, the means whereby musics are created and understood, and the musicians who create pieces and performances. It requires grasping the import of musical rituals and practices and making judgments about the value of these beliefs and practices within the frameworks of expectations and rule sets within specific traditions.

Also, understanding can be thought of in relational terms in the sense of relationships between people who come to arrangements and agreements or who engage in "amicable and friendly relations."[23] For example, two people may have an understanding that they will marry or undertake a business venture together. This notion of understanding recognizes personal relationships between those who have similar mindsets and possess certain knowledge and the interconnectedness between people and things. Seeing understanding as relational recognizes the connectedness between those who share mindsets, beliefs, values, and practices and its ambiguity as abstract and phenomenal, general and specific, individual and social. Taken-for-granted assumptions about which practices are predicated on which beliefs and vice versa provide the basis for sustaining musical traditions that bind together those who share in them; they are the building blocks of societies and cultures and a cohesive force in collective thought and action.

Further, understanding construed as noun and verb entails signification, clarity of meaning, and the exercise of intellect in comprehending the import of ideas and practices. It requires the use of signs and symbols within various languages and discourses. These are grasped deeply in the sense of possessing the intellectual tools to make sense of the symbolic systems understood abstractly and concretely within these languages and discourses. As a type and means of meaning making, understanding goes beyond the superficial appearance of things to grasp how they work and what they mean in a thoroughgoing way. Musical understanding suggests the presence of propositional and procedural knowledge that allows one to constructively and critically interpret music, whether through composition, improvisation, performance, or listening, among other means.[24] Rather than a fixed and immutable point, understanding is ambiguous and developmental over time, with changing intellectual capacity, maturity, and experience.

Among its advantages, the cultivation of understanding acknowledges that education, in whatever field, is a profoundly intellectual and social undertaking. Civil and decent societies and cultures require citizens to think constructively and critically, understand the nature of things and how they are made, evaluate and appraise ideas and practices forwarded in public and private spheres, and work individually and collectively on the basis of shared understandings. Knowing the ground beneath one's feet provides a solid basis for individual and collective action and practice, as actions spring from intellectually held principles. Grasping the significance of relevant facts is the bedrock on which one exercises one's intelligence and plans a reasonable course of action. For me, rather than merely respond to external pressures, understanding empowers collaborative and concerted action guided by principle. Not only is it the means whereby musical traditions are formed, sustained, and transformed, but it is crucial to the flourishing of ensembles and the life of musical institutions such as schools, colleges, academies, concert halls, and opera houses.

Understanding also highlights the importance of the subject matter of instruction or the material on which the intellect is exercised. Some subject matter is more productive of intellection than others that may seem more prosaic and superficial. Musicians and aestheticians sometimes distinguish between the apparent surface of a musical piece and the profundity of its meaning and purpose in their distinctions between musical substance and manner or surface and depth.[25] One might expect music teachers who value understanding to focus on those musics and musical aspects that are most productive of a rich grasp of how music is made and received and its symbolic meaning.[26] Such an approach may favor esoteric or classical traditions in which musicians have cultivated sophisticated systems of musical thought and practice over popular and accessible musics whose structures and meanings do not pretend to offer profundity or intellection but appeal directly, physically and emotionally. Even within classical traditions, some musical pieces may inspire deeper reflection and analysis than others. Musical substance and manner or surface and depth need not be thought of literally as mutually exclusive binaries but can be regarded figuratively as polarities or "weak syndromes" in which one melds into the other.[27]

Also, the relational bonds between those who share common understandings recognize the social qualities of intellection and the assumptive frames of reference shared by community members.[28] For example, shared expectations and assumptions are manifested by adherents to musical traditions and constitute a means of solidifying and promulgating musical practices and their publics. Each sphere of musical validity constitutes a mindset or group of shared understandings that are crucial to fostering certain musical beliefs and practices.[29] Regarding understanding in this way acknowledges the social and individual character of meaning making that is evident in musical practices.

Further, the elasticity of the notion of understanding, as noun and verb, individual and collective, literal and figurative, means and end, formative and summative, seems particularly appropriate to musical and educational milieus encompassing lifelong learning across a gamut of institutions and interests. The specifics may differ from elementary to advanced musical education in formal and informal settings throughout the life cycle. Still, the search for the ground on which one stands and the claims of supporting specific beliefs and practices remains a driving force in the development of intellectual capacity and power viewed individually and collectively. Understanding offers the prospect of empowering those within the educational system as agents able to shape their own lives in ways that bring them the greatest happiness.

Nevertheless, emphasizing the intellectual character of music and education can focus unduly on cognition, to the exclusion of psychomotor and affective dimensions of the self. It may exaggerate the intellectual dimensions of music making and receiving and fail to recognize sufficiently emotional, physical, and felt aspects that may be intuitively sensed rather than rationally apprehended. In the present anti-intellectual climate, I worry that this detraction may be overblown and wonder if an intellectual emphasis on understanding can serve as a corrective to pervasive anti-intellectualism in Western societies.[30] The ambiguity of understanding that encompasses feeling and sense as well as reason may go some way toward resisting an excessively rational approach to understanding. Still, the dangers of overintellectualizing music, teaching it primarily for its cognitive purposes, and failing to grasp sufficiently its felt qualities and physical appeal need to be acknowledged.

Regarding theory as the underpinning of practice can overlook the importance of practical aspects of music education and practice as a generator of theory. In an approach to curriculum that stresses the principles that give rise to practical outcomes, it is possible to ignore the equally important reality that practices often evoke principles as ways of thinking about those practices.[31] This reality turns traditional notions of understanding on their head by thinking about understanding as an outcome of practice rather than the primary generator of practice. My reading of musical history suggests that practices often precede theories that simply codify them in various ways. One might argue, as does David Elliott, following Francis Sparshott and Philip Alperson, that a better approach would focus on the communities of practice that are central to musics and within which they need to be understood.[32] My preference for a dialectical relationship between musical theories and practices suggests a complicated reality in which theory and practice are inextricably linked and essential to a well-rounded musical education.[33] Still, being preoccupied with cultivating understanding raises the possibility that practice may get short shrift, and it may be difficult to find the middle ground and a sense of balance between theory and practice.

Focusing on subject matter and on musical works worthy of contemplation can also unduly privilege some musics over others, especially those that have been the subject of intellectual attention in the academy. I have pointed to the possibility of intellectualizing academic jazz study and treating it as a classical tradition. The idiosyncrasies that once marked jazz performance from one place to another, one performer to another, and that were picked up by informal and oral transmission can be domesticated and sanitized within a broadly systematic formal training within the academy. More esoteric styles can be cultivated in academic circles comfortable with classical traditions. As practiced in the academy, jazz can become separated from ordinary and popular jazz performance in clubs, restaurants, gardens, and other places. This is not to suggest that formal education in jazz is necessarily destructive of the tradition but rather to acknowledge that focusing on an understanding of jazz potentially raises problems that may privilege some jazz performances over others. The same is true of the focus on classical masterworks considered worthy of study in university and college performance programs. Miniatures, or works by lesser known or less prestigious composers, may be de-emphasized when the focus is on works that are determined by musical gatekeepers as worthy of study because they are big and pretentious in scale and profound in their musical requirements of musicians and audiences. In the search for musical depth, accessible music may not be sufficiently valued, thereby driving a wedge between ordinary audiences who do not pretend to know music deeply but who enjoy music that connects more immediately to their experience and academic or sophisticated audiences whose musical training and experience predispose them to enjoy esoteric musics that demand more of performer and listener alike.

KNOWLEDGE

Knowledge was originally thought of as a noun and a verb, although the latter fell into disuse. Its rich history in the English from at least the twelfth century also indicates separate etymologies between the words *knowledge* and *know* and between knowledge as noun and as verb.[34] This broad spectrum of ordinary dictionary meanings of knowledge is complicated by its centrality to educational discourse regarding the subject matter of instruction, the ways in which this subject matter is engaged by teachers and learners, and analysis by means such as types, domains, modes, and levels. Although knowledge is often regarded as a static thing, some modern and postmodern writers have sought to highlight its processual and dynamic quality of coming to know a thing, person, or action, more suggestive of its ancient roots as a verb. In this regard, it shares similarities with the word *music*, thought of by writers such as Alperson, Elliott, and Christopher Small in the active sense of the practice of music.[35]

Among its characteristics, knowledge connotes "acknowledging or owning something" in the sense of a "confession." Its focus on "recognition" requires the application of cognition, particularly, memory in recalling what one has encountered before. There is a "familiarity," a "personal acquaintance, friendship, intimacy" with a person or thing that has been internalized as one's own and even constructed idiosyncratically in ways that render it individual and personal.[36] Even if it is systematically grasped in ways that may be shared collectively, it is, in a sense, a distinctive perspective colored by a person's background, circumstances, and life history. Seeing knowledge in this way requires the proposition that subject matter cannot be separated from the people who engage it. Rather, knowing something requires engaging with ideas and practices from a vantage point shaped physically, psychologically, and socially. Knowledge encompasses the multiple perspectives of people who may share understandings but also differ from each other in important ways. As with wisdom and understanding, it is deeply personal and individual while it is also shared and collective—a crucial ambiguity that is central to its cultivation.

Knowledge dwells particularly in the domain of epistemology, with its roots in questions raised in the West by Plato and others in his train concerning important existential questions that have engaged human beings from time immemorial. It is also thought of as a "branch of science or learning, an art," exemplified in Aristotle's search for systematic knowledge of the natural world through classification and employed in the sense of "knowledge by acquaintance," "knowledge about," and "knowledge by description." In a static sense, it is sometimes taken to be a stock of "knowledge capital"; in contemporary computing parlance, it is incorporated within a "knowledge base" to refer to information that has been compiled and classified and can be retrieved digitally. Thought of more dynamically and processually, it refers to the "apprehension of fact or truth," matters of perception, "mental awareness," "cognizance of fact," and "consciousness" in which one is "conversant with a body of facts, principles, methods, scholarship, learning, erudition."[37] This cognitive emphasis on the ways in which people apprehend and make sense of their own lived existence and the things around them inevitably focuses on ideas and practices that constitute material for reflection. Within music, for example, philosophical questions address an array of ontological, existential, epistemological, aesthetic, and practical questions concerning musical traditions and their practice. Thought and practice of Western and Eastern classical music traditions alike exemplify and express bodies of underlying principles, beliefs, values, and practices that their adherents regard as normative. This knowledge is passed on from one generation to the next, and its acquisition is often a time-consuming process. Research on musical perception, for example, illumines this body of musical knowledge and focuses on musical thought and practice.[38] Other reflective and descriptive musical scholarship is exemplified by the work of Paul Berliner, who reflects on the thought processes involved in the improvisational process in jazz.[39]

Although knowledge necessarily concerns mind and its engagement with important ideas and practices, mind is embodied. Cognition, feeling, affect, and sense are interrelated in holistic and reflexive ways. This is especially true in the practice of music, where music is both known about and done in various ways through composing, improvising, performing, recording, producing, and listening. Langer's notion of music as an expression of feeling and "our myth of the inner life" still rings true for artists and lovers of the arts in our time.[40] Notwithstanding his critique of aspects of her theory, Elliott is also among those to recognize the role of affect in his theory of music.[41] Performers are especially cognizant of the role of feeling in their musical thinking when they talk about what they do. If mind implicates sense and feeling, then knowledge, too, must also be impacted. Distinctions between cognition, affect, and psychomotor domains by Benjamin Bloom and his successors may be important conceptual markers of different processes that together comprise thought, but practically speaking, they are at best weak syndromes or points of emphasis rather than mutually exclusive.[42] So we need to think of knowledge as encompassing not only what we know but all the ways in which we know and come to know the world.

Among the examples of various philosophical typologies of knowledge, I think, for example, of the following important distinctions: between propositional and procedural knowledge, or "knowing that" and "knowing how" highlighted for music education by Howard; between "levels" of knowledge, from basic comprehension to evaluation and appraisal or between elementary and advanced education, forwarded by Benjamin Bloom and his successors; between cycles of knowing, from romance and instrumentation to generalization on the way to wisdom, posited by Whitehead; between domains of knowledge as the basis of education, advanced by Philip Phenix; and between "modes of knowing" through reason (deduction, induction, and analogy), intuition, and imagination, examined by Jerome Bruner, Nelson Goodman, Israel Scheffler, Harvey Siegel, Maxine Greene, and Keith Swanwick.[43] These taxonomies illustrate the varying ways in which knowledge and knowing can be parsed in educational literature.

Postmodern educational discourse has questioned and sometimes upended modernist assumptions concerning knowing and knowledge and stressed the fraught ways in which power impacts personal and collective meaning making.

Within music education, researchers highlight the impact of issues such as race, sexuality, politics, and social justice on musical knowing and knowledge. They interrogate what passes for musical knowing and knowledge, question their subsumed ethical neutrality, focus on the social ways in which they are constructed and deconstructed for purposes that often go counter to humane ends, and recognize the difficulties of challenging the status quo.[44] For these writers, the challenge for music education is to radically critique taken-for-granted assumptions in music education toward ideals of freedom, justice, and human flourishing. It is also to transform musical knowing and knowledge toward democratic ends that empower learners individually and collectively to act as agents in the interest of positive social change. Others disagree with the merits of these claims. They critique the extent to which musical knowing can transform society and whether it should be employed in the interest of social change.[45] In navigating this fraught and sometimes ideologically driven territory, I seek to avoid fallacies of false equivalence and reductionism, exercise care in critiquing the often well-intentioned efforts of musicians and teachers, recognize the limits of philosophy, speak the truth as I have come to know it, and provide a clear and hopeful picture of future possibilities for music and education. This position puts me in "the eye of paradox," where I seek to both transform knowledge and conserve it.[46] I am caught in a dialectic between insights of sometimes opposing claims, unwilling to jettison understandings of either position but seeking my own truth.

Among knowledge's advantages, the ambiguity and elasticity of the notion provide a generative basis for thinking about music education theoretically and practically. In a field that straddles theory and practice, the interconnections of knowledge and knowing address static and dynamic facets and holistic and atomistic aspects of music and education. These qualities of knowledge are synchronous with my view of the dialectical nature of music education and the ironic if often paradoxical dilemmas that face musicians and teachers.[47] Figurative and literal characterizations of knowledge seem appropriate to the conceptualization of the work of education, which itself is understood in these differing ways. They are consistent with music, teaching, learning, instruction, curriculum, and administration—central activities that constitute "common places" in music education.[48]

Also, as with values of wisdom and understanding, thinking of knowledge in terms of subject matter and the constructive engagement of teachers and learners with it highlights the profoundly intellectual character of music and education. The fact of learners' apprehension and internalization of subject matter focuses on the intensely personal work of learning and the importance of learners' active involvement in constructing and deconstructing knowledge. Cultivating understanding is opposed to passive reception of information that is deposited (as in

Paulo Freire's notion of "banking" education).[49] Learners' active involvement in the educational process is transformative as they make sense of their worlds in various ways and are empowered with a sense of agency that enables them to act to change (and hopefully improve) the situations in which they find themselves. Such an educational approach develops the imaginative and critical thought that can help to equip them as citizens prepared to participate fully in a democracy. It can also set learners free to develop in ways that are conducive to their happiness, enable them to better understand, respect, and empathize with those who differ from their own perspectives and circumstances, and foster the dialogue, mutual respect, and civility that characterize decent societies. Democracy can thrive, and authoritarianism can be defeated, only when there is common respect for established facts and intellectual acumen on the part of the citizenry. It is for this reason that public education is intimately connected with democratic governance and necessary for its survival. Taking an embodied view of mind as the basis for knowledge allows for a broad and holistic education that sustains democracy as it also encompasses the mental, spiritual, emotional, and physical needs and aspirations of the people for whom democracy should work. As such, knowledge contributes to a humane education and society.

Acknowledging the different forms of knowledge to which I have referred is consistent with empirical evidence of the varied "ways of knowing" and the degrees to which people and subjects may be known. To take one example, Phenix's taxonomy of various realms of meaning that should be addressed in a comprehensive general education curriculum encompasses symbolics, empirics, esthetics, synnoetics, ethics, and synoptics.[50] This broad range of subject matter echoes the breadth of Plato's prescribed curriculum for citizens in his *Republic*. It also resonates with the ancient Greek notion of *paideia*, revived in different form in the late twentieth century as a plan for comprehensive education.[51] Proponents of these curricula embrace the multiple ways of meaning making that comprise knowledge; their plans for a broadly inclusive curriculum are intended to develop well-rounded individuals. As with the field of philosophy, which examines the arts and the ways in which they are known, aesthetics constitutes an important ground, although not the only ground, for music educational thought and practice.[52] Still, Phenix is not advocating that each way of knowing should be taught in a separate subject.[53] Rather, he acknowledges that although different subjects may focus on specific realms of meaning, they overlap theoretically and practically. So aesthetics can also be evident in fields such as philosophy, mathematics, and the sciences, in which the elegance of an argument, the derivation of a formula, or the design of an experiment respectively may have aesthetic character. Thinking of knowledge in terms of these ambiguities and multiplicities seems particularly appropriate to educators' practical predicaments.

Among its detractions, however, knowledge can be interpreted narrowly and statically rather than broadly and dynamically. One might think of knowledge as a stock or thing rather than a process of becoming. Although Jane Roland Martin considers a stock of "cultural capital," failing to also see it as an evolving reality would overlook this important aspect of cultural knowledge and misinterpret her point.[54] At any one time, a snapshot of cultural reality allows one to take stock of culture and enumerate and describe it; over time, however, were one to take a moving picture of culture, it would change and develop from one time and place to another. Also, interpreting knowledge cognitively, to the exclusion of affect, sense, and physical action, may cause one to miss the multifaceted and holistic dimensions of knowledge and see only a part of the larger whole. If one never arrives at wisdom and understanding and is preoccupied with the acquisition of information, knowledge may be shortsighted.

Focusing on knowledge may also lead to an excessive emphasis on formal rather than informal education. In her description of the ways in which popular musicians learn and the kinds of techniques and means they employ as they come to know their music, Lucy Green shows the significant ways in which these informal approaches differ from the traditional and formal master-disciple approach commonly employed in the transmission of Western and Eastern classical musics.[55] It is possible that a focus on formal education may privilege the study of classical musics of the world and overlook popular, vernacular, and accessible musics that are enjoyed as sources of immediate pleasure rather than for the analysis of their sophisticated techniques of composition, improvisation, or performance. As with understanding, classical traditions have tended toward the erudite and the cultivation of relatively sophisticated cadres of performers and listeners who understand the ways in which these musics are made and who enjoy contemplating their intellectual import as well as their sensory appeal. It is possible that classical musics may become overintellectualized within cadres of academic composers and audiences separate from the mainstream of classical performance in concert halls and other performing spaces. Alternatively, where the focus of knowledge is too limited, a musician may be less preoccupied with the discipline of music and more with its immediate and performative or spectacular character.

Thinking about knowledge within the frame of computing science as digitally collated and disseminated information potentially transforms its character. Since it may be impossible to forget information that is digitally stored, the resulting weight of information can clutter the intellectual landscape. Without a commensurate focus on the acquisition of wisdom and understanding, thinking of knowledge as mere information denigrates it and misses the multiplicity of sorts of knowledge and the richness of ways in which knowledge is acquired. The ability to retrieve information through various technologies can also displace human memory, which has the advantage of remembering and forgetting and sorting new information relevant to the present situation. The accumulating volume of established theories and practices allows less space for the newly created knowledge and can marginalize it. This is often the case with classical concerts that focus on old repertoire and crowd out newly composed pieces. Alternatively, such is the volume of new knowledge that it may crowd out the old. Retrieving information digitally may focus on recent literature and exclude older material not included in digital search parameters. I see this in doctoral-level reviews of research literature that focus on studies undertaken during the last few years and overlook earlier seminal and groundbreaking research. In this way, historical memory and context in music and research can be lost.

Given that theory is often privileged over practice in academic circles, it is possible that theoretical and propositional knowledge will be emphasized over practical and procedural knowledge in the preparation of musicians and educators in higher education. This can come about because propositional knowledge is likely to be more consonant with an interest in theory and carry more weight in the academy than procedural knowledge particularly concerned with musical performance and pedagogy. I have seen this tension in North American conservatory, college, and university music programs over a working lifetime. Teachers and students in these institutions often face a tug-of-war between the claims of theoretical and practical interests in the sorts of knowledge required for a comprehensive musical education. They also encounter pressures as they seek balance or creative tension between these disparate interests.

MASTERY

Originally borrowed from the French and later "remodeled" from the noun *master*, the idea of mastery connotes ideas of "authority, power, dominion, superiority, skill."[56] Its root, *master*, is also a verb with associations of "to get the better of, to rule," suggesting the necessity of a struggle to overcome impediments and "reduce to subjection" the obstacles to one's acquisition of power and skill.[57] Mastery is akin to music as a verb that is now thought of as a noun; it refers to subjects or objects as well as actions.[58] Within music, the master-disciple metaphor is pervasive in the world's musical traditions, notably in classical traditions that require an extended preparation and advanced levels of skill.[59] Master musicians are esteemed and even revered for their wisdom, understanding, knowledge, and virtuosity. Students become their disciples in the hope of coming to possess the selfsame ideas and practices as the master. In music education, mastery also denotes such concepts as a stage of musical development in a model originally developed by Swanwick and extended by Boyce-Tillman.[60] This ambiguity of figurative and literal interpretations of mastery in musical and educational metaphors and models serves to further complicate an analysis of its meaning. As with wisdom, understanding, and knowledge, the word proves evocative, useful to music and education, but also problematic in character.

Mastery is rooted in a masculine metaphor of a battle in which there is a struggle for ascendancy against an adversary for "victory resulting in domination or subjugation." It also encompasses "the state or condition of being master, controller, or ruler" after one has achieved dominion or control.[61] This ambiguous idea of mastery as a means and end of the battle for supremacy and the condition of victor and supreme leader may seem on the surface to be antithetical to the work of education as a nurturing environment in which growth takes place. It also seems at odds with the fact that musicians have often served throughout history as acolytes of rulers and subservient to their whims. Still, although this metaphor may initially jar, looking more deeply, it resonates with the musical challenges in many traditions around the world that are very much a matter of competition and struggle for supremacy as musical stars, prodigies, or virtuosi. I have already referred to Howard's theory of artistic education as a matter of the realization of a "vision of mastery," an ideal that the artist imaginatively grasps and seeks to attain. This vision is won through a disciplined approach to instruction, practice, example, and reflection that results, hopefully, in virtuosity, grace, and a sense of effortlessness.[62] For example, when learning a difficult musical passage or mastering a particular technique, one wrestles with the problem until it is mastered or is no longer a challenge.

For Howard, this struggle is physical in sharpening one's sensory perceptions and learning the technical skills involved in the know-how or procedural knowledge of music. It is also intellectual in acquiring the concepts, beliefs, values, and attitudes that underlie and pervade this music concerning "knowing that" or propositional and felt knowledge. Just as a musician's personal vision of mastery may change throughout life, so the public's "vision of mastery," while more or less agreed on by a music's practitioners, is also contested and dynamic in the process of "becoming" something else.[63] Viewed as social practice, there is likewise a struggle for supremacy among musical practitioners and their publics who hold certain beliefs, values, and attitudes. The winners of these struggles inevitably are regarded and regard themselves as superior to others and may subjugate those whom they vanquish in the struggle. This metaphor is evident in the pervasiveness of musical competitions historically and internationally.

Mastery is also a form of personal empowerment. Among those to advocate it as an educational ideal, Freire sees the acquisition of literacy as a means of empowering those who have been oppressed by others to act politically to improve their lives.[64] For these people, the ability to read and write makes it possible to access languages and knowledge utilized by those who possess political power. Naming the causes of their subjugation, acquiring the knowledge required to improve their lives, and developing self-control and discipline enable them to act in solidarity with others to resist and overcome their oppressors. Facility in language and literature constitute the basis for and means of positive social change. Extending Freire's ideas to music and the other arts suggests that the acquisition of the languages these arts employ empowers people to access ways of knowing and being that would otherwise be outside the realm of their understanding. They are also enabled to make artistic changes that may transform not only the arts but the lives of those who make and receive them. For Shinichi Suzuki, for example, the acquisition and expression of the skills of playing the violin beautifully create "superior people" who not only know and can do what others do not know or cannot do but who know or do things that they might not otherwise have thought possible.[65]

Mastery not only entails personal and collective empowerment, but it constitutes a source of authority. By *authority*, I refer to power that resides in exemplary conduct respected and revered by others or vested in one because of the office that one holds. Authority has the force of commanding obedience and conformity to prescribed beliefs and practices. This normative expectation arises out of respect that is given out of a desire to emulate an exemplar or compelled by external forces, laws, regulations, and the like. The ambiguity of authority that may or may not be enforced suggests that personal empowerment may slip into enforced disempowerment of others. While the language of liberatory education, for example, urges personal empowerment as an unmitigated good, there is also a possibility that it may come to be oppressive because of ambiguity in the ways authority may operate. What once may have been authoritative, in the sense of constituting a valuable reference point and exemplar for musicians, may come to command the acquiescence and obedience of all musicians and thereby constitute a source of their disempowerment. It is important to take this ambiguity into account when thinking of mastery as a means and end of empowerment.

One cannot envision mastery without also thinking of the things, events, or people to whom it relates. Mastery is demonstrated regarding a specific subject matter, tradition, or rule-governed system through virtuosity, grace, sense of style, and an apparent effortlessness that Howard refers to as the epitome of artistic education.[66] Cultivating performative and procedural skills of "know how" differs theoretically from "knowing that" or the theoretical knowledge of the subject matter, although practically speaking, they overlap. One may grasp a theoretical concept of a musical piece quickly and understand how it should go, but achieving a performance that accords with this vision may take extended practice to achieve. When one overcomes the technical and interpretative challenges entailed in bringing the piece to life in a brilliant performance, it seems to have a sense of apparent ease that, as noted earlier, Csikszentmihalyi calls "flow" and Abraham Maslow thinks of as "self-actualization," the highest human experience of spiritual fulfillment.[67] In the moments when one experiences a liquidity and unselfconsciousness or total absorption in the present, this performance fulfills a pervasive and spiritual human need resulting from the exercise of reason, imagination, mental concentration, patience, and discipline that together comprise an intensity of being that is extraordinary. For John Dewey, these are "consummated" experiences that intensify ordinary experience and give it meaning.[68]

In the musical traditions of which I am aware, there is a concern with getting the details precisely right and, beyond this, with having it appear to others as if it is effortless. Things must be done precisely and correctly, whether it be laying down tracks of a recorded popular song, composing a symphony, or re-creating an improvised artistic performance in a life ritual. A performance may seem effortless because of the expenditure of effort, even sacrifice and struggle, in achieving an evocative and captivating result. Mastery is recognized by a music's public because of their consciousness of the rules, norms, and expectations of this tradition. Should a master deliberately break the rules, as many musical composers regularly do, this fact is understood precisely because other exponents and their public are in the know about what is happening. When the details are in place, there is something intensely moving, powerful, and inspiring in the self-forgetfulness for musician and audience alike. These are the moments when one is in a musical experience, forgets about what it has taken or is taking to produce this performance, and becomes absorbed in what is being and has been created.

Among the contributions of mastery to education, the centrality of imagination and its expression as a means and end of learning is intrinsically motivating for teachers and students alike. Focusing on a "vision of mastery," on the end of wisdom, understanding, and knowledge one seeks to achieve, clarifies the objective and renders it more vital. Seeing an end in the mind's eye makes what is needed to realize it more obvious, as it also creates an impulse that motivates one to act to achieve it. In this view, the work of teaching becomes a matter of exemplifying ideals in teachers' lives and practices and prompting students to learn because they desire to emulate their teachers and achieve mastery themselves. Rather than imposing external directives that are passively accepted, this learning is intensely personal and undertaken by those whose imaginations have been fired with a desire to achieve a specific end. As they gradually realize their initial vision, it changes and grows; each progressive vision seems to move further away to yet another more challenging end, and learning becomes a constant state of becoming. Learners' desire constitutes an impulse that generates a process of self-empowerment. For Dewey, as for Freire, this is a transformative process that is encouraging and liberating for the students and their teachers, and its effects ripple outward into the broader society. As students experience success all along the educational process and each objective is attained and surpassed on the way to yet another, the attainment of one objective cultivates the assurance, courage, and power to tackle the next.

Mastery and its demonstration in virtuosity, effortlessness, and grace is an imaginative and spiritual experience that satisfies a human need to transcend other more mundane but essential needs for food, shelter, safety, and so forth. It exemplifies mind at a high level of functioning in an utterly captivating sense of joy, exhilaration, intensity, purpose, meaning, and unselfconsciousness that is play. For me, paradoxically, play exhibits both self-control and freedom—self-control in the discipline of ensuring that everything is in its place and freedom in the abandonment of focusing on the moment of exemplary performance. For the ancients, to play was to approach the supernatural, to be like the gods, and in the millennia since, philosophers have accorded play a central place in general education. Well-rounded curricula typically include the arts as ways in which the sense of joy, wonder, and exhilaration of play may be experienced and cultivated. Their performative character provides the means to clearly demonstrate mastery and thereby meet these spiritual needs.

The struggles and battles to overcome obstacles evoked by mastery resonate especially in some subject matter and at advanced levels of performance. In music, for example, classical traditions around the world often require years, even decades to master at an exemplary level. Still, mastery educational models apply at any educational stage. This training extends into professional life as musicians continue to practice and sometimes take coaching lessons from others throughout their lives. As soloists and members of ensembles, they are challenged to learn new repertoire and perform with musicians who interpret repertoire differently than they do. Youngsters often begin training as violinists or pianists at an early age, and by their midteens they have already spent a decade on private instruction, practice, and performance. Popular professional musicians whose careers span decades are similarly challenged by the changing tastes of their publics, the advent of new technologies, styles, and means of distribution, and the need to remain constantly fresh and attractive to their audiences. Notwithstanding these struggles, all these musicians find joy in their mastery of the musics they perform. They are affirmed and motivated by the moments of exhilaration they and their audiences experience. This fit between mastery and music as a performative art makes it an apt music educational value. Mastery can also be applied more broadly as an appropriate value in other subjects that entail procedural knowledge and where learning physical skills is important.

Among its detractions, however, competition, struggle for supremacy, and the subjugation of others in mastery can be miseducative and dehumanizing. It is one thing to struggle to reach one's ideal of mastery in performance and quite another to struggle against others for supremacy and to win by any means; it is one thing to achieve an exemplary performance and regard it as normative for oneself and quite another to insist on its being normative for others. Yet, too often, mastery becomes a matter of satisfying one's ego and exercising power over others, thereby disempowering them. Musical competitions that from ancient times have constituted the means to display virtuosity and produce a laureate who gives the most exceptional performance have too often been the means of discouraging those who fail to win and institutionalizing a narrow interpretation of the musical ideal. Those musicians who dare to differ from normative, traditional, or orthodox interpretations are prone to give polarizing performances and, as a result, may not win competitions. On winning, some musicians are gracious to their competitors and evidence humility; others gloat and preen over their victory and belittle their fellows. Some personalities may be particularly prone to discouragement and give up prematurely when they fail to win. A master who may have won international competitions in the past and so attracts students to his studio may insist that all the students who perform a specific piece do so only in the "right" way that follows his dictates. Wherever it exists, such subjugation of others is miseducative in that it may not only discourage, stunt, and prevent another's growth but it may have the pernicious effect of stunting one's own growth.[69]

Too often, mastery is associated with elitism, with the cultivation of a select cadre of musicians who display characteristics deemed desirable in classical musics that lie outside the mainstream of vernacular and popular traditions. Musical traditions that are less accessible to the public and require an extended period of education to master then become the focus of general education, too often to the exclusion of those musical traditions that are closer to students' life experiences and interests. Rather than a value that guides the practice of all musics, mastery can become an end that guides the acquisition of beliefs and practices required for elite musics. In so doing, mastery restricts the pool of students selected for musical study and the musical repertoire studied and deprives many students who may benefit from a broad musical study from the experience of studying, creating, and performing music. In these ways, mastery fails to cultivate musical tastes that could broadly benefit the public at large.

When it cultivates authoritarianism, mastery may undermine democracy in decent societies that aspire to values of inclusiveness, diversity, humane conduct, civility, and caring for the most vulnerable in society and those in need. These values are presently under attack in the West, fueled by forces of bigotry, misogyny, and homophobia, fear of different others, alarm at the terror wreaked by fundamentalist ideologues, distrust of the media and political leadership, anger at economic and political disenfranchisement, greed of the rich and powerful, and pervasiveness of new social media that enables the rampant spread of unfettered hate speech. The globalization of the world's information exchange and economy and the toxicity of too much social media have spawned a violent reaction in Western societies and upended a Pax Americana that has stood for democratic values in the wake of tragic world wars that engulfed the world in the twentieth century. As I write, authoritarianism is on the rise, and this development is precisely why music education needs to stand for its antithesis—namely, democratic values of freedom, mutual respect, civility, and inclusiveness. It is in this spirit that Paul Woodford urges the cultivation of critical thinking and resistance to authoritarianism in music education, and Allsup advocates an "open" approach to music education that values diversity, plurality, and an array of possibilities rather than close it within the frame of the traditional master-disciple metaphor.[70]

The four overlapping values of wisdom, understanding, knowledge, and mastery are ambiguous and concerned with the importance of intelligence in music and education. Each value has potential for good and evil if overemphasized, underemphasized, or employed for inhumane ends. Wisdom, grounded in the metaphor of light and enlightenment, is dynamic and holistic in its inclusion of affect and sensation and intellectual capacity. Understanding is based in metaphors of support and power. Construed in relational terms, it is concerned with signification—that is, grasping the symbolic systems concerned with theory or practice. Knowledge draws from the metaphor of ownership and concerns epistemological aspects of the apprehension and acknowledgement of beliefs and practices that comprise music and education. Mastery is associated with the masculine metaphor of battle, struggle, and subjugation; it concerns theoretical and practical matters, issues of authority and power, and right practice. Making judicious decisions that fit the needs of specific music learners is a crucial musical and teaching responsibility, and much hangs on what musicians and educators choose to do. While these values may apply generally, none suffices, and each has a different emphasis and practical effect. Framed at a high level of generality, they are necessarily applied in the context of specific situations. Much depends on how they are interpreted within specific instructional situations. Mulling over this analysis reveals the selectivity of applying general principles to practice, the incompleteness of possibilities, and the unexpected consequences that potentially flow from one's best intentions.

TEN

Justice, Equality, Fairness, and Inclusion

JUSTICE, EQUALITY, FAIRNESS, AND INCLUSION have an important place in contemporary educational literature. Three of these values—justice, equality, and inclusion—have received considerable attention in Anglo-American cultural, educational, and music educational philosophy. John Dewey, R. S. Peters, Jane Roland Martin, Paulo Freire, Seyla Benhabib, and Martha Nussbaum are among those to explore ways in which they contribute to democratic societies and humane education. In music education, writers such as Cathy Benedict, Patrick Schmidt, Gary Spruce, Paul Woodford, and their colleagues, Randall Allsup and his colleagues, and Judith Jellison have examined aspects of justice, equality, inclusion, and, to a lesser degree, fairness.[1]

In putting my own cast on justice, equality, and inclusion and especially forwarding the claims of fairness, I plough the philosophical ground where values of justice, equality, fairness, and inclusion intersect with aspects of musical enculturation.[2] My focus is primarily on what is meant by these values, how they may be exemplified in music and education, and what their advantages and disadvantages for musical and educational beliefs and practices may be. Although they intersect, practically speaking, they are logically distinct, and so I examine each in turn, beginning with justice.

JUSTICE

One way to begin thinking about justice is to associate this word with legal notions of binding rule sets that are legislated and enforced on behalf of the public. Strictly speaking, justice is predicated on the specific rules in place at a given time and place. These rules reflect the beliefs and practices of societies by which they are accepted. A people may aspire to be just or righteous, but specific conceptions of what these words mean are bound up in societal traditions and mores. The rules that are developed depend on determinations of whose perspectives count in the determination of justice and who is rendered invisible, marginal, or beyond the limits of those for whom justice is presumed to be served. In its strict legal sense, justice is meted out in accordance with those rules, and this, too, is a social construction. As with other social conventions, specific notions of justice are in the continuous process of being contested and developed from time to time and from place to place.

Laws carry the presumption of insistence that they be obeyed. Penalties are exacted for failure to comply, and the punitive nature of these laws offers little relief except insofar as the laws can be changed. Marja Heimonen unpacks contrasting continental European and Anglo-American legal traditions and their implications for music education.[3] She shows how the nature of laws and the means of their construction—whether by precedent, as in common law, or through regulation, as in continental law—provide very different contexts in which the work of education is undertaken. Charles Dickens had his character Mr. Bumble in *Oliver Twist* observe that the law can be an "ass" or "idiot" in the bluntness of its specific prescriptions and proscriptions or its unintended practical consequences.[4] Nevertheless, laws constitute a rational and measured approach to aspects of social and cultural life that require, in the view of those who make and carry them out and those who live by them, control and direction of certain behaviors and punishments for deviating from specified prescribed and proscribed beliefs and practices.

I want to go beyond this legalistic view of justice as rule-bound action in pursuit of imagined ideals of what it means to be just. Here, I prefer to think more broadly about these ideals themselves and about individual and social justice. Enlightenment conceptions of an individual's search for wisdom and the importance of personal worth and dignity foster individual claims to justice. People have a claim to justice not only because of membership in a group but because of their individual worth and dignity. More recent movements to ensure that justice is done to everyone recognize that certain groups have traditionally been excluded from those who count as full human beings with the right to justice. Their advocates seek "social justice" and the full recognition of disadvantaged or excluded classes or social groups. For them, justice needs not be done only to individuals but to those social groups who have been disenfranchised, marginalized, or otherwise excluded from full participation in society. Civil rights, feminist, and gay rights advocates are among the proponents for social justice as well as individual justice.[5]

What does it mean to be just? I start with the idea of righteousness, of doing what is morally right. Jacques Derrida, for whom justice constituted a practical impossibility, could not let go of this ideal but sought to frame it problematically in terms of conflicting imperatives for decision and action on the one hand and withholding action and fallibility on the other.[6] The notion of righteousness, for which justice is a synonym, is a lovely old idea. But how is righteousness to be determined? Typically, those things considered to be morally right are justified by appeals to reason and/or revelation. The old French *joust*, sometimes termed a *just*, suggests the notion of engagement and contest in which there is a winner and a loser.[7] The process of justification encapsulates this combat metaphor in the sense that what is morally right can be clearly articulated from what is not and defended on specific grounds. All hangs on this defense. Even claims to supernatural revelation are often tested by appeals to reason. Thus, for example, the biblical Ten Commandments spoken by Moses are justified by arguments regarding the inhumanity of incivility, theft, murder, and the like.

In our time, justice is often depicted as a set of scales in which one thing is held up and measured against another and found wanting or otherwise. This metaphor of comparative weight suggests that means exist to evaluate one thing in terms of another—for example, rightness or wrongness. Not only can one's conduct be measured against certain theoretical and normative prescriptions or proscriptions and evaluated in these terms, but the very rules themselves can be disputed, critically examined, and justified or refuted by argument or the weight of evidence. In law, this disputation often takes the form of combat as, for example, lawyers for the prosecution and defense seek to show the flaws in their opponents' arguments and evidence and examine and cross-examine each other's witnesses. Thinking of a set of scales evokes the idea of balance between complex, competing, conflicting, or differing interests. Determinations of justice are often complicated by various perspectives that need to be considered. Justice is cast not only in terms of rightness and wrongness, or in blacks and whites, but also in shades of gray. Decisions must sometimes be rendered not only between good and evil but between greater and lesser goods and greater and lesser evils. The good that one action may accomplish for some must be weighed against the possibilities of evil to others that may result from that action. Practically speaking, these complexities are navigated through carefully adjudicating and balancing sets of interests against others, as one would do when using a set of scales.

The normative character of justice suggests that its rules and laws have universal application. For example, framers of the US Declaration of Independence assumed that justice applies to all free men and is grounded in natural law predicated on a priori assumptions of justice and the rights to it.[8] This restrictive conception of universality as applying only to free (mainly white) men would later expand to include enslaved persons, minorities, people of color, and women. Still later, the claims of natural law were taken to apply to all living things in the natural world, and notions of "livingness" were construed even more broadly to include planet Earth and the cosmos beyond.[9] Modern notions of universality are rooted, for example, in Enlightenment ideas propounded by thinkers such as Immanuel Kant, who posited that others will agree with one's judgment.[10] This presumption gives rise to what he calls common sense (sensus communis) that is likewise presumed to have universal validity. It is now painfully clear that Kant's presumption of monolithic universal conceptions is problematic. His own perspective was that of a privileged and educated person within a specific societal and cultural milieu. Notwithstanding Isaiah Berlin's efforts to reveal the depth of Kant's insight into human nature, in our own time, we are now more conscious of the ways in which our views are shaped by our varying societal positions and perspectives.[11] Maxine Greene's eloquent conceptions of societal "multiplicities and pluralities" evoke the problematic character of monolithic and universalistic conceptions of justice. In acknowledging justice's ambiguity, both figuratively and literally, individually and socially, I prefer to construe it ambiguously, modestly, and problematically in nuanced and specific as well as comparative and general ways. For me, the pursuit of justice evokes polarities and dialectics that are sometimes difficult to navigate, practically speaking.

Among its contributions, justice facilitates musical transmission and transformation. Its reliance on established rule sets underscores the social and institutional nature of music and education as cultural practices that rely on traditional expectations even as they are in the process of changing and becoming. In emphasizing continuity and tradition, justice contributes to the stability of these practices. Practically speaking, acquiring the rule systems that undergird a given theory or practice is sometimes a messy process that relies on reason and imagination to negotiate civilly. Within education, even though teachers may feel a sense of entitlement in imparting their visions of justice, students may critically deconstruct these taken-for-granted assumptions and this received wisdom and challenge their teachers. The possibility of dissonance between teachers' and students' perceptions of justice can engender conflict between them as rule systems are contested. In decent societies, there is a premium on learning to negotiate civilly the inevitable disagreements and conflicts that arise. This is a high-stakes conversation because musical and educational practices are identity markers that symbolize the people who make and receive them and who are accorded the rights to express themselves musically and pedagogically in particular ways and to have a claim on justice.[12] Martin thinks of music as one of the aspects of cultural wealth that constitutes an important human resource worthy of transmission (and transformation) from one generation to the next.[13] Although on first glance her metaphor of a stock of cultural capital may seem more static than dynamic, it emphasizes the value of the resource constituted by music among the other aspects of culture and the importance of preserving and enhancing it into the future. Considerations of whose musics and which aspects require preservation and transformation, how this should be undertaken, and how musicians and their creations can be protected are important musical considerations for cultural policy makers.[14] The decisions arrived at through dialogue with those who have an interest in music and education are necessarily contingent and subject to change.

Since justice conceives of music and education as forms of moral action, it dignifies and gives meaning to musical and pedagogical undertakings. Its conception of integrity, transparency, and principled action is predicated on the notion of human beings having self-worth and dignity and being worthy of respect. Notwithstanding different conceptions of rightness and goodness, teachers and students who act justly assume that the rules with which they are affiliated carry the imperative of attributes of rightness and goodness. Codes of teacher and student conduct define the expectations of appropriate or "right" behavior and are a source of existential meaning and integrity. Israel Scheffler's "rule" model of teaching constitutes one manifestation of how teachers may approach their work justly.[15] Here, teachers exercise reason in weighing and balancing the relative goods and evils of various approaches. They construe the right way to proceed on behalf of others who may be dependent on them and serve as intermediaries between their students and the "mansions" in which they (these teachers) aspire to live and improve.[16] For Scheffler, these mansions are not up for debate; they represent the good, and teachers who have students' interests at heart aspire for their students to dwell in them, too. This is an aspirational view of education and music in which the teacher leads the student toward the good. Although people do not always act justly, they may seek to live their lives in ways that point to the good, whatever their conception of it may be. Even if justice can never be fully realized in the phenomenal world, it is well worth striving after because of the existential meaning it gives people in their lived situations. Despite the deeply embedded nature of injustice and the practical difficulties of arriving at justice, seeking it values humanity and hopes for the best for and of it.

Thinking in terms of music and education within the frame of justice in situations in which sometimes conflicting interests must be weighed and reconciled, at least for the present, puts a premium on collaboration, community, and contingency that value the human beings involved and the musical and educational processes in which people are central. Dewey's emphasis on the democratic classroom construed as a social system organized around particular rules that constrain students and teachers alike challenges notions of a dictatorial teacher who rules by fiat and powerless students at the mercy of their teacher's whim.[17] For Dewey, rule systems devised collaboratively by teachers and students for the classroom community empower all the participants and prefigure the democratic governance of the wider society. Reason offers the principal means of designing and interpreting these rules and of weighing the conduct of teachers and their students in relation to them. The rules are sometimes contested in the classroom in the manner of a joust as flaws in the rules, their interpretation, or injustices become apparent to some, if not all, participants. Since instruction is a moral undertaking, justice requires civility and dialogue, especially when the rules by which all agree to be bound are disputed and decisions must be made about what to do about the situation.

Justice requires a dynamic and critical engagement between learners and subject matter. Taken-for-granted assumptions are challenged, and privileged traditional knowledge is displaced to refocus on knowledge that heretofore may have been marginalized, repressed, or excluded from study.[18] The subject matter is also examined from the perspective of what has been historically erased from collective memory or denigrated as of little worth. Even though justice contributes to the continuity of tradition, this transformative vision of curriculum ironically emphasizes the imperative of change.[19] Importantly, the rule sets that have guided practice in the past and present are interrogated with a view to exposing injustices that have been unnoticed or hidden. Construing curriculum existentially in terms of the interrelationships between learners who make their own meanings as they come to know a subject and the subject matter of their study shifts the instructional focus. Rather than transmitting a stock of knowledge from one generation to the next, there is a dynamic interplay of meaning making as learners constructively and critically engage the subject of study and make it their own, thereby collectively transforming the subject as much as themselves.[20]

Justice also facilitates a smoothly running social system, be it educational or musical, in which, insofar as possible, contingencies have been accounted for and rules and procedures are applied justly and systematically. For example, in education, teachers, students and their parents and/or guardians, administrators, and the public at large agree to abide by the system's rules and its expectations. Thinking of this system democratically suggests that all have a say in their governance, and all are accountable to the others. For example, teachers and administrators act on behalf of and in the interest of the public good, and their conduct is expected to be ethical and professional. They serve in loco parentis for the young, whose interests they are expected to uphold and protect. Their greater experience, knowledge, and power than their students necessitate a system of checks and balances to ensure that they act ethically, tactfully, and wisely. Students are also expected to observe ethical standards of conduct. In the academy, for example, they are expected to be honest in their claims to authorship of their work and to act civilly and professionally in their relationships with their teachers, fellow students, and support staff. Failing to abide by these agreed-on rules triggers a system of disciplinary review and action that may result in acquittal, sanction, or expulsion from the organizational system.

Various flaws emerge in justice as a value. Among them, unexpected events in the system evoke surprise. Notwithstanding the hope for rationality and omniscience, administratively devised solutions do not always yield appropriate or expected results. Righteousness does not always prevail. The assumption of universality is theoretically and practically problematic. For justice to be done and seen to be done, those within its purview must agree to the principles on which it rests and the ways in which those principles are applied to lived life. In the phenomenal world, people do not always agree on what constitutes justice, and it is difficult to conceive of it without considering its inherently social nature and seeing its claims relatively rather than absolutely.[21] The dynamic nature of justice and its contested quality means that conceptions of what is just change over time. Conservative forces wish to preserve tradition, and liberal forces seek transformation, and there never seems to be an end to this societal struggle. To seek justice when one is outside the mainstream also leaves one in a powerless position and makes the struggle for inclusion more difficult to achieve. Too often, teachers are embroiled in the struggle for justice in circumstances in which they have been or believe themselves to be marginalized or disempowered. Conceptions of justice on the part of the society Establishment are, for those who are effectively marginalized, excluded, or disenfranchised from its purview, unjust; the struggle for justice by those on the margins or outside justice drives the endeavor to forge different conceptions of justice, thereby unsettling those in the Establishment who might otherwise lose power. In our own time, some would set back the clock of justice to an earlier time when they had greater power and control, even if this disadvantages others who have more recently won a claim on justice.

Assumptions of omniscience in forwarding what protagonists consider to be just systems inevitably founder in the face of human fallibility and the unintended consequences of human action. Acting in pursuit of or in the interests of justice assumes that musician teachers possess the know-how to rectify evil and arrive at justice and that, even with the best of intentions, they impose their views of justice on others who are rendered comparatively powerless in the process. For Ivan Illich, this teacher wears "an invisible triple crown like the papal tiara" and "pontificates as pastor, prophet, and priest."[22] The presumptive character of justice is often off the mark in the messy phenomenal world of complexities and nuances, and its prescriptions never seem to encompass the entire gamut of human experience and the natural world. Justice becomes, in a sense, a golden fleece, an impossible ideal, because people lack the very quality of knowing and the action required to identify and redress injustice and achieve justice. One might think that one knows what to do and act as if one does, but one is often wrong. Friedrich Schiller captures this important point when he urges humility on the part of those who, when they are tempted to act on behalf of others, should think of people as they really are; when they seek to inspire others, they should think of them as they could be.[23] His view accords with Berlin's evocation of Kant's metaphor of the "crooked timber of humanity" to make the point that historically, people do not always act as they wish they might or think they should.[24] Instead, there is the reality of fallibility and the impossibility of conceiving of justice without its antithesis, injustice. Undertaking the task of rooting out evildoing and ensuring that righteousness prevails assumes that one is able not only to diagnose what is going wrong but also to remediate the wrong and point toward right doing. Diagnosis is only the first part of the challenge. It is even more daunting to craft appropriate and effective means whereby a problem may be corrected. Devising a correctional strategy presumes wisdom, discernment, and even omniscience in correctly assessing an evil and forging a solution to correct it. So justice, at least in absolute terms, seems to be an ideal always out of reach.

EQUALITY

Thinking of equality in terms of estimations of commensurate value has its basis in mathematical calculations of equivalence. In human affairs, assessments of equality are both theoretical and practical: it is necessary to first articulate a theoretical basis on which equivalence is presumed to rest and then estimate the degree to which this theoretical abstraction is evidenced in the phenomenal world. The worlds of mathematics and human affairs are incommensurate, and notions of equality when applied to the beliefs and actions of human beings are inevitably figurative rather than literal. Nevertheless, in the way of metaphor, the mathematical basis of equality lurks behind the more nebulous conceptions of equality between human beings.

As with justice, the idea of equality in human affairs is rooted in the proposition that all human beings are of value. This sense of being valuable is often construed within religious and mythic traditions. For example, within the Judeo-Christian tradition, people's value arises from theological convictions that they are created in the image of God and are superior to other living things in the natural world.[25] As sentient beings, they possess the consciousness and reason to contemplate their existence and critically examine the various aspects of their lived lives. With a keenly developed social sensibility, they grasp how they fit within their social milieus, and they recognize when they are honored by or subservient to others. For much of human history, people have been willing to accept their place in a social order that accords different status and respect, often determined by birth. At moments throughout recorded history, particularly since the western Enlightenment, influenced by ideas that propounded the value of all human beings and the importance of individual reason and intelligence, this traditional order of things has been challenged, and ordinary people have striven concertedly for equality with those who were more privileged and to overthrow the social systems that rendered them powerless and unequal.[26]

When applied to human conduct, the word *equality* is an ambiguous construct. This ambiguity arises out of a plethora of defining characteristics of human beings—notably, social status and wealth, gender, sexual orientation, intelligence, ethnicity, language, religious and political affiliation, age, and color. Equality variously connotes the "condition of having equal dignity, rank, or privileges with others" and "the fact of being on an equal footing" with them; the idea of "being equal in power, ability, achievement, or excellence"; the notion of "equality of opportunity" or the "equal chance and right to seek success in one's chosen sphere regardless of social factors such as class, race, religion, and sex"; and the idea of "fairness, impartiality, equity."[27] To be equal, at least in mathematical terms, all of these conditions would need to be met. The reality, however, is that people regularly discriminate against different others, and prejudices make it difficult to assure that, notwithstanding the many differences among them, all are on equal footing, are afforded the same dignity and respect, and enjoy the same status, power, and opportunities to succeed. Human nature being what it is, and people being so varied in a host of ways, some are inevitably more privileged than others. George Orwell's astute observation in the commandment on the barn wall of *Animal Farm*, "ALL ANIMALS ARE EQUAL BUT SOME ANIMALS ARE MORE EQUAL THAN OTHERS," captures the reality that notwithstanding the best intentions and the hope that all can be equal, this value seems out of reach in the phenomenal world.[28]

Notice the differing ways in which equality is described in these various ordinary dictionary definitions. It is conceived of as a "condition," or a situation in which people find themselves in various respects. Rather than a unidimensional quality, it is a syndrome—a complex and interrelated array of symptoms that together mark a person's lived reality. Also, equality is described as a chance or an opportunity—that is, something attractive, hoped for, aspirational, and motivational but not yet realized. In this view, it is a perceptual quality. Further, equality is construed as a right to which everyone is entitled, or an expectation with the demand that it be fulfilled. This strong sense of the word combines the conception of a condition with a perception to create an ethical imperative that demands action. Although equality in the strong sense has energized the various political human rights movements during the past century, practically speaking, conditional and aspirational views have dominated in setting educational and musical expectations because they are less radical and demand less change of policy makers and the public at large.

Like justice, equality is evident in comparison to its logical opposite, inequality. Arguments for equality are often cast antithetically against the excesses of inequality, so much so that it is difficult to imagine equality without its opposite. This dialectical vision suggests a struggle for preeminence and the notion of equality (and inequality) as a dynamic concept in the process of being contested and becoming. In the phenomenal world, notions of equality are socially construed and politically charged. Like justice, conceptions of equality in whatever sense are messy constructs forged in the phenomenal world, ideals that remain out of reach yet constitute the source of inspiration, especially for those outside the social mainstream. Oppressed or suppressed people encounter resistance from the powerful who seek to hold on to their privilege and, by their beliefs and actions, ensure the continuation of injustice and inequality.

Among its musical and pedagogical contributions, equality makes it possible for all to share in the psychological benefits of self-actualization and well-being. In Abraham Maslow's view, self-actualization needs to be the objective of education because it epitomizes intellection and sensibility at their pinnacle, and it satisfies the highest of human needs for everyone.[29] For Maslow, attaining such peak experiences constitutes the fullest, highest, deepest, and richest knowing of which human beings are capable. This experience is at once spiritual and sensual, transcendent and immanent, and it encompasses aspiration and reality in the search for oneness and wisdom. Achieving self-actualization requires an educational approach that transcends the acquisition of skills and facts, important though they are, to focus on the search for wisdom and the mastery of procedures manifested by exponents of a given tradition. In a similar vein, June Boyce-Tillman thinks of well-being as a condition in which spiritual as well as material benefits flow to all those involved in the educational process.[30] Regarding people as precious and of equal worth requires ensuring musical and educational experiences that enable everyone to participate in self-actualization.

Thinking of teachers and students as fellow learners, and the teacher as a leader of students, takes a humane approach to music and education. To this end, Freire envisages a radical, cellular, and liberatory pedagogy designed specifically to empower the poor and illiterate to gain equality with those by whom they have been oppressed. Maxine Greene argues, in Freirean vein, that without a community in which one is a respected and valued member, it may be impossible to imagine a different reality.[31] Notions that all human beings are worthy of being treated with dignity and respect in their lived lives, that they can aspire to becoming more fulfilled than they are at present, that nothing external stands in their way to prevent them from realizing their hopes and dreams, and that they have the right to be treated equally to more privileged and powerful others are humane principles that contribute to human happiness and self-realization. Thinking of equality in the strong sense of human rights, as do these writers, empowers those who believe themselves to be disempowered to imagine how things might be different and to act on their convictions.

Embracing equality also suggests affirmative action on behalf of those who have been excluded from certain areas of study or subjects and whose value has been regarded heretofore as questionable or of lesser importance by educational policy makers and their publics. Because there is not a level playing field, affirmative action is required to advocate for and pay special attention to those who have been systematically disadvantaged and to go beyond traditional criteria for inclusion to develop new means by which students and subjects may be included. It is necessary to confront prejudice against different others or certain subjects of study and to open opportunities for students to choose the specific subjects to be studied and the means of their study. Instructional affirmative action is manifestly imaginative and liberatory in empowering students and teachers to grapple with subject matter that all consider worthwhile and intrinsically valuable.[32]

Equality carries the imperatives of accountability and assessment in ensuring and demonstrating that all have the same opportunities to succeed and receive treatment comparable to others. It also requires transparency in the pedagogical process in demonstrating that all are afforded the same access and opportunities and can take full advantages of instruction. In this view, accountability and assessment can serve to correct and ameliorate systemic inequality. Just as it is important for a school system to demonstrate that it is providing equitably for all its participants, teachers can show that all their students receive equal treatment and that instruction is directed toward enabling them to succeed. Since many of the musical and educational benefits are spiritual and hidden from view, accountability and assessment measures are only ever crude indices. Still, insofar as measurement is possible, whether through portfolios or other subjective measures, it provides an important corrective to inequality and data points on which estimations of equality may be made.

Still, among equality's detractions is that, faced with an impossibly high bar of equality in all respects, at least practically speaking, proponents of musical and educational equality may be tempted to retreat to the notion of equality of opportunity, or the idea that all people should have the right and ability to realize their aspirations. This aspirational view does not take account of the fact that even if barriers that prevent people from realizing their aspirations are removed, imaginations may be so hemmed about by prejudice that those aspirations may be severely restricted. Others may be able to take advantage of the same opportunities because their imaginations are open to possibilities and their aspirations seem boundless. Prejudices are institutionalized in the very fabric of society. So deeply are they internalized both individually and collectively that it is difficult to imagine how things might be different or to aspire to the hopes and dreams that may motivate others. Such is the power of imagination and the degree to which it has been impacted by self- or socially imposed limitations that equality of opportunity is difficult to realize in practice. Although as a teacher, one may wish to treat one's students equally, one's own and one's students' prejudices make this a daunting if not impossible task to achieve in practice. It is also possible that those aspects that are more difficult to measure, quantify, or estimate, or are more esoteric or further from the mainstream, may be relegated to the sidelines. Also, resources that might otherwise be devoted to connecting students and certain subjects of study may be diverted into teaching to prepare students for tests or otherwise consumed by the demands and costs, in time and other resources, of assessment. Engaging in aspects that have previously been accorded less value also displaces those matters that hitherto have been central and invites resistance from people with a vested interest in the status quo.

Some notions of equality before the law link ideas of justice to those of equality in the proposition that all people have the same legal protections and claims despite their diversity; this conception also turns out to be an ideal that is difficult if not impossible to achieve. For example, all people may have the right to a fair trial and the protections of the law insofar as they are spelled out. Despite the social prejudices that may abound in society, all people may be presumed to have equal standing or be on an equal footing with different others who appeal to or are brought before legal authorities. Much depends on the laws that are enacted and the degree to which they embody principles that seek to value all human beings equally, notwithstanding the evident differences that characterize them. When laws are enacted that privilege men, white people, specific religious affiliations, or languages, others, such as women, persons of color, members of other religions, and those who speak different languages than those the law privileges cannot expect to be treated equally before the law. Should they be rich, they may be able to afford a spirited defense; should they be poor, the legal counsel appointed to represent them may not be of the same caliber as the rich person's, and they may have fewer resources with which to mount a defense. Equality before the law is thus problematic and difficult to realize in practice.

Organizational and administrative problems arise in seeking an equitable distribution of resources throughout the system so that all participants have equal opportunities and means to achieve widely commensurate ends. The search for equality requires determining the criteria and instruments by which equality is to be assessed. In this case, educational policy makers are likely to take a data-driven and rational approach to the management of human and other resources in the system. Through this means, they hope to demonstrate accountability to teachers, students, parents and guardians, boards of education, accrediting agencies, and the wider public. In practice, though, this is a fraught task. Issues arise in respect to the assessment of the degree to which equality in whatever sense is to be measured. Problems of estimating equality arise because of the plethora of ways in which human beings may be unequal and the invisibility of some of the effects of educational and musical inequality (as well as equality). Factors that make it difficult to measure equality in a social system include the dynamism and complexity of social systems; the short time scales of social events (measured in minutes, hours, days, weeks, months, or years); the problems of definitively establishing causation; the fact that people's behaviors do not correspond exactly with their beliefs, values, and attitudes; and the fact that their position within or outside a social group impacts what they can or cannot observe or notice. It is likely that even the most sophisticated instruments are somewhat limited and even crude—at best, indices of the phenomena they are intended to measure. In the strictest sense, equality relies on accurate estimations of the degrees and ways in which it is and is not manifested, and, practically speaking, these estimations remain difficult to achieve.

Thinking about musical equality requires acknowledging the comparative worth of musics and regarding them as meriting study and practice for a variety of reasons. Estimating the value of musical traditions and the practices that exemplify them is particularly difficult because musics manifest in a plethora of ways, and their effects are not always evident. Musical prejudices arise from the differing musical values that undergird each musical practice as well as the values ascribed to those musics by virtue of how they function in society—meanings that Lucy Green terms "delineated" as opposed to "inherent" to the music.[33] As I read her work, Green would not suppose these binaries to be dichotomous; she would see them as "weak syndromes" in which one blends into another in a mix somewhere between two theoretical extremes. Once one opens the door to the social value of music as a part of wider aesthetic and specifically musical concerns, prejudices must be admitted as part of the baggage. These prejudices are difficult to overcome in the search for a comparative and egalitarian musical view that espouses all musics in their myriad manifestations as of equivalent worth in one respect or another. For example, it is challenging to dislodge the racialized nature of Western music, the societal preference for whiteness over blackness, and the higher valuation of musics associated with whiteness over those associated with blackness. A crucial and daunting problem in seeking musical equality, as cultural equality more generally, is also to determine (justify and contest) bases on which assessments of value are to be made. Practically speaking, although this is sometimes a fraught task, musicians and educators regularly determine that some musical beliefs and practices are more important and defensible than others for their specific purposes.

Too often, equality has been thought of in ways such as color-blindness and meritocracy, which render invisible the distinctive differences among human beings in terms of such things as language, gender, age, and race. This conception, while thought of as egalitarian and inclusive, can result in demeaning those whose identities are bound up in these differences and, by failing to recognize, notice, and respect them, treats those characterized by them as of lesser value. For these reasons, some may prefer to use the word *equity* because it concerns notions of "fairness, impartiality; even-handed dealing" that suggest accommodation, repair, and restitution.[34] Equity seeks to restore equality rather than observing it. It attempts to rectify inequalities, whether by seeking adjustments between differing persons, approaches, mindsets, or practices, remedying evident inequalities, or treating others fairly. By going further to eradicate invisibility, inequity, and social injustice, equity has a more transformative purpose.[35] As such, it seems closer to the value of fairness, to which I come next.

FAIRNESS

The word *fairness* has an aesthetic and feminine ring. As the "quality or condition of being fair," it has been used variously to describe qualities as different as women's "beauty" and "lightness in color of complexion, skin, or hair," or weather that is pleasant, fine, or "free from rain, winds." The lightness and calmness evident in the flow, transparency, and gentleness of fairness is in counterpoint to the storminess, disagreeableness, and darkness of its antithesis, foulness. Here, I use *fairness* to connote qualities such as "honesty; impartiality, equitability, justness; fair dealing," which I see metaphorically through the prisms of lightness and femininity.[36] In forwarding this word, I also return to my Australian roots and the myth of the "fair go."[37] This value is deeply rooted in the white Australian ethos where people must often rely on each other to survive in a harsh physical environment. It refers to a deeply held and egalitarian belief in the importance of fairness, in considering all the angles of a situation and dealing honestly and impartially with others so that everyone has an opportunity to succeed. Rather than rig a system to privilege some over others or mislead or trick others, the idea of the "fair go" requires integrity, forthrightness, evenhandedness, trust, and transparency in one's dealings with others.

Thinking about fairness from a pedagogical standpoint suggests that the rule systems that govern the situation are transparent and do not favor some or disadvantage others.[38] All the participants are accountable for their actions and expected to treat each other dispassionately. Differing beliefs and practices are weighed and critically examined with a view to finding ways through differing and sometimes conflicting perspectives on the situation. Interpersonal relationships in the instructional situation are predicated on the smoothness and flow that arise out of clear expectations of all the participants about what should be done under specific circumstances. The instructional rules also need to be revisited from time to time, especially when contested by those who regard the taken-for-granted conceptions of fairness as manifestly unfair and even evil and who demand systemic change that supplants present rules. Moreover, the claims of fairness require that policy makers create and maintain a transparent organizational system that is evenhanded and dispassionate. Rules and procedures whereby the organization operates need to be clearly articulated and enforced without special favor to individuals or groups. Administrators seek to create a smoothly flowing system with a minimum of uncertainty, interruption, conflict, and chaos. Having set this system in motion, the hope is that the clarity of expectations and roles on the part of all those within it will render leaders more or less invisible. Rather than micromanage every organizational decision, administrative effort and time can then be directed toward solving those problems that prevent the system from working smoothly.

The notion of transparency implicit within fairness suggests it is possible to clearly apprehend and evaluate all the relevant aspects of a situation, everything needed for a decision is disclosed, ideas and practices are consistent, and nothing is deliberately hidden from view, glossed over, or rendered opaque or misleading. Persons whose beliefs and actions are transparent are thought of as having integrity—that is, they exhibit a wholeness and unity of thought, purpose, and action that others can readily perceive as utterly consistent and clear. Figuratively, there is a lightness and even brightness in their belief and conduct. When others deal with them, they know with whom they are dealing and can interact without the fear of negotiating hidden currents or unexpected storms. This same transparency also applies to the workings of social systems; fairness suggests that people clearly understand how a system works and grasp that the rules in place are dispassionately applied to everyone. Those in positions of power are accountable for the exercise of that power to the public to whom they are responsible, and their actions can be clearly discerned.

It is difficult to envisage fairness without also acknowledging its opposite: foulness. Here, notions of opacity, murkiness, and distastefulness stand opposed to the transparency, clarity, and attractiveness of fairness. This aesthetic quality of fairness renders it, like any art, somewhat in the eye of the beholder; what may be beautiful for one may be ugly for another. The implicit conflict of the attractiveness, lightness, whiteness, and brightness of fairness with the ugliness, darkness, blackness, and dullness of foulness privileges the light and white against the dark and black and reflects a racial perspective. The roots of the Australian myth of the "fair go" are colonial rather than indigenous. Many of the first colonists were transported as convicts, often for minor offenses. They felt a sense of injustice at their plight and the need for fairness in all their dealings with others. As they were cast adrift in an alien environment, this notion of fairness took root as a fundamental value in the Australian psyche. The aboriginal peoples did not view their world as hostile but lived within it; it was the white men who saw the natural world as threatening and needing to be tamed and subdued. What might be regarded as a "fair go" for white Australians was viewed as foul by the first peoples. Indeed, the project of reclaiming the dignity of people of color necessitated rescuing aesthetic values of ugliness, darkness, and blackness and asserting the value of foulness as opposed to fairness.

Among its potential contributions, fairness suggests that decisions are reasonable and made dispassionately. By this, I mean that an individual's judgment is not clouded by emotional attachments or dislikes. Susanne Langer invokes the notion of "psychic distancing" as a means of making judgments about the arts.[39] This dispassion has its roots in Kantian convictions about the power of reason in negotiating aspects of human life that are felt and enacted. For Langer, the arts, religions, myths, and dreams express the greater part of the life of the mind that resists encapsulation within ordinary discourse. Since emotion and reason are closely connected, whether as cognitive emotions or emotional cognitions, practicing a measure of restraint and distancing oneself from phenomena constitute mechanisms for negotiating this territory.[40] Fairness highlights the complexity of practical decision-making and the difficulty of achieving transparency in thought and action in one's interpersonal relationships. This is the case when compromises need to be made in the phenomenal world that reflect greater and lesser goods and evils. Reason constitutes a means of thinking about and working through sometimes intractable issues in the lived world. In exercising reason, teachers seek to weigh multiple and sometimes conflicting interests, pressures, and possibilities. They may need to compromise and identify points of consensus as well as dissensus in finding practical paths forward. Their approach may be provisional, and the uncertainties arising from the impact of their actions in the phenomenal world may require revisiting their aims and methods from time to time.

Fairness also suggests an educational approach that emphasizes personal integrity, transparency of goals and methods, and a calm demeanor that navigates sometimes problematic, confusing, and messy practical realities and weighs matters reasonably and dispassionately. When applied to learning, fairness suggests that the procedures and goals are transparent and that all that is relevant to the performance of all students is understood clearly before and during the process.

As teachers and students grapple with the complexities of approaching the subject matter and the possibilities of disparate values that are employed in adjudicating it, they need to develop a dispassionate approach to weighing and accounting for varying points of view. Their own integrity and honesty are relied on in the instructional situation, and cheating and other forms of academic dishonesty are viewed as grievous sins that must be punished. A curriculum construed within the frame of fairness requires a transparent process whereby the students come to know various subjects of study, and subject matter is constructed by the students in an interactive process. The material to be studied is approached dispassionately, even objectively in the sense of students coming to the public knowledge of a subject and acquiring the wisdom possessed by its exponents and practitioners. In so doing, the competing and conflicting claims of various perspectives, traditions, and interests are treated evenhandedly through the exercise of reason.

The reality of musical systems that too often are rigged in favor of certain individuals and groups demands the value of fairness so that these systems may be rendered transparent and accessible to all who wish to participate in them. As I have noted, racism lurks everywhere and predisposes Western systems to whiteness over blackness. Notions of musical fairness suggest that compromise will be necessary in adjudicating sometimes conflicting, competing, and differing interests and traditions. Where choices need to be made between the lesser of evils or the greater of goods, fairness may remain out of reach. Musical fairness recognizes and honors the presence of marginalized or ostracized persons and groups and the difficulties of reconciling differing interests. For example, Pete Gale grapples with this array of practical and pedagogical issues in his inner-city classroom as he works with DJ microphones and a turntable and figures out who he will call on next.[41]

Among fairness's detractions, the assumption of dispassion as its basis has come under fire by those who argue that this is exactly the wrong approach and who resist conceptions of decision-making rooted in Enlightenment notions of the supremacy of reason.[42] Rather than judgments based purely on reason, passion and desire as parts of one's being are embraced and accounted for so that one becomes intimate with rather than remains distant from the phenomena in question when deciding what to do.[43] In this view, a holistic view of human beings suggests that "psychic distancing" is not only ill-advised but impossible to achieve, as it flies in the face of the passional nature of judgment. Women's decision-making is often situated and requires that one deliberately take account of feeling; the dispassionate reason lauded by Enlightenment writers is at odds with the ways women see the world.[44] Thinking of the Australian "fair go" from this perspective suggests a quite masculine view of the world that assumes dispassion rather than compassion in making judgments in the interests of transparency and evenhandedness.

The tensions between fairness and foulness raise problems about what to do about them, practically speaking, and how to balance their competing interests. For example, thinking of education in terms of fairness may turn out to be a quite ethnocentric and masculine view that contrasts with the ways in which minorities and women see the world. In proposing other aesthetics such as blackness in counterpoint to whiteness, bell hooks is among those to interrogate Establishment views of fairness and to suggest that teachers ought to transgress them in favor of the perspectives of women and minorities.[45] The racialized basis of learning and the prejudices that flow from deeply ingrained habits of thought and practice and ethnocentric and classist perspectives on subject matter are difficult for teachers and students to overcome. It is also possible that women and girls may find themselves "outsiders," "interlopers," and "immigrants" in what seems to be a masculine approach to learning.[46] Overcoming the many barriers between people—among them racism, ethnocentrism, homophobia, classism, and sexism—remains a resilient objective in learning that aspires to be fair. Still, it is difficult to overcome the prejudices of educational policy makers, publics, teachers, and students against certain persons, beliefs, and practices, and those with vested interests in the status quo.

Although calmness, dispassion, and reason may be helpful in negotiating these complexities, multiple possibilities and viewpoints need to be adjudicated in achieving fairness. To do this comprehensively would require omniscience—a quality that human beings lack. This reality puts fairness ultimately out of reach. Still, acknowledging the variety, even plethora of angles and considerations, the objective need not be achieving the correct decision or the "one right way." Fairness can be construed more ambiguously as a matter of weighing differing interests and attempting to reach a solution that takes them all into account while also eschewing preferential treatment of interests, persons, or considerations. This is a broad view because it hopes to consider the sweep of cultural multiplicity and the variety and differences of viewpoints represented. Accomplishing this objective probably means the entire exercise is something of a compromise and necessarily fallible and shortsighted. I admit this is a very practical and pragmatic view of the situation that accepts the murkiness of the phenomenal world but hopes to shine the clear light of dispassionate reason on it insofar as possible. One may seek to take all the differing and sometimes competing and conflicting interests into account in coming to a decision of what would be fair. Still, everything hangs on one's ability to see possibilities and a broad picture and one's confidence that reason provides a basis on which to judge which beliefs and actions need to be arrived at and applied in practice. Practically speaking, and despite one's best intentions, fairness may take insufficient cognizance of the difficulties of negotiating differing possibilities and viewpoints and arriving at a point of decision.

INCLUSION

At its root, inclusion is an ambiguous quality. In its ordinary usage, it is construed as noun and verb, as "an act of including something or someone" or "the fact or condition of being included." The verb means "to enclose" or "incorporate as part of a whole." In the United States, inclusion means an "action, practice, or policy of including any person in an activity, system, organization, or process, irrespective of race, gender, religion, age, ability, etc." Within education, it refers specifically to the "action, practice, or fact of enabling all students, especially those with disabilities or learning difficulties, to participate in mainstream education while having their special needs supported."[47] Its comprehensive and all-embracing quality suggests that the focus is on "taking in" contra its opposite of exclusion or "leaving out." Its construal in terms of avoiding bias and its broad reference to encompassing previously marginalized persons and groups within the mainstream of society link it directly to justice, equality, and fairness in this present quartet. I use it here in the sense of thought, language, and action that include all people regardless of gender, religion, politics, race, ethnicity, language, color, age, intellectual ability, different physical ability, or social class, among the host of differences that separate them.[48] In this writing, thinking about inclusion is particularly fraught since space precludes both forwarding my own ideas and giving voice comprehensively to every author who has addressed social justice and inclusiveness in music education. The selective and sometimes categorical nature of my references illustrates how talk about inclusion can itself be exclusive even if this is not one's intention. This dilemma exemplifies the challenges of realizing inclusion in music education thought and practice.

The value of inclusion in American public education is grounded in the democratic ideal of the participation of the public in its own governance. Inclusion is forwarded by philosophers of education and the arts such as Dewey and Herbert Read. In their view, since all citizens need to participate collectively in decision-making regarding the common good, it is necessary that they be educated to do so intelligently. For Dewey, this education is manifestly scientific and artistic; for Read, it is necessarily artistic.[49] Both writers take their cues from Plato's embrace of the arts and sciences as the building blocks of a common education.[50] As the definition of a citizen broadened from a small group of wealthy and free men to, in more recent times, most adults within a society, irrespective of their age, social class, economic wealth, gender, sexual orientation, religious or political affiliation, language, or color, the idea of inclusion as an ideal expanded to take in this broader notion of the citizenry. In educational thought and practice, this value impacted who should be included within the compass of mandated schooling and who might be considered educable. Differently challenged children with an array of physical, cognitive, and emotional conditions were now, where possible, to be mainstreamed within general education. The ideal of including everyone within the compass of education, irrespective of where they fit within the spectrum of human difference, became a central concern of publicly supported education.

Contra notions of the psychic distancing implicated in fairness, inclusion thrives in the spirit of intimacy and closeness to the subjects of study.[51] Rather than a matter of rational judgment, this psychic nearness also implicates feeling for the other, whether similar or different from oneself. Drawing on the metaphor of the family, for example, inclusion wants to enlarge the circle to embrace different others within it. It aspires to draw on the love, fellowship, affection, and mutual respect family members hopefully have toward each other and extend that feeling outward, passionately rather than dispassionately, to the wider community. Inclusion is forever pressing against the restrictive bounds of social groups, organizations, societal institutions, and societies. It cannot be content with the present but, like the universe, is in a state of perpetual and dynamic expansion. Never satisfied or complete, it is in a constant state of becoming ever more inclusive. In the process of unsettling and challenging social barriers, it can also destroy, transform, and reconstruct groups, institutions, and societies.

The implication of cognitive emotions and emotional cognitions in all their forms renders the study, practice, and assessment of inclusion more an artistic than a scientific enterprise.[52] Immanence in counterpoint with transcendence suggests sorts of knowing and social engagement in the social group that are difficult to measure. Inclusion is a more communitarian than individualistic value. One is identified as a member of a group and is valued as much for one's membership within it as for one's individuality. The arts, myths, rituals, and religions provide particularly appropriate ways of enacting knowledge that is felt rather than grasped intellectually and propositionally.

Among its advantages, inclusion offers a humane view of people in the wider natural world and cosmos. It provides the bedrock for democratic institutions of government, takes a compassionate approach to individual and social affairs, and constitutes a dynamic process of becoming in search of a broader worldview. Seen in its more recent sense of political and legal engagement, it seeks to overcome the restrictiveness of too much thought and practice. It also transforms ideas practically in ways that resonate with the interests of justice, equality, and fairness.

Thinking of music inclusively involves the role of compassion and empathy in the work of incorporating disenfranchised traditions into the mainstream. There is the possibility, even the hope, that this inclusion may result in displacing the focus on other musical traditions to those that have been heretofore excluded or marginalized. Musical traditions are approached with a desire for intimacy rather than with the dispassion and psychic distance of fairness. One hopes to feel, insofar as possible, the experience of exponents or devotees of these musics. This view of music is also enactive in the sense that musics must be performed and undergone, as closely as possible to the ways in which their exponents experience them. Since music relates intimately to other aspects of culture, be they the other arts, religions, familial traditions, governance, or commercial interests, one also needs to grasp musics contextually. Since there is never an end to inclusion, and its borders are constantly expanding, so, too, does this view of music have a dynamic quality as one musical tradition and practice intersects with others, sometimes creating new traditions and practices, other times remaining separate from the others. The musical horizons of those who learn new musics are also being pushed outward so that music takes on a dynamic, living quality that animates its making and receiving. This emphasis on inclusion is also a humane view that accords dignity to the people identified with certain musics. Importantly, the vitality and animated quality of music, as culture more broadly, resonates with people who make and receive it, and music becomes inextricably connected with other aspects of life.

Inclusion takes a comprehensive view of teaching and thinks of enculturation as an important educational means and end. Such a broad view entails living a way of life as well as communicating propositional and procedural knowledge about subject matter. It means seeing teaching as integrally related to other aspects of culture and lived life. Teachers focus on establishing the conditions for personal and interpersonal growth. From time to time, doing this may require some exclusiveness so that teachers and their students can develop in specific ways and directions. This is a processual and dynamic view of teaching that is enacted and practical, reflective and theoretical. Importantly, since teachers are interested in widening the instructional community and bringing different others into the educational process, they approach their work compassionately rather than dispassionately. They seek to come close to their students, especially those who face various intellectual, emotional, or physical challenges that would otherwise leave them outside the mainstream.

An inclusive learning environment emphasizes the role of communities in which learners are fully present to and respectful of others and in which solitary learners may not imagine how things could be different from how they are in such a community.[53] "Communities of practice" emphasize procedural as well as propositional knowledge and seek not only to selectively transmit wisdom from one generation to the next but to transform that practice. It is not surprising to encounter porous boundaries that permit learners to freely enter and exit the instructional situation.[54] This being the case, rather than excluding students prematurely because of their educational pedigree or past performance, the onus is on them to demonstrate that they can do the work. This open approach to education is likely to result in wider differences in student aptitude and ability than might otherwise be the case if the borders of the instructional situation were harder and less porous. Moreover, learning is more likely passionate rather than dispassionate, and emotional responses to the pedagogical situation play an important role in what is learned and how it is learned. Here, practice rather than theory is emphasized, and doing rather than just learning propositional knowledge about what is done is central to instruction.

The boundaries of this ever-widening community of fellow learners are drawn generously. In its hard sense of insisting on moral and legal rights to be incorporated within the mainstream of society, inclusion combats prejudice against minorities and different others and acts affirmatively on their behalf as it seeks to bring all into the instructional situation. Its reliance on empathy and compassion values cooperation and mutual support of those within and without the instructional situation's present borders. Those who are excluded from or on the margins of instruction are invited to its center, possibly displacing those who heretofore have enjoyed a privileged position and special treatment. Such a move may be resisted by those who no longer enjoy preferential status and who must now wait their turn, as do less privileged others. In drawing the borders of this community so generously, a wider range of students and teachers may now work together. This reality complicates the interaction between the participants in the instructional situation, and negotiating these complexities civilly relies on generosity, affection, and empathy toward others.

An inclusive curriculum is construed as a dynamic process that enlarges the boundaries of fields of study as much as the horizons of those who come to know to know these subjects. In emphasizing the multiple perspectives and interests of pluralities within the public at large, the designers of this curriculum seek a way through dissensus and consensus by empathizing and coming close to different others. Inclusion makes a place for feeling as central to intellection and challenges unbridled reason and dispassion. It admits those ways of knowing that are enacted and that may be grounded in thought about emotion in the way of the religions, arts, myths, and rites, which Yob calls "emotional cognitions," as well as regarding emotion as parasitic on reason in what Scheffler terms "cognitive emotions."[55]

Inclusion suggests that educational policy makers' focus is on leading an organization by means of appealing to the hearts as well as the minds of its members. The organization is rooted in the metaphor of the family, and effort is expended to build teams of people around bonds of affection and shared interests and goals. This is an informal approach to leadership that values intimacy, sharing, bringing people with disparate backgrounds (many of whom may have been marginalized or excluded from membership) into the organization, and empowering all its members to take ownership of it. Educational policy makers seek to include women and minorities within leadership teams and welcome students who might otherwise not have an opportunity to attend a particular school. They reach out into the communities in which their schools are located to provide services such as continuing education programs and invite participation by community experts in their educational programs. Moreover, since lifelong learning constitutes the grand project of education, collaboration blurs the boundaries between the institutions that foster formal and informal education such as the home, religion, state, artistic and cultural institutions, and commerce.

Among its detractions, inclusion as a value is difficult to imagine without its antithesis, exclusion. While inclusion is a useful value in educating citizens for democratic participation, a necessary part of education concerns exclusion, or the value of separating people without specific knowledge or skills from those with them. The point of certifying teachers, doctors, accountants, lawyers, and clergy members, among other professionals, for example, is to draw such a line and keep those without the requisite knowledge and skills from acting as if they possess them. In medicine, for example, excluding some by setting high standards of admission criteria and performance levels can help save lives. Only those with a high degree of medical knowledge are permitted to practice as masters of their art or craft. This is true of other professions in which the implications of malpractice may be less directly life-threatening but nevertheless harmful in other ways. From medieval times, guilds excluded all but those with the demonstrated expertise from practicing a profession. In music guilds, for example, those with requisite music skills were enabled to earn a livelihood, and guild membership provided a monopoly of sorts that protected members from interlopers. Today's musician teachers also act as if exclusion has value in musical performance. If they wish to create outstanding performing ensembles, they may audition students for membership and exclude those without the necessary expertise or interest.

The notion of inclusion as an educational value is based on the metaphor of growth. Here, the teacher is the gardener who cultivates the soil and tends the plant so that it grows to maturity. Shinichi Suzuki, like Dewey and Maria Montessori, suggests that this cultivation of the environment in which the student is situated needs to be a central pedagogical focus.[56] While this may be good, and teachers seek to help all their students develop, growth takes insufficient cognizance of the other side of cultivation—the need to weed out and exclude some plants from the garden. As I have commented on this metaphor elsewhere, gardeners realize that over time the exclusion of weeds and plants of various kinds takes on more prominence.[57] This is especially the case if the gardener hopes to shape the garden to a certain vision or if plants are to have the space to thrive. Enhancing student growth necessarily requires excluding some things. Scheffler notes that realizing human potential requires choices along the way that exclude the development of some aspects and require the development of others.[58] In this view, unbridled inclusion can do potential harm by failing to make the kinds of choices that would permit and encourage growth in certain ways by excluding development in others. Also, as June Boyce-Tillman points out, the fact that artistic, mythic, religious, and ritualistic ways of knowing are subjugated in Western societies makes it difficult to see them as equally powerful to those ways of knowing that rely on propositional discourse and reason.[59] Further, there may be insufficient critical attention to contesting dubious claims for inclusion of certain subjects or methods, or agreement on what subject matter and instructional approaches should be included.[60]

Crucial to the notion of exclusion is the question of who is responsible for doing the excluding and how this task is to be undertaken. Much of the more recent literature on the value of inclusion recognizes the systemic factors that stand in the way of individuals developing in certain ways.[61] For Scheffler, the question regarding human potential is resolved by assuming that no external factors prevent John from learning to play the piano (either physically or in terms of his environment), and he also has a choice in the matter (or his parents or guardians on his behalf in loco parentis).[62] If he is prevented from learning to play the piano by reason of his gender, his parents' lack of money to buy him an instrument on which to practice or afford private lessons, or his own physiognomy (if, for example, his hands are small and he is unable to negotiate particular piano repertoire), he may not realize his potential to learn to play the piano. Even if he is not prevented by these factors, there is the further consideration of whether he wishes to learn to play. The final decision, Scheffler hopes, will be his own to take (or will belong to those who have his best interests at heart). Would that he might get to this point! Too often, external factors intervene to exclude him from learning to play the piano before he can exercise his own choice in the matter.[63]

Seeing inclusion along with exclusion requires the notion of boundedness—namely, the presence of identifiable boundaries that define inner and outer, individual and others, among other aspects that include some and exclude others. Inclusion takes on importance only because of the presence of these borders and boundaries. In this Cartesian worldview, separating inner and outer, and self and other, comes under fire from writers such as Gilles Deleuze and Felix Guattari, who believe everything to be interconnected and included and who prefer a smooth and dynamic flow between disparate elements rather than a static reality of hard surfaces between things.[64] Notwithstanding the importance of these insights, in the phenomenal world, boundaries, borders, and binaries are facts of life. Nor do Deleuze and Guattari succeed in escaping them: their analysis is replete with binaries.[65] Despite the fact that music and education are hedged about with borders, inclusion serves to challenge, expand, transcend, and even destroy those that constitute barriers in the way of realizing human potential.

Thinking of justice, equality, fairness, and inclusion, justice can be construed metaphorically as combat and a set of scales and legally in terms of rule-bound action, in terms of what it means to be just, righteous, or morally right. Equality is conceived in terms of estimations of commensurate value, drawing on the metaphor of mathematical equivalence, and predicated on the assumption of the preciousness of humanity. Fairness evokes honesty, calmness, and gentleness thought of metaphorically as lightness and femininity and the white Australian myth of the "fair go." Inclusion connotes the ideas of surrounding, enclosing, and incorporating into a whole. These values share several attributes and differ sometimes markedly in other respects. As ambiguous constructs seen in antithesis with their opposites (injustice, inequality, foulness, and exclusion, respectively), practically speaking, they seem impossible to reach. Their rootedness in metaphors gives them distinctive flavors, and they are known imaginatively and emotionally from multiple perspectives. Enacted to some degree, their associated skills have distinctive attributes, and they require artistry and skill to negotiate in the phenomenal world. When they inevitably intersect, practically speaking, harmony and synergy do not always emerge, and they point in different directions, suggest alternative approaches, and evoke tensions, discontinuities, and irreconcilable differences as their ambiguities only multiply. Despite their contributions, they represent a double-edged sword. Still, this is the stuff of musical and educational thought and practice. Notwithstanding the challenges in determining what should be done in circumstances in which there are no easy solutions, musicians and educators need to learn to celebrate these ambiguities and love the questions they raise.

ELEVEN

Commonalities, Resonances, Applications, and Decisions

I BEGIN WITH THE QUESTIONS that have guided this study—namely, the values that ought to characterize music and education, their contributions and detractions, and their application to practice. In the preceding chapters, I sketched nine quartets of interrelated yet distinctive values with a view to their theoretical and practical interrelationships to music and education. In every case, it was clear that musicians, teachers, and students find themselves on the horns of a dilemma as to how to interpret, respond to, and apply these values in their various musical and pedagogical situations. Returning to these questions at book's end, and taking a meta-view of the foregoing chapters, I reflect on the meaning of this analysis, especially how my approach might apply to the practice as well the theory of music education. In keeping with my search for common ground in this plurality of values, I am interested in the features common to these value sets, how they resonate theoretically with music and education, how they apply to the practical predicaments faced by musicians and teachers, and what my approach offers music education more generally. Since music and education are practical activities, the proof of the worth of thinking through these values lies in the pudding of action. I assume that all those interested in music and education are likely to approach this writing from differing perspectives on the values and their likely resonance with their specific and divergent musical and instructional situations. I have illustrated how I have thought about these values and their meanings; it is then up to others to reach their own conclusions and determine how they might or should be applied in practice.

WHAT ARE THE COMMON FEATURES OF THESE VALUES?

Among the commonalities in the values I have examined, I have shown that all these values are ambiguous. They are rational (intellectual), emotional (felt), and embodied (sensed) commitments that are lived by and even loved. Their ambiguity opens the prospect of figurative and literal interpretation and nuance. The values I have discussed often rest in metaphors, sometimes in multiple metaphors, that evoke various interpretations and suggest different nuances. For example, the metaphors of justice as a joust or contest and as a set of scales in which things are weighed comparatively invite differing views of the character of justice as a value, the musical and education purposes it serves, and the methods by which it should be carried forward. Whether or to what degree justice is to be interpreted literally or figuratively also impacts its conception. For example, I have suggested in another writing that there are multiple justices, each situated and viewed comparatively, and no monolithic justice is perfectly attainable in the phenomenal world.[1] Each value in a cluster (for example, justice, equality, fairness, and inclusion) emphasizes different qualities, and there are overlaps between one cluster and another. Practically speaking, values seem to be soft-boundaried as one merges into another.[2] For practitioners, it may be difficult to definitively and authoritatively define each value, agree on its interpretation as a basis for collective action, and determine the suitable requisite action. Joseph Schwab describes this challenge as a principal curricular predicament (I also see it as characteristic of all aspects of music education), as a messy and tangled ground where beliefs spawn practices that in turn prompt beliefs.[3] Ambiguity opens the prospect for musical and educational "multiplicities and pluralities."[4] These appeal to imagination and critical thought in forging creative ways to construe values and apply them in the specific musical and pedagogical situations in which music teachers and students meet in coming to know music.[5]

All these values are two-edged swords with bright and dark possibilities. In every case, with Aristotle, I want to avoid the worst that each value when carried to excess might suggest while embracing the best. I am inevitably caught in the predicament of seeking to put "this-with-that" in tension and paradox, prone to critique from all sides.[6] My position puts the onus on musical and educational policy makers and all their constituencies not only to find a fraught path and avoid the possible evils that may arise from their best intentions but to work out how these values apply in their individual situations. For me, this is the reality of the pedagogical and musical situations I have faced during a lifetime. This intellectual position is exhilarating and requires intelligence and imagination to solve sometimes intractable problems often in disparate situations that are already underway. The values I have described serve as examples and reminders of my premise in this book that wisdom lies in the middle ground between extremes: values carried to extremes may constitute evils, goods may constitute evils, and evils may be goods. My challenge as a musician and educator is to embrace those values that I see as musical and educational goods and avoid the evils evoked if these values are taken to extremes. Given the social as well as individual roots of values, there is a sense in which values are ultimately situational or relational, at least practically speaking—a point that Nel Noddings argues regarding the value of caring.[7] There is no single definitive solution that fits all situations. My own moral and spiritual commitments also play an important role. While these personal commitments also have social roots, the values I hold and apply do not rely entirely on the situations in which I find myself. In the way of dialectic, sorting through what I am to do in the phenomenal world opens the urgent question of how my values relate to those of others and how my commitments should play out in the musical and instructional situations in which I find myself.

The work of analysis, deconstruction, and redemption in making sense of these values, grasping their meaning, and applying them in the phenomenal world is as crucial as the solutions arrived at. The journey is as important as the destination. I have demonstrated that values serve principally for their corrective, inspirational, and aspirational character. In the dynamic process of becoming, while useful in illumining where beliefs and practices may be mistaken and in need of change, they are all ultimately unattainable by fallible people made of "crooked timber" (to invoke Kant's metaphor).[8] They are all being contested, defended, and critiqued within the communities of belief and practice they serve. With respect to justice, for example, Jacques Derrida's insight into the importance of a struggle through and toward justice that is aspired to but ultimately unattainable is especially useful in grasping justice as a means as well as an end.[9] This idea also finds a home in the work of John Dewey, who is among those educational philosophers to recognize the principle of interrelationship between means and ends.[10] Musicians, teachers, and students who reflect critically and productively on how justice might apply in their classrooms and studios, and all the other places in which they experience music, teach, and learn, do the work of justice.[11] All the values I have discussed are dynamic, in process of becoming as they are contemplated, contested, and more or less agreed on and applied in musical and educational communities.

The individual and communal character of values requires dialogue as a means of negotiating meanings and applications in a democratic society. Seyla Benhabib argues persuasively that where dialogue fails, as it sometimes does, laws and regulations are needed to solve matters peacefully and equitably in decent societies.[12] Dialogue in democracies that aspire to be decent is made more difficult in polarized and inequitable societies where the forces of corruption, anti-intellectualism, fundamentalism, tribalism, and radicalization are rife. As public spaces shrink, many people are unable or unwilling to dialogue with different others, arrive at a measure of consensus in public spaces, and act cooperatively for the common good in accordance with values characteristic of decent and humane societies. Although it lies beyond the scope and power of musicians and educators to correct all these evils, at least in the short term, music education policy makers can create musical and educational spaces for dialogue and model such spaces for the wider society.

Dialogue writ large requires intelligence, fidelity, critical thought, and imagination. From antiquity, philosophers have argued for the importance of developing intellectual capacity as a principal educational task.[13] For example, Dewey understands that democracies survive only when the arts and education are valued and citizens have a developed capacity to reason and think critically and creatively.[14] Paul Woodford likewise posits intellectual development and critical thought as critical to democratic music education.[15] The natural outcome of anti-intellectualism is a breakdown in the ability to dialogue respectfully and empathetically with others who hold different beliefs and values. Since values are naturally contested, it is necessary to reclaim an intellectual focus in all the institutions under whose aegis music and education are conducted, be they family, religion, politics, commerce, or the music profession.[16] Maxine Greene suggests that without a community of those who are respectful, honest, forthright, and willing and able to listen to each other intelligently and empathetically, it may be impossible to imagine how things might be better than they are and work effectively in concert with others. For her, the struggle for freedom can best be realized through dialogue in community.[17] Other seekers of educational equality, freedom, justice, and an inclusive and humane society concur with her.[18] Throughout the foregoing chapters I have emphasized the importance of dialogue as a peaceful way of contesting values and arriving at shared perspectives that constitute the basis for collective action. Doing this requires musical and educational transformations that rely on and emphasize the life of the mind.[19]

Values may be applied variously in the phenomenal world. Beyond the discontinuities between theory and practice, musical and educational policy makers and all those who are involved or invested in music and education (or, for the very young, those who seek to make decisions on their behalf and in their best interest) need to decide how to apply the values they hold to the specific situations in which they find themselves. It is also necessary to ask which values, when, where, how, and so forth are to be applied to a specific situation. Asking these questions requires that all those involved in the work of music and education have the agency and power to make meaningful choices and carry forward musical and educational programs based on personal and collective commitments. One size does not fit all. My earlier theoretical work comparing music instructional situations with assumptions of differing teacher and student choice supports the premise that the most productive musical engagement, teaching, and learning occurs where all those involved are empowered to decide for themselves: these situations are the most conducive to humane music and education.[20] The fact that musical and educational transformation needs to be systemic makes it difficult to forge change in the absence of concerted effort on the part of a large and determined constituency.[21] It may be easier to find agreement on the musical and educational values to be defended and the ways to apply them in practice if one appeals to generalities rather than specifics. Even if there is agreement on general principles, reconciling the tensions around specifics requires flexibility that allows for individual agency and difference in the system.

I have suggested that these values cover all aspects of musical education including music, teaching, learning, instruction, curriculum, and administration.[22] Taken together as a whole, their practical application requires intelligence in interpreting and prioritizing them and applying them to specific situations. I prefer the term *intelligence* over *reason* because it is more open-ended and evocative of the whole person's engagement with values and their application. The exercise of what Liora Bresler calls "knowing bodies" and "moving minds" is central to the work of music and education and constitutes a direct challenge to the pervasive anti-intellectualism present in too much of today's society and to the inhumanity of too much music and education.[23] Intellectual qualities of thought in making sense of the values I have discussed in this writing and the possibilities of enacting them require thoughtful reflection about the musical and educational situation, a humane commitment to music and education, transparency and integrity in a consonance between beliefs and practices, the application of reason (deduction, induction, analogical thought), an imaginative approach to possibilities, passionate and spiritual engagement in the work of music and education, and the employment of all the senses in grasping musical and educational predicaments. These dispositions need to be developed in every aspiring musician and teacher and cultivated in every student. Ethical and aesthetic commitments to put people at the heart of music and education matter deeply in fostering well-being, sustaining humane music and education, enriching culture, and developing a decent society.

HOW DO THESE VALUES APPLY THEORETICALLY?

Among the ways in which the values I have described apply theoretically, I consider three that illustrate a range of considerations. First, these values may apply differently across the various phases of life. Perhaps the work of Erik and Joan Erikson encapsulates a way of thinking that encompasses the entirety of life's journey and not just the school-age years that have typically been the focus of music education. In *In Search of Music Education,* I critique the narrowness of music education that focuses on the school-age years of organized preschool, primary or elementary, and secondary schools.[24] Over my working lifetime, preschool or early childhood and tertiary education, community music, music therapy, and elder music education have increasingly been considered to be a part of the formation of musicians, students, and teachers, and I am grateful for these developments. Still, the thrust of music education as it is commonly construed in teacher preparation courses and music education publications remains focused on primary or elementary and secondary schooling. The school-age years in publicly supported primary or elementary and secondary schools are crucially important, and it is imperative to take full advantage of the opportunities they afford and to ensure that education is available to all children and young people. Widening our view opens possibilities for musical and educational thought and practice over the entire life span. There are rich opportunities in prenatal and early life before formal schooling, as well as for musical and educational experiences after formal education, during the world of work, and well into old age. We should also take full advantage of all these possibilities. The Eriksons divide life into nine stages exemplifying differing values and purposes. Their work implies that musical and educational experiences at each point in life need to be consonant, with differing emphases and values that are applicable throughout life. For example, reflecting on gerotranscendence, a stage beyond old age that Joan recognized at ninety, and that she added after their eight stages had been more or less codified, it seems that values of consolation, courage, equipoise, inclusion, hope, and wisdom are among those that are particularly important when or if things begin to fall apart toward the end of life. Joan acknowledged that although one might wish to think of life as a continuum of joy and growth, she had to admit that this is often not the way it is. Elder and geriatric music education needs to concern the changing realities of life after work or during old age and the differing purposes and methods that directly address them. Pretending that the selfsame vision of unending life, openness, and possibility at life's beginning also remains at life's end and every stage in between is a mistake. Instead, the growing desire for closure and reflection on experience as people mature into old age needs to be addressed. A frank discussion is required involving music education elders, scholars in fields such as psychology and gerontology, and experienced professionals who have offered music education for the elderly about which values are needed at this point and the ways in which they might be applied. Such a conversation would be helpful in forging plans to meet the needs, interests, and values of this burgeoning population. One could also imagine such conversations with people or those who care for them at every other phase of life.

Second, these values may apply differently in terms of the various conceptions of education that apply in thinking about music education. Among these, I have written about schooling, training, pedagogy, apprenticeship, eduction, socialization, and enculturation.[25] Whether the specific purpose of music education is to prepare specialized and expert musicians or to engage the public widely in coming to know music, different values are likely to prevail. Whether one is learning a way of life as a musician or including music within one's lived experience significantly affects the character of the values that may assume greater or lesser importance. For example, cultivating artistry, taste, skill, and style or fidelity, persistence, patience, and loyalty may be critical values for the formation of musicians whereas cultivating curiosity, imagination, wonder, and open-mindedness or joy, happiness, pleasure, and celebration may loom large in audience development and general education. Of course, all these values could be expected to be present across the board, but the profiles of values may differ significantly in emphasis from one educational purpose to another. One would want, for example, to prepare audiences with an appreciation of artistry, taste, skill, and style and qualities of fidelity, persistence, patience, and loyalty, just as one would want to ensure that musicians value curiosity, imagination, wonder, and open-mindedness along with joy, happiness, pleasure, and celebration. Still, their differing roles and livelihoods, and the fact that musicians must be steeped in the musical traditions of which they are exponents while audience members have the luxury of time to sample a host of differing traditions without the necessity of spending the time to be able to do all the musics they enjoy are important practical considerations in determining which values are foregrounded and which recede in importance. David Elliott, Marissa Silverman, Wayne Bowman, and their colleagues propose the creation of "artistic citizens" as an important purpose for general music education. Even if musicians and educators were to agree with this purpose, the ways in which artistry, taste, style, and skill are forwarded and the specific foci, whether on artistry, taste, style, or skill, are likely to differ depending on the particular instructional circumstances in which teachers and students gather in music and education.[26]

Third, the societal institutions and cultural milieus in which music and education are conducted and the character of individual and social engagement with music may also significantly affect the character of these values, their relative importance, and their application to practice. In *In Search of Music Education,* I write about several of the institutions involved in music education including family, religion, politics, commerce, and music profession, each of which is associated with certain beliefs, practices, and values.[27] One might imagine, for example, that the family may be particularly associated with values of love, friendship, desire, and devotion; religion may be characterized by values of reverence, humility, awe, and spirituality; politics may be concerned with justice, equality, fairness, and inclusion; commerce may exemplify dignity, dispassion, restraint, and discipline; and the music profession may forward artistry, taste, skill, and style. Even though all these values may be important in every institution, the specific character of an institution suggests that different values may resonate with a particular raison d'être and ethos. In thinking broadly about music and education, it is necessary to account for the natural propensities of institutions to forward some values over others. It is also possible that revitalizing certain values might transform these institutions.[28] I think, for example, of the potential impact of embracing values of joy, happiness, pleasure, and celebration on the character of music education that too often may have focused on wisdom, understanding, knowledge, and mastery. Nel Noddings, Lucy Green, and Randall Allsup hope for this effect in transforming the character of education and music education toward greater happiness, inclusion, informality, and open-mindedness.[29] Situating societal institutions in the wider cultures of which they are a part only complicates the possibilities and inevitably results in a heterogeneity of values and associated cultural practices. Facing this veritable riot of cultural richness, rather than seeking to domesticate and narrow their possibilities, I prefer to rejoice in the resulting profusion and diversity and celebrate the joy of musical life in all its distinctiveness. This view is entirely consistent with my dialectical view of the nature of music and education as phenomena that, notwithstanding their insistence on rightness or fitness for specific occasions within certain traditions, also foster multiplicity and difference.

HOW DO VALUES APPLY TO THE PRACTICAL PREDICAMENTS OF MUSICIANS AND TEACHERS?

I turn now to crucial matters concerning how musicians and teachers might think through their values in deciding what they should do in their rehearsals, classes, and lessons and among all the situations in which they teach, learn, and engage in music. In addressing these concerns in my own experience of music, teaching, and learning, I have found it helpful to practice a way of self-reflexive thinking. What does this mean? Practically speaking, self-reflexivity means opening myself to the idea that I may be wrong, I may find a better way to think about and do this thing, and I need to seek constantly to interrogate my ideas and practices and search for an improved way of thinking and doing. This is a kind of "reflection-in-action" about which Donald Schön writes, in which I do not necessarily have the luxury to think ahead of what I am doing, but I must improvise and think "on the fly."[30] There may be times in which I can reflect at more leisure, on vacations or breaks away from lessons, terms, concert seasons, commissions, or projects. These opportunities for reflection-after-action allow me to contemplate my purposes and approaches, evaluate what I have done in the past, and imaginatively construct an action plan. More often, I discover what I need to do differently during a lesson, rehearsal, term, season, or commissioned task. Every decision regarding every aspect of music and education, whether it be musical, teaching, learning, instructional, curricular, or administrative, constitutes a practical predicament. I unpack several here with a view to illustrating the various questions musicians and teachers might ask themselves.

I begin with the predicament of deciding whether to affiliate or remain with an institution, organization, or client. At the point at which one accepts employment or contracts to teach music, it is important to consider the alignment of one's values with those of the institutions, organizations, or persons with whom one considers working. This is a critical decision because it determines the administrative or organizational context for one's work, the aspects that one can control, and the constraints on one's freedom to act. It is rare to find a perfect fit with an organization that is dynamic and comprised of people with differing commitments, interests, and priorities. Practically speaking, some accommodation and compromise are needed in working with others. There are myriad choices open to musicians and teachers. Among them, one may elect to open a private music studio, work for a corporation, serve as a minister of music, take a position on a school board or in a state department of education, teach in a parochial or private school, play in a symphony orchestra, join a military music organization, serve as a music teacher for the department of defense or the foreign service, develop instructional computer programs related to music, direct a performing arts organization, or become a music entrepreneur. Each option offers a bounded frame in which one accepts certain limitations and possesses some freedom for musical activity, teaching, and learning. A "zone of tolerance" represents the limits within which one is willing to accept a certain degree of misalignment of one's values with those of one's employers or clients and constraints on one's freedom of choice of students, repertoire, instructional methods, musical expectations, and the like.[31] I have found that when I am able to change the things I can control, the satisfaction of doing so may allow me to remain in a position even if the fit is not perfect. If these changes still do not suffice and I go beyond my zone of tolerance, holding this position may be uncomfortable, stressful, and deleterious to my health and well-being and that of my family, and I need to critically review my situation.

When I first began to teach, I did not grasp the importance of a synergy of my values with those of the entities with which I affiliated. I accepted positions that allowed me little freedom to do what I needed, and this lack of freedom became irksome. Later, after I realized the imperative of a fit between my values and those of the organizations I considered joining, I could only partially discover this in advance. The organizations with which I affiliated also changed over time. For example, the somewhat leisurely academic world I entered as a young teacher developed into today's frenetic, exploitative, materialistic, and corporately driven enterprise.[32] Tenured appointments, the state of a lifetime sinecure that brought a sense of security to faculty with a vested interest in the university or college community, began to disappear, and more faculty were employed in less secure term appointments, as adjuncts, or in for-profit online institutions at will. As this occurred, the tasks typically performed by tenured faculty were shared by fewer faculty members whose teaching and service loads increased while the selfsame expectations for research and creative work remained. Administrative and personnel changes also impacted the context and circumstances in which I worked. The situation sometimes improved, hummed along, or worsened. Economic imperatives and personal circumstances occasionally made it difficult or impractical to move to more congenial situations, and it was often necessary to subvert the system if I was to remain true to my values.

At critical moments, when I reflected on the contexts in which I worked, I asked questions such as the following: Are the strictures I accepted on my work as a musician and teacher in the past still acceptable? Can I alter my teaching and musical activities to stay in this position, or must I go elsewhere? What would it take to find happiness in this position? Where might I go to enable a better fit between my values and those of the organization or persons with whom I work? Do I need to rethink my values? Should I broaden my horizons beyond their previous limits, be willing to go to other places and do other things? What will be the costs in disrupting my family or taking a position I might not have considered previously? Do I need to retrain myself for a different position, and if so, how can I accomplish this? Arriving at answers to these and other questions required reflecting on the values to which I was committed and the practical possibilities for realizing them insofar as possible in imperfect and dynamic situations about which I was not omniscient.

There is also the predicament of human nature. Even if one believes that one should do such and such, one sometimes does not do it. Granting agency to all involved in music and education does not suffice, and what is does not equate to what ought to be. One may fear risking criticism and retribution if one follows what one believes one should do; the desire to sustain a livelihood, especially during times of economic distress, even if this means compromising principles in which one believes, may overcome one's wish to do things differently. Students may be pulled away from their commitments to study such and such or with so and so by pressures from other people or seductive attractions. In thinking of our humanity, Parker Palmer regards fear and the lack of courage as common problems in the lives and work of teachers.[33]

The risk of alienating powerful persons in an organization, fear of repudiation by one's colleagues, or loss of a position effectively normalize, domesticate, and pacify those who think and act in divergent ways. Over the years, I have seen behavior on the part of musicians, administrators, teachers, and students that has shaken me to my core. I have witnessed evils of abuse, intimidation, bullying, marginalization, and alienation. Such moments are distressing precisely because one's values are expressions of who one is; one personifies the values one holds. I have discovered that academic freedom comes at a high price: it is far easier to go along with harmful policies and actions than to resist, especially if one is in a minority position. Sometimes, it takes a concerted effort to withstand pressure from within or without the institutions in which music is made, taught, and learned and act according to one's values. Where cohesion is lacking among musicians and teachers who are fearful and lack courage to resist, if one cannot subvert those policies with which one disagrees or do one's work according to the values by which one loves to live, one must either seek to transform those things within one's control or find other opportunities. It is sometimes possible to live through difficult situations and sometimes not. Although one may not always do as one believes one should, and one is caught in a human predicament of fallibility, fear, and lack of courage, there is comfort in the hope that one may do better in the future. It is for this reason that Friedrich Schiller reminds artists and teachers to "think of [people] as they ought to be when called upon to influence them; think of them as they are when tempted to act on their behalf."[34]

Musicians and teachers are also caught in the predicament of choosing musical repertoire and subject matter. In making these choices, one applies the values one holds dear to specific situations. On these decisions hang the processes of instruction, teaching, learning, and music making and receiving.[35] Yet too many musicians and teachers build curricula to fill the time available rather than dig beneath the skin of their practical activities to ask relevant questions: What does this curriculum say about what I value? What are the gaps I need to fill or the imbalances I need to remedy? What are the surprises that emerge when I critically examine my repertoire selection and subject matter? Is playing and singing this repertoire and teaching and learning this subject matter enjoyable to my students and me? Do we value this repertoire and subject matter? Is it vital and living to us? Are we growing musically and educationally because of what we are doing together? Can we stretch ourselves further? What do we need to experience and know now and in the foreseeable future? Obviously, my own values drive these questions. Others with different values will have different questions relating to the situations in which they experience music, teach, and learn.

Engaging repertoire and subject matter critically and constructively from the perspective of one's values requires skill in thinking reflexively: this disposition is too important a matter to be left to chance and needs to be cultivated in musical and teacher preparation programs. How can this be accomplished? One way is to use curricular case studies and set intriguing problems. Here, for example, teachers and students can plan a specific program of repertoire for an ensemble or class of their choice under limiting conditions and think critically about what they have created and what this repertoire suggests about their values. Alternatively, they may begin with values to which they are most committed and develop a program of repertoire that illustrates and cultivates them. They can write reflectively about what they learn from the experiences of thinking ethically about music and education, speculate about what they might have done differently, and share their perspectives with each other. Alternatively, they may create responses in different modalities through art, theater, dance, film, or some other form. Despite the ambiguity between values and repertoire, such problem-focused exercises allow teachers and students to discover important approaches to thinking about planning, teaching, learning, rehearsing, improvising, performing, composing, producing, promoting, listening, and defending repertoire and other subject matter.

There is also the predicament of realizing that one's conceptions of values need to be rethought: they do not suffice or need to be repudiated, are too narrowly construed or insufficiently focused, or need to be foregrounded or backgrounded in a given situation. I have often made these discoveries during musical activities, teaching, and learning where I must act immediately. When I first began to teach, the White Australia Policy governed immigration to the country of my birth and indigenous people (whose culture flourished millennia before the arrival of white people) were alien, out of sight, and on the margins of my consciousness. I had yet to awaken to and interrogate issues of race, ethnocentrism, immigration, and colonial experience. Immigrating to Canada, and later to the United States, and teaching students from sometimes widely different backgrounds was often challenging, especially when I was completely unprepared for these moments. One of the most dramatic was when, as a master's degree student recently arrived in the United States, I was appointed as a part-time substitute teacher of music in an urban school in which most of my students were black. This was a time of racial unrest, and I shall never forget my first day at that school, with armed guards in the corridor, substandard third-world physical conditions and equipment, no textbooks or musical instruments in sight save a solitary out-of-tune upright grand piano, and sometimes hostile groups of children who needed to be won over before we could begin to teach or learn anything. In meeting these children, I realized how little I knew about them and how much they had to teach me about themselves, music, and education. I needed to act now, to reflect-in-action, but what was I to do when my musical and educational values needed to be urgently recast for this alien situation? My view of music and teaching needed to change, my values needed to broaden, and I had to rely on values such as honesty, determination, courage, love, and inclusion if I was to find a way to commune with these children. Connecting with my students was more important than covering the day's subject matter. I had to reach into myself and draw on reserves I did not know I possessed. It has been this way in all the moments in which I realized that my values were too narrow, misconstrued, or out of sync with my teaching situation.

I discovered that if I am to solve the dilemmas I face and build bridges with my students, I need to rethink my values differently and critically, imagine possibilities that I cannot be sure will work, and live dangerously and sometimes transgressively, often at the borders of my knowledge. If I am to change the situation toward the good in ways that benefit students, colleagues, and wider society, I need the courage to do so and the willingness to take risks. Travel and the opportunities to experience an array of different cultural experiences have broadened my sensitivities, enlarged my musical and educational understandings, and reshaped my values, and I recommend such experiences for all teachers and students. Still, my education continues to this day as I now confront the exigencies of online for-profit doctoral education, and I seek to help mostly women and minority students who might otherwise not have the opportunity for a doctoral education write and defend their dissertations. For musicians and teachers caught in such dilemmas, it is up to each person to discover how to reconstruct, realign, and broaden their values and simply do their best in the situations in which they find themselves.

Changing times provide opportunities to rethink one's values. At a moment of racial and social unrest, Julia Koza clarifies the relationship between white power relations and white supremacy that have historically infected the field.[36] The uncomfortable yet persuasive evidence she offers of Carl Seashore's and others' close ties with eugenics and white supremacist ideology and the ways in which this ideology impacted American music education during the last century and into the twenty-first are hard to bear. Equally disturbing are the ways in which broader psychological and educational movements for sorting, categorizing, and testing people with respect to attributes such as musical ability and intelligence and the stress on musical competitions and the like continue to shape music education thought and practice in the United States. To read her account is to come face to face with the complicity of music education in the West in forwarding whiteness and patriarchy. Still, Koza lives in hope of a better and more equitable and inclusive world. She realizes that change comes only when the truth of one's situation is directly confronted and one determines to change. Her writing reminds me of the importance of humility in my whiteness, of the limits to what I may and should authentically teach, and of the necessity of diverse racial, cultural, and musical perspectives and expertise in music education so that each may bring what others lack and everyone can be valued and included as fully human and of equal worth.

Adam Kruse tells a poignant story of a white music teacher with a class consisting mostly of students of color who attempted to teach hip-hop that he did not know well. In his students' eyes, he "didn't know what he was doin'."[37] All students have a right to expect their teachers not only to know them and care about them but to be exponents of and knowledgeable about the subject matter they teach; understanding one's subject is an expression of one's caring.[38] I imagine how this teacher must have felt as he sought to do his best. That positive results came from the class speaks to the teacher's caring and his students' good will and generosity. Nevertheless, as I contemplate this tale, I wish for a very different reality. In my mind's eye, I see a musician-teacher who intimately understands the lived lives of these students of color and the music she teaches, and who desires to open their hearts and minds to worlds of music beyond their immediate experience. Although she may sometimes live dangerously on the edges of her knowledge, imagine the possibilities when she brings to these students a cultural sensibility and rich musicality that is inspirational and a competence that they respect so that her students agree that "she knows what she is doing." This does not mean that only people of color may teach hip-hop to students of color authentically and carefully. In her response to David Carr's question, "Can White Men Play the Blues?" Patrice Madura posits that audiences are unable to distinguish the color of blues players' skin when they hear sound recordings by blues exponents.[39] She understands that it is crucial that all musician teachers be steeped in the music they teach and know it intimately. Only then can one say that these students of color are truly valued and regarded as worthy of the best-informed musical instruction that can be afforded. I have seen transformations like this, and I long for every student to experience such musical education.

Movements for racial and social justice require conversations about how to put these values into action. The voices of musicians, teachers, and students of color, women, the differently gendered and abled, the dispossessed, strangers, and immigrants need to be welcomed as full participants in music and education. White male patriarchy is difficult to unseat. For ages, women have known what it is to be considered as inferiors of men; they have known enslavement and violence when treated as men's chattel. In the United States, black men were enfranchised before white women, and women of every color still know the heavy hand of governmental and religious institutions on their bodies. Their right to control their bodies and their equality with men is not yet enshrined in the Constitution. The intersectionality of attributes such as race and gender demands solidarity of people of every background on behalf of those who are oppressed. Although I stand in solidarity with movements for racial and social justice, I do not presume to know and forge solutions on behalf of everyone. I am obliged to listen to and learn from those whose backgrounds and perspectives differ from mine. I should not seek to design and build the house of music education on their behalf and think that they will want to dwell there; all need to be full participants in designing and building it together. Stepping aside to create space for women, people of color, the differently gendered and abled, immigrants, and newcomers may be difficult for those who are empowered, especially when the interests of others need to be forwarded ahead of their own. As Akosua Addo argues, systemic power issues arise in knowledge construction and stand in the way of improving the situation.[40] Changing present realities in music education requires nothing short of the redistribution of musical and educational power, and if history is any guide, resistance from those who prefer the status quo is likely to follow. This conversation is also challenging because of the need to build bridges of understanding, trust, and intimacy between people of different backgrounds, cultures, and languages. There will doubtless be difficult things for all to hear, and humility, generosity, diplomacy, and empathy are needed from all participants. Nevertheless, conversations with those who have experienced being regarded and treated as of lesser value and more dispensable than others can be an agent of healing and wholeness. In our diversity, together we can accomplish the work of music education more effectively and humanely and point the way to a more civil and inclusive society.

The predicament of effecting positive change toward the good in music and education is also a crucial decision point in putting values into action. It is important for music teachers to create "spaces for individual and collective action toward the good" and cultivate "skills for improving culture and society."[41] What are these skills? Iris Yob suggests an array of important skills that educators need in order to bring about change—notably, scholarship, systematic thinking, and reflection; application, advocacy, collaboration, and political engagement; and ethics, commitment, and courage.[42] If one wishes to transform one's situation for the better, it is crucial to think not only about the values that drive one's work but about practical ways in which one may work together collectively to create the change one envisages. bell hooks offers a compelling argument for the importance of "sisterhood," or solidarity with one's fellow teachers, and her advice also resonates with musicians.[43] I admire my colleagues who possess these skills and can transform less than ideal situations into communities that breathe inspiration into all the participants and create islands of humanity amid inhumanity. Their example reminds me that rather than leaving a difficult situation prematurely, it is important to first ask whether and how I can work with others to redeem it. Importantly, how can I better prepare others with the skills to enact change in the institution or wider society?

WHAT DO THESE VALUES OFFER MUSIC EDUCATION?

I conclude this book on a personal note because the onus is on all those who are invested and interested in the work of music and education to consider and come to a personal decision concerning it. I have not sought to forge a definitive list of values that will be adopted by all music educators and that will govern them all but rather to forward a list of values to which I am committed and that I propose as worthy of consideration by others. I hope that the values I have discussed will be augmented by others I have overlooked or bypassed in this writing and that this analysis might exemplify the reflection that needs to precede and accompany all musical and educational action in the phenomenal world.

The values about which I have written are among those to collectively constitute a north star that has guided and continues to shape my thinking, being, and doing as a student, teacher, and musician. They are inspiring and a source of meaning despite my failure to live up to all of them as I wish I might do. When I see them exemplified in the lives and work of my family, friends, colleagues, and fellow students and in the writings of musicians, philosophers, and teachers, I am inspired to do better than I have done in the past. In the communities of which I am a part, I am often reminded of values I already knew but had forgotten or apprised of values I had not thought of before. I am also prompted to reexamine my views when, in the way of life, my former students become my teachers. These communities are sources of encouragement and friendship and sites where imagination may take flight and hope is fostered. Seeing others committed to different values and engaged variously in music and music education fosters humility as I realize that each person sees a part of a wider truth. Admitting fallibility engenders humility, but it should not prevent me from claiming the power to courageously seek my own truth. Still, I also need the company of others who may grasp what I have missed.

These values are also a reminder that those things I regard as goods may be taken to extremes, just as those things that may be regarded as evils may have redeeming qualities. Adjudicating and applying them requires caution, open-mindedness, and critical thinking about all the ideas and practices that claim my attention and adherence. Interrogating practices in the light of the values that underlie them is a particularly fraught process. In communities of theory and practice, motivations are often unseen, humanity is flawed, and it is important to resist a rush to judgment. Just as written texts are ambiguous, so too are the indices of values at work in practice. Philosophizing necessarily takes the work of practice as its text, but undertaking this task risks the possibilities of misunderstanding, misconstruing, or oversimplifying what is going on. For example, Christopher Small's analysis of concert halls and orchestral concerts in the Western classical tradition evidences a specific ethical view of musical ritual that views it from a certain perspective. Small pictures musicians as actors in a larger social process in which they are (maybe unwittingly) complicit. His account does not project these events from the perspective of those musicians whose lives are bound up with a deep respect, spirituality, even reverence for the very places that Small sees as inhumane and socially exclusive, and whose motives may not be those he describes.[44] Could one be an angel or a god and grasp the complete picture? One may see an institution and place that is deeply beneficial and deeply flawed, and the resulting social picture may be much more complex than the one Small has painted. Still, while limited in scope, Small's perspective merits consideration, and it remains to also include others that necessarily complicate the picture.

The possibility that the values to which I am committed may be taken to extremes to become evils and those that might be regarded as evils may have redeeming qualities requires intellectual qualities of caution, open-mindedness, imagination, and critical thinking about all the ideas and practices that claim my attention and adherence. Ronald Dworkin regards equality as the "supreme virtue."[45] While I agree that equality is crucial, I am less interested in the supremacy of any one value than in the necessity of intelligence in weighing the sometimes conflicting and competing claims of familial, religious, political, economic, and music institutional prescriptions and proscriptions. Thinking about the values that ought to underlie musical and educational thought and practice draws on philosophical argument and empirical evidence. Israel Scheffler thinks of the intellectual qualities required in adjudicating and applying values as the exercise of reason, and he is right that reason plays a central role in education.[46] Still, as I have already indicated, I prefer a broader vision of intelligence, embodied mind and "knowing body," or the whole person grappling with important ethical questions.[47] These questions include the following: What is of value? Which values am I committed to? How shall I apply my commitments to my situation to seek the best but avoid the worst? What if I make a mistake? Given the unintended consequences of thought and practice, I need to approach these questions with great care and intellectual verve. My decisions are necessarily contingent. Still, paradoxically, having arrived at a point of decision, I am also bound to act with integrity and boldness. Not to do so is also an abdication of my ethical responsibilities as a musician and educator committed to humane music and education. When I err, as I doubtless shall, I need the humility to reorient my thinking and practice.

Acknowledging the tension and ambiguity between theory and practice in values and their application to music and education is helpful in navigating matters relating to how values apply in practice and in working out how to act in the phenomenal world. That music and education are pervasively social undertakings inevitably raises the possibilities of criticism and disagreement within even the most generous-hearted and inclusive communities. Because our commitments are lived and even loved, conflicts may carry emotional valence and may be easily personalized. It is sometimes difficult to love the questions when they assail our most precious commitments or when others misunderstand or undermine our work or impugn our motives. As I noted earlier, Gilles Deleuze's metaphor of smooth surfaces is useful in understanding the interrelationship of values in theory and practices where both may be intermingled one with the other, and it seems impossible, practically speaking, to disentangle them.[48] Deleuze's metaphor of striated surfaces also serves to highlight the fact that values are distinctive and subjective commitments that are more or less evidenced in practice. The possibility of misattributing or misapplying values evokes disagreement and conflict. In this messy ground, there is wisdom in humility and carefulness in seeking to transform society and culture toward greater civility and humanity.[49]

In taking a general view of the questions that guide this investigation, the common features of these values, how they resonate theoretically with music and education, how they apply to practical predicaments faced by musicians and teachers, and what they offer music education are evident. Throughout this book, I have sought to clarify these values and their possibilities for music and education. This task is incomplete, and it will fall to others to further conceptualize and critique these and other values and apply them to practice. Although no one value suffices or is without possible detractions, values can enable musicians and educators to navigate toward more humane and civil societies through storm and calm alike. Nothing could be more important to the future of music and education and to the societies and cultures of which they are a part than decisions about which values to espouse and why and how to interpret and apply them to all the situations in which music and education are underway. This task is never finished. Musicians and educators of every generation are challenged to reconsider them anew.

Epilogue

I PAUSE AT THE END of this writing to reflect on the questions that remain and the importance of surprise. I wonder: Do the values that I have discussed resonate or align with the metaphorical models or modular metaphors described in my earlier *Pictures of Music Education*?[1] These images include music education conceived as boutique and consumption, village and community, artist and apprenticeship, revolutionary and transgression, factory and production, garden and growth, therapist and healing, court and rule, seashore and energy, home and informality, guide and pedagogy, web and connectivity. Although I did not plan the foregoing chapters of quartets of values with these pictures in mind, correspondences emerge out of my writing. I briefly sketch resonances between those values and pictures for which I see an immediate connection, point to nuances in values that may relate to other pictures as well, and raise matters that await attention in the future.

Artistry, taste, skill, and style, examined in chapter 2, immediately evoke the artist and apprenticeship pictures that are common to classical and vernacular music traditions around the world.[2] These values are applicable to artistic knowledge and its practice. As I have already noted, in all the musical traditions of which I am aware, exponents, adherents, and their publics alike exemplify these values although in a host of different ways and to different degrees. These values also may apply in the guide and pedagogy pictures of music education, and philosophers of education have proposed that they should apply much more widely to forms of knowledge beyond music and the other arts.[3] For example, Philip Phenix supposes the aesthetic realm as one of what he sees as a comprehensive list of realms that need to be addressed in general education, and Vernon Howard believes that the arts constitute a metaphor for learning writ large and ought to infuse the educational curriculum.[4] The arts and sciences also overlap, for example, in the exquisitely executed and botanically accurate models for academic study in the Ware Collection of Blaschka Glass Models of Plants, popularly known as the Glass Flowers and held in the Harvard Museum of Natural History.[5] Importantly, these values are often associated with transgression and revolutionary pictures.[6] As they challenge, sometimes overturn, otherwise transgress traditional beliefs and practices, and forge new artistic beliefs and practices, artists subvert the status quo and prompt revolution not only in art but in society and culture. The power of the arts in evoking social change is such that writers such as Jacques Attali have long seen them as prophetic of societal change.[7]

Reverence, humility, awe, and spirituality, examined in chapter 3, seem especially linked with the therapist-healing pictures.[8] With their emphasis on a holistic approach to healing and well-being and aspects of mind, body, and spirit, these pictures are often associated with unseen benefits of linkages with myth, ritual, the religions, and the arts. This is the spiritual world described by Susanne Langer as the expression of feeling and the use of presentational or performative symbols to express a part of human communication that transcends propositional discourse.[9] Insofar as the religions also cultivate these values, music and education carried on in religious contexts that also stress the healing of mind, body, and soul are especially likely to foster these values. This quartet may also be characteristic of music education in secular contexts in the artist-apprenticeship pictures where students revere their teachers, express humility in their presence, and are in awe of their teachers' prowess, and the practice of their tradition constitutes a spiritual experience.[10]

I think of dignity, dispassion, restraint, and discipline sketched in chapter 4 as especially related to the factory-production pictures.[11] The formality of the process and of those involved in it, the rational (even emotionless) planning and execution of the creation of a product, the restraint evident in the design of the system, which is geared to be as independent of individual persons as possible, and the discipline in sticking with this system until or unless it breaks down or otherwise becomes obsolete fit especially well with the rationality of the factory-production pictures. These values might also be characteristic of court-rule in their emphasis on formality in teacher and student interaction and of web-connectivity when they mirror factory-production and are conducted within the purview of corporate entities for financial gain.[12]

Love, friendship, desire, and devotion, analyzed in chapter 5, resonate particularly with the home-informality pictures, aptly captured in Maria Montessori's *casa dei bambini* and Jane Roland Martin's schoolhome.[13] These values may also be associated with my seashore-energy pictures, where friends and families gather in mutual enjoyment of each other, like-minded souls commune, teachers and students choose each other and the subjects of study, and all are engaged in play.[14] The attraction and empathy of the participants to each other and to the subject of study constitute the glue that binds music and education in home and informality.[15] In the case of seashore and energy, mutual attraction and play energize participants in moving from impulse and desire to action. Love, friendship, desire, and devotion are likely to play out differently in these pictures, regarding the grounding metaphor and specific musical, teaching, learning, instructional, curricular, and administrative characteristics of home-formality and seashore-energy in music education.

Joy, happiness, pleasure, and celebration, sketched in chapter 6, relate particularly to the seashore and energy pictures but also apply to home and informality.[16] These values constitute the raison d'être for play and prompt and energize musical education construed as seashore-energy. Positive reinforcement for teaching and learning is presumed to be most efficacious in motivating people to expend the energy required to come to know and do music. These values light up otherwise prosaic or dull lives and invest them with meaning and the desire to live life fully. It is to be hoped that these values also fill the home and informality. Without joy, happiness, pleasure, and celebration, it is hard to imagine why people would create and sustain homes in the first place. Regrettably, this is not always the case; still, one hopes that homes and the home-informality pictures are characterized by expressions of joy, happiness, pleasure, and celebration, albeit in differing ways than they may be manifested in the seashore and energy pictures.

I think of fidelity, persistence, patience, and loyalty, described in chapter 7, particularly regarding the garden and growth pictures.[17] Maybe this association is deeply ingrained by devotion to the gardens in which I have lived for decades. Growth, especially as John Dewey and Shinichi Suzuki describe it, requires fidelity and persistence to sustain effort through good seasons and bad, patience in waiting until the fullness of time when plants produce their flowers and fruits and grow to maturity, and loyalty to all the plants in one's garden which one must attend to, trim, reposition, or give every opportunity to thrive if one is to have a beautiful garden.[18] These values may also apply somewhat differently to the artist-apprenticeship pictures, where there is fidelity to the musical tradition, persistence in practice, patience to gradually become a musician, and loyalty to one's teachers and fellows.

Pictures to which the values of curiosity, imagination, wonder, and open-mindedness, discussed in chapter 8, apply include the web-connectivity and maybe, surprisingly to some, the boutique-consumption and factory-production.[19] This may be especially the case in the era of "post-shopping malls" transforming into entertainment and experiential spaces that vie for consumer patronage.[20] For Ivan Illich, who foresaw the possibility of deschooling through the democratic possibilities of online access to education, these values are the spark of all education and the means of promoting education for all.[21] The web and its associated model of connectivity rely on individual curiosity, arousing imagination, evoking wonder, and cultivating open-mindedness. If one thinks of the boutique-consumption pictures from the perspective of attracting people to musical education, these values would also be evident in the ways in which educational products are packaged for prospective consumers to evoke their curiosity, imagination, wonder, and open-mindedness. Of course, it is apparent that these values would be emphasized and applied differently than in the web-connectivity pictures. For example, web-connectivity relies on an individual's agency, initiative, and desire whereas in boutique-consumption, an individual chooses among available products and is prompted or enticed to participate. Also, proponents of the factory and production may see curiosity, imagination, wonder, and open-mindedness as necessities in producing products that consumers want to buy. Although these emphases may blur in practice as the web increasingly uses corporate tactics to produce goods and services and attract people to buy them, the pictures of web-connectivity, boutique-consumption, and factory-production, while conceptually distinct, may, practically speaking, interrelate with one another.

Wisdom, understanding, knowledge, and mastery, analyzed in chapter 9, seem immediately applicable to the guide and pedagogy pictures that rely on a wise musician and teacher who has been this way before and knows the territory over which instruction will travel and the challenges for students who seek to acquire these intellectual qualities.[22] Emphasizing the acquisition of wisdom, understanding, knowledge, and mastery of a field of study also evokes the artist-apprenticeship pictures in their grasp of the imperative of students willing to study with an exponent of a practice for an intensive period with the intent of becoming exponents themselves. Wisdom, understanding, knowledge, and mastery may play out differently, especially given the intellectual focus of the guide-pedagogy and the practical and artistic focus of artist-apprenticeship. Still, there is a clear practical overlap in that both sets of pictures concern propositional and procedural knowledge, and instrumental music teachers often refer to their work in developing artists as a form of pedagogy.

Justice, equality, fairness, and inclusion, described in chapter 10, immediately relate to the court and rule pictures of music education.[23] The philosophical notions of justice on which I have drawn—notably, those of John Rawls, Amartya Sen, and Jacques Derrida—have constructive, deconstructive, and rule-oriented connotations that would be at home in the court-rule approach to music education, with its emphasis on formality and rule-bound behavior.[24] Notions of equality such as those proposed by Ronald Dworkin and Danielle Allen likewise resonate with the court-rule picture, although they might also relate to the village-community pictures.[25] Fairness, especially the idea forwarded by John Rawls, is interconnected with justice and would be consonant with the court-rule picture as it might also be with the village-community pictures.[26] Inclusion, especially as thought about judicially and politically by Dworkin and Allen, could be expected to characterize court-rule as it might also exemplify the village-community.[27] With respect to this quartet, it is also likely that while they more or less exemplify court-rule, these values characterize other pictures as well—for example, the village-community pictures.

These interconnections between the quartets of values and the metaphoric models or modular metaphors of music education illustrate how the ambiguity of the values I have discussed is further amplified when they are applied to the various pictures of music education. Ambiguity begets ambiguity—a reality that complicates the work of music and education. Although I suggest ways in which musicians and educators can think through their values and relate them to the practical situations in which they find themselves, the questions multiply, and the predicaments are more fraught.

I was surprised to discover my exclusion of value quartets that speak especially and immediately to my earlier pictures of the village and community, revolutionary and transgression, and boutique and consumption, even though, as I indicate, the values examined in this writing can also be applied to them. These pictures might be expected to relate, respectively, to values such as cooperation and mutuality, opposition and resistance, and seduction and choice. Cooperation and mutuality are among those positively construed values in music education not addressed in this study. Opposition and resistance, and seduction and choice, may be too easily dismissed by musicians and educators committed to mutuality and cooperation. Others that may carry a negative valence, such as transgression and exclusion, lurk within this analysis but are largely on its margins.[28] Although these values may be thought of as music educational sins, they can be construed redemptively.[29] Given my natural optimism, it was reasonable to begin with those values that have been taken to be educational goods, are in wide use in music and education, or have been forgotten and are in need of rescuing. Still, it is also important to examine those things that are often considered to be evil but may serve musical and educational goods. For want of space, this task must await a future writing.

Among unresolved matters beyond the scope of this book are the ambiguity between musical and educational values and the possibility of construing music as a metaphor for education and education as a metaphor for music.[30] These potentially transformative ideas challenge traditional conceptions of music, education, and music education and generate ambiguities concerning musical and educational values.[31] There is also a premium on figurative as well as literal thinking about music and education when each is seen as a metaphor for the other. While implicit in this book, the task of systematically examining these ideas remains beyond this study.

It may be the case that the values of greatest personal importance lie so close that one fails to see them. I think, for example, of the value of self-reflexivity, whereby one asks oneself critically whether one's beliefs and actions are on the mark and whether they need to be jettisoned or sustained. I have relied on this value as a means of determining how to navigate the various quartets throughout the preceding chapters and explicitly in chapter 11, as I sketch the application of values to practical predicaments. Also, there is the value of generosity, which I ask the reader for in chapter 1 and return to throughout this book. By generosity, I mean open-mindedness, hospitality, and friendship—to expect the best from and see the best in another. Notwithstanding their importance, neither self-reflexivity nor generosity is unpacked in this writing. Coming to this realization illustrates that as one excavates musical and educational practices to disclose some values, one may encounter blind spots. Some values may be invisible although they are in plain sight, as was the case for me with self-reflexivity and generosity. Uncovering them may be a surprise. Once they are exposed, it remains to interrogate them. This reality highlights the importance of surprise, of writing to learn, and of doing so within a community of those who see what one may not see, hear what one may not hear, and do as one may not otherwise think of doing.[32] I owe a profound debt to those generous-minded readers who have been my teachers and the community of those with whom I am privileged to travel, who love the questions, and who are in search of wisdom.

NOTES

CHAPTER 1 - CULTURE, HUMANITY, TRANSFORMATION, AND VALUE

1. Alfred North Whitehead, *The Aims of Education and Other Essays* (1929; repr., New York: Free Press, 1967).
2. See Estelle R. Jorgensen, *In Search of Music Education* (Bloomington: Indiana University Press, 1997).
3. Vernon A. Howard, *Learning by All Means: Lessons from the Arts: A Study in the Philosophy of Education* (New York: Peter Lang, 1992) is among those to grasp this possibility.
4. Jorgensen, *In Search of Music Education*; Estelle R. Jorgensen, *Transforming Music Education* (Bloomington: Indiana University Press, 2003), *The Art of Teaching Music* (Bloomington: Indiana University Press, 2008), and *Pictures of Music Education* (Bloomington: Indiana University Press, 2011). Stephen L. Carter, *Civility: Manners, Morals, and the Etiquette of Democracy* (New York: Basic Books, 1998), writes about the necessity of civility as a means of sustaining democratic conversation and society.
5. Philip Alperson, ed., *Worlds of Music: New Directions for the Philosophy of Music* (University Park, PA: Penn State University Press, 1998); Julian Johnson, *Who Needs Classical Music? Cultural Choice and Musical Value* (New York: Oxford University Press, 2002); Liz Garnet, *The British Barbershopper: A Study in Socio-Musical Values* (Aldershot, UK: Ashgate, 2005); Keith Moore Chapin and Lawrence Kramer, eds., *Musical Meaning and Human Values* (New York: Fordham University Press, 2009); Jerrold Levinson, *Musical Concerns: Essays in Philosophy of Music* (Oxford: Oxford University Press, 2015); Jayson Beaster-Jones, *Music Commodities, Markets, and Values: Music as Merchandise* (New York: Routledge, 2016).
6. Thomas A. Regelski, "Ethical Dimensions of School-Based Music Education," in *The Oxford Handbook of Philosophy in Music Education*, ed. Wayne

D. Bowman and Ana Lucia Frega (New York: Oxford University Press, 2012), 284–304; Paul Woodford, *Democracy and Music Education: Liberalism, Ethics, and the Politics of Practice* (Bloomington and Indianapolis: Indiana University Press, 2005); Robert Walker, *Music Education: Cultural Values, Social Change and Innovation* (Springfield, IL: Charles C. Thomas, 2007); Randall Everett Allsup and Heidi Westerlund, "Methods and Situational Ethics in Music Education," *Action, Criticism, and Theory for Music Education* 11, no. 1 (2012, March): 124–148, http://act.maydaygroup.org/articles/AllsupWesterlund11_1.pdf; Elizabeth Gould, "Feminist Imperative(s) in Music Education: Philosophy, Theory, or What Matters Most," *Educational Philosophy and Theory* 43, no. 2 (2011): 130–147, https://doi.org/10.1111/j.1469-5812.2008.00424.x; Hildegard C. Froehlich, *Sociology for Music Teachers: Perspectives for Practice* (New York: Routledge, 2016); David J. Elliott, Marissa Silverman, and Wayne D. Bowman, eds., *Artistic Citizenship: Artistry, Social Responsibility, and Ethical Praxis* (New York: Oxford University Press, 2016).

7. See, for example, David Carr, "Moral Values and the Arts in Environmental Education: Towards an Ethics of Aesthetic Appreciation," *Journal of Philosophy in Education* 38, no. 2 (2004): 221–239, https://doi.org/10.1111/j.0309-8249.2004.00377.x; Joe Winston, *Beauty and Education* (New York: Routledge, 2010); Donald S. Blumenfeld-Jones, *Ethics, Aesthetics, and Education: A Levinasian Approach* (New York: Palgrave McMillan, 2016).

8. See John Richmond, "Ethics and the Philosophy of Music Education," *Journal of Aesthetic Education* 30, no. 3 (Autumn 1996): 3–22, https://doi.org/10.2307/3333319. For a discussion of the cultural tensions in music's role in public schools, see J. Scott Goble, *What's So Important about Music Education?* (New York: Routledge, 2010), especially chap. 1.

9. Thomas Byrne Edsall, *The Age of Austerity: How Scarcity Will Remake American Politics* (New York: Doubleday, 2012).

10. See, for example, Robert D. Putnam and David E. Campbell, *American Grace: How Religion Divides and Unites Us* (New York: Simon and Schuster, 2012); Paul Maltby, *Christian Fundamentalism and the Culture of Disenchantment* (Charlottesville: University of Virginia Press, 2013); Darara Timotewos Gubo, *Blasphemy and Defamation of Religions in a Polarized World: How Religious Fundamentalism Is Challenging Fundamental Human Rights* (Lanham, MD: Rowan and Littlefield, 2014).

11. For example, journalists such as Fiona Maddocks, "The Future of the Arts: 'The Classical Music World Has Been Transfigured," *Guardian*, June 21, 2020, https://www.theguardian.com/music/2020/jun/21/the-future-of-the-arts-the-classical-music-world-has-been-transfigured, have documented the impact of the COVID-19 pandemic on classical music. Music educators have formed Facebook groups such as "Higher Ed Music Lessons in the Time of COVID-19" and "Music Educators Creating Online Learning" to converse about music teaching and learning and to rethink the use of technology in musical performance and distance learning.

12. See June Boyce Tillman, *Constructing Musical Healing: The Wounds That Sing* (London: Jessica Kingsley, 2000).

13. Friedrich Schiller, *On the Aesthetic Education of Man, in a Series of Letters*, ed. and trans. Elizabeth M. Wilkinson and L. A. Willoughby (Oxford: Clarendon, 1967), ninth letter, 61.

14. Herbert Read, *Education through Art*, 3rd edition (New York: Pantheon Books, 1956).

15. Jacques Maritain, *The Responsibility of the Artist* (New York: Charles Scribner's Sons, 1960). I am indebted to Deanne Bogdan for reminding me of Maritain's advice on the artist's duty.

16. Hannah Arendt, *The Origins of Totalitarianism*, new edition and added prefaces (1968; repr., Boston: Houghton, Mifflin, Harcourt, c. 1994).

17. Aristotle, *Nicomachean Ethics*, trans. and ed. Roger Crisp (Cambridge: Cambridge University Press, 2000), book 2, para. 1109b, 36. James Legge, *The Chinese Classics (Confucian Analects)* (London, 1861; Project Gutenberg, 2005), book 1, VI, "Yung Yeh," para. 27, https://www.gutenberg.org/ebooks/3330: "The Master said, 'Perfect is the virtue which is according to the Constant Mean!'" This ancient idea of taking nothing to excess is exemplified in the Greek myth of Icarus, whose father, Daedalus, constructed wings of feathers and wax for Icarus to fly from Crete. Daedalus instructed his son to fly neither too high nor too low; unfortunately, Icarus flew too close to the sun, the wax melted, and he fell into the sea that bears his name.

18. I am indebted to Randall Everett Allsup for the suggestion of this metaphor.

19. Deanne Bogdan, "Dissociation/Reintegration of Literary/Musical Sensibility," in *Humane Music Education for the Common Good*, ed. Iris M. Yob and Estelle R. Jorgensen (Bloomington: Indiana University Press, 2020), 232–247.

20. Maxine Greene, *Releasing the Imagination: Essays on Education, the Arts, and Social Change* (San Francisco: Jossey-Bass, 1995), 43. This transformative approach is consistent with my earlier *Transforming Music Education* (Bloomington: Indiana University Press, 2003).

21. Deanne Bogdan uses this phrase to refer to my dialectical bent in her review of my *In Search of Music Education*, *Philosophy of Music Education Review* 6, no. 1 (Spring 1998): 71–73.

22. See Øivind Varkøy, Frederik Pio, Hanne Fossum, Eva Georgii-Hemming, and Christian Rolle, "Perspectives on Uniformity, Sameness, and Homogeneity, and Proclamations of Pluralism, Diversity, and Heterogeneity," *Philosophy of Music Education Review* 25, no. 1 (Spring 2017): 4–99, https://www.jstor.org/stable/10.2979/philmusieducrevi.25.issue-1.

23. Claude Lévi-Strauss, *The Raw and the Cooked: Mythologiques*, vol. 1, trans. John and Doreen Wieghtman (1969; repr., Chicago: University of Chicago Press, 1983).

24. Northrop Frye, *The Educated Imagination* (1963; repr., Toronto: House of Anansi, 1993).

25. Deanne Bogdan, *Re-educating the Imagination: Towards a Poetics, Politics, and Pedagogy of Literary Engagement* (Portsmouth, NH: Boynton/Cook-Heinemann, 1992).

26. For a philosophical discussion of the relationship between culture and education in the arts, see Ralph A. Smith, ed., *Culture and the Arts in Education: Critical Essays on Shaping Human Experience* (New York: Teachers College Press, 2006).

27. Jorgensen, *In Search of Music Education*, 23–29.

28. Werner Jaeger, *Paideia: The Ideals of Greek Culture*, 3 vols., trans. Gilbert Highet (New York: Oxford University Press, 1939, 1943, 1944). The translation of this monumental work of German scholarship was published during the war years in New York. This achievement speaks to a scholarly commitment to the classics and internationalism during this fraught period.

29. John Dewey wondered about replacing the word *education* with *culture*. Among his writings on culture, see his *Art as Experience* (1934; repr., New York: Paragon Books, 1979). His followers capture this close connection between culture and education in the title of the journal of the John Dewey Society, *Education and Culture*.

30. On these conceptions of education, see Jorgensen, *In Search of Music Education*, chap. 1.

31. Lévi-Strauss, *The Raw and the Cooked*.

32. The complexity of Mesopotamian liturgies is well established. See, for example, Henry George Farmer, "The Music of Ancient Mesopotamia," in *The New Oxford History of Music, Vol. 1: Ancient and Oriental Music*, ed. Egon Wellesz (London: Oxford University Press, 1957), 228–254. For an overview of more recent scholarship, see Grove Music Online, s.v. "Mesopotamia," by Anne Kilmer and Sam Mirelman, accessed February 22, 2021, https://doi.org/10.1093/gmo/9781561592630.article.18485.

33. Donald Arnstine, *Democracy and the Arts of Schooling* (Albany: State University of New York Press, 1995).

34. Neil Postman, *Technopoly: The Surrender of Culture to Technology* (New York: Vintage Books, 1992).

35. Arnstine, *Democracy and the Arts of Schooling*; Howard, *Learning by All Means*; and June Boyce-Tillman, *Constructing Musical Healing: The Wounds That Sing* (London: Jessica Kingsley, 2000).

36. Harry S. Broudy, *Enlightened Cherishing: An Essay on Aesthetic Education* (Urbana: University of Illinois Press, 1994); Philip H. Phenix, *Realms of Meaning: A Philosophy of the Curriculum for General Education* (1964; repr., Ventura, CA: Ventura County Superintendent of Schools Office, 1986); Howard, *Learning by All Means*; James Fowler, *Strong Arts, Strong Schools: The Promising Potential and Shortsighted Disregard of the Arts in American Schooling* (New York: Oxford University Press, 1996); Ralph A. Smith, *Culture and the Arts in Education: Critical*

Essays on Shaping Human Experience (New York: Teachers College Press, 2006), and his edited collection, *Aesthetics and Problems of Education: Readings in the Philosophy of Education* (Urbana and Chicago: University of Illinois Press, 1971); Maxine Greene, *Releasing the Imagination: Essays on Education, the Arts, and Social Change* (San Francisco: Jossey-Bass, 1995) and her *Variations on a Blue Guitar: The Lincoln Center Institute Lectures on Aesthetic Education* (New York: Teachers College Press, 2001).

37. Herbert Read, *Education through Art* (London: Faber and Faber, 1943).

38. Jorgensen, *Pictures of Music Education.*

39. See Peter Kivy, "Music and Liberal Education," and John Shepherd, "Music and the Last Intellectuals," in *The Philosopher, Teacher, Musician: Contemporary Perspectives on Music Education*, ed. Estelle R. Jorgensen (Urbana: University of Illinois Press, 1993), 79–93, 95–114.

40. See Börje Stålhammar, ed., *Musical Identities and Music Education* (Aachen, Germany: Shaker, 2006); Lucy Green, ed., *Learning, Teaching, and Musical Identity: Voices across Cultures* (Bloomington and Indianapolis: Indiana University Press, 2011).

41. Martha C. Nussbaum, *Cultivating Humanity: A Classical Defense of Reform in Liberal Education* (Cambridge, MA: Harvard University Press, 1997), draws on the classics to make her case for a humanistic education.

42. Friedrich Schiller, *On the Aesthetic Education of Man in a Series of Letters*, trans. Elizabeth M. Wilkinson and L. A. Willoughby (1967; repr., Oxford: Clarendon, 1986). When John Dewey, *Democracy and Education: An Introduction to the Philosophy of Education* (1916; repr., New York: Free Press, 1966) speaks of the "live organism" interacting with the environment, he evokes this physical view of humankind, although he does not stop here.

43. William Golding, *Lord of the Flies* (London: Faber and Faber, 1954).

44. Maxine Greene, *The Dialectic of Freedom* (New York: Teachers College Press, 1988).

45. Amy Gutmann and Dennis Thompson argue in *Democracy and Disagreement* (Cambridge, MA: Belknap Press of Harvard University Press, 1996) that moral conflicts are inevitable in politics, and they proffer the process of "deliberative democracy" as a way of working through these moral dilemmas.

46. See R. S. Peters, *Ethics and Education* (London: George Allen and Unwin, 1966) and his *Moral Development and Moral Education* (London: George Allen and Unwin, 1981); David Carr, *Professionalism and Ethics in Teaching* (London and New York: Taylor and Francis, 1999); David Carr and J. W. Steutel, eds., *Virtue Ethics and Moral Education* (London and New York: Routledge, 1999).

47. Regelski, "Ethical Dimensions of School-Based Music Education."

48. Carol Gilligan, *In a Different Voice: Psychological Theory and Women's Development* (Cambridge, MA: Harvard University Press, 1982); Nel Noddings, *Caring: A Feminine Approach to Ethics and Moral Education* (Berkeley: University

of California Press, 1984) and her *Critical Lessons: What Our Schools Should Teach* (Cambridge: Cambridge University Press, 2006); Raimond Gaita, *A Common Humanity: Thinking about Love and Truth and Justice* (London and New York: Routledge, 2014).

49. See Carr, *Professionalism and Ethics in Teaching*; Carr and Steutel, eds., *Virtue Ethics and Moral Education.*

50. Israel Scheffler, *In Praise of the Cognitive Emotions and Other Essays on the Philosophy of Education* (New York: Routledge, Chapman and Hall, 1991); Iris M. Yob, "The Cognitive Emotions and Emotional Cognitions," *Studies in Philosophy and Education* 16, no. 1–2 (1997): 43–57, https://doi.org/10.1023/A:1004990702983.

51. Vernon A. Howard, *Artistry: The Work of Artists* (Indianapolis, IN: Hackett, 1982).

52. See, for example, Elliot W. Eisner, *Cognition and Curriculum Reconsidered*, 2nd ed. (New York: Teachers College Press, 1994); Doris Sommer, *Bilingual Aesthetics: A New Sentimental Education* (Durham, NC: Duke University Press, 2004); Thomas A. Regelski and J. Terry Gates, eds., *Music Education for Changing Times: Guiding Visions for Practice* (Dordrecht, Netherlands: Springer, 2009); Gayatri Chakravorty Spivak, *An Aesthetic Education in the Era of Globalization* (Cambridge, MA: Harvard University Press, 2012); Donald S. Blumenfeld-Jones, *Curriculum and the Aesthetic Life: Hermeneutics, Body, Democracy, and Ethics in Curriculum Theory and Practice* (New York: Peter Lang, 2012).

53. See Estelle R. Jorgensen, "William Channing Woodbridge's Lecture 'On Vocal Music as a Branch of Common Education' Revisited," *Studies in Music* (University of Western Australia) 18 (1984): 1–32. Reprinted in *Visions of Music Education* 14 (June 2009), http://www-usr.rider.edu/~vrme/v14n1/vision/woodbridge.pdf.

54. For histories of music education, see Michael L. Mark and Charles L. Gary, *A History of American Music Education*, 3rd ed. (Lanham, MD: Rowman and Littlefield Education, 2007); James A. Keene, *A History of Music Education in the United States*, 2nd ed. (Centennial, CO: Glenridge, 2009); Michael Mark and Patrice Madura, *Contemporary Music Education*, 4th ed. (Boston: Schirmer, 2014).

55. On the dialectic of music making and receiving, see Jorgensen, *In Search of Music Education*, 83–87.

56. Estelle R. Jorgensen, "Engineering Change in Music Education: A Model of the Political Process Underlying the Boston School Music Movement (1829–1838)," *Journal of Research in Music Education* 31 (1983): 67–75, https://doi.org/10.2307/3345111.

57. See Jorgensen, *In Search of Music Education.*

58. Jorgensen, *Transforming Music Education.*

59. Gilles Deleuze and Felix Guattari, *A Thousand Plateaus: Capitalism and Schizophrenia*, trans. Brian Massumi (Minneapolis and London: University of Minnesota Press, 1987).

60. Howard, *Artistry*, chap. 6.

61. In Estelle R. Jorgensen, "On the Development of a Theory of Musical Instruction," *Psychology of Music* 8 (1980): 25–30, https://doi.org/10.1177/030573568082003, I described music educational commonplaces such as music, teaching, learning, curriculum, instruction, and administration in order to think about aspects of music education in a music educational way, and I drew on this approach in Jorgensen, *Pictures of Music Education*.

62. Henry A. Giroux, *Border Crossings: Cultural Workers and the Politics of Education* (1992; repr., New York and London: Routledge, 1993) employs the expression *cultural workers* to refer generally to all of those engaged in cultural policy. This term includes politicians and others who may not think of themselves, strictly speaking, as educators or teachers. Giroux's perspective is consonant with my own view of the state and its institutions as involved, broadly speaking, in the work of education even though it may be ongoing beyond the borders of schools and formal general education.

CHAPTER 2 - ARTISTRY, TASTE, SKILL, AND STYLE

1. See Vernon A. Howard, *Learning by All Means: Lessons from the Arts: A Study in the Philosophy of Education* (New York: Peter Lang, 1992).

2. See Werner Jaeger, *Paideia: The Ideals of Greek Culture*, 3 vols., trans. Gilbert Highet (New York: Oxford University Press, 1939, 1943, 1944).

3. John Dewey, *Art as Experience* (1934; repr., New York: Paragon Books, 1979).

4. On the arts, culture, and education, see, for example, Donald Arnstine, *Democracy and the Arts of Schooling* (Albany: State University of New York Press, 1995); Seyla Benhabib, *The Claims of Culture: Equality and Diversity in the Global Era* (Princeton, NJ: Princeton University Press, 2002); Harry S. Broudy, *Enlightened Cherishing: An Essay on Aesthetic Education* (Urbana and Chicago: University of Illinois Press, 1994); Maxine Greene, *Releasing the Imagination: Essays on Education, the Arts, and Social Change* (San Francisco: Jossey-Bass, 1995), and her *Variations on a Blue Guitar: The Lincoln Center Institute Lectures on Aesthetic Education* (New York: Teachers College Press, 2001); Jane Roland Martin, *Cultural Miseducation: In Search of a Democratic Solution* (New York: Teachers College Press, 2002), and her *School Was Our Life: Remembering Progressive Education* (Bloomington: Indiana University Press, 2018); Martha C. Nussbaum, *Cultivating Humanity: A Classical Defense of Reform in Liberal Education* (Cambridge, MA: Harvard University Press, 1997), and her *Poetic Justice: The Literary Imagination and Public Life* (Boston: Beacon, 1995); Herbert Read, *Education through Art* (London: Faber and Faber, 1943).

5. See, for example, Plato, *The Republic of Plato*, trans. Francis Macdonald Cornford (1941; repr., Oxford: Oxford University Press, 1942); Aristotle, *Aristotle's Poetics*, trans. George Whalley, eds. John Baxter and Patrick Atherton (Montreal,

PQ: McGill-Queen's University Press, 1997); Friedrich Schiller, *On the Aesthetic Education of Man in a Series of Letters*, trans. Elizabeth M. Wilkinson and L. A. Willoughby (1967; repr., Oxford: Clarendon, 1986); Dewey, *Art as Experience.*

6. See, for example, Vernon A. Howard, *Artistry: The Work of Artists* (Indianapolis, IN: Hackett, 1982), and his *Charm and Speed: Virtuosity in the Performing Arts* (New York: Peter Lang, 2008); Bennett Reimer, *A Philosophy of Music Education: Advancing the Vision*, 3rd edition (Upper Saddle River, NJ: Prentice-Hall, 2003); David J. Elliott and Marissa Silverman, *Music Matters: A Philosophy of Music Education*, 2nd edition (New York: Oxford University Press, 2014); Wayne D. Bowman and Ana Lucia Frega, eds., *The Oxford Handbook of Philosophy in Music Education* (New York: Oxford University Press, 2012).

7. On institutions and music education, see Estelle R. Jorgensen, *In Search of Music Education* (Urbana: University of Illinois Press, 1997), chap. 2.

8. OED Online, s.v. "Artist, n.," accessed October 17, 2018, https://www.oed.com/view/Entry/11237?; also, Online Etymology Dictionary, s.v. "Artist," accessed October 17, 2018, https://www.etymonline.com/word/artist.

9. Nan Cooke Carpenter, *Music in the Medieval and Renaissance Universities* (Norman: University of Oklahoma Press, 1958), especially chap. 3.

10. OED Online, s.v. "artist, n."

11. OED Online s.v. "Artistry, n.," accessed October 17, 2018, https://www.oed.com//view/Entry/11246?.

12. Estelle R. Jorgensen, "'This-with-That': A Dialectical Approach to Teaching for Musical Imagination," *Journal of Aesthetic Education* 40, no. 4 (Winter 2006): 1–20, https://doi.org/10.1353/jae.2006.0035.

13. Howard, *Artistry*, chap. 6.

14. See, for example, Aaron Copland, *Music and Imagination* (Cambridge, MA: Harvard University Press, 1980); Susanne K. Langer, *Feeling and Form: A Theory of Art Developed from Philosophy in a New Key* (London: Routledge, 1953); Northrop Frye, *The Educated Imagination* (1963; repr., Toronto: House of Anansi, 1993).

15. See Philip Alperson, *What Is Music? An Introduction to the Philosophy of Music* (1987; University Park: Pennsylvania State University Press, 1994); Elliott and Silverman, *Music Matters*; David J. Elliott, ed., *Praxial Music Education: Reflections and Dialogues* (New York: Oxford University Press, 2005).

16. See David J. Elliott, Marissa Silverman, and Wayne D. Bowman, eds., *Artistic Citizenship: Artistry, Social Responsibility, and Ethical Praxis* (New York: Oxford University Press, 2016).

17. David Ward-Steinman, "On Composing: Doing It, Teaching It, Living It," *Philosophy of Music Education Review* 19, no. 1 (Spring 2011): 5–23, https://doi.org/10.2979/philmusieducrevi.19.1.fm, makes the point of a niggling spot in an otherwise good composition that the composer insists on getting right. I am indebted to Iris M. Yob for reminding me of this article.

18. On the dialectic between music making and music receiving, see Jorgensen, *In Search of Music Education*, 83–87.

19. For a wide-ranging and interdisciplinary critical view of improvisation, see *The Oxford Handbook of Critical Improvisation Studies*, vol. 1, ed. George Lewis and Benjamin Piekut (New York: Oxford University Press, 2016).

20. On the relationships between music and social class, see Derek B. Scott, ed., *Music, Culture, and Society: A Reader* (2000; repr., New York: Oxford University Press, 2002), part 3. Also, on the relation between music and power, see Jacques Attali, *Noise: The Political Economy of Music*, trans. Brian Massumi (Minneapolis: University of Minnesota Press, 1985).

21. This point is well documented in musicological and ethnomusicological scholarship by the twentieth century; see, for example, Karl Geiringer and Irene Geiringer, *The Bach Family: Seven Generations of Creative Genius* (New York: Oxford University Press, 1954); Christoph Wolff, *The New Grove Bach Family* (New York: W. W. Norton, 1983); George Martin, *The Dambrosch Dynasty: America's First Family of Music* (Boston: Houghton Mifflin, 1983); Daniel M. Neuman, *The Life of Music in North India: The Organization of an Artistic Tradition* (Detroit: Wayne State University Press, 1980).

22. On the present predicament of the American Federation of Musicians and the Actors Equity Association in the United States, see Rachel Shane, "Resurgence or Deterioration? The State of Cultural Unions in the 21st Century," *Journal of Arts Management, Law and Society* 43, no. 3 (2013): 139–152, https://doi.org/10.1080/10632921.2013.817364.

23. Donald Francis Tovey, *Essays in Musical Analysis*, 6 vols. (London: Oxford University Press, Humphrey Milford, 1935–1939).

24. Thomas A. Regelski, "The Aristotelian Bases for Praxis for Music and Music Education," *Philosophy of Music Education Review* 6, no. 1 (Spring 1998): 22–59, https://www.jstor.org/stable/40327113.

25. See, for example, J. Scott Goble, "Perspectives on Practice: A Pragmatic Comparison of the Praxial Philosophies of David Elliott and Thomas Regelski," *Philosophy of Music Education Review* 11, no. 1 (Spring 2003): 23–44, https://www.jstor.org/stable/40327196.

26. Doreen Rao, "Craft, Singing Craft, and Musical Experience: A Philosophical Study with Implications for Vocal Music Education as Aesthetic Education" (PhD diss., Northwestern University, 1988), sees the craft of singing as a building block of musical artistry and a part of a broader aesthetic education. Her performance-based approach to music education presaged that of Elliott and Silverman, *Music Matters*.

27. See Johan Huizinga, *Homo Ludens: A Study of the Play-element in Culture* (1950; repr., Boston: Beacon, 1955); Armand D'Angour, "Plato and Play: Taking Play Seriously," *American Journal of Play* 5, no. 3 (Spring 2013): 293–307, https://www.journalofplay.org/sites/www.journalofplay.org/files/pdf-articles/5-3-article-plato-and-play.pdf.

28. Despite the many musical odes, anthems, hymns, and other musical offerings to St. Cecilia, women's contributions to music have been largely ignored

or marginalized in the classical canon and its history. In their edited collection, *Cecilia Reclaimed: Feminist Perspectives on Gender and Music* (Urbana: University of Illinois Press, 1994), Susan C. Cook and Judy S. Tsou seek to recognize women's contributions as deserving of a central place in the canon of Western music.

29. Among the writers on spirituality, music, and musical education, I think of June Boyce-Tillman, "Towards an Ecology of Music Education," *Philosophy of Music Education Review* 12, no. 2 (2004): 102–125, https://www.jstor.org/stable/40327232, and her *Experiencing Music—Restoring the Spiritual: Music as Well-Being* (Bern, Switzerland: Peter Lang, 2016), and June Boyce-Tillman, ed., *Spirituality and Music Education: Perspectives from Three Continents* (Oxford: Peter Lang, 2017); Iris M. Yob, "If We Knew What Spirituality Was, We Would Teach for It," *Music Educators Journal* 98, no. 2 (December 2011): 41–47, https://doi.org/10.1177/0027432111425959, and her "Why Is Music a Language of Spirituality?" *Philosophy of Music Education Review* 18, no. 2 (Fall 2010): 145–151, https://doi.org/10.2979/pme.2010.18.2.145; Liora Bresler, ed., *International Handbook of Research in Arts Education* (Dordrecht, Netherlands: Springer, 2007), section 13: "Spirituality."

30. See Neuman, *Life of Music in North India*, chap. 2.

31. For a study of the relationship between music and trance, see Gilbert Rouget, *Music and Trance: A Theory of the Relations between Music and Possession*, trans. Brunhilde Biebuyk with the author (Chicago: University of Chicago Press, 1985). Also, on the notion of music as a simulacrum of sacrifice, see Attali, *Noise*, especially chap. 2.

32. Estelle R. Jorgensen, "Another Perspective: The Joyous Composer," *Music Educators Journal* 102, no. 3 (March 2016): 71–74, https://doi.org/10.1177/0027432115621864.

33. On know-how, see Howard, *Artistry*, chap. 3.

34. See Israel Scheffler, *In Praise of the Cognitive Emotions and Other Essays on the Philosophy of Education* (New York: Routledge, Chapman and Hall, 1991), chap. 3. Also see Scheffler's analysis of knowledge and skill in his *Conditions of Knowledge: An Introduction to Epistemology and Education* (Chicago: University of Chicago Press, 1965), chap. 5.

35. See Susanne K. Langer, *Philosophy in a New Key: A Study in the Symbolism of Reason, Rite, and Art*, 3rd edition (Cambridge, MA: Harvard University Press, 1957), her *Feeling and Form: A Theory of Art Developed from Philosophy in a New Key* (London: Routledge, 1953), and her trilogy, *Mind: An Essay on Human Feeling*, 3 vols. (Baltimore: Johns Hopkins Press, 1967, 1972, 1982).

36. For an examination of Langer's ideas, see a special issue of the *Philosophy of Music Education Review* 1, no. 1 (spring 1993), https://www.jstor.org/stable/i40013909.

37. Philip H. Phenix, *Realms of Meaning: A Philosophy of the Curriculum for General Education* (1964; repr., Ventura, CA: Ventura County Superintendent of Schools Office, 1986), section entitled "The Third Realm: Esthetics."

38. Nelson Goodman, *Ways of Worldmaking* (Indianapolis, IN: Hackett, 1978).

39. Lucy Green, *How Popular Musicians Learn: A Way Ahead for Music Education* (2002; repr., Abingdon, UK, and New York: Routledge, 2016).

40. See Hilary Hahn, "What Did You Bring to Play for Me Today? The Concertos—and Lessons—I Learned from My Two Greatest Teachers," *Slate*, July 19, 2015, https://slate.com/culture/2015/07/violinist-hilary-hahn-on-her-two-greatest-teachers-and-on-the-mozart-and-vieuxtemps-concertos-they-taught-her.html.

41. Scheffler, *In Praise of the Cognitive Emotions*, chap. 3.

42. OED Online. "Taste, n.1," accessed October 24, 2018, https://www.oed.com/view/Entry/198050?.

43. OED Online, s.v. "Taste, v.," accessed October 24, 2018, https://www.oed.com/view/Entry/198052?.

44. Max Van Manen, *The Tact of Teaching: The Meaning of Pedagogical Thoughtfulness* (Albany: State University of New York Press, 1991).

45. On the role and unavoidability of surprise, see Scheffler, *In Praise of the Cognitive Emotions*, 12–15, 35–36.

46. Randall Everett Allsup, *Remixing the Classroom: Toward an Open Philosophy of Music Education* (Bloomington: Indiana University Press, 2016).

47. Maxine Greene, *The Dialectic of Freedom* (New York: Teachers College Press, 1988), chap 4.

48. See John Dewey, *Experience and Education* (1938; repr., New York: Collier Books, 1963).

49. For example, see Percy A. Scholes, *Music, the Child, and the Masterpiece: A Comprehensive Handbook of Aims and Methods in All That Is Usually Called "Musical Appreciation"* (London: Oxford University Press, Humphrey Milford, 1935).

50. See Alexandra Kertz-Welzel, "'Two Souls, Alas, Reside Within My Breast': Reflections on German and American Music Education Regarding the Internationalization of Music Education," *Philosophy of Music Education Review* 21, no. 1 (Spring 2013): 52–65, https://doi.org/10.2979/philmusieducrevi.21.1.52; Leonard Tan, "Response to Alexandra Kertz-Welzel's '"Two Souls, Alas, Reside within My Breast": Reflections on German and American Music Education Regarding the Internationalization of Music Education,'" *Philosophy of Music Education Review* 23, no. 1 (Spring 2015): 113–117, https://doi.org/10.2979/philmusieducrevi.23.1.113.

51. Immanuel Kant, *Critique of Judgment*, trans. James Creed Meredith (1952; repr., Oxford: Clarendon, 1982), part 1, §§5-8, 50–57.

52. Jorgensen, *In Search of Music Education*, chap. 2.

53. Among the seminal studies to explore the psychological and social roots of musical taste, I think of Paul R. Farnsworth, *Musical Taste: Its Measurement and Cultural Nature* (Stanford, CA: Stanford University Press, 1950).

54. Self-actualization is evident in peak experiences. See Abraham H. Maslow, "Music Education and Peak Experience," *Music Educators Journal* 54, no. 6

(February 1968), 72+, 171, https://doi.org/10.2307/3391274, and his *The Farther Reaches of Human Nature* (1971; repr., Harmondsworth, UK: Penguin, 1976), chap. 3.

55. Bernarr Rainbow and Gordon Cox, *Music in Educational Thought and Practice: A Survey from 800BC* (Woodbridge, Suffolk, UK: Boydell, 2006), 19.

56. See Plato, *Republic*, §§401d-403c, 100–102; §§509d-511e, 236–248; §§535a-541b, 268–276.

57. Zoltán Kodály, *The Selected Writings of Zoltán Kodály*, ed. Ferenc Bónis, trans. Lili Halápy and Fred Macnicol (London: Boosey and Hawkes, 1974), 140. Kodály also claims that "only art of intrinsic value is suitable for children! Everything else is harmful" (122).

58. See James A. Keene, *A History of Music Education in the United States*, 2nd ed. (Centennial, CO: Glenridge, 2009).

59. See, for example, Ann Margaret Daniel, "Violins and Fiddles: Roots Reigns at Boston's Conservatories," *The Journal of Roots Music: No Depression*, February 26, 2015, at https://www.nodepression.com/violins-and-fiddles-roots-music-reigns-at-bostons-conservatories/; and Nathaniel J. Olson, "The Institutionalization of Fiddling in Higher Education: Three Cases" (EdD diss., Columbia University, 2014). I am indebted to Randall Allsup for his assistance in securing this dissertation.

60. See Sean Steel, "The Birth of Dionysian Education (The Spirit of Music)?: Part 1," *Philosophy of Music Education Review* 22, no. 1 (Spring 2014): 38–60, https://doi.org/10.2979/philmusieducrevi.22.1.38, and his "The Birth of Dionysian Education (The Spirit of Music)?: Part 2," *Philosophy of Music Education Review* 23, no. 1 (Spring 2015): 67–81, https://doi.org/10.2979/philmusieducrevi.23.1.67.

61. See Judith Vander, *Songprints: The Musical Experience of Five Shoshone Women* (Urbana: University of Illinois Press, 1996).

62. OED Online, s.v. "Skill, n.1," accessed October 29, 2018, https://www.oed.com/view/Entry/180865?.

63. OED Online, s.v. "Skill, v.1," accessed October 29, 2018, https://www.oed.com/view/Entry/180867?.

64. Scheffler, *In Praise of the Cognitive Emotions*, chap. 3.

65. Scholes, *Music, the Child, and the Masterpiece*, 99.

66. On the learner's predicament, see Howard, *Artistry*, especially chap. 2.

67. Mary J. Reichling, "Images of Imagination," *Journal of Research in Music Education* 38, no. 4 (1990): 282–293, https://doi.org/10.2307/3345225.

68. On feeling, see Langer, *Philosophy in a New Key*, her *Feeling and Form*, and her trilogy, *Mind*.

69. On wisdom, see Alfred North Whitehead, *The Aims of Education and Other Essays* (1929; repr., New York: Free Press, 1967), 30. Whitehead emphasizes the application of knowledge and the power its mastery enables and conveys.

70. See Rainbow and Cox, *Music in Educational Thought and Practice*, chap.1.

71. On the "demonstration effect," see Estelle R. Jorgensen, "Engineering Change in Music Education: A Model of the Political Process Underlying the Boston School Music Movement (1829–1838)," *Journal of Research in Music Education* 31 (1983): 67–75, https://doi.org/10.2307/3345111.

72. See Estelle R. Jorgensen, "William Channing Woodbridge's Lecture 'On Vocal Music as a Branch of Common Education' Revisited," *Studies in Music* (University of Western Australia) 18 (1984): 1–32. Reprinted in *Visions of Music Education* 14, no. 1 (June 2009) http://www-usr.rider.edu/~vrme/v14n1/vision/woodbridge.pdf.

73. On the dialectic of making and receiving music, see Jorgensen, *In Search of Music Education*, 83–87.

74. On the "noncategorical distinction between art and craft," see Howard, *Artistry*, 24, also chap. 1.

75. OED Online, s.v. "Style, n.," accessed October 30, 2018, https://www.oed.com/view/Entry/192315?.

76. OED Online, s.v. "Style, v.," accessed October 30, 2018, https://www.oed.com/view/Entry/192316?.

77. The notion of communities of practice was developed by Jean Lave and Etienne Wenger, *Situated Learning: Legitimate Peripheral Participation* (Cambridge: Cambridge University Press, 1991), and subsequently revised by Etienne Wenger, *Communities of Practice: Learning, Meaning, and Identity* (Cambridge: Cambridge University Press, 1998).

78. Jorgensen, *In Search of Music Education*, chap. 2.

79. See Kant, *Critique of Judgment*, part 1, §§5-8, 50–57. I see this characteristic of style as one of the overlapping features of style and taste.

80. See, for example, Scholes, *Music, the Child, and the Masterpiece*.

81. On articulated life-symbols, see Langer, *Philosophy in a New Key*, 153, 205, 240, 246, 251. On generalization, see Whitehead, *Aims of Education*, 36, 37. Whitehead writes, "Education is the guidance of the individual towards a comprehension of the art of life; and by art of life I mean the most complete achievement of varied activity of that living creature in the face of its actual environment" (39).

82. Whitehead, *Aims of Education*, 12.

83. Phenix, *Realms of Meaning*, The Third Realm—Esthetics, 139–185.

84. Kodály, The Selected Writings of Zoltán Kodály, 140.

CHAPTER 3 - REVERENCE, HUMILITY, AWE, AND SPIRITUALITY

1. See, for example, David Carr and John Haldane, eds., *Spirituality, Philosophy and Education* (London: RoutledgeFalmer, 2003); Iris V. Cully, *Education for Spiritual Growth* (San Francisco: Harper and Row, 1984); Michael Patrick Lynch, "Teaching Humility in an Age of Arrogance," *The Chronicle of Higher Education*, June 5, 2017, https://www.chronicle.com/article/teaching-humility-in-an-age-of-arrogance/;

Michael Patrick Lynch, *The Internet of Us: Knowing More and Understanding Less in the Age of Big Data* (New York: Liveright Publishing Corp, 2016); Parker J. Palmer, *The Active Life: A Spirituality of Work, Creativity, and Caring* (San Francisco: Jossey-Bass, 1990); Kirk J. Schneider, *Rediscovery of Awe: Splendor, Mystery, and the Fluid Center of Life* (St. Paul, MN: Paragon House, 2004); Paul Woodruff, *Reverence: Renewing a Forgotten Virtue* (Oxford: Oxford University Press, 2001).

2. See, for example, June Boyce-Tillman, ed., *Spirituality and Music Education: Perspectives from Three Continents* (Oxford: Peter Lang, 2017); June Boyce-Tillman, *Experiencing Music—Restoring the Spiritual: Music as Well-Being* (Bern, Switzerland: Peter Lang, 2016); Karin Hendricks and June Boyce-Tillman, eds., *Queering Freedom: Music, Identity, and Spirituality* (Oxford: Peter Lang, 2018).

3. See OED Online, s.v. "Reverence, n.," accessed November 12, 2017, https://www.oed.com/view/Entry/164755?; OED Online, s.v. "Reverence, v.," accessed November 12, 2017, https://www.oed.com/view/Entry/164756?.

4. Jacques Attali, *Noise: The Political Economy of Music*, trans. Brian Massumi (Minneapolis: University of Minnesota Press, 1985), 4, describes music as originating as a "simulacrum" of "ritual murder" or "sacrifice."

5. This veneration is described by Christopher Small, *Musicking: The Meanings of Performing and Listening* (Hanover, NH: Wesleyan University Press, University Press of New England, 1998).

6. On *riaz* in the North Indian tradition, see Daniel M. Neuman, *The Life of Music in North India: The Organization of an Artistic Tradition* (Detroit: Wayne State University Press, 1980), chap. 2; *Grove Music Online*, s.v. "India, subcontinent of," by Regula Qureshi et al., accessed March 1, 2021, https://doi.org/10.1093/gmo/9781561592630.article.43272.

7. See David Buckley and John Shepherd, "Stardom," *Continuum Encyclopedia of Popular Music of the World*, vol. 1, Media, Industry, and Society, ed. John Shepherd, David Horn, Dave Laing, Paul Oliver, and Peter Wicke (New York: Continuum, 2003), 366–369; Alexis Patridis, "Streaming In: The New Wave of Pop Stars Created by YouTube," *Guardian*, February 20, 2014, https://www.theguardian.com/music/2014/feb/20/ward-alvord-days-boyce-avenue-youtube-pop-stars; John Shepherd and Kyle Devine, eds., *The Routledge Reader on the Sociology of Music* (New York: Routledge, 2015), 274–275; Mathieu Deflem, *Lady Gaga and the Sociology of Fame: The Rise of a Pop Star in an Age of Celebrity* (New York: Palgrave Macmillan, 2017).

8. On psychical distancing, see Susanne K. Langer, *Philosophy in a New Key: A Study in the Symbolism of Reason, Rite, and Art*, 3rd edition (Cambridge, MA: Harvard University Press, 1957), 222–223.

9. See Israel Scheffler, *In Praise of the Cognitive Emotions and Other Essays on the Philosophy of Education* (New York: Routledge, Chapman and Hall, 1991), on the cognitive emotions and Iris M. Yob, "The Cognitive Emotions and Emotional Cognitions," *Studies in Philosophy and Education* 16, no. 1–2 (1997):43–57, https://doi.org/10.1023/A:1004990702983, on the emotional cognitions.

10. On music's celebratory and alienating roles, see Lucy Green, *Music on Deaf Ears: Musical Meaning, Ideology and Education* (Manchester, UK: Manchester University Press, 1988).

11. On making and receiving music among the other arts, see Estelle R. Jorgensen, *In Search of Music Education* (Urbana: University of Illinois Press, 1997), 83–87.

12. See Iris M. Yob, "School and Sacred Time," paper presented at Tenth International Society for Philosophy of Music Education Conference, Frankfurt, Germany, 2015, and her "School as Sacred Space," paper presented at Reasons of the Heart Conference, Edinburgh, Scotland, September 2004.

13. Parker J. Palmer, *Courage to Teach: Exploring the Inner Landscape of a Teacher's Life* (San Francisco: Jossey-Bass, 1998); Maxine Greene, *The Dialectic of Freedom* (New York: Teachers College Press, 1988).

14. On the Guide and Pedagogy pictures, see Estelle R. Jorgensen, *Pictures of Music Education* (Bloomington: Indiana University Press, 2011), chap. 12.

15. John Dewey, *Art as Experience* (1934; repr. New York: Paragon Books, 1979), chap. 3.

16. See, for example, Abraham H. Maslow, "Music Education and Peak Experience," *Music Educators Journal* 54, no. 6 (February 1968), 72+, 171, https://doi.org/10.2307/3391274, and his *The Farther Reaches of Human Nature* (1971; repr., Harmondsworth, UK: Penguin, 1976), chap. 12, entitled "Education and Peak Experiences."

17. On embodied teaching and learning, see Liora Bresler, ed., *Knowing Bodies, Moving Minds: Towards Embodied Teaching and Learning* (New York: Springer, 2004).

18. See Langer, *Philosophy in a New Key*, chap. 4.

19. On a Dionysian philosophy of music education, see Sean Steel, "The Birth of Dionysian Education (The Spirit of Music)?: Part 1," *Philosophy of Music Education Review* 22, no. 1 (Spring 2014): 38–60, https://doi.org/10.2979/philmusieducrevi.22.1.38, and his "The Birth of Dionysian Education (The Spirit of Music)?: Part 2," *Philosophy of Music Education Review* 23, no. 1 (Spring 2015): 67–81, https://doi.org/10.2979/philmusieducrevi.23.1.67.

20. On the "thermostatic" view of education, see Neil Postman, *Teaching as a Conserving Activity* (New York: Dell, 1979), chap. 1.

21. On subjugated ways of knowing, see, for example, June Boyce-Tillman, *Constructing Musical Healing: The Wounds That Sing* (London: Jessica Kingsley, 2000), chap. 1, and her "Towards an Ecology of Music Education," *Philosophy of Music Education Review* 12, no. 2 (2004): 102–125.

22. On the tyranny of colonization in music education thought, see Deborah Bradley, "Good for What? Good for Whom?: Decolonizing Music Education Philosophies," in *The Oxford Handbook of Philosophy in Music Education*, ed. Wayne D. Bowman and Ana Lucia Frega (New York: Oxford University Press, 2012), 409–433.

23. Ivan Illich, *Deschooling Society* (1971; repr., London and New York: Marion Boyars, 2004), 31.

24. Paulo Freire, *Pedagogy of the Oppressed*, New Revised 20th Anniversary Edition, trans. Myra Bergman Ramos (New York: Continuum, 1993), chap. 2.

25. See OED Online, s.v. "Humility, n.," accessed November 12, 2017, https://www.oed.com/view/Entry/89375?.

26. See excerpts of Johann Heinrich Pestalozzi's *Evening Hour of the Hermit* and *Leonard and Gertrude* in *Three Thousand Years of Educational Wisdom: Selections from Great Documents*, 2nd edition, ed. Robert Ulich (Cambridge, MA: Harvard University Press, 1954), 480–507.

27. For example, William Channing Woodbridge, a Congregationalist minister, emphasizes Christian virtues as the values that should exemplify vocal music instruction in elementary or "common" schools. See Estelle R. Jorgensen, "William Channing Woodbridge's Lecture 'On Vocal Music as a Branch of Common Education' Revisited," *Studies in Music* (University of Western Australia) 18 (1984): 1–32. Reprinted in *Visions of Music Education* 14, no. 1 (June 2009), http://www-usr.rider.edu/~vrme/v14n1/vision/woodbridge.pdf.

28. See Baldesar Castiglione, *The Book of the Courtier*, trans. George Bull (1967; repr., Harmondsworth, UK: Penguin, 1976); Judith Tick, "Passed Away Is the Piano Girl: Changes in American Musical Life, 1870–1900," in *Women Making Music: The Western Art Tradition, 1150–1950*, ed. Jane Bowers and Judith Tick (Urbana: University of Illinois Press, 1986), 325–348.

29. See OED Online, s.v., "Humility, n." Also, see David Hume, *A Treatise on Human Nature: A Critical Edition*, ed. David Fate Norton and Mary J. Norton, vol. 1: Texts (Oxford: Clarendon, 2007), especially Book 2: Of the Passions, Part 1: Of Pride and Humility.

30. See Mircea Eliade, *The Myth of the Eternal Return or, Cosmos and History*, trans. Willard R. Trask (1954; repr., Princeton, NJ: Princeton University Press, 1974). Also, see Mircea Eliade, *Symbolism, the Sacred, and the Arts*, ed. Diane Apostolos-Cappadona (New York: Crossroad, 1988).

31. Vernon A. Howard, *Artistry: The Work of Artists* (Indianapolis, IN: Hackett, 1982), especially chap. 6, "Practice and the Vision of Mastery."

32. Aaron Copland, *Music and Imagination* (Cambridge, MA: Harvard University Press, 1980), 53–55.

33. Aristotle, *Nicomachean Ethics*, trans. and ed. Roger Crisp (Cambridge: Cambridge University Press, 2000), book 2, para. 1109b, p. 36.

34. See OED Online, s.v. "Meekness, n.," accessed November 12, 2017, https://www.oed.com/view/Entry/115837?.

35. Max Van Manen, *The Tact of Teaching: The Meaning of Pedagogical Thoughtfulness* (Albany: State University of New York Press, 1991).

36. Nel Noddings, *Caring: A Feminine Approach to Ethics and Moral Education* (Berkeley: University of California Press, 1984).

37. On the power of dialogue in education, see Freire, *Pedagogy of the Oppressed*, chap. 3; Maxine Greene, *Variations on a Blue Guitar: The Lincoln Center Institute Lectures on Aesthetic Education* (New York: Teachers College Press, 2001), 104–109; Palmer, *Courage to Teach*, especially chaps. 4, 5, and 6. Also, see David Bohm *On Dialogue*, ed. Lee Nichol (London and New York: Routledge, 1996).

38. See Vernon A. Howard, *Charm and Speed: Virtuosity in the Performing Arts* (New York: Peter Lang, 2008).

39. Mihaly Csikszentmihalyi, *Flow: The Psychology of Optimal Experience* (New York: Harper and Row, 1990). Interestingly, Schneider, *Rediscovery of Awe*, sees awe as the "fluid center" of life. Both these psychologists regard optimal experience as fluid and dynamic rather than solid and static.

40. See OED Online, s.v. "Grace, n.," accessed November 12, 2017, https://www.oed.com/view/Entry/80373?; OED Online, s.v. "Grace, v.," accessed November 12, 2017, https://www.oed.com/view/Entry/80374?.

41. See Isaiah Berlin, *The Crooked Timber of Humanity: Chapters in the History of Ideas*, ed. Hardy Henry (Princeton, NJ: Princeton University Press, 1990).

42. Scheffler, *In Praise of the Cognitive Emotions*, 13–15, discusses skepticism, gullibility, and dogmatism as defenses against surprise.

43. Ellen Koskoff, "The Sound of a Woman's Voice: Gender and Music in a New York Hasidic Community," in *Women and Music in Cross Cultural Perspective*, ed. Ellen Koskoff, (1987; repr., Urbana: University of Illinois Press, 1989), 213–223.

44. Freire, *Pedagogy of the Oppressed*, especially chap. 4.

45. See OED Online, s.v. "Awe, n.1.," accessed November 12, 2017, https://www.oed.com/view/Entry/13911?.

46. Iris M. Yob, "If We Knew What Spirituality Was, We Would Teach for It," *Music Educators Journal* 98, no. 2 (December 2011): 41–47, https://doi.org/10.1177/0027432111425959.

47. Mark St. Germain, *Freud's Last Session*, suggested by *The Question of God* by Dr. Armand M. Nicholi Jr., acting edition (New York: Dramatists Play Service, c.2010).

48. Rudolf Otto, *The Idea of the Holy: An Inquiry into the Non-rational Factor in the Idea of the Divine and Its Relation to the Rational*, trans. John W. Harvey, 2nd ed. (Oxford: Oxford University Press, 1950), especially chap. 4.

49. See Dianna T. Kenny, *The Psychology of Music Performance Anxiety* (Oxford: Oxford University Press, 2011).

50. Dewey, *Art as Experience*, 35.

51. See Estelle R. Jorgensen, "On Excellence in Music Education," *McGill Journal of Education* 15, no. 1 (1980): 94–103, https://mje.mcgill.ca/article/view/7313/5252.

52. "Music in the Heart of the Congo," reported by Bob Simon, *60 Minutes*, CBS, April 8, 2012, https://www.cbsnews.com/news/music-in-the-heart-of-the-congo.

53. Bennett Reimer, "The Experience of Profundity in Music," *Journal of Aesthetic Education* 29, no. 4 (Winter 1995): 1–21, https://doi.org/10.2307

/3333288. Philip Fisher, *Wonder, the Rainbow, and the Aesthetics of Rare Experiences* (Cambridge, MA: Harvard University Press, 1998), chap. 1, links wonder (for him, the beginning of philosophy) and the sublime.

54. On the arousal theory of music, see Stephen Davies, *Musical Meaning and Expression* (Ithaca, NY: Cornell University Press, 1994); Peter Kivy, *Sound Sentiment: An Essay on the Musical Emotions, Including the Complete Text of The Corded Shell* (Philadelphia: Temple University Press, 1989) and his *Introduction to a Philosophy of Music* (Oxford: Clarendon, 2002).

55. Matthew Fox, ed., *Hildegard of Bingen's Book of Divine Works with Letters and Songs* (Santa Fe, NM: Bear and Co., 1987), 348, invokes the metaphor of a "feather . . . carried on the wind." Also, see Gothic Voices with Emma Kirkby and directed by Christopher Page, *Hildegard von Bingen: Feather on the Breath of God* (Hyperion, 1983), CDA 66039. The metaphor for music of breath evokes the notion of "tala" in Indian classical music. See Lewis Rowell, *Thinking about Music: An Introduction to the Philosophy of Music* (Amherst: University of Massachusetts Press, 1983), 208–209.

56. See "Music in the Heart of the Congo."

57. See Scheffler, *In Praise of the Cognitive Emotions*; Yob "The Cognitive Emotions and Emotional Cognitions."

58. On virtual or psychic time in perceiving a musical image, see Susanne K. Langer, *Feeling and Form: A Theory of Art Developed from Philosophy in a New Key* (London: Routledge, 1953), especially chap. 7, and her *Philosophy in a New Key.*

59. Schneider, *Rediscovery of Awe*, especially chaps. 2 and 5.

60. Zoltán Kodály, *The Selected Writings of Zoltán Kodály*, ed. Ferenc Bónis, trans. Lili Halápy and Fred Macnicol (London: Boosey and Hawkes, 1974), 120, 122, 125.

61. See Kenny, *Psychology of Music Performance Anxiety.*

62. See OED Online, s.v. "Spirituality, n.," accessed November 12, 2017, https://www.oed.com/view/Entry/186904?.

63. For example, see Sequentia's recording of Hildegard of Bingen, *Ordo Virtutum* (Freiburg, Breisgau, Germany: BMG Entertainment, 1998) under its Deutsche Harmonia Mundi label, 05472 77394 2, available in mp3, audio cd, and vinyl formats.

64. See Kivy, *Sound Sentiment*; Deanne Bogdan, "The Shiver-Shimmer Factor: Music Spirituality, Emotion, and Education," *Philosophy of Music Education Review* 18, no. 2 (Fall 2010): 111–129, https://doi.org/10.2979/pme.2010.18.2.111, and her "Musical Spirituality: Reflections on Identity and the Ethics of Embodied Aesthetic Experience in/and the Academy," *Journal of Aesthetic Education* 37, no. 2 (Summer 2003): 80–98, https://doi.org/10.2307/3527457.

65. On imagination and the sense of vitality and livingness in music and the arts, see Susanne K. Langer, *Problems of Art: Ten Philosophical Lectures* (New York: Charles Scribner's Sons, 1957). Also, see her *Philosophy in a New Key* and her *Feeling*

and Form. The role of imagination as an element of cognition is also elaborated in her trilogy, *Mind: An Essay on Human Feeling*, 3 vols. (Baltimore: Johns Hopkins Press, 1967, 1972, 1982).

66. For composers' perspectives on listening, see, for example, classic texts by Copland, *Music and Imagination*; Roger Sessions, *The Musical Experience of Composer, Performer, Listener* (New York: Atheneum, 1962). Among those to argue for the need to contextualize musical listening and study it in natural as well as clinical settings, see Nicholas Cook, *Music, Imagination, and Culture* (Oxford: Oxford University Press, 1990); Adrian C. North and David J. Hargreaves, "Experimental Aesthetics and Everyday Music Listening," in *The Social Psychology of Music*, David J. Hargreaves and Adrian C. North, eds. (New York: Oxford University Press, 1997), 84–103.

67. Yob, "If We Knew What Spirituality Was, We Would Teach for It." Also, see Iris M. Yob, "Images of Spirituality: Traditional and Contemporary," in Carr and Haldane, eds., *Spirituality, Philosophy and Education*, 112–126.

68. For example, see Small, *Musicking*, especially the prelude.

69. On the aspects of imagination, see Mary J. Reichling, "Images of Imagination," *Journal of Research in Music Education* 38, no. 4 (1990): 282–293, https://doi.org/10.2307/3345225.

70. Donald Schön, *Educating the Reflective Practitioner: Toward a New Design for Teaching and Learning in the Professions* (San Francisco: Jossey-Bass, 1987), chap. 2.

71. Langer, *Feeling and Form*, 121.

72. Langer, *Philosophy in a New Key*, 241.

73. See David Carr, "Music, Spirituality, and Education," *Journal of Aesthetic Education* 42, no. 1 (Spring 2008): 16–29, https://www.jstor.org/stable/25160263.

74. See Carr and Holdane, eds., *Spirituality, Philosophy and Education*, especially chap. 15, on definitions of spirituality.

75. Music's power on character formation is such that Plato found it necessary to censor music that was played, sung, and danced to. See Plato, *The Republic of Plato*, trans. Francis Macdonald Cornford (1941; repr., Oxford: Oxford University Press, 1942), especially books 3 and 10.

76. Kodály, *The Selected Writings of Zoltán Kodály*.

77. Shinichi Suzuki, *Nurtured by Love: A New Approach to Education*, trans. Waltraud Suzuki (New York: Exposition, 1969).

78. Leonard Tan, "Towards a Transcultural Philosophy of Music Education" (PhD diss., Indiana University, 2012).

79. On the importance of balance or homeostasis, see Postman, *Teaching as a Conserving Activity*, 23.

80. Illich, *Deschooling Society*, 24, observes that this bifurcation creates a situation where "education becomes unworldly and the world becomes noneducational."

81. See Steel, "The Birth of Dionysian Education (The Spirit of Music)?" parts 1 and 2.

82. Friedrich Schiller, *On the Aesthetic Education of Man in a Series of Letters*, ed. and trans. Elizabeth M. Wilkinson and L. A. Willoughby (Oxford: Oxford University Press, 1967).

CHAPTER 4 - DIGNITY, DISPASSION, RESTRAINT, AND DISCIPLINE

1. Among the music educators to argue for informality and embrace passion in music education, Sean Steel, "The Birth of Dionysian Education (The Spirit of Music)?: Part 1," *Philosophy of Music Education Review* 22, no. 1 (Spring 2014): 38–60, https://doi.org/10.2979/philmusieducrevi.22.1.38, places abandon, passion, sensuality, and informality central to musical and educational experience. Randall Everett Allsup, *Remixing the Classroom: Toward an Open Philosophy of Music Education* (Bloomington: Indiana University Press, 2016) refuses the mantle of the master and prefers a more open and egalitarian approach to music education. Lucy Green, *How Popular Musicians Learn: A Way Ahead for Music Education* (2002; repr., Abingdon, UK, and New York: Routledge, 2016) advocates the importance of informality and popular culture in music education.

2. OED Online, s.v. "Dignity, n.," accessed March 2, 2018, https://www.oed.com/view/Entry/52653?.

3. Friedrich Schiller, *On the Aesthetic Education of Man in a Series of Letters*, edited and translated by Elizabeth M. Wilkinson and L. A. Willoughby (Oxford: Oxford University Press, 1967); excerpts of Johann Heinrich Pestalozzi's *Leonard and Gertrude* and *Evening Hour of the Hermit* in *Three Thousand Years of Educational Wisdom: Selections from Great Documents*, 2nd edition, ed. Robert Ulich (Cambridge, MA: Harvard University Press, 1954), 440–507.

4. On dispositions, see Donald Arnstine, *Democracy and the Arts of Schooling* (Albany: State University of New York Press, 1995).

5. Irving Goffman, *The Presentation of Self in Everyday Life* (1959; repr., New York: Anchor Books, 1990).

6. Howard Gardner, *Frames of Mind: The Theory of Multiple Intelligences*, 2nd paper edition, 10th anniversary edition (New York: Basic Books, 2011).

7. See John Dewey, *Experience and Education* (1938; repr., New York: Collier Books, 1963), chaps. 4 and 5.

8. Among the twentieth-century Anglo-American philosophers of education on self-control and discipline, see John Dewey, *Democracy and Education: An Introduction to the Philosophy of Education* ([1916]; repr., New York, Free Press, 1966), and his *Art as Experience* (1934; repr., New York: Paragon Books, 1979); R. S. Peters, *Ethics and Education* (London: George Allen and Unwin, 1966); Israel Scheffler, *Reason and Teaching* (1973; repr., Indianapolis, IN: Bobbs-Merrill, 1973).

Ideals of decency, discipline, and self-control also exemplify ancient Chinese ideas on music education; see Leonard Tan, "Towards a Transcultural Philosophy of Music Education" (PhD diss., Indiana University, 2012); C. Victor Fung, *A Way of Music Education: Classic Chinese Wisdoms* (New York: Oxford University Press, 2018).

9. On the idea of decent peoples and societies, see John Rawls, *The Law of Peoples with The Idea of Public Reason Revisited* (Cambridge, MA: Harvard University Press, 1999).

10. Iris M. Yob, "School as Sacred Space," paper presented at Reasons of the Heart Conference, Edinburgh, Scotland, September 2004, and "School and Sacred Time," paper presented at Tenth International Society for Philosophy of Music Education Conference, Frankfurt, Germany, June 2015.

11. Scheffler, *Reason and Teaching*, 80.

12. Paulo Freire, *Pedagogy of the Oppressed*, New Revised 20th Anniversary Edition, trans. Myra Bergman Ramos (New York: Continuum, 1993).

13. See Estelle R. Jorgensen, "Music and International Relations," in *Culture and International Relations*, ed. Jongsuk Chay (New York: Praeger, 1990), 56–71. On music as propaganda and the use of power, see Jacques Attali's classic *Noise: The Political Economy of Music*, trans. Brian Massumi (Minneapolis: University of Minnesota Press, 1985).

14. See David Hebert and Alexandra Kertz-Welzel, eds., *Patriotism and Nationalism in Music Education* (Farnum, Surrey, UK: Ashgate, 2012), especially chap. 2: Alexandra Kertz-Welzel, "Lesson Learned? In Search of Patriotism and Nationalism in the German Music Education Curriculum." On music education and fascism, see Deborah Bradley, "Oh, That Magic Feeling! Multicultural Human Subjectivity, Community, and Fascism's Footprints," *Philosophy of Music Education Review* 17, no. 1 (Spring 2009): 56–74, https://www.jstor.org/stable/40327310.

15. Brenda Brenner provides this opportunity in her Fairview Project in Bloomington, Indiana, in which concerts educate parents and grandparents as much as children. On the Fairview Project, see https://intranet.music.indiana.edu/precollege/year-round/fairview-violin-project/. See her "Reflecting on the Rationales for String Study in Schools," *Philosophy of Music Education Review* 18, no. 1 (Spring 2010): 45–64, https://doi.org/10.2979/pme.2010.18.1.45.

16. OED Online, s.v. "Dispassion, n.," accessed September 8, 2014, https://www.oed.com/view/Entry/54938?.

17. OED Online, s.v. "Passion, n.," accessed September 8, 2014, https://www.oed.com/view/Entry/138504?.

18. OED Online, s.v. "Passion, v.," accessed September 8, 2014, https://www.oed.com/view/Entry/138505?.

19. Epicurus, *The Extant Remains*, trans. Cyril Bailey (Oxford: Oxford University Press, 1926), V. Fragments, 139, https://archive.org/details/EpicurusThe ExtantRemainsBaileyOxford1926_201309.

20. Epicurus, *Extant Remains,* I, To Heroditus, 58.

21. Epicurus, *Extant Remains,* V. Fragments, 137.

22. William Temple, "Upon the Gardens of Epicurus; or of Gardening in the Year 1685," in *Sir William Temple upon the Gardens of Epicurus, with other XVIIth Century Garden Essays,* Introduction, eds. Albert Forbes Sieveking, William Temple, Abraham Cowley, Thomas Browne, Andrew Marvel, and John Evelyn (London: Chatto and Windus, 1908), 13–65.

23. Temple, "Upon the Gardens of Epicurus," 19–20.

24. Temple, 20.

25. Albert Sieveking, "Introduction," in William Temple, *Sir William Temple upon the Gardens of Epicurus,* xix.

26. Jean Jacques Rousseau, *Émile,* trans. Barbara Foxley (1911; repr., London: Dent; New York, Dutton, 1972).

27. See Estelle R. Jorgensen, "William Channing Woodbridge's Lecture 'On Vocal Music as a Branch of Common Education' Revisited," *Studies in Music* (University of Western Australia) 18 (1984): 1–32. Reprinted with permission in *Visions of Music Education* 14, no. 1 (June 2009), http://www-usr.rider.edu/~vrme/v14n1/vision/woodbridge.pdf.

28. See Jorgensen, "William Channing Woodbridge's Lecture."

29. For a recent restatement of the garden metaphor for music education, see Hanne Rinholm, "Rethinking the Good, the True, and the Beautiful for Music Education: New Visions from an Old Garden," in *The Road Goes Ever On: Estelle Jorgensen's Legacy in Music Education,* ed. Randall Everett Allsup and Cathy Benedict (London, ON: Western University, December 2019), 253–270, https://doi.org/10.5206/Q1144262.jorgensen.2019.

30. On the virtue of idleness, among other perceived educational sins, see Israel Scheffler, "Vice into Virtue: or Seven Deadly Sins of Education Redeemed," in his *In Praise of the Cognitive Emotions and Other Essays on the Philosophy of Education* (New York: Routledge, Chapman and Hall, 1991), 126–139. On music education, see Kevin Shorner-Johnson, "Music and the Sin of Sloth: The Gendered Articulation of Worthy Musical Time in Early American Music," *Philosophy of Music Education Review* 27, no. 1 (Spring 2019): 51–67, https://doi.org/10.2979/philmusieducrevi.27.1.05.

31. In his *Art as Experience,* Dewey unpacks the passive and "undergoing" aspects of artistic experience. This principle also applies to his educational project.

32. Susanne K. Langer, *Philosophy in a New Key: A Study in the Symbolism of Reason, Rite, and Art,* 3rd edition (Cambridge, MA: Harvard University Press, 1957).

33. On subjugated knowledge, see June Boyce-Tillman, "Towards an Ecology of Music Education," *Philosophy of Music Education Review* 12, no. 2 (2004): 102–125, https://www.jstor.org/stable/40327232, and her *Constructing Musical Healing: The Wounds That Sing* (London: Jessica Kingsley, 2000).

34. Dewey, *Art as Experience,* 62.

35. Scheffler, *In Praise of the Cognitive Emotions*, chap. 1; Iris M. Yob, "The Cognitive Emotions and Emotional Cognitions," in *Reason and Education: Essays in Honor of Israel Scheffler*, ed. Harvey Siegel (Dordrecht, Netherlands: Kluwer Academic Publishers, 1997), 43–57.

36. See, for example, Liora Bresler, ed., *Knowing Bodies, Moving Minds: Towards Embodied Teaching and Learning* (New York: Springer, 2004).

37. OED Online, s.v. "Restraint, n.," accessed September 19, 2014, https://www.oed.com/view/Entry/164011?.

38. Dewey, *Experience and Education*, chap. 4.

39. Freire, *Pedagogy of the Oppressed*.

40. See, for example, Maria Montessori, *The Discovery of the Child*, trans. M. Joseph Costelloe (1967; repr., New York: Ballantine Books, 1972), and her *The Absorbent Mind* (1967; repr., New York: Dell, 1980).

41. Estelle R. Jorgensen, *Transforming Music Education* (Bloomington: Indiana University Press, 2003).

42. See OED Online, s.v. "Discipline, n.," accessed September 26, 2014, https://www.oed.com/view/Entry/53744?; OED Online, s.v. "Discipline, v.," accessed September 26, 2014, https://www.oed.com/view/Entry/53745?.

43. See Estelle R. Jorgensen, "Western Classical Music and General Education," *Philosophy of Music Education Review* 11, no. 2 (Fall 2003): 130–140, https://www.jstor.org/stable/40327206, and her "To Love or Not to Love (Western Classical Music): That is the Question (for Music Educators," *Philosophy of Music Education Review* 28, no. 2 (Fall 2020): 128–144, https://doi.org/10.2979/philmusieducrevi.28.2.02.

44. On means and ends, see Dewey, *Democracy and Education*, 106, 323, 346–347.

45. Bennett Reimer, "Would Discipline-Based Music Education Make Sense?" *Music Educators Journal* 77, no. 9 (May 1991): 21–28, https://doi.org/10.2307/3398187; Jeffrey Patchen, "Overview of Discipline-Based Music Education," *Music Educators Journal* 83, no. 2 (September 1996): 19–26+, 44, https://doi.org/10.2307/3398961.

46. On the dialectic of making and receiving music, see Estelle R. Jorgensen, *In Search of Music Education* (Urbana: University of Illinois Press, 1997), 83–87.

47. On the ethical and aesthetic dimensions of jazz, see "Herbie Hancock | The Ethics of Jazz | 2014 Norton Lectures," lecture by Herbie Hancock, Mahindra Humanities Center, playlist of six videos, last updated March 2, 2020, https://www.youtube.com/playlist?list=PLtxVM47qfVNCuPUKzbGB15-8vbhaeJAZz; Paul F. Berliner, *Thinking in Jazz: The Infinite Art of Improvisation* (Chicago: University of Chicago Press, 1994).

48. On the "rule" model, see Scheffler, *Reason and Teaching*, 76–79.

49. On the structure of subject matter, see Jerome Bruner's classic *The Process of Education* (1960; repr., Cambridge, MA: Harvard University Press, 1977). Bruner

wrote on behalf of the conferees—scientists, scholars, and educators—gathered at Woods Hole, Massachusetts, in 1959.

50. This is true more generally of artists who create a sense of order in their lives through daily rituals. For example, Mason Currey, ed., *Daily Rituals: How Artists Work* (New York: Alfred A. Knopf, 2013), illustrates the multifarious ways in which artists live their lives in order to work and the need they have for time and space in which to focus on their work apart from the distractions of ordinary lived life. For women such as Virginia Wolff, there is a need for "a room of one's own" or a sacred space in which to create. See Virginia Wolff, *A Room of One's Own* (1929; repr., New York: Harcourt Brace Jovanovich, 1991).

51. Joshua Kosman, "Classical Music May Never Be the Same: How Esa-Pekka Salonen Is a Game Changer for SF Symphony," *San Francisco Chronicle*, December 6, 2018, https://datebook.sfchronicle.com/music/with-esa-pekka-salonen-hire-look-for-some-high-impact-innovation-at-sf-symphony, describes the impact that a new conductor may have on the San Francisco Orchestra.

52. Scheffler, *In Praise of the Cognitive Emotions*, chap. 3: "Making and Understanding."

53. On the power of procedural knowledge in the preparation of performers, see Estelle R. Jorgensen, "Face-to-Face and Distance Teaching and Learning in Internationalized Higher Education: Lessons from the Preparation of Professional Musicians," *Journal of Music, Technology & Education* 7, no. 2 (2014): 187–197, https://doi.org/10.1386/jmte.7.2.181_1.

54. Vernon A. Howard, *Artistry: The Work of Artists* (Indianapolis, IN: Hackett, 1982).

55. On the arts as a metaphor for education, see Vernon A. Howard, *Learning by All Means: Lessons from the Arts: A Study in the Philosophy of Education* (New York: Peter Lang, 1992); Jorgensen, "Face-to-face and Distance Teaching and Learning."

56. Despite the American Academy of Pediatricians' recommendations against spanking, see Robert D. Sege and Benjamin S. Siegel, "Effective Discipline to Raise Healthy Children," Council on Child Abuse and Neglect, Committee on Psychosocial Aspects of Child and Family Health, *Pediatrics* (November 2018): e20183112, https://doi.org/10.1542/peds.2018-3112. As recently as 2017, corporal punishment was still practiced in North Carolina and Arkansas schools. See Jess Clark, "At Opposite Ends of the State, Two NC Schools Keep Paddling Alive," last modified February 23, 2017, https://www.wunc.org/post/opposite-ends-state-two-nc-schools-keep-paddling-alive#stream/0; Ibby Caputo, "Bid to Eliminate Corporal Punishment in Schools Fails but Another School Discipline Bill Advances," *Arkansas Times*, March 22, 2017, https://www.arktimes.com/arkansas/bid-to-eliminate-corporal-punishment-in-schools-fails/Content?oid=5728358; Jess Clark, "Where Corporal Punishment Is Still Used in Schools, Its Roots Run Deep," *All Things Considered*, NPR, April 12, 2017, 6:00 AM ET, https://www.npr.org/sections/ed/2017/04/12/521944429/where-corporal-punishment-is-still-used-its-roots-go-deep.

57. Corporal punishment was also used in European music schools. Although the church banned corporal punishment in 1980, Melissa Eddy describes a persistent continuing problem of sexual abuse at the Regensburg Cathedral Choir School until the 1990s in her article "'Culture of Silence' Abetted Abuse of at Least 547 German Choir Boys, Inquiry Finds," *New York Times*, July 18, 2017, https://www.nytimes.com/2017/07/18/world/europe/germany-sexual-abuse-boys-choir.html.

58. See Pestalozzi, *Leonard and Gertrude* and *Evening Hour of the Hermit*.

59. On Alice Dewey's influence on John Dewey, see Nancy Bunge, "Love & Logic," *Philosophy Now*, no. 45, https://philosophynow.org/issues/45/Love_and_Logic. I also think of Montessori's *casa dei bambini* and Jane Roland Martin's schoolhome. See Montessori, *The Absorbent Mind*, and her *The Discovery of the Child*; Jane Roland Martin, *The Schoolhome: Rethinking Schools for Changing Families* (Cambridge, MA: Harvard University Press, 1992), and her *School Was Our Life: Remembering Progressive Education* (Bloomington: Indiana University Press, 2018).

60. Shinichi Suzuki, *Nurtured by Love: A New Approach to Education*, trans. Waltraud Suzuki (New York: Exposition, 1969).

61. Estelle R. Jorgensen, *The Art of Teaching Music* (Bloomington: Indiana University Press, 2008), 89–93; Iris M. Yob and Estelle R. Jorgensen, eds., *Humane Music Education for the Common Good* (Bloomington: Indiana University Press, 2020).

62. Susanne K. Langer, *Problems of Art: Ten Philosophical Lectures* (New York: Charles Scribner's Sons, 1957).

CHAPTER 5 - LOVE, FRIENDSHIP, DESIRE, AND DEVOTION

1. My article—Estelle R. Jorgensen, "To Love or Not to Love (Western Classical Music): That Is the Question (for Music Educators)," *Philosophy of Music Education Review* 28, no. 2 (Fall 2020): 128–144, https://doi.org/10.2979/philmusieducrevi.28.2.02—is drawn from an earlier version of this chapter and reworked to focus on Western classical music.

2. See, for example, Wayne Booth, *For the Love of It: Amateuring and Its Rivals* (Chicago: University of Chicago Press, 1999); Johann Heinrich Pestalozzi, excerpts from *The Evening Hour of a Hermit* and *Leonard and Gertrude*, in *Three Thousand Years of Educational Wisdom: Selections from Great Documents*, 2nd edition, ed. Robert Ulich (Cambridge, MA: Harvard University Press, 1954), 480–507; Maria Montessori, *The Discovery of the Child*, trans. M. Joseph Costelloe (1967; repr., New York: Ballantine Books, 1972), and her *The Absorbent Mind* (1967; repr., New York: Dell, 1980); Max Van Manen, *The Tact of Teaching: The Meaning of Pedagogical Thoughtfulness* (Albany: State University of New York Press, 1991); Shinichi Suzuki, *Nurtured by Love: A New Approach to Education*, trans. Waltraud Suzuki (New York: Exposition, 1969). Donald Phillip Verene, *The Art of Humane Education* (Ithaca, NY: Cornell University Press, 2002), posits qualities of pedagogical

eloquence and authority as qualities of humane education, and Stephen L. Carter, *Civility: Manners, Morals, and the Etiquette of Democracy* (New York: Basic Books, 1998), argues that love for one's fellow human beings is at the root of the value of civility, which is crucial to democratic discourse and society.

3. This is akin to C. S. Lewis's task in his *The Four Loves* (New York: Harcourt, Brace, 1960), in which he unpacks the notions of affection, friendship, erotic love, and love of God from a Christian perspective.

4. OED Online, s.v. "Love, n.1," accessed May 2, 2018, http://www.oed.com /view/Entry/110566?.

5. OED Online, s.v. "Love, n.1."

6. See Nancy Ellen Abrams, *A God That Could Be Real: Spirituality, Science, and the Future of Our Planet* (Boston: Beacon, 2015), on a notion of God compatible with the science of emergence.

7. Among my colleagues at the Indiana University Jacobs School of Music, Menahem Pressler was beloved by his students. His love of the music he taught and performed was legendary. This love was exemplified in the care with which he approached his students and the repertoire, his devotion to his pianistic heritage, and his artistic expectations of his students and of himself in his long performing career as a chamber musician and soloist. See William Brown, *Menahem Pressler: Artistry in Piano Teaching* (Bloomington: Indiana University Press, 2008).

8. OED Online, s.v. "Love, n.1."

9. Samuel Taylor Coleridge, *Coleridge's Notebooks: A Selection*, ed. Seamus Perry (Oxford: Oxford University Press, 2002), III. 70, (1809), also cited in OED Online, s.v. "Love, n.1."

10. Virginia Woolf, *Between the Acts* (New York: Harcourt, Brace and Co., 1941), 92, also cited in OED Online, s.v. "Love, n.1." This book was published shortly after Woolf's death, and the manuscript had not been finally revised by the author. A more recent edition edited by Mark Hussey was published by Cambridge University Press in 2011.

11. OED Online, s.v. "Love, v.1.," accessed March 4, 2021, https://www.oed.com /view/Entry/110568?.

12. OED Online, s.v. "Love, n.1."

13. Nel Noddings, *Caring: A Relational Approach to Ethics and Moral Education*, 2nd edition updated (Berkeley: University of California Press, 2013). Noddings originally published this book with the same publisher under the title *Caring: A Feminine Approach to Ethics and Moral Education* (1984). While updated and possibly more inclusive, something is also lost in this revised title.

14. In Estelle R. Jorgensen, "On a Choice-Based Instructional Typology in Music," *Journal of Research in Music Education* 29 (1981): 97–102, https://doi.org /10.2307%2F3345018, I hypothesize that mutual attraction between teacher and student is a more productive basis for musical instruction than its logical opposite of mutual antipathy.

15. For example, see John Shepherd, *Music as Social Text* (Cambridge, MA: Polity, 1991); Christopher Small, *Musicking: The Meanings of Performing and Listening* (Hanover, NH: Wesleyan University Press, University Press of New England, 1998); Derek B. Scott, ed., *Music, Culture, and Society: A Reader* (2000; repr., New York: Oxford University Press, 2002); Martin Clayton, Trevor Herbert, Richard Middleton, eds., *The Cultural Study of Music: A Critical Introduction* (New York: Routledge, 2003); Tia DeNora, *After Adorno: Rethinking Music Sociology* (Cambridge: Cambridge University Press, 2003); John Shepherd and Kyle Devine, eds., *The Routledge Reader on the Sociology of Music* (London: Routledge, 2015). On the dialectic between music making and receiving, see Estelle R. Jorgensen, *In Search of Music Education* (Urbana: University of Illinois Press, 1997), 83–87.

16. For example, Small, *Musicking*, criticizes the concert hall rituals of Western classical music.

17. I make this point explicitly in Estelle R. Jorgensen, "Western Classical Music and General Education," *Philosophy of Music Education Review* 11, no. 2 (Fall 2003): 130–140, https://www.jstor.org/stable/40327206; Jorgensen, "To Love or Not to Love."

18. See *Itzhak*, Alison Chernick, director. Documentary film (US: Greenwich Entertainment, 2018); *The Music of Strangers: Yo-Yo Ma and the Silk Road Ensemble*, Morgan Neville, director. Documentary film (US: Tremolo Productions, 2016).

19. Alexandra Kertz-Welzel, *Globalizing Music Education: A Framework* (Bloomington: Indiana University Press, 2018).

20. Zoltán Kodály, *The Selected Writings of Zoltán Kodály*, ed. Ferenc Bónis, trans. Lili Halápy and Fred Macnicol (London: Boosey and Hawkes, 1974), especially section III: "On Music Education," which is particularly concerned with the deleterious impact of mediated music on young people. He advocates the teaching of Hungarian folk songs to inculcate this music into the hearts and minds of young Hungarians. For him, classical and folk musics are integrally related and spring from the selfsame roots.

21. Suzuki, *Nurtured by Love*, 8, states, "What is man's ultimate direction in life? It is to look for love, truth, virtue, beauty."

22. On the self-reflexive character of love, see Jorgensen, "To Love or Not to Love," 138.

23. OED Online, s.v. "Friendship, n.," accessed May 3, 2018, http://www.oed.com /view/Entry/74661?.

24. OED Online, s.v. "Friend, n. and adj.," accessed May 3, 2018, http://www.oed.com /view/Entry/74646?.

25. George Herbert, "The Best Mirror Is an Old Friend," in John Bartlett, *Familiar Quotations: A Collection of Passages, Phrases and Proverbs Traced to Their Sources in Ancient and Modern Literature*, 13th and centennial edition (Boston: Little, Brown, and Co., 1955), 234a.

26. Forest Hansen, "In Dialogue: The Principle of Civility in Academic Discourse," *Philosophy of Music Education Review* 19, no. 2 (Fall 2011): 198–200, https://doi.org/10.2979/philmusieducrevi.19.2.198.

27. Jean Jacques Rousseau, *Émile*, trans. Barbara Foxley ([1911]; repr., London: Dent, 1972).

28. bell hooks, *Teaching to Transgress: Education as the Practice of Freedom* (New York: Routledge, 1994).

29. On Rousseau, see Jane Roland Martin, *Reclaiming a Conversation: The Ideal of the Educated Woman* (New Haven, CT: Yale University Press, 1985), chap. 3. On women's experience in the academy, see Jane Roland Martin, *Coming of Age in Academe: Rekindling Women's Hopes and Reforming the Academy* (New York: Routledge, 2000).

30. Randall Everett Allsup, *Remixing the Classroom: Toward an Open Philosophy of Music Education* (Bloomington: Indiana University Press, 2016), especially chap. 4.

31. On the need for hospitality among the religions, see, for example, Martin E. Marty, *When Faiths Collide* (Malden, MA: Wiley-Blackwell, 2008); his *The One and the Many: America's Struggle for the Common Good* (Cambridge, MA: Harvard University Press, 1997). On hospitality in music education, see Patrick Schmidt, "Authority and Pedagogy as Framing," *Philosophy of Music Education Review* 24, no 1 (Spring 2016): 8–23, https://doi.org/10.2979/philmusieducrevi.24.1.03.

32. Charlene Morton, "Boom Diddy Boom Boom: Critical Multiculturalism and Music Education," *Philosophy of Music Education Review* 9, no. 1 (Spring 2001): 32–41, https://www.jstor.org/stable/40495451.

33. Kertz-Welzel, *Globalizing Music Education.*

34. See Maxine Greene, *The Dialectic of Freedom* (New York: Teachers College Press, 1988); her *Releasing the Imagination: Essays on Education, the Arts, and Social Change* (San Francisco: Jossey-Bass, 1995); Allsup, *Remixing the Classroom.*

35. Raimond Gaita, *A Common Humanity: Thinking about Love and Truth and Justice* (London and New York: Routledge, 2014).

36. See, for example, Bennett Reimer, *A Philosophy of Music Education: Advancing the Vision*, 3rd edition (Upper Saddle River, NJ: Prentice-Hall, 2003); David J. Elliott and Marissa Silverman, *Music Matters: A Philosophy of Music Education*, 2nd edition (New York: Oxford University Press, 2014).

37. Isaiah Berlin, *The Crooked Timber of Humanity: Chapters in the History of Ideas*, ed. Hardy Henry (Princeton, NJ: Princeton University Press, 1990), evokes Immanuel Kant's metaphor "*aus so krummen Holze, als woraus der Mensch gemacht ist, kann nichts ganz Gerades gezimmert warden*" ["out of timber so crooked as that from which man is made, nothing entirely straight can be built"]. Immanuel Kant, "Idee zu einer allgemeinen Geschichte in weltbürgerlicher Absicht" (1774), *Kant's gesammelte Schriften*, vol. 8 (Berlin: G. Reimer, 1912), 23.

38. On feminist scholarship in education, see, for example, Madeline R. Grumet, *Bitter Milk: Women and Teaching* (Amherst: University of Massachusetts Press, 1988); Liora Bresler, *Knowing Bodies, Moving Minds: Towards Embodied Teaching and Learning* (New York: Springer, 2004); Marjorie O'Loughlin, *Embodiment and Education: Exploring Creatural Existence* (Dordrecht, Netherlands: Springer, 2006); Anna L. Peterson, *Everyday Ethics and Social Change: The Education of Desire* (New York: Columbia University Press, 2009); Barbara Thayer-Bacon, Lynda Stone, and Katharine M. Specher, eds., *Education Feminism: Classic and Contemporary Readings* (Albany: State University of New York Press, 2013).

39. See Bernarr Rainbow and Gordon Cox, *Music in Educational Thought and Practice: A Survey from 800BC* (Woodbridge, Suffolk, UK: Boydell, 2006), 19.

40. For example, just as North Indian musicians traditionally chose who they would teach and how much they should impart to them (Daniel M. Neuman, *The Life of Music in North India: The Organization of an Artistic Tradition* [Detroit: Wayne State University Press, 1980]), so teachers in Western conservatories audition their students, and much hangs on the students' desire to learn (Henry Kingsbury, *Music, Talent, and Performance: A Conservatory Cultural System* [Philadelphia: Temple University Press, 1988]; Bruno Nettl, *Heartland Excursions: Ethnomusicological Reflections on Schools of Music* [Urbana: University of Illinois Press, 1995]).

41. Walden University is among those universities to appeal to competency-based education (CBE) in the present century. See Walden University, "What Is Competency-Based Education?" accessed May 4, 2018, https://www.waldenu.edu/experience/tempo-learning/resource/what-is-competency-based-education. CBE approaches to music education were evident in the latter part of the twentieth century—for example, Clifford K. Madsen and Cornelia Yarbrough, *Competency-Based Music Education* (Englewood Cliffs, NJ: Prentice-Hall, 1980). This approach to education has appeal for its systematic approach to skill acquisition and the possibility of quantitative and even scientific approaches to measurement and evaluation.

42. Among the feminist writers in music education, see Deanne Bogdan, "Pythagoras' Rib or, What Does Music Education Want?" *Philosophy of Music Education Review* 2, no. 2 (Fall 1994): 122–131, https://www.jstor.org/stable/40327078; her "Situated Sensibilities and the Need for Coherence: Musical Experience Reconsidered," *Philosophy of Music Education Review* 10, no. 2 (Fall 2002): 125–128, https://www.jstor.org/stable/40327186; and her "The Shiver-Shimmer Factor: Music Spirituality, Emotion, and Education," *Philosophy of Music Education Review* 18, no. 2 (Fall 2010): 111–129, https://doi.org/10.2979/pme.2010.18.2.111; Eleanor Stubley, "Meditations on the Letter A: The Hand as Nexus between Music and Language," *Philosophy of Music Education Review* 14, no. 1 (Spring 2006): 42–55, https://www.jstor.org/stable/40316828; Julia Eklund Koza, "My Body Had a Mind of Its Own: On Teaching, the Illusion of Control, and the Terrifying Limits of

Governmentality (Part 2)," *Philosophy of Music Education Review* 18, no. 1 (Spring 2010): 4–25, https://doi.org/10.2979/pme.2010.18.1.4; Roberta Lamb, "Feminism as Critique in Philosophy of Music Education," *Philosophy of Music Education Review* 2, no. 2 (Fall 1994): 59–74, https://www.jstor.org/stable/40327073; Marie McCarthy, "Gendered Discourse and the Construction of Identity: Toward a Liberated Pedagogy in Music Education," *Journal of Aesthetic Education* 33, no. 4 (Winter 1999): 109–125, https://doi.org/10.2307/3333724; Elizabeth Gould, "Nomadic Turns: Epistemology, Experience, and Women University Band Directors," *Philosophy of Music Education Review* 13, no. 1 (Fall 2005): 147–164, https://www.jstor.org/stable/40495509, and her "Women Working in Music Education: The War Machine," *Philosophy of Music Education Review* 17, no. 2 (Fall 2009): 126–143, https://www.jstor.org/stable/40495496. Also, see Allsup, *Remixing the Classroom*, especially chap. 4.

43. OED Online, s.v. "Desire, n.," accessed May 4, 2018, http://www.oed.com/view/Entry/50880?.

44. OED Online, s.v. "Desire, v.," accessed May 4, 2018, http://www.oed.com/view/Entry/50881?.

45. Susanne K. Langer, *Philosophy in a New Key: A Study in the Symbolism of Reason, Rite, and Art*, 3rd edition (Cambridge, MA: Harvard University Press, 1957).

46. Iris M. Yob, "The Cognitive Emotions and Emotional Cognitions," *Studies in Philosophy and Education* 16, no. 1–2 (1997), https://doi.org/10.1023/A:1004990702983; Israel Scheffler, *In Praise of the Cognitive Emotions and Other Essays on the Philosophy of Education* (New York: Routledge, Chapman and Hall, 1991), 3–17.

47. On personal impulse and desire, see John Dewey, *Experience and Education* (1938; repr., New York: Collier Books, 1963), 70, 71.

48. On the instinctual and primal basis for musical imagination, see Aaron Copland, *Music and Imagination* (Cambridge, MA: Harvard University Press, 1980), especially chap. 1.

49. Susan Laird, "Musical Hunger: A Philosophical Testimonial of Miseducation," *Philosophy of Music Education Review* 17, no. 1 (Spring 2009): 4–21, https://www.jstor.org/stable/40327307.

50. See Dewey, *Experience and Education*, 70–71.

51. On consummatory experience, see John Dewey, *Art as Experience* (1934; repr., New York: Paragon Books, 1979); Philip W. Jackson, *John Dewey and the Lessons of Art* (New Haven, CT: Yale University Press, 1998); Herbert Read, *Education through Art* (London: Faber and Faber, 1943).

52. Vernon A. Howard, *Artistry: The Work of Artists* (Indianapolis, IN: Hackett, 1982), especially chap. 6.

53. Bresler, ed., *Knowing Bodies, Moving Minds*.

54. Irving Goffman, *The Presentation of Self in Everyday Life* (1959; repr., New York: Anchor Books, 1990).

55. Nel Noddings, *Happiness and Education* (Cambridge: Cambridge University Press, 2003).

56. On the "gaze" as applied to medicine, see Michel Foucault, *The Birth of the Clinic: An Archaeology of Medical Perception*, trans. A. M. Sheridan Smith (1973; repr., New York: Vintage Books, 1994), for a critique of the atomistic and objective view that disempowers the patient. Foucault rethinks the notion of the gaze in ways that recognize its relation to power and its culturally and socially situated character. For a survey of feminist critiques of Foucault, see Monique Deveaux, "Feminism and Empowerment: A Critical Reading of Foucault," *Feminist Studies* 20, no. 2, (Summer 1994): 223–247, https://doi.org/10.2307/3178151. Others have leaned on Foucault's notion of the gaze to articulate the gendered, racist, classist character of the gaze and unpack its role in teacher and student interaction. See, for example, Sherene H. Razack, *Looking White People in the Eye: Gender, Race, and Culture in Courtrooms and Classrooms* (1998; repr., Toronto: University of Toronto Press, 2001); Jan Masschelein, "E-ducating the Gaze: The Idea of a Poor Pedagogy," *Ethics and Education* 5, no. 1 (2010): 43–53, https://doi.org/10.1080/17449641003590621.

57. Langer, *Philosophy in a New Key*, 97, 153, 240.

58. On wisdom, see Alfred North Whitehead, *The Aims of Education and Other Essays* (1929; repr., New York: Free Press, 1967). Plato's notion of unity and diversity is evident, for example, in his line between the intelligible world and the world of appearances and his allegory of the cave. See Plato, *The Republic*, trans. Robin Waterfield (Oxford; New York: Oxford University Press, 1993), books 6 and 7.

59. See Sean Steel, "The Birth of Dionysian Education (The Spirit of Music)?: Part 1," *Philosophy of Music Education Review* 22, no. 1 (Spring 2014): 38–60, https://doi.org/10.2979/philmusieducrevi.22.1.38, and his "The Birth of Dionysian Education (The Spirit of Music)?: Part 2," *Philosophy of Music Education Review* 23, no. 1 (Spring 2015): 67–81, https://doi.org/10.2979/philmusieducrevi.23.1.67.

60. See Lucy Green, *Music on Deaf Ears: Musical Meaning, Ideology and Education* (Manchester, UK: Manchester University Press, 1988), especially chap. 10.

61. Greene, *Dialectic of Freedom*, chap. 4.

62. *Så som I himmelen* (*As It Is in Heaven*), directed by Kay Pollak (Sweden: Lorber Films, 2004), https://www.imdb.com/title/tt0382330.

63. See Randall J. Stephens, *The Devil's Music: How Christians Inspired, Condemned, and Embraced Rock 'n' Roll* (Cambridge, MA: Harvard University Press, 2018); Nasim Niknafs, "Tehran's Epistemic Heterotopia: Resisting Music Education," *Philosophy of Music Education Review* 26, no. 2 (Fall 2018): 155–175, https://doi.org/10.2979/philmusieducrevi.26.2.04.

64. OED Online, s.v. "Devotion, n.," accessed May 4, 2018, http://www.oed.com/view/Entry/51579?.

65. Neuman, *Life of Music in North India*, 45–50.

66. See Kingsbury, *Music, Talent, and Performance*; Nettl, *Heartland Excursions*, on studio relationships between teacher and students.

67. See Yob, "The Cognitive Emotions and Emotional Cognitions"; Scheffler, *In Praise of the Cognitive Emotions*, 3–17.

68. Lucy Green, *How Popular Musicians Learn: A Way Ahead for Music Education* (2002; repr., Abingdon, UK, and New York: Routledge, 2016).

69. On mental concentration and excellence, see Estelle R. Jorgensen, "On Excellence in Music Education," *McGill Journal of Education* 15, no. 1 (1980): 94–103, https://mje.mcgill.ca/article/view/7313/5252.

70. This is evident, for example, in the ancient notion of paideia. See Werner Jaeger, *Paideia: The Ideals of Greek Culture*, 3 vols., trans. Gilbert Highet (New York: Oxford University Press, 1939, 1943, 1944).

71. See Jorgensen, "On a Choice-Based Instructional Typology in Music."

72. Langer, *Philosophy in a New Key*, chap. 1.

73. Steel, "The Birth of Dionysian Education (The Spirit of Music)?," parts 1 and 2.

74. Judith Vander, *Songprints: The Musical Experience of Five Shoshone Women* (Urbana: University of Illinois Press, 1996).

75. Catherine A. Dobris and Rachel D. Davidson, "From Dirty Little Secrets to Prime Time: Values, Metaphors, and Social Change at the 2015 Grammy Awards," *Gender, Education, Music, Society* 8, no. 4 (April 2015): 4–18, https://ojs.library.queensu.ca/index.php/gems/issue/view/534.

CHAPTER 6 - JOY, HAPPINESS, PLEASURE, AND CELEBRATION

1. OED Online, s.v. "Joy, n.," accessed May 16, 2018, http://www.oed.com/view/Entry/101795?.

2. Johann Heinrich Pestalozzi extols joy in the home life among the poor he depicts in *Leonard and Gertrude* in *Three Thousand Years of Educational Wisdom: Selections from Great Documents*, 2nd edition, Robert Ulich, ed. (Cambridge, MA: Harvard University Press, 1954), 485–507. For him, this joy should also be evident in education. Also, evoking the home, Maria Montessori, *The Discovery of the Child*, trans. M. Joseph Costelloe (1967; repr. New York: Ballantine Books, 1972), 320, 321, envisages children's houses as educational places where joy should be experienced; Jane Roland Martin, *The Schoolhome: Rethinking Schools for Changing Families* (Cambridge, MA: Harvard University Press, 1992), addresses the intersection of family life and schooling. On educational means-ends, see John Dewey, *Democracy and Education: An Introduction to the Philosophy of Education* ([1916]; repr., New York: Free Press) and his *Experience and Education* ([1938]; repr., New York: Collier Books, 1963).

3. See Susanne K. Langer, *Philosophy in a New Key: A Study in the Symbolism of Reason, Rite, and Art*, 3rd edition (Cambridge, MA: Harvard University Press, 1957).

4. Northrop Frye, *The Educated Imagination* (1963; repr., Toronto: House of Anansi, 1993).

5. I discuss Campbell's notion of following one's bliss in Estelle R. Jorgensen, *The Art of Teaching* Music (Bloomington: Indiana University Press, 2008), 14–15. See Joseph Campbell with Bill Moyers, *The Power of Myth*, ed. Betty Sue Flowers (New York: Doubleday, 1988), 120–121.

6. On the joyful virtuoso, see Leonard Tan, "Towards a Transcultural Philosophy of Music Education" (PhD diss., Indiana University, 2012).

7. Mihaly Csikszentmihalyi, *Flow: The Psychology of Optimal Experience* (New York: Harper and Row, 1990).

8. Israel Scheffler, *In Praise of the Cognitive Emotions and Other Essays on the Philosophy of Education* (New York: Routledge, Chapman and Hall, 1991), 10–11.

9. Bennett Reimer, "The Experience of Profundity in Music," *Journal of Aesthetic Education* 29, no. 4 (Winter 1995): 1–21, https://doi.org/10.2307/3333288, focuses on several aspects of being deeply moved by music. Among the most compelling, for me, is a grasp not only of the social and cultural contexts in which music is made but of the musical tradition itself. When traveling in China, I watched various operatic traditions and was acutely aware of the gulf between these traditions and my own Western operatic and musical experiences; I also intuitively apprehended many similarities between these disparate traditions. Both are revered and prized by the musicians who perform them. Both are expressions of feeling. Both are dramatic and sonic evocations that are disciplined, intense, and bodily.

10. See Scheffler, *In Praise of the Cognitive Emotions*; Iris M. Yob, "The Cognitive Emotions and Emotional Cognitions," *Studies in Philosophy and Education* 16, no. 1–2 (1997): 43–57, https://doi.org/10.1023/A:1004990702983.

11. See Immanuel Kant, *Critique of Judgment*, trans. James Creed Meredith (1952; repr., Oxford: Clarendon, 1982).

12. The idea of a comprehensive musical education including composition, performance, and listening as the basis for school music was forwarded by twentieth-century Anglo-American music education philosophers. See, for example, Bennett Reimer, *A Philosophy of Music Education* (Englewood Cliffs, NJ: Prentice-Hall, 1970); Keith Swanwick, *A Basis for Education* (1979; reprinted, Windsor, Berkshire, UK: NFER-Nelson, 1981); David J. Elliott, *Music Matters: A New Philosophy of Music Education* (New York: Oxford University Press, 1995).

13. On the "vision of mastery," see Vernon A. Howard, *Artistry: The Work of Artists* (Indianapolis, IN: Hackett, 1982), chap. 6.

14. C. S. Lewis, *Surprised by Joy: The Shape of My Early Life* (1955; repr., New York: HarperCollins, 1955).

15. See Scheffler, *In Praise of the Cognitive Emotions*, chap. 1.

16. See R. Murray Schafer, *The Thinking Ear: Complete Writings on Music Education* (1986; repr., Toronto: Arcana Publications, 1988).

17. Randall Everett Allsup, *Remixing the Classroom: Toward an Open Philosophy of Music Education* (Bloomington: Indiana University Press, 2016), advocates an open-ended philosophy and practice of music education.

18. This writing on happiness draws on Estelle R. Jorgensen, "Life, Liberty, and the Pursuit of Happiness: Values for Music Education," *Bulletin of the Council for Research in Music Education* no. 226 (Fall 2020): 66–79, https://doi.org/10.5406/bulcouresmusedu.226.0066. For the US Declaration of Independence, see National Archives, "Declaration of Independence: A Transcription," accessed May 18, 2018, https://www.archives.gov/founding-docs/declaration-transcript.

19. See Danielle Allen, *Our Declaration: A Reading of the Declaration of Independence in Defense of Equality* (New York: W. W. Norton, 2014).

20. Nel Noddings, *Happiness and Education* (Cambridge: Cambridge University Press, 2003).

21. In her discussion of "subjugated ways of knowing," June Boyce-Tillman, "Towards an Ecology of Music Education," *Philosophy of Music Education Review* 12, no. 2 (2004): 102–125, https://www.jstor.org/stable/40327232, draws on Michel Foucault's notion of subjugated knowledges.

22. OED Online, s.v. "Happiness, n.," accessed May 18, 2018, http://www.oed.com/view/Entry/84070?.

23. Noddings, *Happiness and Education.* Also see Nel Noddings, *Caring: A Relational Approach to Ethics and Moral Education*, 2nd edition updated (Berkeley: University of California Press, 2013).

24. See Noddings, *Happiness and Education.*

25. Noddings, *Happiness and Education.*

26. See Lucy Green, *How Popular Musicians Learn: A Way Ahead for Music Education* (2002; repr., Abingdon, UK, and New York: Routledge, 2016), on informality. Also, see Estelle R. Jorgensen, "On Informalities in Music Education," in *The Oxford Handbook of Philosophy in Music Education*, ed. Wayne D. Bowman and Ana Lucia Frega (New York: Oxford University Press, 2012), 453–471.

27. The notion of play as an element of informal education, evident in the mid-twentieth century in Madeleine Carabo-Cone, *The Playground as Music Teacher: An Introduction to Music through Games* (New York: Harper and Brothers, 1959), is regularly included as an aspect of formal elementary school music instruction. Also, see Mary J. Reichling, "Music, Imagination, and Play," *Journal of Aesthetic Education* 31, no. 1 (1997): 41–55, https://doi.org/10.2307/3333470.

28. John Dewey, *Experience and Education* (1938; repr., New York: Collier Books, 1963), 70–71.

29. OED Online, s.v. "Pleasure, n.," accessed May 18, 2018, http://www.oed.com/view/Entry/145578?.

30. Kant, *Critique of Judgment.*

31. See Langer, *Philosophy in a New Key,* and her *Feeling and Form: A Theory of Art Developed from Philosophy in a New Key* (London: Routledge, 1953), especially chap. 3.

32. This is the case, for example, in Plato, *The Republic of Plato,* trans. Francis Macdonald Cornford (1941; repr., Oxford: Oxford University Press, 1942), books 3, 6, 7. Plato allowed only the Dorian and Phrygian *harmoniai.* See Grove Music Online, s.v. "Plato," by Warren J. Anderson and Thomas J. Mathiesen, accessed February 26, 2021, https://www.oxfordmusiconline.com/grovemusic/view/10.1093/gmo/9781561592630.001.0001/omo-9781561592630-e-0000021922?.

33. See, for example, Lucy Green, *Music, Gender, Education* (Cambridge: Cambridge University Press, 1997); contributors to Cathy Benedict, Patrick Schmidt, Gary Spruce, and Paul Woodford, eds., *The Oxford Handbook of Social Justice in Music Education* (New York: Oxford University Press, 2015); Elizabeth Gould, "Companion-able Species: A Queer Pedagogy for Music Education," *Bulletin of the Council for Research in Music Education,* no. 197 (Summer 2013): 63–75, https://doi.org/10.5406/bulcouresmusedu.197.0063. For an empirical study on gender identity and music teacher practice, see, for example, Matthew L. Garrett and Fred P. Spano, "An Examination of LGTBQ-inclusive Strategies Used by Practicing Music Teachers," *Music Education Research* 39, no. 1 (2017): 39–56, https://doi.org/10.1177/1321103X17700702.

34. See St. Augustine, *Confessions,* book 10, chap. 33, excerpted in Michael L. Mark, ed., *Music Education Source Readings from Ancient Greece to Today,* 2nd edition (New York: Routledge, 2002), 23–24.

35. See Martin Luther, *Preface to Georg Rhau's Symphoniae incundae,* in Mark, ed., *Music Education Source Readings from Ancient Greece to Today,* 32–33.

36. See Jean Jacques Rousseau, *Émile,* trans. Barbara Foxley (1911; repr., London: Dent; New York: Dutton, 1972).

37. See Sean Steel, "The Birth of Dionysian Education (The Spirit of Music)?: Part 1," *Philosophy of Music Education Review* 22, no. 1 (Spring 2014): 38–60, https://doi.org/10.2979/philmusieducrevi.22.1.38, and his "The Birth of Dionysian Education (The Spirit of Music)?: Part 2," *Philosophy of Music Education Review* 23, no. 1 (Spring 2015): 67–81, https://doi.org/10.2979/philmusieducrevi.23.1.67.

38. See Friedrich Schiller, *On the Aesthetic Education of Man in a Series of Letters,* trans. Elizabeth M. Wilkinson and L. A. Willoughby (1967; repr., Oxford: Clarendon, 1986).

39. On the dialectic of making and receiving music, see Estelle R. Jorgensen, *In Search of Music Education* (Urbana: University of Illinois Press, 1997), 83–87.

40. Maxine Greene, *Variations on a Blue Guitar: The Lincoln Center Institute Lectures on Aesthetic Education* (New York: Teachers College Press, 2001), 120.

41. See Peter Kivy, *Sound Sentiment: An Essay on the Musical Emotions, Including the Complete Text of The Corded Shell* (Philadelphia: Temple University Press, 1989).

42. See, for example, Carabo-Cone, *The Playground as Music Teacher*; Reichling, "Music, Imagination, and Play."

43. Alfred North Whitehead, *The Aims of Education and Other Essays* (1929; repr., New York: Free Press, 1967), 1.

44. On the persistence of corporal punishment and abuse, see chap. 4, "Dignity, Dispassion, Restraint, Discipline," nn. 56 and 57.

45. Kris Chesky, "Preventing Music-Induced Hearing Loss," *Music Educators Journal* 94, no. 3 (January 2008): 36–41, https://doi.org/10.1177%2F00274321080 9400308, points to a significant public health problem among music teachers and students caused by significantly higher levels of exposure than is allowable by the National Institute for Occupational Safety and Health standards.

46. OED Online, s.v. "Celebration, n.," accessed May 18, 2018, http://www.oed .com/view/Entry/29415?.

47. Langer, *Philosophy in a New Key*, chap. 6, draws on the sacred roots of ritual in thinking of sacrament as one of her "life-symbols."

48. Christopher Small, *Musicking: The Meanings of Performing and Listening* (Hanover, NH: Wesleyan University Press, University Press of New England, 1998), unpacks the meanings associated with the concert hall ritual.

49. Iris M. Yob, "The Cognitive Emotions and Emotional Cognitions," in *Reason and Education: Essays in Honor of Israel Scheffler*, ed., Harvey Siegel (Dordrecht, Netherlands: Kluwer Academic Publishers, 1997), 43–57.

50. Dewey, *Art as Experience*, 82.

51. See Lucy Green, *Music on Deaf Ears: Musical Meaning, Ideology and Education* (Manchester, UK: Manchester University Press, 1988), fig. 1, 138.

52. On spheres of musical validity, see Jorgensen, *In Search of Music Education*, chap. 2.

53. See Allsup, *Remixing the Classroom*.

54. Philip Alperson, "Robust Praxialism and the Anti-Aesthetic Turn," *Philosophy of Music Education Review* 18, no. 2 (2010): 171–193, https://doi.org/10 .2979/pme.2010.18.2.171.

55. Martin Luther, "Luther on Education: Studies and Methods," in Mark, ed., *Music Education Source Readings from Ancient Greece to Today*, 32.

CHAPTER 7 - FIDELITY, PERSISTENCE, PATIENCE, AND LOYALTY

1. On difference and music education, see Cathy Benedict, Patrick Schmidt, Gary Spruce, and Paul Woodford, eds., *The Oxford Handbook of Social Justice in Music Education* (New York: Oxford University Press, 2015), section II.

2. On dialectics in music education, see Estelle R. Jorgensen, *In Search of Music Education* (Urbana: University of Illinois Press, 1997), chap. 3; and Estelle R. Jorgensen, "A Dialectical View of Theory and Practice," *Journal of Research in Music Education* 49, no. 1 (2001): 343–359, https://doi.org/10.2307/3345617.

3. See Estelle R. Jorgensen, *Pictures of Music Education* (Bloomington: Indiana University Press, 2011), chap. 4; Randall Everett Allsup, *Remixing the Classroom: Toward an Open Philosophy of Music Education* (Bloomington: Indiana University Press, 2016).

4. OED Online, s.v. "Fidelity, n.," accessed May 29, 2018, http://www.oed.com/view/Entry/69888?.

5. See Donald Arnstine, *Democracy and the Arts of Schooling* (Albany: State University of New York Press, 1995), especially chap. 3.

6. OED Online, s.v. "Fidelity, n."

7. Israel Scheffler, *In Praise of the Cognitive Emotions and Other Essays on the Philosophy of Education* (New York: Routledge, Chapman and Hall, 1991), 25, notices that human potential is a decision to do such and such, as John decides to play the piano. In this essay entitled "Human Nature and Potential," Scheffler argues that it is impossible to be "all that one can be" since choices made preclude other possibilities that are not pursued.

8. Alfred North Whitehead, *The Aims of Education and Other Essays* (1929; repr., New York: Free Press, 1967).

9. See Scheffler, *In Praise of the Cognitive Emotions*, chap. 1.

10. OED Online, s.v. "Fidelity, n."

11. On Western conservatories, see Bruno Nettl, *Heartland Excursions: Ethnomusicological Reflections on Schools of Music* (Urbana: University of Illinois Press, 1995); Henry Kingsbury, *Music, Talent, and Performance: A Conservatory Cultural System* (1988; Philadelphia: Temple University, 2001).

12. See Daniel M. Neuman, *The Life of Music in North India: The Organization of an Artistic Tradition* (Detroit: Wayne State University Press, 1980).

13. Iris M. Yob and Linda Crawford, "Conceptual Framework for Mentoring Doctoral Students," *Higher Learning Research Communications* 2, no. 2 (June 2012); 37–50, https://doi.org/10.18870/hlrc.v2i2.66.

14. Silkroad, founded by the cellist Yo-Yo Ma, is a nonprofit organization with a social change mission. It fosters "radical cultural collaboration" among musicians of various traditions to "build a more hopeful and inclusive world." See https://www.silkroad.org, accessed March 2, 2021.

15. See Christopher Small, *Musicking: The Meanings of Performing and Listening* (Hanover, NH: Wesleyan University Press, University Press of New England, 1998).

16. For the PBS Great Performances broadcast of the Vienna Philharmonic Summer Night Concert 2016, see "Vienna Philharmonic Summer Night Concert 2016: Full Episode," PBS, recorded live, May 26, 2016, https://www.pbs.org/wnet/gperf/vienna-philharmonic-summer-night-concert-2016-concert/5334/. On sexism in music education, see Estelle R. Jorgensen, *Transforming Music Education* (Bloomington: Indiana University Press, 2003) 20–25.

17. See Susanne K. Langer, *Philosophy in a New Key: A Study in the Symbolism of Reason, Rite, and Art*, 3rd edition (Cambridge, MA: Harvard University Press, 1957), chap. 1; Allsup, *Remixing the Classroom*.

18. Émile Jaques-Dalcroze, *Rhythm, Music, and Education*, trans. Harold F. Rubinstein (1921; repr., New York: Arno, 1976), 16.

19. Scheffler, *In Praise of the Cognitive Emotions*, 13, 14.

20. Paul Woodford, *Democracy and Music Education: Liberalism, Ethics, and the Politics of Practice* (Bloomington and Indianapolis: Indiana University Press, 2005).

21. See Jorgensen, *Pictures of Music Education*.

22. OED Online, s.v. "Persist, v.," accessed May 30, 2018, https://www.oed.com/view/Entry/141465?.

23. OED Online, s.v. "Persistence, n.," accessed May 30, 2018, https://www.oed.com/view/Entry/141466?.

24. On the "vision of mastery," see Vernon A. Howard, *Artistry: The Work of Artists* (Indianapolis, IN: Hackett, 1982), chap. 6.

25. John Dewey, *Art as Experience* (1934; repr., New York: Paragon Books, 1979).

26. See, for example, Herbert Read, *Education through Art* (London: Faber and Faber, 1943); Maxine Greene, *The Dialectic of Freedom* (New York: Teachers College Press, 1988), her *Releasing the Imagination: Essays on Education, the Arts, and Social Change* (San Francisco: Jossey-Bass, 1995), and her *Variations on a Blue Guitar: The Lincoln Center Institute Lectures on Aesthetic Education* (New York: Teachers College Press, 2001); Howard, *Artistry*, his *Learning by All Means: Lessons from the Arts: A Study in the Philosophy of Education* (New York: Peter Lang, 1992), and his *Charm and Speed: Virtuosity in the Performing Arts* (New York: Peter Lang, 2008).

27. See Leonard B. Meyer, *Emotion and Meaning in Music* (Chicago: University of Chicago Press, 1956).

28. Carl Orff and Gunild Keetman, *Musik für Kinder*, 5 vols. (Mainz, Germany: B. Schott's Söhne, 1950).

29. John Blacking, *How Musical Is Man?* (1973; London: Faber and Faber, 1976).

30. Lucy Green, *How Popular Musicians Learn: A Way Ahead for Music Education* (2002; repr. Abingdon, UK, and New York: Routledge, 2016).

31. For a history of curricular discourses in the United States, see William F. Pinar, William M. Reynolds, Patrick Slattery, and Peter M. Taubman, *Understanding Curriculum: An Introduction to the Study of Historical and Contemporary Curriculum Discourses* (New York: Peter Lang, 1995).

32. See David B. Tyack and Larry Cuban, *Tinkering toward Utopia: A Century of Public School Reform* (Cambridge, MA: Harvard University Press, 1995).

33. On the transfer effect of music listening and training to other areas, see E. Glenn Schellenberg and Michael W. Weiss, "Music and Cognitive Abilities," in *Psychology of Music*, ed. Diana Deutsch (New York: Elsevier, 2013), 449–550. I am indebted to Peter Miksza for bringing this reference to my attention.

34. On "dogmatism" as a defense against surprise, see Scheffler, *In Praise of the Cognitive Emotions*, 13, 14.

35. On the "fundamentalist imagination," see Randall Everett Allsup, "Hard Times: Philosophy and the Fundamentalist Imagination," *Philosophy of Music Education Review* 13, no. 2 (Fall 2005): 139–142, https://www.jstor.org/stable/40495507.

36. Whitehead, *The Aims of Education*, chap. 3.

37. On miseducative experience, see John Dewey, *Experience and Education* (1938; repr., New York: Collier Books, 1963), 25.

38. Interview with Sergei Babayan and Daniil Trifonov in the Greene Performing Space, New York, broadcast live on Medici-TV, November 9, 2015.

39. OED Online, s.v. "Patience, n.1 (and int.)," accessed May 31, 2018, https://www.oed.com/view/Entry/138816?.

40. Maggie Berg and Barbara K. Seeber, *The Slow Professor: Challenging the Culture of Speed in the Academy* (Toronto: University of Toronto Press, 2016).

41. See Jane Roland Martin, *School Was Our Life: Remembering Progressive Education* (Bloomington: Indiana University Press, 2018); Nel Noddings, *Happiness and Education* (Cambridge: Cambridge University Press, 2003).

42. OED Online, s.v. "Patience, n.1 (and int.)."

43. OED Online, s.v. "Patience, n.1 (and int.)."

44. OED Online, s.v. "Patience, n.1 (and int.)."

45. OED Online, s.v. "Patience, n.1 (and int.)."

46. See Howard, *Charm and Speed*, his *Artistry*, and his *Learning by All Means*.

47. Robert K. Merton's widely accepted notion of the self-fulfilling prophecy in his article entitled "The Self-fulfilling Prophecy," *Antioch Review* 8 (1948): 193–210, https://doi.org/10.2307/4609267, is developed in John M. Darley and Russell H. Fazio, "Expectancy Confirmation Processes Arising in the Social Interaction Sequence," *American Psychologist* 35, no. 10 (1980): 867–881, https://doi.org/10.1037/0003-066X.35.10.867. Empirical research in music education has demonstrated an expectancy effect between parental support and student musical success—for example, Gary Macpherson, "The Role of Parents in Children's Musical Development," *Psychology of Music* 37, no. 1 (2009): 91–110, https://doi.org/10.1177/0305735607086049. (I am indebted to Peter Miksza for bringing this reference to my attention.) Teacher expectations have been linked to other aspects of music—see Peter D. MacIntyre, Gillian K. Potter, and Jillian N. Burns, "The Socio-Educational Model of Music Motivation," *Journal of Research in Music Education* 60, no. 2 (July 2012): 129–144, https://doi.org/10.1177/0022429412444609. At the time of this writing, I am unaware of empirical research that definitively supports my hypothesized connection between music teacher expectations and student musical performance quality.

48. On a thermostatic approach to education, see Neil Postman, *Teaching as a Conserving Activity* (New York: Dell, 1979).

49. Martin, *School Was Our Life*.

50. On the importance of present experience in the context of an experiential continuum of life lived in the past and projecting forward into the future, see Dewey, *Experience and Education*, especially chap. 3.

51. Jaques-Dalcroze, *Rhythm, Music, and Education*, especially chap. 2. He comments that it would be better if music were not offered in schools if it is to be treated as "superfluous." If conventional timetables prove an obstacle to the requisite instructional time in music, "remove the obstacle" (168).

52. Martin, *School Was Our Life*, 59.

53. OED Online, s.v. "Loyalty, n.," accessed May 31, 2018, http://www.oed.com/view/Entry/110759?.

54. Werner Jaeger, *Paideia: The Ideals of Greek Culture*, trans. Gilbert Highet, 3 vols. (New York: Oxford University Press, 1943–1945).

55. Parker J. Palmer, *Courage to Teach: Exploring the Inner Landscape of a Teacher's Life* (San Francisco: Jossey-Bass, 1998), especially chap. 5.

56. This occurs, for example, in international music competitions where hundreds of aspiring musicians are whittled down to a small group of finalists, with a laureate winning the grand prize and chief among the winners. For a social analysis of music competitions, see Lisa McCormick, *Performing Civility: International Competitions in Classical Music* (Cambridge: Cambridge University Press, 2015). Also, see Joseph Horowitz, *The Ivory Trade: Music and the Business of Music at the Van Cliburn International Piano Competition* (New York: Summit Books, 1990) for an insider exposé of the machinations within a piano competition.

57. On the difficulty if not impossibility of grasping imaginative possibilities in the absence of attachment to others, see Greene, *The Dialectic of Freedom*, 17.

58. See Iris M. Yob, her "School as Sacred Space," paper presented at Reasons of the Heart Conference, Edinburgh, Scotland, September 2004, and her "School and Sacred Time," paper presented at Tenth International Society for Philosophy of Music Education Conference, Frankfurt, Germany, June 2015.

59. On enculturation and cultivating a "way of life" in music education, see Jorgensen, *In Search of Music Education*, her *The Art of Teaching Music* (Bloomington: Indiana University Press, 2008), and her *Pictures of Music Education*.

60. See June Boyce-Tillman, "Towards an Ecology of Music Education," *Philosophy of Music Education Review* 12, no. 2 (2004): 102–125, https://www.jstor.org/stable/40327232.

61. See Langer, *Philosophy in a New Key*.

62. See Iris M. Yob, "If We Knew What Spirituality Was, We Would Teach for It," *Music Educators Journal* 98, no. 2 (December 2011): 41–47, https://doi.org/10.1177/0027432111425959.

63. On reciprocal empathy, see Estelle R. Jorgensen, "On a Choice-Based Instructional Typology in Music," *Journal of Research in Music Education* 29 (1981): 97–102, https://doi.org/10.2307/3345018.

64. For the use of classic microeconomic modeling techniques in music education, see Estelle R. Jorgensen, "An Analysis of Aspects of Type IV Music Instruction in a Teacher-Student Dyad," *The Quarterly Journal of Music Teaching and Learning* 6, no. 1 (1995): 16–31, reprinted with permission in *Visions of Research in Music Education* 16, no. 6 (Autumn 2010), http://www-usr.rider.edu/~vrme/v16n1/volume6/visions/spring3; her "Modeling Aspects of Type IV Music Instructional Triads," *The Bulletin of the Council for Research in Music Education*, no. 137 (1998): 43–56, https://www.jstor.org/stable/40318931; and her "On a Choice-Based Instructional Typology in Music," https://doi.org/10.2307/3345018. Although interesting for their logical possibilities, these modeling techniques are grounded in unrealistic assumptions of rationality and perfect knowledge. Their conclusions may seem to fit some intuitively perceived and anecdotal evidence, but these instructional models require systematic empirical testing.

65. I am indebted to Deanne Bogdan for introducing me to performances by the pianist Daniel Trifonov; for accompanying Iris Yob and me on a field trip from Sarasota to Miami, Florida, on March 1, 2015 to hear Sergei Babayan perform for the first time at a chamber concert sponsored by the Chopin Foundation of the United States. For an analysis of Trifonov's performance, see Deanne Bogdan, "Incarnating the Shiver-Shimmer Factor: Toward a Dialogical Sublime," *Philosophy of Music Education Review* 28, no. 2 (Fall 2020): 145–167, https://doi.org/10.2979/philmusieducrevi.28.2.03.

CHAPTER 8 - CURIOSITY, IMAGINATION, WONDER, AND OPEN-MINDEDNESS

1. See John Shepherd, "Music and the Last Intellectuals," in *The Philosopher, Teacher, Musician: Contemporary Perspectives on Music Education*, ed. Estelle R. Jorgensen (Urbana: University of Illinois Press, 1993), 95–114.

2. OED Online, s.v. "Curiosity, n.," accessed June 8, 2018, https://www.oed.com/view/Entry/46038?.

3. See, for example, Donald Arnstine, *Democracy and the Arts of Schooling* (Albany: State University of New York Press, 1995), 100–114.

4. On the teacher's responsibility to transform impulse into desire and educational growth, see John Dewey, *Experience and Education* (1938; repr., New York: Collier Books, 1963), especially 70–72.

5. Martin Buber, *I and Thou*, trans. Walter Kaufmann (New York: Charles Scribner's Sons, 1970).

6. See Percy A. Scholes, *Music, the Child, and the Masterpiece: A Comprehensive Handbook of Aims and Methods in All that is Usually Called 'Musical Appreciation'* (London: Oxford University Press, Humphrey Milford, 1935).

7. See, for example, Bennett Reimer, "Once More with Feeling: Reconciling Discrepant Accounts of Musical Affect," *Philosophy of Music Education Review* 12, no. 1 (Spring 2004): 4–16, https://www.jstor.org/stable/40327216.

8. On music as power, see Jacques Attali, *Noise: The Political Economy of Music*, trans. Brian Massumi (Minneapolis: University of Minnesota Press, 1985).

9. See Henry Kingsbury, *Music, Talent, and Performance: A Conservatory Cultural System* (Philadelphia: Temple University Press, 1988); Bruno Nettl, *Heartland Excursions: Ethnomusicological Reflections on Schools of Music* (Urbana: University of Illinois Press, 1995).

10. Arnstine, *Democracy and the Arts of Schooling*, 100–114, notes the necessity of teachers and schools providing intellectual stimulation that prompts and prods curiosity.

11. Paulo Freire, *Pedagogy of the Oppressed*, New Revised 20th Anniversary Edition, trans. Myra Bergman Ramos (New York: Continuum, 1993), especially chap. 2.

12. See Maxine Greene, *The Dialectic of Freedom* (New York: Teachers College Press, 1988).

13. See Raimond Gaita, *A Common Humanity: Thinking about Love and Truth and Justice* (London and New York: Routledge, 2014).

14. See William B. Turner, *A Genealogy of Queer Theory* (Philadelphia: Temple University Press, 2000).

15. See Philip Brett, Elizabeth Wood, Gary C. Thomas, eds., *Queering the Pitch: The New Lesbian and Gay Musicology*, 2nd ed. (New York: Routledge, 2006); Doris Leibetseder, *Queer Tracks: Subversive Strategies in Rock and Pop Music*, trans. Rebecca Carbery (2012; revised trans., New York: Routledge, 2016); Judith Ann Peraino, "Listening to the Sirens: Music as Queer Ethical Practice," *GLQ: A Journal of Lesbian and Gay Studies* 9, no. 4 (2003): 433–470, https://doi.org/10.1215/10642684-9-4-433, and her *Listening to the Sirens: Musical Technologies of Queer Identity from Homer to Hedwig* (Berkeley: University of California Press, 2006); Jodie Taylor, *Playing It Queer: Popular Music, Identity and Queer World-Making* (Bern, Switzerland: Peter Lang, 2012); Nelson M. Rodriguez, Wayne J. Martino, Jennifer C. Ingrey, and Edward Brockenbrough, eds., *Critical Concepts in Queer Studies and Education: An International Guide for the Twenty-First Century* (New York: Palgrave Macmillan, 2016); Elizabeth Gould, "Companion-able Species: A Queer Pedagogy for Music Education," *Bulletin of the Council for Research in Music Education* no. 197 (Summer 2013): 63–75, https://doi.org/10.5406/bulcouresmusedu.197.0063; Elizabeth Gould, "Ecstatic Abundance: Queer Temporalities in LGBTQ Studies and Music Education," *Bulletin of the Council for Research in Music Education* no. 207–208 (Winter/Spring 2016): 123–138, https://doi.org/10.5406/bulcouresmusedu.207-208.0123; Karin Hendricks and June Boyce-Tillman, eds., *Queering Freedom: Music, Identity, and Spirituality* (Oxford: Peter Lang, 2018).

16. Gould, "Companion-able Species," 64, and "Ecstatic Abundance, 123–124.

17. On the "stickiness" of songs, see Estelle R. Jorgensen, foreword to *School Was Our Life: Remembering Progressive Education*, by Jane Roland Martin (Bloomington: Indiana University Press, 2018), x.

18. David R. Gillham, *City of Women* (New York: Berkley Pub. Group, 2013).

19. Among social histories of musical families, see Daniel M. Neuman, *The Life of Music in North India: The Organization of an Artistic Tradition* (Detroit: Wayne State University Press, 1980); Karl Geiringer, *The Bach Family: Seven Generations of Creative Genius* (New York: Oxford University Press, 1954); George Martin, *The Damrosch Dynasty: America's First Family of Music* (Boston: Houghton Mifflin, 1983). On jazz lineage and the role of memory in knowledge transmission among musicians, see Gabriel Solis, *Monk's Music: Thelonius Monk and Jazz History in the Making* (Berkeley: University of California Press, 2007).

20. On musicians' unions, see, for example, John Williamson and Martin Cloonan, *Players' Work Time: A History of the British Musicians' Union 1893–2013* (Manchester, UK: Manchester University Press, 2016).

21. On the Boston School Music Movement, see Estelle R. Jorgensen, "Engineering Change in Music Education: A Model of the Political Process Underlying the Boston School Music Movement (1829–1838)," *Journal of Research in Music Education* 31 (1983): 67–75, https://doi.org/10.2307/3345111, and her "William Channing Woodbridge's Lecture 'On Vocal Music as a Branch of Common Education' Revisited," *Studies in Music* (University of Western Australia) 18 (1984): 1–32. Reprinted with permission in *Visions of Music Education* 14, no. 1 (June 2009), http://www-usr.rider.edu/~vrme/v14n1/vision/woodbridge.pdf. Also, see Émile Jaques-Dalcroze, *Rhythm, Music and Education*, trans. Harold F. Rubinstein (1921; repr., New York: Arno, 1976), 16, and especially chap. 2.

22. Austin B. Caswell, "Canonicity in Academia: A Music Historian's View," in *Philosopher, Teacher, Musician: Perspectives on Music Education*, ed. Estelle R. Jorgensen (Urbana: University of Illinois Press, 1993), 129–145.

23. On the principle of antecedence, see Estelle R. Jorgensen, *The Art of Teaching Music* (Bloomington: Indiana University Press, 2008), 155, 221.

24. OED Online, s.v. "Imagination, n." accessed June 12, 2018, https://www.oed.com/view/Entry/91643?

25. Mary J. Reichling, "Images of Imagination," *Journal of Research in Music Education* 38, no. 4 (1990): 282–293, https://doi.org/10.2307/3345225.

26. OED Online, s.v. "Imagination, n."

27. See Vernon A. Howard, *Artistry: The Work of Artists* (Indianapolis, IN: Hackett, 1982), chap. 6.

28. OED Online, s.v. "Imagination, n."

29. See Susanne K. Langer, *Philosophy in a New Key: A Study in the Symbolism of Reason, Rite, and Art*, 3rd edition (Cambridge, MA: Harvard University Press, 1957); her *Feeling and Form: A Theory of Art Developed from Philosophy in a New Key* (London: Routledge, 1953); and her *Problems of Art: Ten Philosophical Lectures* (New York: Charles Scribner's Sons, 1957).

30. OED Online, s.v. "Imagination, n."

31. On feeling as central to mind, see Susanne K. Langer, *Mind: An Essay on Human Feeling*, 3 vols. (Baltimore: Johns Hopkins Press, 1967, 1972, 1982). On the cognitive emotions and emotional cognitions, see Israel Scheffler, *In Praise of the Cognitive Emotions and Other Essays on the Philosophy of Education* (New York: Routledge, Chapman and Hall, 1991), chap. 1; Iris M. Yob, "The Cognitive Emotions and Emotional Cognitions," in *Reason and Education: Essays in Honor of Israel Scheffler*, ed. Harvey Siegel (Dordrecht, Netherlands: Kluwer Academic Publishers, 1997), 43–57.

32. See Israel Scheffler, *The Language of Education* (Springfield, IL: Charles C. Thomas, 1960), his *Beyond the Letter: A Philosophical Inquiry into Ambiguity, Vagueness and Metaphor in Language* (London: Routledge and Kegan Paul, 1979), and his *Science and Subjectivity*, 2nd edition (Indianapolis, IN: Hackett, 1982).

33. See Greene, *The Dialectic of Freedom*. Also, see her *Releasing the Imagination: Essays on Education, the Arts, and Social Change* (San Francisco: Jossey-Bass, 1995), and *Variations on a Blue Guitar: The Lincoln Center Institute Lectures on Aesthetic Education* (New York: Teachers College Press, 2001).

34. OED Online, s.v. "Imagination, n."

35. See Herbert Read, *Education through Art* (London: Faber and Faber, 1943).

36. See Vernon A. Howard, *Learning by All Means: Lessons from the Arts: A Study in the Philosophy of Education* (New York: Peter Lang, 1992).

37. Northrop Frye, *The Educated Imagination* (1963; repr., Toronto: House of Anansi, 1993).

38. Deanne Bogdan, *Re-educating the Imagination: Towards a Poetics, Politics, and Pedagogy of Literary Engagement* (Portsmouth, NH: Boynton/Cook-Heinemann, 1992).

39. See, for example, Robert W. Mitchell, ed., *Pretending and Imagination in Animals and Children* (Cambridge: Cambridge University Press, 2002). Also, for an examination of overlooked cartoons and animations from the early twentieth century that became the basis for a surging interest in animated and science fiction films in the latter part of century, see J. P. Telotte, *Animating the Science Fiction Imagination* (New York: Oxford University Press, 2018). On thinking of artificial intelligence as having imagination, see Igor Aleksander, *How to Build a Mind: Toward Machines with Imaginations* (New York: Columbia University Press, 2001).

40. Greene, *Releasing the Imagination*, 35, 133, chap. 10.

41. On the Anthropocene, see Elizabeth Kolbert, *The Sixth Extinction: An Unnatural History* (New York: Henry Holt, 2014).

42. See Abraham H. Maslow, "A Theory of Human Motivation," *Psychological Review* 50 (1943): 370–396, https://doi.org/10.1037/h0054346; his *Toward a Psychology of Being*, 2nd edition (New York: D. Van Nostrand, 1968); and his *The Farther Reaches of Human Nature* (1971; repr., Harmondsworth, UK: Penguin, 1976).

43. Mihaly Csikszentmihalyi, *Flow: The Psychology of Optimal Experience* (New York: Harper and Row, 1990).

44. See, for example, Johan Huizinga, *Homo Ludens: A Study of the Play-Element in Culture* (1950; repr., Boston: Beacon, 1955); Armand D'Angour, "Plato and Play: Taking Play Seriously," *American Journal of Play* 5, no. 3 (Spring 2013): 293–307, https://www.journalofplay.org/sites/www.journalofplay.org/files/pdf-articles/5-3-article-plato-and-play.pdf.

45. I make this point in Estelle R. Jorgensen, "The Concert Hall and the Web," last modified December 15, 2015, https://www.estellejorgensen.com/blog/the-concert-hall-and-the-web.

46. On the dark side of technology, see Michael Harris, *The End of Absence: Reclaiming What We've Lost in a World of Constant Connection* (2014; repr., New York: Penguin, 2015).

47. See Howard, *Artistry*, especially chap. 2.

48. Since the original publication of his *Frames of Mind: The Theory of Multiple Intelligences*, 2nd paper edition, 10th anniversary edition (New York: Basic Books, 2011), Howard Gardner has continued to develop his theory. Among his critics, see, for example, Joe L. Kincheloe, ed., *Multiple Intelligences Reconsidered* (New York: Peter Lang, 2004).

49. Philip H. Phenix, *Realms of Meaning: A Philosophy of the Curriculum for General Education* (1964; repr., Ventura, CA: Ventura County Superintendent of Schools Office, 1986); Nelson Goodman, *Ways of Worldmaking* (Indianapolis, IN: Hackett, 1978).

50. See, for example, the seminal writing of Carol Gilligan, *In a Different Voice: Psychological Theory and Women's Development* (Cambridge, MA: Harvard University Press, 1982); Jerome Bruner, *Actual Minds, Possible Worlds* (Cambridge, MA: Harvard University Press, 1986), and his *Acts of Meaning* (Cambridge, MA: Harvard University Press, 1990); Greene, *Dialectic of Freedom*, and her *Releasing the Imagination*; Michael Apple, *Ideology and Curriculum*, 2nd edition (New York: Routledge, 1990); Bogdan, *Re-educating the Imagination*; Henry A. Giroux, *Border Crossings: Cultural Workers and the Politics of Education* (1992: repr., New York and London: Routledge, 1993) and his *Fugitive Cultures: Race, Violence, and Youth* (New York: Routledge, 1996).

51. See Erik H. Erikson with Joan M. Erikson, *The Life Cycle Completed* (New York: W. W. Norton, 1998).

52. Dewey, *Experience and Education*.

53. See Greene, *The Dialectic of Freedom*.

54. OED Online, s.v. "Wonder, n.," accessed June 13, 2018, http://www.oed.com/view/Entry/229936?.

55. OED Online, s.v. "Wonder, v.," accessed June 13, 2018, http://www.oed.com/view/Entry/229938?.

56. See Iris M. Yob, "If We Knew What Spirituality Was, We Would Teach for It," *Music Educators Journal* 98, no. 2 (December 2011): 41–47, https://doi.org/10.1177/0027432111425959.

57. See William James, *The Varieties of Religious Experience* (Cambridge, MA: Harvard University Press, 1985).

58. See David Carr and J. W. Steutel, eds., *Virtue Ethics and Moral Education* (London: Routledge, 1999); David Carr and John Haldane, eds., *Spirituality, Philosophy, and Education* (London and New York: RoutledgeFalmer, 2003); David Carr, "The Significance of Music for the Moral and Spiritual Cultivation of Virtue," *Philosophy of Music Education Review* 14, no. 2 (Fall 2006): 103–117, https://www.jstor.org/stable/40327249, and his "Music, Spirituality, and Education," *Journal of Aesthetic Education* 42, no. 1 (Spring 2008): 16–29, https://www.jstor.org/stable/25160263; Iris M. Yob, "School as Sacred Space," paper presented at Reasons of the Heart Conference, Edinburgh, Scotland, September 2004, and her "School and Sacred Time," paper presented at Tenth International Society for Philosophy of Music Education Conference, Frankfurt, Germany, June 2015.

59. Howard, *Learning by All Means.*

60. See Yob, "If We Knew What Spirituality Was, We Would Teach for It."

61. Deanne Bogdan, "The Shiver-Shimmer Factor: Music Spirituality, Emotion, and Education," *Philosophy of Music Education Review* 18, no. 2 (Fall 2010): 111–129, https://doi.org/10.2979/pme.2010.18.2.111.

62. See Scheffler, *In Praise of the Cognitive Emotions,* chap. 1; Yob, "The Cognitive Emotions and Emotional Cognitions."

63. Howard, *Artistry,* chap. 6.

64. Shinichi Suzuki, *Nurtured by Love: A New Approach to Education,* trans. Waltraud Suzuki (New York: Exposition, 1969).

65. Israel Scheffler, *Reason and Teaching* (1973; repr., Indianapolis, IN: Bobbs-Merrill, 1973), 80.

66. On the fear of freedom, the fright of surprise, and the unbearable burden of uncertainty and vulnerability, particularly at times of rampant change, see Erich Fromm, *Escape from Freedom* (New York: Rinehart, 1941).

67. See the discussion of corporal punishment in chap. 4, n. 55 and n. 56.

68. On the role of fear in instrumental music education, see Timothy Lautzenheiser, "The Essential Elements to a Successful Band: The Teacher, the Conductor, the Director, the Leader," in *Teaching Music through Performance in Band,* ed. Richard Miles (Chicago: GIA Publications, 1997), 63; Ken Murakami, "Building a Great Junior High Band" DVD (Hiroshima, Japan: Brain Co., 2006), minute 1:21. I am indebted to Leonard Tan for bringing these references to my attention. Also, see Randall Allsup and Cathy Benedict, "The Problems of Band: An Inquiry into the Future of Instrumental Music Education," *Philosophy of Music Education Review* 16, no. 2 (Fall 2008): 156–173, https://www.jstor.org/stable/40327299; Leonard Tan, "Towards a Transcultural Philosophy of Music Education" (PhD diss., Indiana University, 2012).

69. On musical substance and manner, see Charles E. Ives, "Essays Before a Sonata," in *Three Classics in the Aesthetic of Music* (1920; repr., New York: Dover,

1962), 103–185. More recently, notions of surface and depth are examined by Richard Shusterman, *Surface and Depth: Dialectics of Criticism and Culture* (Ithaca, NY: Cornell University Press, 2002).

70. OED Online, s.v. "Open-mindedness, n.," accessed June 14, 2018, http://www.oed.com/view/Entry/259301?; OED Online, s.v. "Open-minded, adj.," accessed June 14, 2018, http://www.oed.com/view/Entry/259299?.

71. On virtue as a mean, see, for example, Aristotle, *Nicomachean Ethics*, trans. and ed.X Roger Crisp (Cambridge: Cambridge University Press, 2000), book 2, para. 1106b, 30.

72. On critical thinking in music education, see Paul Woodford, *Democracy and Music Education: Liberalism, Ethics, and the Politics of Practice* (Bloomington and Indianapolis: Indiana University Press, 2005).

73. For philosophical discussions of difference and cosmopolitanism in music education, see, for example, June Boyce-Tillman, "Music and the Dignity of Difference," *Philosophy of Music Education Review* 20, no. 1 (Spring 2012): 25–44, https://doi.org/10.2979/philmusieducrevi.20.1.25; Patrick Schmidt, "Cosmopolitanism and Policy: A Pedagogical Framework for Global Issues in Music Education," *Arts Education Policy Review* 114, no. 3 (2013): 103–111, https://doi.org/10.1080/10632913.2013.803410; his "A Rabi [*sic*], an Imam, and a Priest Walk into a Bar . . . Or, What Can Music Education Philosophy Learn from Comparative Cosmopolitanism?" *Philosophy of Music Education Review* 21, no. 1 (Spring 2013): 23–40, https://doi.org/10.2979/philmusieducrevi.21.1.23; Geir Johanssen, "Music Education and the Role of Comparative Studies in a Globalized World," *Philosophy of Music Education Review* 21, no. 1 (Spring 2013): 41–51, https://doi.org/10.2979/philmusieducrevi.21.1.41; Lauren Kapalka Richerme, "Difference and Music Education," in *Music Education*, ed. Clint Randles (New York: Routledge, 2014); 30–42; her "Uncommon Commonalities: Cosmopolitan Ethics as a Framework for Music Education Analysis," *Arts Education Policy Review* 117 (2016): 87–95, https://doi.org/10.1080/10632913.2015.1047002; and her "A Feminine and Poststructural Extension of Cosmopolitan Ethics in Music Education," *International Journal of Music Education* 35, no. 3 (2016): 414–424, https://doi.org/10.1177/0255761416667470.

74. See, for example, Suzuki, *Nurtured by Love*; Brenda Brenner, "Reflecting on the Rationales for String Study in Schools," *Philosophy of Music Education Review* 18, no. 1 (Spring 2010): 45–64, https://doi.org/10.2979/pme.2010.18.1.45; Leonard Tan, "Towards a Transcultural Theory of Democracy for Instrumental Music Education," *Philosophy of Music Education Review* 22, no. 1 (Spring 2014): 61–77, https://doi.org/10.2979/philmusieducrevi.22.1.61; Merlin Thompson, "Authenticity, Shinichi Suzuki, and 'Beautiful Tone with Living Soul, Please,'" *Philosophy of Music Education Review* 24, no 2 (Fall 2016): 170–190, https://doi.org/10.2979/philmusieducrevi.24.2.03.

75. Among those to engage theoretical and practical issues in world musics, see, for example, Keith Swanwick, *Music, Mind, and Education* (London: Routledge,

1988); Therese Volk, *Music Education and Multiculturalism* (New York: Oxford University Press, 1998); Patricia Shehan Campbell, *Lessons from the World: A Cross-Cultural Guide to Music Teaching and Learning* (New York: Schirmer Books, 1991), and her *Music, Education, and Diversity: Bridging Cultures and Communities* (New York: Teachers College Press, 2017); June Boyce-Tillman, "Towards an Ecology of Music Education," *Philosophy of Music Education Review* 12, no. 2 (Fall 2004): 102–125, https://www.jstor.org/stable/40327232, and her "Music and the Dignity of Difference"; Huib Schippers, *Facing the Music: Shaping Music Education from a Global Perspective* (New York: Oxford University Press, 2010).

76. Scheffler, *In Praise of the Cognitive Emotions*, 13.

77. Thomas Regelski, "On 'Methodolatry' and Music Teaching as Critical and Reflective Praxis," *Philosophy of Music Education Review* 10, no. 2 (Fall 2002): 102–123, https://www.jstor.org/stable/40327184.

78. See Giroux, *Border Crossings*; Claire Detels, *Soft Boundaries: Re-visioning the Arts and Aesthetics in American Education* (Westport, CT: Bergin and Garvey, 1999).

79. On teaching and learning for openings, see Greene, *The Dialectic of Freedom*, and her *Releasing the Imagination*; Randall Everett Allsup, *Remixing the Classroom: Toward an Open Philosophy of Music Education* (Bloomington: Indiana University Press, 2016).

80. Dewey, *Experience and Education*.

81. On dispositions, see Arnstine, *Democracy and the Arts of Schooling*.

82. R. S. Peters, *Moral Development and Moral Education* (London: George Allen and Unwin, 1981); Carr and Steutel, eds., *Virtue Ethics and Moral Education*.

83. See Estelle R. Jorgensen, "The Curriculum Design Process in Music," *College Music Symposium* 28 (1988): 94–105, https://www.jstor.org/stable/40374590.

84. Freire, *Pedagogy of the Oppressed*.

85. On caring and its educational implications, see Nel Noddings, *Caring: A Feminine Approach to Ethics and Moral Education* (Berkeley: University of California Press, 1984), her *The Challenge to Care in Schools: An Alternative Approach to Education* (New York: Teachers College Press, 1992), and her *Educating Moral People: A Caring Alternative to Character Education* (New York: Teachers College Press, 2002).

86. See Israel Scheffler, *Of Human Potential: An Essay in the Philosophy of Education* (Boston: Routledge and Kegan Paul, 1985), and his *In Praise of the Cognitive Emotions*, chap. 2.

87. See, for example, Joe L. Kincheloe and William Pinar, eds., *Curriculum as Social Psychoanalysis: The Significance of Place* (Albany: State University of New York Press, 1991); Nel Noddings, *Taking Place Seriously in Education* (Ann Arbor, MI: Caddo Gap, 1998), which was the 22nd Garles DeGarmo Lecture of the Society of Professors of Education; David M. Callejo-Pérez, Donna Adair Brealt, and William L. White, *Curriculum as Spaces: Aesthetics, Community and the Politics of Place* (New York: Peter Lang, 2014).

88. Plato, *The Republic of Plato,* trans. Francis Macdonald Cornford (1941; repr., Oxford: Oxford University Press, 1942), book 7, para. 514–521, 240–249.

CHAPTER 9 - WISDOM, UNDERSTANDING, KNOWLEDGE, AND MASTERY

1. See Parker J. Palmer, *Courage to Teach: Exploring the Inner Landscape of a Teacher's Life* (San Francisco: Jossey-Bass, 1998).
2. OED Online, s.v. "Wisdom, n.," accessed June 28, 2018, http://www.oed.com/view/Entry/229491?.
3. See Lorin W. Anderson, ed., *A Taxonomy of Teaching, Learning, Assessing: A Revision of Bloom's Taxonomy of Educational Objectives,* abridged edition (2001; repr., Upper Saddle River, NJ: Pearson, 2013).
4. In the Jerusalem faiths, wisdom is often attributed to the deity, and one speaks of sacred texts as "wisdom literature." In Christian Scripture, Jesus is spoken of as the "Wisdom of the Father," (1 Cor. 1:24, 30); in Jewish Scripture, the writings of Solomon in the books of Ecclesiastes and Song of Songs are referred to as wisdom literature.
5. OED Online, s.v. "Wisdom, n."
6. See Keith Swanwick and June Boyce-Tillman, "The Sequence of Musical Development," *British Journal of Music Education* 3, no. 3 (1986): 305–339, https://www.doi.org/10.1017/S0265051700000814; Keith Swanwick, *Music, Mind, and Education* (London: Routledge, 1988), 76. For an extension of the original spiral, see June Boyce-Tillman, *Experiencing Music—Restoring the Spiritual, Music as Wellbeing* (New York: Peter Lang, 2016).
7. Alfred North Whitehead, *The Aims of Education and Other Essays* (1929; repr., New York: Free Press, 1967).
8. Whitehead, *The Aims of* Education, 14.
9. Plato, *Phaedrus,* trans. Benjamin Jowett (Oxford, 1892; Project Gutenberg, 2008), http://www/gutenberg.org/ebooks/1636, has Socrates say, "If I find any man who is able to see a 'One and Many' in nature, him I follow and 'walk in his footsteps as if he were a god.'" Jowett's translation is also quoted by Jacob Loewenberg, "Classic and Romantic Trends in Plato," *Harvard Theological Review* 10, no. 3 (July 1917): 215, https://www.jstor.org/stable/1507077, who observes that the problem of the "One and the Many" is a central Platonic concern.
10. On the ambiguity of language, see Israel Scheffler, *Beyond the Letter: A Philosophical Inquiry into Ambiguity, Vagueness and Metaphor in Language* (London: Routledge and Kegan Paul, 1979).
11. See Susanne K. Langer, *Philosophy in a New Key: A Study in the Symbolism of Reason, Rite, and Art,* 3rd edition (Cambridge, MA: Harvard University Press, 1957), 222–223, and her *Mind: An Essay on Human Feeling,* 3 vols. (Baltimore: Johns Hopkins Press, 1967, 1972, 1982).

12. John Dewey, *Art as Experience* (1934; repr., New York: Paragon Books, 1979).

13. On self-actualization, see Abraham H. Maslow, "A Theory of Human Motivation," *Psychological Review* 50 (1943): 370–396, https://doi/10.1037/h0054346; his *Toward a Psychology of Being*, 2nd edition (New York: D. Van Nostrand, 1968); and his *The Farther Reaches of Human Nature* (1971; repr., Harmondsworth, UK: Penguin, 1976). On flow, see Mihaly Csikszentmihalyi, *Flow: The Psychology of Optimal Experience* (New York: Harper and Row, 1990).

14. On grace, style, and virtuosity, see Vernon A. Howard, *Charm and Speed: Virtuosity in the Performing Arts* (New York: Peter Lang, 2008).

15. On the vision of mastery, see Vernon A. Howard, *Artistry: The Work of Artists* (Indianapolis, IN: Hackett, 1982), chap. 6.

16. Matt. 22:14, KJV.

17. See Cynthia S. Hawkins, "Aspects of the Musical Education of Choristers in Church of England Choir Schools" (MA thesis, McGill University, Montreal, Canada, 1985); Bernarr Rainbow with Gordon Cox, *Music in Educational Thought and Practice: A Survey from 800BC* (Woodbridge, Suffolk, UK: Boydell, 2006), especially chaps. 2 and 3.

18. Randall Allsup and Cathy Benedict, "The Problems of Band: An Inquiry into the Future of Instrumental Music Education," *Philosophy of Music Education Review* 16, no. 2 (Fall 2008): 156–173. For an early history of school instrumental music, see James A. Keene, *A History of Music Education in the United States*, 2nd ed. (Centennial, CO: Glenridge, 2009), chaps. 16 and 17.

19. For an anthropological view of academic jazz as a paradoxical undertaking, see Eitan Wilf, *School for Cool: The Academic Jazz Program and the Paradox of Institutionalized Creativity* (Chicago: University of Chicago Press, 2014).

20. OED Online, s.v. "Understanding, n.," accessed June 28, 2018, http://www.oed.com/view/Entry/212090?.

21. OED Online, s.v. "Understand, v.," accessed June 28, 2018, http://www.oed.com/view/Entry/212085?.

22. Langer, *Philosophy in a New Key*; her *Feeling and Form: A Theory of Art Developed from Philosophy in a New Key* (London: Routledge, 1953); her *Mind: An Essay on Human Feeling.*

23. OED Online, s.v. "Understanding, n."

24. See Howard, *Artistry*; Israel Scheffler, *In Praise of the Cognitive Emotions and Other Essays on the Philosophy of Education* (New York: Routledge, Chapman and Hall, 1991), chap. 3.

25. See, for example, Charles E. Ives, "Essays Before a Sonata," in *Three Classics in the Aesthetic of Music* (1920; repr., New York: Dover, 1962), which distinguishes between musical substance and manner; and Richard Shusterman, *Surface and Depth: Dialectics of Criticism and Culture* (Ithaca, NY: Cornell University Press, 2002), who thinks rather of surface and depth.

26. On the dialectic of music making and receiving see Jorgensen, *In Search of Music Education* (Urbana: University of Illinois Press, 1997), 83–87.

27. On weak syndromes, see Estelle R. Jorgensen, "Four Philosophical Models of the Relation between Theory and Practice," *Philosophy of Music Education Review* 13, no. 1 (Spring 2005): 21–36, https://www.jstor.org/stable/40495465.

28. The term "assumptive frame of reference" was defined by Edward Tiryakian, "Sociology and Existential Phenomenology," in *Phenomenology and the Social Sciences*, I, ed. Maurice Natanson (Evanston, IL: Northwestern University Press, 1973), 199–201.

29. See Jorgensen, *In Search of Music Education*, chap. 2.

30. This idea resonates with Neil Postman's thermostatic approach to education advocated in his *Teaching as a Conserving Activity* (New York: Dell, 1979).

31. Estelle R. Jorgensen, "The Curriculum Design Process in Music," *College Music Symposium* 28 (1988): 94–105, https://www.jstor.org/stable/40374590.

32. David J. Elliott, *Music Matters: A New Philosophy of Music Education* (New York: Oxford University Press, 1995); Francis E. Sparshott, *The Theory of the Arts* (Princeton, NJ: Princeton University Press, 1982); Philip Alperson, *What Is Music?: An Introduction to the Philosophy of Music* (1987; University Park: Pennsylvania State University Press, 1994). Also, see Philip Alperson, "What Should One Expect from a Philosophy of Music Education?" *The Journal of Aesthetic Education* 25, no. 3 (Fall 1991): 215–242, https://doi.org/10.2307/3333004; and his "Robust Praxialism and the Anti-Aesthetic Turn," *Philosophy of Music Education Review* 18, no. 2 (2010): 171–193, https://doi.org/10.2979/pme.2010.18.2.171.

33. The idea of complicating music education is seeing a revival, for example, in Lauren Kapalka Richerme, *Complicating, Considering, and Connecting Music Education* (Bloomington: Indiana University Press, 2020).

34. OED Online, s.v. "Knowledge, n.," accessed June 29, 2018, http://www.oed.com/view/Entry/104170?; OED Online, s.v. "Knowledge, v.," accessed June 29, 2018, http://www.oed.com/view/Entry/104171?.

35. Alperson, "What Should One Expect from a Philosophy of Music Education?" and his "Robust Praxialism"; Elliott, *Music Matters*; Christopher Small, *Musicking: The Meanings of Performing and Listening* (Hanover, NH: Wesleyan University Press, University Press of New England, 1998).

36. OED Online, s.v. "Knowledge, n."

37. OED Online, s.v. "Knowledge, n."

38. For a survey of literature on music perception and cognition, see, for example, Diana Deutsch, ed., *Psychology of Music*, 3rd ed. (London: Academic Press, 2013).

39. Paul F. Berliner, *Thinking in Jazz: The Infinite Art of Improvisation* (Chicago: University of Chicago Press, 1994).

40. Langer, *Philosophy in a New Key*, 245.

41. David J. Elliott, "Music as Affect," *Philosophy of Music Education Review* 8, no. 2 (Fall 2000): 79–88, https://www.jstor.org/stable/40495437.

42. See Lorin W. Anderson, ed., *A Taxonomy of Teaching, Learning, Assessing: A Revision of Bloom's Taxonomy of Educational Objectives*, abridged edition (2001; repr., Upper Saddle River, NJ: Pearson, 2013).

43. See, for example, Howard, *Artistry*, 49, 67–71; Anderson, ed., *A Taxonomy of Teaching, Learning*; Whitehead, *The Aims of Education*; Philip H. Phenix, *Realms of Meaning: A Philosophy of the Curriculum for General Education* (1964; repr., Ventura, CA: Ventura County Superintendent of Schools Office, 1986); Jerome Bruner, *On Knowing: Essays for the Left Hand* (1962; repr., New York: Atheneum, 1970), and his *Acts of Meaning* (Cambridge, MA: Harvard University Press, 1990); Nelson Goodman, *Ways of Worldmaking* (Indianapolis, IN: Hackett, 1978); Israel Scheffler, *Conditions of Knowledge: An Introduction to Epistemology and Education* (Chicago, IL: University of Chicago Press, 1965); Harvey Siegel, *Educating Reason: Rationality, Critical Thinking and Education* (London: Routledge, 1990); Maxine Greene, *Releasing the Imagination: Essays on Education, the Arts, and Social Change* (San Francisco: Jossey-Bass, 1995); Keith Swanwick, *Musical Knowledge: Intuition, Analysis and Music Education* (London and New York: Routledge, 1994).

44. Regarding social justice, for example, see Cathy Benedict, Patrick Schmidt, Gary Spruce, and Paul Woodford, eds., *The Oxford Handbook of Social Justice in Music Education* (New York: Oxford University Press, 2015); Randall Everett Allsup, ed., "Music Education, Equity and Social Justice," *Music Education Research* 9, no. 2 (July 2007), https://doi.org/10.1080/14613800701424841.

45. See Hanne Fossum and Øivind Varkøy, "A Call for Moderation—Between Hubris and Resignation: Music Education for Humane Ends and a Common Good," in *Humane Music Education for the Common* Good, ed. Iris M. Yob and Estelle R. Jorgensen (Bloomington: Indiana University Press, 2020); Sigrid Røyseng and Øivind Varkøy, "What Is Music Good For? A Dialogue on Technical and Ritual Rationality," *ACT. Action, Criticism, and Theory of Music Education* 13, no. 1 (2014): 101–125, http://www.act.maydaygroup.org/articles/RøysengVarkøy13_1.pdf; Alexandra Kertz-Welzel, "The Pied Piper of Hamelin: Adorno on Music Education," *Research Studies in Music Education* 25, no. 1 (2005), http://dx.doi.org/10.1177/1321103X050250010301. I am indebted to Øivind Varkøy and Alexandra Kertz-Welzel, respectively, for bringing my attention to these sources.

46. Deanne Bogdan, "Book Review: Estelle R. Jorgensen, *In Search of Music Education.* Urbana and Chicago: University of Illinois Press, 1997," *Philosophy of Music Education Review* 6, no. 1 (Spring 1998): 73, https://www.jstor.org/stable/40327115.

47. See Jorgensen, *In Search of Music Education*, chap. 3, and her "A Dialectical View of Theory and Practice."

48. See Estelle R. Jorgensen, *Pictures of Music Education* (Bloomington: Indiana University Press, 2011); Joseph J. Schwab, "The Practical: Arts of Eclectic," *The School Review* 79, no. 4 (August 1971): 493–542, https://doi.org/10.1086/442998.

49. See Paulo Freire, *Pedagogy of the Oppressed*, New Revised 20th Anniversary Edition, trans. Myra Bergman Ramos (New York: Continuum, 1993), chap. 2.

50. See Phenix, *Realms of Meaning.*

51. Plato, *The Republic of Plato*, trans. Francis Macdonald Cornford (1941; repr., Oxford: Oxford University Press, 1942); Werner Jaeger, *Paideia: The Ideals of Greek*

Culture, 3 vols., trans. Gilbert Highet (New York: Oxford University Press, 1939, 1943, 1944); Mortimer J. Adler on behalf of the members of the Paideia Group, *The Paideia Proposal: An Educational Manifesto* (New York: Collier Books, 1982); their *Paideia Problems and Possibilities: A Consideration of Questions Raised by* The Paideia Proposal (New York: Collier Books, 1983); their *The Paideia Program: An Educational Syllabus* (New York: Collier Books, 1984).

52. See Bennett Reimer, *A Philosophy of Music Education* (Englewood Cliffs, NJ: Prentice-Hall, 1970).

53. Phenix, *Realms of Meaning*, especially chaps. 12–15 on "Esthetics."

54. Jane Roland Martin, *Cultural Miseducation: In Search of a Democratic Solution* (New York: Teachers College Press, 2002), especially chap. 1.

55. Lucy Green, *How Popular Musicians Learn: A Way Ahead for Music Education* (2002; repr., Abingdon, UK, and New York: Routledge, 2016).

56. OED Online, s.v. "Mastery, n.," accessed July 3, 2018, http://www.oed.com/view/Entry/114791?.

57. OED Online, s.v. "Master, v.," accessed July 3, 2018, http://www.oed.com/view/Entry/114753?.

58. See Elliott, *Music Matters*; Small, *Musicking*.

59. Jorgensen, *Pictures of Music Education*, chap. 4.

60. See Keith Swanwick, *Music, Mind, and Education* (London: Routledge, 1988); Boyce-Tillman, *Experiencing Music*.

61. OED Online, s.v. "Mastery, n."

62. See Howard, *Artistry*, his *Learning by All Means: Lessons from the Arts: A Study in the Philosophy of Education* (New York: Peter Lang, 1992), and his *Charm and Speed*.

63. On the distinction between "knowing-that" and "knowing-how," see Howard, *Artistry*, 49–50; on the artist's "vision of mastery, see Howard, *Artistry*, chap. 6. Also, on the distinction between making and understanding, see Scheffer, *In Praise of the Cognitive Emotions*, chap. 3.

64. Freire, *Pedagogy of the Oppressed*.

65. Shinichi Suzuki, *Nurtured by Love: A New Approach to Education*, trans. Waltraud Suzuki (New York: Exposition, 1969).

66. Howard, *Charm and Speed*.

67. See Csikszentmihalyi, *Flow*; Maslow, "A Theory of Human Motivation."

68. See Dewey, *Art as Experience*, especially chap. 3.

69. On music competitions, see, for example, Lisa McCormick, *Performing Civility: International Competitions in Classical Music* (Cambridge: Cambridge University Press, 2015); Joseph Horowitz, *The Ivory Trade: Music and the Business of Music at the Van Cliburn International Piano Competition* (New York: Summit Books, 1990). For a study of the effect of competition on musical performance, see Jacob Eisenberg and William Forde Thompson, "The Effects of Competition on Improvisers' Motivation, Stress, and Creative Performance," *Creativity Research Journal* 23, no. 2 (2011): 129–136, https://doi.org/10.1080/10400419.2011.571185.

70. Paul Woodford, Democracy and Music Education: Liberalism, Ethics, and the Politics of Practice (Bloomington and Indianapolis: Indiana University Press, 2005); Randall Everett Allsup, Remixing the Classroom: Toward an Open Philosophy of Music Education (Bloomington: Indiana University Press, 2016).

CHAPTER 10 - JUSTICE, EQUALITY, FAIRNESS, AND INCLUSION

1. See, for example, John Dewey, *Democracy and Education: An Introduction to the Philosophy of Education* (1916; repr., New York: Free Press, 1966); R. S. Peters, *Ethics and Education* (London: George Allen and Unwin, 1966) and his *Moral Development and Moral Education* (London: George Allen and Unwin, 1981); Jane Roland Martin, *Reclaiming a Conversation: The Ideal of the Educated Woman* (New Haven, CT: Yale University Press, 1985); Paulo Freire, *Pedagogy of the Oppressed*, New Revised 20th Anniversary Edition, trans. Myra Bergman Ramos (New York: Continuum, 1993); Seyla Benhabib, *The Claims of Culture: Equality and Diversity in the Global Era* (Princeton, NJ: Princeton University Press, 2002); Martha C. Nussbaum, *Frontiers of Justice: Disability, Nationality, Species Membership* (Cambridge, MA: Belknap, 2006). On social justice in music education, see, for example, Cathy Benedict, Patrick Schmidt, Gary Spruce, and Paul Woodford, eds., *The Oxford Handbook of Social Justice in Music Education* (New York: Oxford University Press, 2015); Randall Everett Allsup, "Music Education, Equity and Social Justice," *Music Education Research* 9, no. 2 (July 2007), https://doi.org/10.1080/14613800701424841. On inclusion in music education, see Judith A. Jellison, "Inclusive Music Classrooms and Programs," in *The Oxford Handbook of Music Education*, vol. 2 (2nd ed.), ed. Gary E. McPherson and Graham F. Welch, *Oxford Handbooks Online* (November 2012), https://doi.org/10.1093/oxfordhb/9780199928019.013.0005, and her *Including Everyone: Creating Music Classrooms Where All Children Learn* (New York: Oxford University Press, 2015).

2. See my earlier writing on social justice in Estelle R. Jorgensen, "Intersecting Social Justices and Music Education," in *The Oxford Handbook of Social Justice and Music Education*, ed. Cathy Benedict, Patrick Schmidt, Gary Spruce, and Paul Woodford (New York: Oxford University Press, 2015), 7–28.

3. See Marja Heimonen, "Music Education and Law: Regulation as an Instrument," *Studia Musica* 17 (Helsinki, FI: Sibelius Academy, 2002), and her "Justifying the Right to Music Education," *Philosophy of Music Education Review* 14, no. 2 (Fall 2006): 119–141, https://www.jstor.org/stable/40327250.

4. Charles Dickens, *Oliver Twist, Or, the Parish Boy's Progress* (New York, 1909; Project Gutenberg, 2014), chap. 51, http://www.gutenberg.org/ebooks/46675.

5. In music education, see, Cathy Benedict, Patrick Schmidt, Gary Spruce, and Paul Woodford, eds., *The Oxford Handbook of Social Justice in Music Education* (New York: Oxford University Press, 2015).

6. Unlike John Rawls, who envisions justice as a matter of fairness guided by a set of rules (see his *A Theory of Justice*, rev. ed. [Cambridge, MA: Harvard University Press, 1999], and his *Justice as Fairness: A Restatement*, ed. Erin Kelly [Cambridge, MA: Harvard University Press, 2001]), Jacques Derrida sees justice as beyond the law, inestimable, contingent, responsive to the "other," and hopeful. See his "Force of Law: The 'Mystical Foundation of Authority,'" trans. Mary Quaintance, in *Acts of Religion*, ed. Gil Anidjar (London: Routledge, 2002), 230–298, where he comments that "justice is deconstruction" (243). For an application of Derridean justice to music education, see Pete Gale, "Derridean Justice and the DJ: A Classroom Impossibility?" *Philosophy of Music Education Review* 20, no. 2 (Fall 2012): 135–153, https://doi.org/10.2979/philmusieducrevi.20.2.135. Others who go beyond Rawls include Amartya Sen, *The Idea of Justice* (Cambridge, MA: Harvard University Press, 2009).

7. For dictionary definitions of just, the root of justice, as noun and verb, see OED Online, s.v. "Just, n.1.," accessed August 30, 2017, http://www.oed.com/view/Entry/339763?; OED Online, s.v. "Joust just, v.," accessed August 30, 2017, http://www.oed.com/view/Entry/101755?; OED Online, s.v. "Just, v.," accessed August 30, 2017, http://www.oed.com/view/Entry/102191?.

8. For a further discussion of justice and music education, see Jorgensen, "Intersecting Social Justices and Music Education."

9. See, for example, Martha C. Nussbaum, *Frontiers of Justice: Disability, Nationality, Species Membership* (Cambridge, MA: Belknap, 2006). Nel Noddings, *Caring: A Feminine Approach to Ethics and Moral Education* (Berkeley: University of California Press, 1984), makes a case for the wider ethical claims of the natural world in education.

10. Immanuel Kant, *Critique of Judgment*, trans. James Creed Meredith (1952; repr., Oxford: Clarendon, 1982), § 22, 84–85. Also, on taste as a sort of sensus communis, see Kant, § 20–22, 40, 82–85, 150–154.

11. Isaiah Berlin, *The Crooked Timber of Humanity: Chapters in the History of Ideas*, ed. Hardy Henry (Princeton, NJ: Princeton University Press, 1990).

12. On the dialectic of music making and receiving, see Estelle R. Jorgensen, *In Search of Music Education* (Urbana: University of Illinois Press, 1997), 83–87.

13. Jane Roland Martin, *Cultural Miseducation: In Search of a Democratic Solution* (New York: Teachers College Press, 2002), chap. 2.

14. See David Carr, "The Significance of Music for the Promotion of Moral and Spiritual Value," *Philosophy of Music Education Review* 14, no. 2 (Fall 2006): 103–117, https://www.doi.org/10.1353/pme.2007.0001.

15. Israel Scheffler, *Reason and Teaching* (1973; repr., Indianapolis, IN: Bobbs-Merrill, 1973).

16. Scheffler, *Reason and Teaching*, 80.

17. See John Dewey, *Experience and Education* (1938; repr., New York: Collier Books, 1963), chap. 4.

18. I think, for example, of the problems of displacement evident in contemporary music education (see Kinh T. Vu and Andre de Quadros, eds., *My Body Was Left on the Street: Music Education and Displacement* [Rotterdam, The Netherlands: Brill | Sense, 2020]); marginalized voices in music education (see Estelle R. Jorgensen, "On Mediated Qualitative Scholarship and Marginalized Voices in Music Education," in *Narratives and Reflections in Music Education: Listening to Voices Seldom Heard*, ed. Tawnya D. Smith and Karin S. Hendricks [Cham, Switzerland: Springer, 2020], 193–206; Tawnya D. Smith, "Belonging in Moments: A 'Becoming-Out' Ethnodrama as Told through Spiritual, Social, and Musical Reflections," in *Queering Freedom: Music, Identity, and Spirituality*, ed. Karin S. Hendricks and June Boyce-Tillman [Oxford: Peter Lang, 2018], 263–279; Brent C. Talbot, *Marginalized Voices in Music Education* [New York: Routledge, 2018]); colonization (see Lise Vaugeois, "Social Justice and Music Education: Claiming the Space of Music Education as a Site of Post-colonial Contestation," *Action, Criticism and Theory for Music Education* 6, no. 4 [2007]: 163–200, http://act.maydaygroup.org/articles/Vaugeois6_4.pdf; and her "White Subjectivities, the Arts, and Power in Colonial Canada: Classical Music as White Property," in *The Palgrave Handbook of Race and the Arts in Education*, ed. Amelia M. Kraehe, Rubén Gaztambide-Fernández, and B. Stephen Carpenter II [New York: Palgrave Macmillan, 2018], 45–67; Guillermo Rosabal-Coto, "'I Did It My Way!' A Case Study of Resistance to Coloniality in Music Learning and Socialization," *Action, Criticism, and Theory for Music Education* [2014], http://act.maydaygroup.org/articles/Rosabal-Coto13_1.pdf; Deborah Bradley, "Good for What, Good for Whom?: Decolonizing Music Education Philosophies," *The Oxford Handbook of Philosophy in Music Education*, ed. Wayne Bowman and Ana Lucía Frega [New York: Oxford, 2012], 409–433, and her "The Sounds of Silence: Talking Race in Music Education," *Action, Criticism, and Theory for Music Education* 6, no. 4 [2007]: 132–162, http://act.maydaygroup.org/articles/Bradley6_4.pdf; Guillermo Rosabal-Coto, "The Day after Music Education," *Action, Criticism, and Theory for Music Education* 18, no. 3 [September 2019]: 1–24, https://doi.org/10.22176/act18.3.1); racism (Juliet Hess, "Upping the 'Anti-': The Value of an Anti-racist Theoretical Framework in Music Education," *Action, Criticism, and Theory for Music Education* 14, no. 1 [2015]: 66–92, http://act.maydaygroup.org/articles/Hess14_1.pdf); and disability (see Deborah VanderLinde Blair and Kimberly A. McCord, eds., *Exceptional Music Pedagogy for Children with Exceptionalities: International Perspectives* [New York: Oxford University Press, 2015] [I am indebted to Warren Churchill for bringing this reference to my attention.]).

19. Hanna M. Nikkanen and Heidi Westerlund, "More Than Just Music: Reconsidering the Educational Value of Music in School Rituals," *Philosophy of Music Education Review* 25, no. 2 (Fall 2017): 112–127, https://doi.org/10.2979/philmusieducrevi.25.2.02, point to the ironies between performative rituals that both reinforce tradition and suggest change.

20. On existentialism and music education, see Frederik Pio and Øivind Varkøy, "A Reflection on Musical Experience as Existential Experience: An Ontological Turn," *Philosophy of Music Education Review* 20, no. 2 (Fall 2012): 99–116, https://doi.org/10.2979/philmusieducrevi.20.2.99.

21. See Jorgensen, "Intersecting Social Justices and Music Education."

22. Ivan Illich, *Deschooling Society* (1971; repr., London and New York: Marion Boyars, 2004), 31.

23. Friedrich Schiller, *On the Aesthetic Education of Man in a Series of Letters*, Neunter brief/Ninth letter, trans. Elizabeth M. Wilkinson and L. A. Willoughby (1967; repr., Oxford: Clarendon, 1986), 60, 61.

24. Berlin, *The Crooked Timber of Humanity*, front matter.

25. See, for example, H. Wheeler Robinson, *The Christian Doctrine of Man*, 3rd ed. (1926; repr., Edinburgh, Scotland: T. & T. Clark, 1974); Erdman Harris, *God's Image and Man's Imagination* (New York: Charles Scribner's Sons, 1959), chap. 10: "Man's Image and God's."

26. See, for example, Danielle Allen, *Our Declaration: A Reading of the Declaration of Independence in Defense of Equality* (New York: W. W. Norton, 2014).

27. OED Online, s.v. "Equality, n.," accessed November 7, 2017, http://www.oed.com/view/Entry/63702?.

28. George Orwell, *Animal Farm*, Classics Library (New Delhi, India: Rupa, 2010), 114.

29. See Abraham Maslow, *Religions, Values, and Peak-Experiences* (1964; repr., Harmondsworth, UK: Penguin, 1976).

30. See June Boyce-Tillman, *Constructing Musical Healing: The Wounds That Sing* (London: Jessica Kingsley, 2000); June Boyce-Tillman, *Experiencing Music—Restoring the Spiritual: Music as Well-being* (Bern, Switzerland: Peter Lang, 2016).

31. On the imperative of community, see Freire, *Pedagogy of the Oppressed*; Maxine Greene, *The Dialectic of Freedom* (New York: Teachers College Press, 1988).

32. Parker J. Palmer, *Courage to Teach: Exploring the Inner Landscape of a Teacher's Life* (San Francisco: Jossey-Bass, 1998), especially chap. 4.

33. On inherent and delineated meanings, see Lucy Green, *Music on Deaf Ears: Musical Meaning, Ideology and Education* (Manchester, UK: Manchester University Press, 1988), especially chaps. 2 and 3.

34. OED Online, s.v. "Equity," accessed on March 5, 2021, https://www.oed.com/view/Entry/63838?. I am indebted to Randall Allsup and Julia Eklund Koza for emphasizing the distinction between equality and equity.

35. See, for example, Omionota N. Ukpokodu and P. O. Ojiambo, *Erasing Invisibility, Inequities, and Social Injustice of African Immigrants in the Diaspora and the Continent* (Newcastle, UK: Cambridge Scholars Publishing, 2017). I am indebted to Akosua Addo for bringing my attention to the work of Omionota Ukpokodu and her colleagues.

36. OED Online, s.v. "Fairness, n.," accessed November 7, 2017, http://www.oed.com/view/Entry/67729?.

37. This idea also crops up in other countries. For example, in the United States, it is the colloquialism "no fair."

38. This analysis shares commonalities with that of Rawls, *Justice as Fairness*, in its emphasis on rule-governed thought and practice. This writing is a rethinking of his earlier *A Theory of Justice*.

39. See Susanne K. Langer, *Philosophy in a New Key: A Study in the Symbolism of Reason, Rite, and Art*, 3rd ed. (Cambridge, MA: Harvard University Press, 1957). This term was earlier proposed by Edward Bullough, "'Psychical Distance' as a Factor in Art and an Aesthetic Principle," *British Journal of Psychology* 5 (1912): 87–117, https://doi.org/10.1111/j.2044-8295.1912.tb00057.x.

40. Israel Scheffler, *In Praise of the Cognitive Emotions and Other Essays on the Philosophy of Education* (New York: Routledge, Chapman and Hall, 1991), on the cognitive emotions and Iris M. Yob, "The Cognitive Emotions and Emotional Cognitions," *Studies in Philosophy and Education* 16, no. 1–2 (1997): 43–57, https://doi.org/10.1023/A:1004990702983, on the emotional cognitions.

41. Gale, "Derridean Justice and the DJ."

42. The critique of disembodied reason is especially evident in feminist literature over the past decades—e.g., in Carter Heyward, *Our Passion for Justice: Images of Power, Sexuality, and Liberation* (New York: Pilgrim, 1984); Mary Daly, *Pure Lust: Elemental Feminist Philosophy* (New York: Harper Collins, 1984); Elizabeth Grosz, *Volatile Bodies: Toward a Corporeal Feminism* (Bloomington: Indiana University Press, 1994); Judith Butler, *Gender Trouble: Feminism and the Subversion of Identity* (New York: Routledge, 1990), and her *Senses of the Subject* (New York: Fordham, 2015).

43. Eleni Lapidaki, "Towards the Discovery of Contemporary Trust and Intimacy in Higher Music Education," in *Humane Music Education for the Common Good*, ed. Iris M. Yob and Estelle R. Jorgensen (Bloomington: Indiana University Press, 2020).

44. For a landmark study on this point, see Carol Gilligan, *In a Different Voice: Psychological Theory and Women's Development* (Cambridge, MA: Harvard University Press, 1982).

45. bell hooks, *Teaching to Transgress: Education as the Practice of Freedom* (New York: Routledge, 1994).

46. Madeline R. Grumet, *Bitter Milk: Women and Teaching* (Amherst: University of Massachusetts Press, 1988), writes of going into the school as her "father's house," and Jane Roland Martin, *Coming of Age in Academe: Rekindling Women's Hopes and Reforming the Academy* (New York: Routledge, 2000), refers to her experience in academe as an immigrant and outsider.

47. OED Online, s.v. "Inclusion, n.," accessed November 7, 2017, http://www.oed.com/view/Entry/93579?; OED Online, s.v. "Include, v.," accessed November 7, 2017, http://www.oed.com/view/Entry/93571?; OED Online, s.v. "Inclusive, n. and adj.," accessed November 7, 2017, http://www.oed.com/view/Entry/93581?; OED

Online, s.v. "Inclusive, adv.," accessed November 7, 2017, http://www.oed.com/view/Entry/49995329?.

48. See n. 18. Regarding gender, for example, following Lucy Green's groundbreaking *Music, Gender, Education* (Cambridge, UK: Cambridge University Press, 1997), there is a growing music educational literature on the differently gendered—for example, Gregory F. DeNordo et al., "Establishing Identity: LGBT Studies & Music Education—Select Conference Proceedings," *Bulletin of the Council for Research in Music Education* no. 188 (Spring 2011): 9–64, https://www.jstor.org/stable/41162329. On the intersection of gender and colonialization, see Guillermo Rosabal-Coto, "I Did It My Way!" On indigeneity, see Anita Prest and J. Scott Goble, "Language, Music, and Revitalizing Indigeneity: Effecting Cultural Restoration and Ecological Balance via Music Education," *Philosophy of Music Education Review* 29, no. 1 (Spring 2021): 24–46, https://doi.org/10.2979/philmusieducrevi.29.1.03.

49. Dewey, *Democracy and Education*, and his *Art as Experience* (1934; repr., New York: Paragon Books, 1979); Philip W. Jackson, *John Dewey and the Lessons of Art* (New Haven, CT: Yale University Press, 1998); Herbert Read, *Education through Art* (London: Faber and Faber, 1943).

50. Plato, *The Republic of Plato*, trans. Francis Macdonald Cornford (1941; repr., Oxford: Oxford University Press, 1942).

51. See Lapidaki, "Towards the Discovery of Contemporary Trust and Intimacy in Higher Music Education."

52. Scheffler, *In Praise of the Cognitive Emotions*; Yob, "The Cognitive Emotions and Emotional Cognitions."

53. Greene, *The Dialectic of Freedom*; Palmer, *Courage to Teach*.

54. Jean Lave, "Situating Learning in Communities of Practice," in *Perspectives on Socially Shared Cognition*, ed. Lauren B. Resnick, John M. Levine, and Stephanie Teasley (Washington, DC: American Psychological Association, 1991), 63–82; Jean Lave and Etienne Wenger, *Situated Learning: Legitimate Peripheral Participation* (Cambridge: Cambridge University Press, 1991); Etienne Wenger, *Communities of Practice: Learning, Meaning, and Identity* (Cambridge: Cambridge University Press, 1998).

55. Scheffler, *In Praise of the Cognitive Emotions*; Yob, "The Cognitive Emotions and Emotional Cognitions."

56. On growth, see Shinichi Suzuki, *Nurtured by Love: A New Approach to Education*, trans. Waltraud Suzuki (New York: Exposition, 1969); Maria Montessori, *The Absorbent Mind* (1967; repr., New York: Dell, 1980) and her *From Childhood to Adolescence*, 2nd ed. (New York: Schocken Books, 1973); Dewey, *Democracy and Education*, chap. 4.

57. Estelle R. Jorgensen, *Pictures of Music Education* (Bloomington: Indiana University Press, 2011).

58. Israel Scheffler, *Of Human Potential: An Essay in the Philosophy of Education* (Boston: Routledge and Kegan Paul, 1985), and his *In Praise of the Cognitive Emotions*, chap. 2.

59. June Boyce-Tillman, "Towards an Ecology of Music Education," *Philosophy of Music Education Review* 12, no. 2 (2004): 102–125, https://www.jstor.org/stable/40327232, draws on Michel Foucault's notion of subjugated knowledge.

60. Antia Gonzalez-Ben, "Here Is the Other, Coming / Come In: An Examination of Spain's Contemporary Multicultural Music Education Discourses," *Philosophy of Music Education Review* 26, no. 2 (Fall 2018): 118–138, https://doi.org/10.2979/philmusieducrevi.26.2.02, makes the crucial point that music educators may mouth values of inclusion while practicing exclusion and othering of those who are supposedly included.

61. The large literature on educational inclusion, also attending to the needs of special learners, includes Lani Florian, "Inclusion: Special or Inclusive Education: Future Trends," *British Journal of Special Education* 35, no. 4 (December 2008): 202–208, https://doi.org/10.1111/j.1467-8578.2008.00402.x; Yusef Sayed and Crain Soudien, "(Re)Framing Education Exclusion and Inclusion Discourses: Limits and Possibilities," *IDS Bulletin* 34, no. 1 (January 2003): 9–19, https://doi.org/10.1111/j.1759-5436.2003.tb00055.x; Alan Dyson, "Inclusion and Inclusions: Theories and Discourses in Inclusive Education," in *World Yearbook of Education 1999: Inclusive Education*, ed. Harry Daniels and Philip Garner (London and New York: Routledge, 2012). In music education, see, for example, Thomas S. Popkewitz and Ruth Gustafson, "Standards of Music Education and the Easily Administered Child/Citizen: The Alchemy of Pedagogy and Inclusion/Exclusion," *Philosophy of Music Education Review* 10, no. 2 (Fall 2002): 80–90, https://www.jstor.org/stable/40327182; Pamela Burnard, Steve Dillon, Gabriel Rusinek, and Eva Saether, "Inclusive Pedagogies in Music Education: A Comparative Study of Music Teachers' Perspectives from Four Countries," *International Journal of Music Education* 26, no. 2 (2008): 109–126, https://doi.org/10.1177/0255761407088489.

62. Scheffler, *In Praise of the Cognitive Emotions*, chap. 2.

63. Susan Laird, "Musical Hunger: A Philosophical Testimonial of Miseducation," *Philosophy of Music Education Review* 17, no. 1 (Spring 2009): 4–21, https://www.jstor.org/stable/40327307.

64. Gilles Deleuze and Felix Guattari, *A Thousand Plateaus: Capitalism and Schizophrenia*, trans. Brian Massumi (Minneapolis and London: University of Minnesota Press, 1987).

65. Estelle R. Jorgensen and Iris M Yob, "Deconstructing Deleuze and Guattari's *A Thousand Plateaus* for Music Education," *The Journal of Aesthetic Education* 47, no. 3 (Fall 2013): 36–55, https://doi.org/10.5406/jaesteduc.47.3.0036.

CHAPTER 11 - COMMONALITIES, RESONANCES, APPLICATIONS, AND DECISIONS

1. See Estelle R. Jorgensen, "Intersecting Social Justices and Music Education," in Cathy Benedict, Patrick Schmidt, Gary Spruce, and Paul Woodford, eds., *The*

Oxford Handbook of Social Justice in Music Education (New York: Oxford University Press, 2015), 7–28.

2. Claire Detels, *Soft Boundaries: Re-visioning the Arts and Aesthetics in American Education* (Westport, CT: Bergin and Garvey, 1999); Gilles Deleuze and Felix Guattari, *A Thousand Plateaus: Capitalism and Schizophrenia*, trans., Brian Massumi (Minneapolis and London: University of Minnesota Press, 1987), 492–499, contrast smooth and striated aesthetics.

3. Joseph J. Schwab, "The Practical: Arts of Eclectic," *The School Review* 79, no. 4 (August 1971): 493–542, https://doi.org/10.1086/442998.

4. Maxine Greene, *The Dialectic of Freedom* (New York: Teachers College Press, 1988), chap. 4, on "multiplicities and pluralities."

5. For Schwab, "The Practical," the "arts of eclectic" are invoked as the means whereby beliefs and practices are sorted through, settled on, and implemented.

6. Estelle R. Jorgensen, "'This-with-That': A Dialectical Approach to Teaching for Musical Imagination," *Journal of Aesthetic Education* 40, no. 4 (Winter 2006): 1–20, https://doi.org/10.1353/jae.2006.0035.

7. Nel Noddings, *Caring: A Feminine Approach to Ethics and Moral Education* (Berkeley: University of California Press, 1984).

8. Isaiah Berlin, *The Crooked Timber of Humanity: Chapters in the History of Ideas*, ed. Hardy Henry (Princeton, NJ: Princeton University Press, 1990), frontispiece, invokes Kant's metaphor: "Out of timber so crooked as that from which man is made nothing entirely straight can be built." From Kant, "*Idee zu einer allgemeinen Geschichte in weltbürgerlicher Absicht.*"

9. For Jacques Derrida, "Force of Law: The 'Mystical Foundation of Authority,'" trans. Mary Quaintance, *Acts of Religion*, ed., Gil Anidjar (London: Routledge, 2002), 243, "justice is deconstruction." As such, it is in the process of becoming.

10. See John Dewey, *Democracy and Education: An Introduction to the Philosophy of Education* (1916; repr., New York: Free Press, 1966), 106.

11. For Juliet Hess, *Music Education for Social Change: Constructing an Activist Music Education* (New York: Routledge, 2019), reflection and agency are intertwined and translate necessarily into action.

12. See Seyla Benhabib, *The Claims of Culture: Equality and Diversity in the Global Era* (Princeton, NJ: Princeton University Press, 2002), chap. 5, on resolving challenges of diversity and equality in deliberative democracies within legal frameworks.

13. See Robert Ulich, ed., *Three Thousand Years of Educational Wisdom: Selections from Great Documents*, 2nd edition (Cambridge, MA: Harvard University Press, 1954).

14. See Dewey, *Democracy and Education.*

15. See Paul Woodford, *Democracy and Music Education: Liberalism, Ethics, and the Politics of Practice* (Bloomington and Indianapolis: Indiana University Press, 2005).

16. For an examination of the role of institutions as agents of music education, see Estelle R. Jorgensen, *In Search of Music Education* (Urbana: University of Illinois Press, 1997), chap. 2.

17. See Greene, *The Dialectic of Freedom*, 17.

18. See, for example, Paulo Freire, *Pedagogy of the Oppressed*, New Revised 20th Anniversary Edition, trans. Myra Bergman Ramos (New York: Continuum, 1993); bel hooks, *Teaching to Transgress: Education as the Practice of Freedom* (New York: Routledge, 1994).

19. See Estelle R. Jorgensen, *Transforming Music Education* (Bloomington: Indiana University Press, 2003).

20. Estelle R. Jorgensen, "On a Choice-Based Instructional Typology in Music," *Journal of Research in Music Education* 29 (1981): 97–102, https://doi.org/10.2307/3345018; her "An Analysis of Aspects of Type IV Music Instruction in a Teacher-Student Dyad," *The Quarterly Journal of Music Teaching and Learning* 6, no. 1 (1995): 16–31, http://www-usr.rider.edu/~vrme/v16n1/volume6/visions/spring3, and her "Modeling Aspects of Type IV Music Instructional Triads," *The Bulletin of the Council for Research in Music Education*, no. 137 (1998): 43–56, https://www.jstor.org/stable/40318931.

21. See Jorgensen, *Transforming Music Education.*

22. On these theoretical commonplaces in music education, see Estelle R. Jorgensen, "On the Development of a Theory of Musical Instruction," *Psychology of Music* 8 (1980): 25–30, https://doi.org/10.1177/030573568082003.

23. Liora Bresler, *Knowing Bodies, Moving Minds: Towards Embodied Teaching and Learning* (New York: Springer, 2004), prelude.

24. See Jorgensen, *In Search of Music Education*, chap. 1.

25. See Jorgensen, *In Search of Music Education*, and Estelle R. Jorgensen, *Pictures of Music Education* (Bloomington: Indiana University Press, 2011).

26. See David J. Elliott, Marissa Silverman, and Wayne D. Bowman, eds., *Artistic Citizenship: Artistry, Social Responsibility, and Ethical Praxis* (New York: Oxford University Press, 2016).

27. See Jorgensen, *In Search of Music Education*, chap. 2.

28. Estelle R. Jorgensen and Iris M. Yob, "Metaphors for a Change," *Journal of Aesthetic Education* 53, no. 2 (Summer 2019): 19–39, https://doi.org/10.5406/jaesteduc.53.2.0019.

29. Nel Noddings, *Happiness and Education* (Cambridge: Cambridge University Press, 2003); Lucy Green, *Music, Informal Learning and the School: A New Classroom Pedagogy* (Aldershot, Hampshire, UK: Ashgate, 2008); Randall Everett Allsup, *Remixing the Classroom: Toward an Open Philosophy of Music Education* (Bloomington: Indiana University Press, 2016).

30. See Donald Schön, *Educating the Reflective Practitioner: Toward a New Design for Teaching and Learning in the Professions* (San Francisco: Jossey-Bass, 1987), chap. 2.

31. See Jorgensen, "On a Choice-Based Instructional Typology in Music."

32. Randall Everett Allsup, "The Eclipse of a Higher Education or Problems Preparing Artists in a Mercantile World," *Music Education Research* 17, no. 3 (2015): 251–261, https://doi.org/10.1080/14613808.2015.1057996.

33. Parker J. Palmer, *The Courage to Teach: Exploring the Inner Landscape of a Teacher's Life* (San Francisco: Jossey-Bass, 1998).

34. Friedrich Schiller, *On the Aesthetic Education of Man in a Series of Letters*, ed. and trans. Elizabeth M. Wilkinson and L. A. Willoughby (Oxford: Clarendon, 1967), ninth letter, 61.

35. On the dialectic of music making and receiving, see Jorgensen, *In Search of Music Education*, 83–87.

36. See Julia Eklund Koza, *"Destined to Fail": Carl Seashore's World of Eugenics, Psychology, Education, and Music* (Ann Arbor: University of Michigan Press, 2021).

37. Adam J. Kruse, "'He Didn't Know What He Was Doin'': Student Perspectives of a White Teacher's Hip-Hop Class," *International Journal of Music Education* 38, no. 2 (May 2020), https://doi.org/10.1177/0255761420924316.

38. See Omionota Nelly Ukpokodu, *You Can't Teach Us If You Do Not Know Us and Care About Us: Becoming an Ubuntu, Responsive and Responsible Urban Teacher* (New York: Peter Lang, 2016).

39. See Patrice D. Madura, "A Response to David Carr, 'Can White Men Play the Blues? Music, Learning Theory, and Performance Knowledge,'" *Philosophy of Music Education Review* 9, no. 1 (Spring 2001): 60–62, https://www.jstor.org/stable/40495455; David Carr, "Can White Men Play the Blues? Music, Learning Theory, and Performance Knowledge," *Philosophy of Music Education Review* 9, no. 1 (Spring 2001): 23–31, https://www.jstor.org/stable/40495450.

40. Akosua Addo, "Socio-cultural Power and Music Knowledge Construction," in *On the Sociology of Music Education II: Papers from the Music Education Symposium at the University of Oklahoma*, ed. Roger R. Rideout and Stephen J. Paul (Amherst: University of Massachusetts, published by the editors as a service to music education, 2000),75–90. For an interrogation of her experience, see her "African Education through the Arts," in *Contemporary Voices from the Margin: African Educators on African and American Education*, ed. Omionota N. Ukpokodu and Peter Ukpokodu (Charlotte, NC: Information Age Publishing, 2012), 22–66.

41. Estelle R. Jorgensen, "Some Challenges for Music Education: What Are Music Teachers to Do?" Keynote lecture to the International Conference CIPEM (Centro de Investigação em Psicologia da Música e Educação Musical), 2019, Porto, Portugal, September 19–21, 2019, published in Portuguese as "Alguns Desafios Para a Educação Musical. O Que Podem Fazer os Professores de Música," trans. Graça Boal-Palheiros, in *Desafios em Educação Musical*, ed., Graça Boal-Palheiros and Pedro S. Boia (Porto, Portugal: CIPEM, 2020).

42. Iris M. Yob, Steven Danver, Sheryl Kristensen, William Schulz, Kathy Simmons, Henry Brashen, Rebecca Sidler, Linda Kiltz, Linda Gatlin, Suzanne

Wesson, and Diane Penland, "Curriculum Alignment with a Mission of Social Change in Higher Education," *Innovative Higher Education* (October 2015), https://doi.org/10.1007/s10755-015-9344-5.

43. On sisterhood, see bell hooks, *Teaching to Transgress: Education as the Practice of Freedom* (New York: Routledge, 1994), 102, 103.

44. Christopher Small, *Musicking: The Meanings of Performing and Listening* (Hanover, NH: Wesleyan University Press, University Press of New England, 1998).

45. See Ronald Dworkin, *Sovereign Virtue: The Theory and Practice of Equality* (Cambridge, MA: Harvard University Press, 2000).

46. See Israel Scheffler, *Reason and Teaching* (1973; repr., Indianapolis, IN: Bobbs-Merrill, 1973).

47. See Bresler, *Knowing Bodies*, Prelude.

48. Deleuze and Guattari, *A Thousand Plateaus*, 492–299.

49. Hanne Fossum and Øivind Varkøy, "Music Education for the Common Good? Between Hubris and Resignation: A Call for Temperance," in *Humane Music Education for the Common* Good, ed. Iris M. Yob and Estelle R. Jorgensen (Bloomington: Indiana University Press, 2020), 40–53.

EPILOGUE

1. See Estelle R. Jorgensen, *Pictures of Music Education* (Bloomington: Indiana University Press, 2011), chap. 1.

2. Jorgensen, *Pictures of Music Education*, chap. 4.

3. Jorgensen, *Pictures of Music Education*, chap. 12.

4. On the arts as a central part of general education, see Philip Phenix, *Realms of Meaning: A Philosophy of the Curriculum for General Education* (1964; repr., Ventura, CA: Ventura County Superintendent of Schools Office, 1986); Vernon A. Howard, *Learning by All Means: Lessons from the Arts: A Study in the Philosophy of Education* (New York: Peter Lang, 1992).

5. See Harvard Museum of Natural History, "Glass Flowers: The Ware Collection of Blaschka Glass Models of Plants," accessed November 7, 2018, https://hmnh.harvard.edu/glass-flowers.

6. Jorgensen, *Pictures of Music Education*, chap. 5.

7. Jacques Attali, *Noise: The Political Economy of Music*, trans. Brian Massumi (Minneapolis: University of Minnesota Press, 1985).

8. Jorgensen, *Pictures of Music Education*, chap. 8.

9. Susanne K. Langer, *Philosophy in a New Key: A Study in the Symbolism of Reason, Rite, and Art*, 3rd edition (Cambridge, MA: Harvard University Press, 1957).

10. See Iris M. Yob, "If We Knew What Spirituality Was, We Would Teach for It," *Music Educators Journal* 98, no. 2 (December 2011): 41–47, https://doi.org/10.1177/0027432111425959. Examples can be found in Western and Eastern classical music traditions. See Daniel M. Neuman, *The Life of Music in North India: The*

Organization of an Artistic Tradition (Detroit: Wayne State University Press, 1980); Bruno Nettl, *Heartland Excursions: Ethnomusicological Reflections on Schools of Music* (Urbana: University of Illinois Press, 1995); Henry Kingsbury, *Music, Talent, and Performance: A Conservatory Cultural System* (1988; Philadelphia: Temple University, 2001).

11. Jorgensen, *Pictures of Music Education*, chap. 6.

12. Jorgensen, *Pictures of Music Education*, chaps. 9 and 6.

13. Jorgensen, *Pictures of Music Education*, chap. 11. See Maria Montessori, *The Absorbent Mind* (1967; repr., New York: Dell, 1980); Jane Roland Martin, *The Schoolhome: Rethinking Schools for Changing Families* (Cambridge, MA: Harvard University Press, 1992).

14. Jorgensen, *Pictures of Music Education*, chap. 10.

15. Jorgensen, *Pictures of Music Education*, chap. 11.

16. Jorgensen, *Pictures of Music Education*, chaps. 10 and 11.

17. Jorgensen, *Pictures of Music Education*, chap. 7.

18. On growth and nurture, see John Dewey, *Experience and Education* (1938; repr., New York: Collier Books, 1963); Shinichi Suzuki, *Nurtured by Love: A New Approach to Education*, trans. Waltraud Suzuki (New York: Exposition, 1969).

19. Jorgensen, *Pictures of Music Education*, chaps. 2, 6, and 13.

20. Amanda Hess, "Welcome to the Era of the Post-Shopping Mall: As the Mall Declines, American Dream—a 'Destination' at the Height of Capitalism—Rises," *New York Times*, December 27, 2019, https://www.nytimes.com/2019/12/27/arts/american-dream-mall-opening.html.

21. Ivan Illich, *Deschooling Society* (1971; repr., London and New York: Marion Boyars, 2004).

22. Jorgensen, *Pictures of Music Education*, chap. 12.

23. Jorgensen, *Pictures of Music Education*, chap. 9.

24. John Rawls, *A Theory of Justice*, rev. ed. (Cambridge, MA: Harvard University Press, 1999); Amartya Sen, *The Idea of Justice* (Cambridge, MA: Harvard University Press, 2009); Jacques Derrida, "Force of Law: The 'Mystical Foundation of Authority,'" trans. Mary Quaintance, in *Acts of Religion*, ed. Gil Anidjar (London: Routledge, 2002).

25. Ronald Dworkin, *Sovereign Virtue: The Theory and Practice of Equality* (Cambridge, MA: Harvard University Press, 2000); Danielle Allen, *Our Declaration: A Reading of the Declaration of Independence in Defense of Equality* (New York: W. W. Norton, 2014); Danielle Allen, Tommie Shelby, Marcelo Suárez-Oroczco, Michael Rebell, and Quiara Alegría Hudes, *Education and Equality* (Chicago: Chicago University Press, 2016). On the village-community pictures, see Jorgensen, *Pictures of Music Education*, chap. 3.

26. See John Rawls, *Justice as Fairness: A Restatement*, ed., Erin Kelly (Cambridge, MA: Harvard University Press, 2001). Also, see Jorgensen, *Pictures of Music Education*, chaps. 9 and 3.

27. See Dworkin, *Sovereign Virtue*; Allen, *Our Declaration*; Allen et. al., *Education and Equality*; Jorgensen, *Pictures of Music Education*, chaps. 9 and 3.

28. For an analysis of two faces of transgression, see Panagiotis A. Kanellopoulos, "Rethinking the Transgressive: A Call for 'Pessimistic Activism' in Music Education," in *The Road Goes Ever On: Estelle Jorgensen's Legacy in Music Education*, ed. Randall Everett Allsup and Cathy Benedict (London, ON: Western University, December 2019), 119–137, https://doi.org/10.5206/Q1144262.jorgensen.2019.

29. Israel Scheffler, *In Praise of the Cognitive Emotions and Other Essays on the Philosophy of Education* (New York: Routledge, Chapman and Hall, 1991), chap. 12, entitled "Vice into Virtue, or Seven Deadly Sins of Education Redeemed."

30. Vernon A. Howard, *Learning by All Means: Lessons from the Arts: A Study in the Philosophy of Education* (New York: Peter Lang, 1992) is among those to grasp this possibility.

31. Thinking of music educations rather than music education is advanced in Patrick Schmidt, "Becoming a Story: Searching for Music Educations," in *The Road Goes Ever On: Estelle Jorgensen's Legacy in Music Education*, ed. Randall Everett Allsup and Cathy Benedict (London, ON: Western University, December 2019), 141–150, https://doi.org/10.5206/Q1144262.jorgensen.2019.

32. On writing as a means of learning, see Vernon A. Howard and James H. Barton, *Thinking on Paper* (New York: William Morrow, 1986). On the importance of being in community as a means of awakening imagination, see Maxine Greene, *The Dialectic of Freedom* (New York: Teachers College Press, 1988), 17. Writing also enables one to remember and relearn what might have been forgotten or overlooked. I think, for example, of the philosophical conversation on musical values over a quarter century ago prompted by Forest Hansen's seminal article, "Values in Music Education," *Philosophy of Music Education Review* 2, no. 1 (Spring 1994): 3–13, https://www.jstor.org/stable/40327065, in which he addresses important matters concerning the intrinsic value of music; David J. Elliott's "Musical Values Revisited: A Reply to Forest Hansen's 'Values in Music Education,'" *Philosophy of Music Education Review* 3, no. 1 (Spring 1995): 52–55, https://www.jstor.org/stable/40327088; and Forest Hansen's "Musical Values Again: A Response to David Elliott's Critique of 'Values in Music Education,'" *Philosophy of Music Education Review* 3, no. 2 (Fall 1995): 125–127, https://www.jstor.org/stable/40327098.

INDEX

ESTELLE R. JORGENSEN is Professor Emerita of Music Education at the Indiana University Jacobs School of Music and University Research Reviewer, Research Methodologist, and Contributing Faculty Member at the Richard W. Riley College of Education and Leadership at Walden University. Recipient of the 2020 Senior Researcher Award from the National Association for Music Education, she is author of *In Search of Music Education, Transforming Music Education* (IUP, 2002), *The Art of Teaching Music* (IUP, 2008), and *Pictures of Music Education* (IUP, 2011) and coeditor of *Humane Music Education for the Common Good* (IUP, 2020).

Lightning Source UK Ltd.
Milton Keynes UK
UKHW042148081021
391776UK00008B/191